CW01514108

CULTURAL HISTORY AND LITERARY IMAGINATION

EDITED BY CHRISTIAN EMDEN & DAVID MIDGLEY

VOL. 5

PETER LANG

Oxford · Bern · Berlin · Bruxelles · Frankfurt am Main · New York · Wien

Memory Traces

1989 and the Question of German Cultural Identity

Silke Arnold-de Simine

PETER LANG

Oxford · Bern · Berlin · Bruxelles · Frankfurt am Main · New York · Wien

Bibliographic information published by Die Deutsche Bibliothek
Die Deutsche Bibliothek lists this publication in the Deutsche Nationalbibliografie;
detailed bibliographic data is available on the Internet at ‹http://dnb.ddb.de›.

British Library and Library of Congress Cataloguing-in-Publication Data:
A catalogue record for this book is available from *The British Library*, Great Britain, and
from *The Library of Congress*, USA

ISSN 1660-6205
ISBN 3-03910-297-4
US-ISBN 0-8204-7223-9

© Peter Lang AG, European Academic Publishers, Bern 2005
Hochfeldstrasse 32, Postfach 746, CH-3000 Bern 9, Switzerland
info@peterlang.com, www.peterlang.com, www.peterlang.net

All rights reserved.
All parts of this publication are protected by copyright.
Any utilisation outside the strict limits of the copyright law, without the permission of the
publisher, is forbidden and liable to prosecution.
This applies in particular to reproductions, translations, microfilming, and storage and
processing in electronic retrieval systems.

Printed in Germany

Contents

Silke Arnold-de Simine

Introduction

The way we deal with the past has become one of the key issues of modern cultural studies and 'memory' its leading term.[1] Whereas in the past the humanities played a major part in providing us with a canon of our cultural heritage, they have now become more and more self-reflexive by scrutinizing the workings of those processes of selection, exclusion and preservation which characterize our dealings with the past. How we remember, individually and collectively, has become almost as important an issue as what we remember, as the former is seen to determine the latter. Given the ever increasing number of publications on the topic it seems necessary to begin with a few words which outline the conceptual and theoretical framework in which the essays collected in this volume are situated.

A rupture such as the end of the GDR and the reunification of East and West Germany naturally provokes questions about what might have changed in the way we preserve, reinterpret and commemorate the post-war period, and it consequently elicits a wide range of attempts to answer those questions. The two German nations differed profoundly in their interpretation of German history and in their official cultures of commemoration. Although one can hardly describe the process after reunification as fair negotiations over those differing interpretations, reunified Germany still battles over the adequate and legitimate interpretation of its past but also over the role

---

1   Aleida Assmann, Gedächtnis als Leitbegriff der Kulturwissenschaften, in Lutz Musner and Gotthart Wunberg (eds.), *Kulturwissenschaften. Forschung – Praxis – Positionen*, Freiburg i.B. 2003, pp.27–47: p.27; Alon Cofino, 'Collective Memory and Cultural History: Problems of the Method', *American Historical Review*, 102 (December 1997), 1386–1403: 1386; Mieke Bal, Jonathan Crewe and Leo Spitzer (eds.), *Acts of Memory: Cultural Recall in the Present*, Hanover-London 1999, p.vii.

of various memory media and institutions, such as the musem, in that process. However, this is not just a German issue. In reaction to the failing of utopian ideologies and the breaches of civilization that the twentieth century experienced, it has become equally fashionable to proclaim the end of history and at the same time to indulge in a 'memory hype', which could be seen as an attempt to replace one way of dealing with the past by the other.

The paradigm of a collective memory as it was described by Maurice Halbwachs and others at the beginning of the twentieth century was in response to the concept of history as it had emerged in the course of the nineteenth century: 'Der Begriff des Gedächtnisses [...] kann unschwer als Wiederkehr dessen identifiziert werden, was aus dem modernistischen Geschichtsbegriff verdrängt wurde.' ('The concept of memory [...] can easily be identified as the return of what was suppressed in the modernistic idea of history.')[2] Halbwachs has established a clear distinction between memory and history, though clearly based on the positivistic historiography of his time.[3] In his view history takes over once tradition, shared by the community as a whole, dissolves. History aims to reconstruct the past in an impartial and objective account, whereas memory relates to the past as an emotional presence. The past that is not gone but is perceived as eternal presence creates what Pierre Nora calls the *milieux de mémoire*, the real environments of memory. He claims that the ritual and with it the *milieux de mémoire* have vanished, leaving us with the *lieux de mémoire*, sites which remind us of the past, of a (broken) memory. The term *lieux de mémoire* indicates that it is not a repetition but only a representation of the past, a 'meaningful entity of a real or imagined kind, which has become a symbolic element of a given community as a result of human will or the effect of time.'[4] Nora's ideas are clearly influenced by a nostalgic and conservative longing for a stable and equally uncritical sense of identity in social communities in general and the (French) nation in particular. Nora's

---

2   Assmann, Gedächtnis als Leitbegriff, p.35.
3   Maurice Halbwachs, *La mémoire collective*, Paris 1950, p.75.
4   Pierre Nora (ed.), *Les Lieux de Memoire*, III/3, Les France: De l'archive à l'emblème, Paris 1992, p.1004.

example shows that however we choose to define (collective) memory, it clearly relies on our concept of history.

History is still seen to establish distance and focuses on change, on the differences and discontinuities between present and past. The subject of memory, on the other hand, does not reflect on the past but recognizes itself in the past. Memories are highly selective and are based on a reduction of complexity. They establish continuity and a stable and coherent identity. There are as many collective memories and stories as there are communities and these memory cultures claim no authority outside their specific community. History, on the other hand, aims to discover and portray a past on which potentially everybody should be able to agree, the universal history of mankind. These distinctions between memory and history are in one form or the other still supported by contemporary theorists such as Pierre Nora[5] and Paul Ricoeur,[6] even if theorists such as Hayden White have drawn attention to the poetical and ideological nature of historical writing and research.[7]

Nora's ideas are based on the traditional differentiation between natural memory and artificial memory (*ars memoriae*). Plato in his dialogue *Phaedrus* was one of the first thinkers to give preference to the natural human capacity to remember over the artificiality of media-based memory. He had severe doubts concering the enhancement of memory through rhetorical aids and devices such as writing, which, in his view, would only encourage forgetfulness. But these days the distinction between natural and artificial memory on the one hand and memory and history on the other has become porous, given that the concept of memory is already used to enhance the concept of history, open up its fields of research, diversify its objects and revise

---

5   Pierre Nora, 'Between Memory and History: Les Lieux de Mémoire', *Representations* 26 (Spring 1989), 7–25: 8.

6   Paul Ricoeur, 'Gedächtnis – Vergessen – Geschichte', in Klaus E. Müller and Jörn Rüsen (eds.), *Historische Sinnbildung. Problemstellungen, Zeitkonzepte, Wahrnehmungshorizonte, Darstellungsstrategien*, Reinbek bei Hamburg 1997, pp.433–454.

7   Hayden White, *Metahistory. The Historical Imagination in Nineteenth-Century Europe*, Baltimore-London 1973.

its methods.[8] Whereas history used to be deployed to correct and differentiate memories, now the personal memories of contemporary witnesses 'have emerged as privileged mode of access to the past and its traumatic occurences'.[9] Memory seems to allow for a wider diversity than the concept of history with its ideal of objectivity. Thereby the competition begins over who can rightfully claim authority over the past. The past is a hard contested territory, and '[h]e who recovers the lost past wins control of the future.'[10]

We have to ask if the individual case studies put into perspective history's established claim to have an objective, verified and therefore privileged access to the past. Or if, on the contrary, the individual perspectives become sanctified and authorized by being included in the master discourse, which has widened its claim of relevance by including and highlighting personal experience. The false memory debate focuses on the fact that our memory is closely connected to our imagination and that a memory is never a simple recalling of the past but always more or less a recreation. Remembering is a creative process and memories can only be transmitted as narratives.[11] These narratives are not so much concerned with the truthful reconstruction of the past, but constitute a collective interpretation of past events according to the necessities of the community in regard to its present social and historical context. However, the scandal surrounding Binjamin Wilkomirski's sham Holocaust-memoir[12] in the late 1990s clearly shows that we still expect historical truth from personal recollections and that we want to draw a clear line between fact and

---

8   This rigid distinction has been challenged among others by Peter Burke, 'History as Social Memory', in Thomas Butler (ed.), *Memory: History, Culture and the Mind,* Oxford 1989, pp.97–113.

9   Dominick LaCapra, *History and Memory after Ausschwitz,* Ithaca 1998, p.11.

10   Hagen Schulze, *Gibt es überhaupt eine deutsche Geschichte?,* Berlin 1989, p.8.

11   Taking this notion one step further, Pierre Nora even claims that our excessive preoccupation with the past has become a substitute for our (literary) imagination: 'Die Geschichte ist unser Ersatz-Imaginäres.' ('History is our surrogate imaginary'). Pierre Nora, *Zwischen Gedächtnis und Geschichte,* trans. Wolfgang Kaiser, Berlin 1990, p.33.

12   Binjamin Wilkomirski, *Bruchstücke. Aus einer Kindheit 1939–1948,* Frankfurt/M. 1995.

fiction. This differentiation has not been given up at all, on the contrary, it has even become ethically recharged.[13]

Narratives of the past address the memories of contemporary witnesses, but are also directed towards those who have no experiential connection to an historical event and who can thereby – to a certain extent – participate in performing the past. In order to ensure the potential participation of future generations, valuable memories that are supposed to endure have to be preserved by ritual and repetition or transferred into a material form. In our society there are several institutions responsible for the preservation and presentation of remains of the past: the library, the archive, the museum. What these institutions store is determined by choice as much as by chance. Objects perceived as treasures can be destroyed by fire or other catastrophes, some artefacts or documents may have been deemed irrelevant at one point and were subsequently lost. But once these objects have found their way into storage, they do not simply vanish because society loses interest. These institutions can be seen to constitute society's 'cold memory'. The term 'hot memory' covers what is still actively remembered and practiced, a lived memory, whereas 'cold memory' refers to those remains which are stored, preserved and registered, not necessarily motivated by any specific idea of their further use, such as mechanically collected daily newspapers in an archive.[14] They might sink into oblivion but the knowledge and information they hold can be rediscovered at any time if they are deemed important for the present.

Although there is an undeniable element of chance in each act of preservation that should not be overlooked, it is still necessary to ask about the motives for preservation: The question is not only what is remembered by whom but also how and why is it remembered? On the basis of a number of case studies this volume sets out to illuminate the role of several coexisting memory media in that process. These

---

13   Even an acclaimed author such as W.G. Sebald was critized for feeding off the tragic biographies of real-life people for his novel *Austerlitz* (2001) and making it thereby difficult for the reader to distinguish between fact and fiction.

14   Jan Assmann, *Das kulturelle Gedächtnis. Schrift, Erinnerung und politische Identität in frühen Hochkulturen*, Munich 1997, p.66–86.

media constitute the means through which different narratives vie for a place in our collective memory. They affect different memory communities in different ways, and the respective technological and semiotic shifts they bring about influence our prevailing concepts of memory.

Collective Memory

The title of this essay collection alludes to the fact that memories can be perceived as traces, as indications of something that has disappeared, but has nevertheless left its marks and therefore in some sense still prevails. These marks might be perceived as signs, pointing to something that would otherwise be overlooked and helping to trace what has vanished and its lasting influence on our present. Memories are often seen as the individual's creative ability to refer to his/her past by cognitive and emotional recollections. But as Maurice Halbwachs has showed in his groundbreaking study *Les cadres sociaux de la mémoire* (1925, *The social frameworks of memory*) all memory has a social dimension and function that evokes and enables memories in the first place. Society strongly influences people's personal memories: 'It is in society that man acquires his memories, that he recalls them, that he recognizes them, and that he locates them. [...] the groups to which I belong continuously offer me the means to reconstruct them.'[15] Halbwachs stresses the fact that social groups, be it families, generations, institutions or nations, share narratives of the past and hand them down, retell and modify them. Aleida Assmann has suggested replacing the term 'collective memory', which has given rise to many misunderstandings, by three distinct terms, namely

---

15 'Der Mensch [erlangt] normalerweise seine Erinnerungen, ruft sie sich in das Gedächtnis zurück [...] und lokalisiert sie in der Gesellschaft. [...] die Gruppen, denen ich angehöre, bieten mir in jedem Augenblick die Mittel, sie zu rekonstruieren'. Maurice Halbwachs, *Das Gedächtnis und seine sozialen Bedingungen*, Berlin, Neuwied 1966 [1952], p.20f.

'social memory', 'political memory' and 'cultural memory'.[16] These formats are a rough approximation in the effort to indicate different collectives as sources, bearers and performers of those memories, as well as different motivations for and different modes of preservation. That is not to say that a collective can be treated as if it would command a common consciousness or memory, capacities which we are used to ascribing to individual biophysical entities. Groups create their own memory with the aid of performative actions such as rites and ceremonies on the one hand and more material and durable forms of transmission such as texts, images, buildings or monuments on the other.[17]

The most important difference between the 'social memory' on the one hand and the 'political' and 'cultural memory' on the other is its duration: Social memory spans what is orally and personally communicated and vanishes with the direct contact to its bearers. The 'social' or, in Jan Assmann's terminology, 'communicative memory'[18] can, for example, represent the shared experience and value-system of a generation. Applying Assmann's concept, Anne Friederike Müller's essay assesses the decisive remodeling of the German polity in 1989–90 which followed closely the moment when the all-important forty-year threshold was reached, when the recollections of the National-Socialist past moved from communicative to cultural memory. The essay examines the treatment of old men in media reports about prominent court cases as well as in fictional literature. The literary works considered include so-called 'father novels' (*Väterromane*) of the eighties as well as pre-1989 and post-1989 texts by East and West German authors. While the media coverage of the court cases shows that old men can stand as symbols for German state power in the past,

---

16   Aleida Assmann, 'Four Formats of Memory: From Individual to Collective Constructions of the Past', in Christian Emden and David Midgley (eds.), *The Fragile Tradition: The German Cultural Imagination since 1500. I: Cultural Memory and Historical Consciousness,* Oxford 2004, pp.19–37: p.22.

17   Assmann, Four Formats of Memory. p.24. See also Renate Lachmann, 'Kultursemiotischer Prospekt', in Anselm Haverkamp and Renate Lachmann (eds.), *Poetik und Hermeneutik XV: Memoria – Vergessen und Erinnern,* Munich 1993, p.xvii.

18   Jan Assmann, *Das kulturelle Gedächtnis,* p.50ff.

the examination of the literary texts makes it possible to paint a more differentiated picture of various attitudes towards old men as authority figures.

Social, Political and Cultural Memory

Whereas social memory is established through shared experience, political and cultural memory denote the processes by which societies actively construct, shape and transmit collective memories by material or procedural representations. It has to be emphasized that there are no strict boundaries between those formats of memory: As Marc Oliver Huber's contribution in this volume reveals, family memories such as photo albums, diaries and letters can become part of the cultural memory, as is the case with the Manns, a family exceptionally deeply involved in twentieth-century German history. However, as Huber goes on to argue, the current memory debate focuses too much on isolated figures, thus neglecting the configurations or social poetics of memory. The Manns have been most prominent in developing familial memory relations, with several of their members putting them at the heart of their literary productions. Not surprisingly, they have recently been termed a German *lieu de mémoire* ('deutscher Erinnerungsort').[19] Huber investigates the discourse framework of the post-1989 memory boom by looking at the Manns. In crucial respects the Mann family novel parallels a national family romance firmly rooted in the political imaginary of the Federal Republic. Both offer narratives about an overwhelming and repressive bourgeois father and his anti-bourgeois children struggling for an autonomous existence, and thereby releasing the repressed. Nevertheless, the national family novel delineated by the generation of 1968 differs significantly from the account of history the Mann family is able to provide. After 1989, the Manns develop into a prominent object of memory simply because

---

19   Etienne François and Hagen Schulze (eds.), *Deutsche Erinnerungsorte*, Munich 2001.

they also function as a reminder of the achievements of the bourgeois way of life which the harsh critique by the generation of 1968 has denied. A narrative of achievement counterbalances a narrative of guilt and this tension mirrors the German cultural self-perception which is in constant flux between the two extremes.

This example shows that the question of how long memories will continue to be passed on does not so much depend on whether they are considered to be social, political or cultural memories but rather on whether they are meaningful contributions to our making sense of the present and whether they are preserved in some material representation so that after a period of falling into neglect they can be rediscovered. They do not even have to be intended as reminders (such as memorials) but can acquire this status by constituting the site of an epochal event and becoming 'unintended monuments' (Alois Riegl). Simon Ward's essay examines the processes by which 'unintended monuments' operate in public space. He investigates the discourses that surround them and the various ways they are imbued with 'memory value' (Andreas Huyssen). The essay focuses on ruin sites from the post-war era, all still present in the memory landscape of Berlin in 2005. They show how the 'memory value' of these unintended monuments has been established and changed over time, with particular reference to the period since 1989. A building such as the Kaiser Wilhelm-Gedächtniskirche in Berlin might have been built as a monument to the Prussian Monarchy but in the course of time it acquired several more memorial functions, thus demonstrating that it is hardly possible to fix, stabilize or restrict the memories attached to intended or unintended monuments. The Gedächtniskirche illustrates a number of paradigms of the workings of memory value in public space after 1945: 1) the relationship between memory value and exchange value, 2) the irrelevance of previous ideological functions and architectural merit and 3) the need for signs and borders to stabilize the workings of memory value and establish the exhibition value of the remnant. The *Gestapo-Gelände*, best known now as the *Topographie des Terrors* (Topography of Terror), is symptomatic for how a more critical form of memory value, which has developed since the seventies, has shaped the discussion of public space following German reunification. As a remnant of the GDR state, the *Palast der*

Republik tests the strategies by which the memory value of this particular building is played off against the demands of the new unified state as well as the plans for a reconstruction of the imperial 'Schloss' previously located on its site.

Intertwined with the question of how we deal with the past, is the question of how we perceive the process of present turning into past. This process can take on various forms. It can be slow or abrupt, it can involve complete oblivion or a form of storage which provides the basis for a recovery in the future. German history in the twentieth century is marked by a succession of ruptures in which different political systems experienced their ideological and existential bankruptcies. These caesuras have shaped people's lives in that from one day to another they turned a lived present into an invalid past, thus contradicting the notion of an evolutionary pattern of growth and decay. In his essay *Der Erzähler* (1936/37) Walter Benjamin described this loss of valid experience that could be communicated and handed on as a consequence of industrialization and the First World War, and outlined the implications for narration. For Benjamin, experiences were the raw material of every story and the narrative enabled the audience to relate to them.[20] This sense of continuity seems to be lost in the twentieth century. Even so it does not simply result in a feeling of alienation towards the past. It triggers a desire to overcome the distance by creating a consciously contructed relation to the past.[21]

---

20   Walter Benjamin, 'Der Erzähler. Betrachtungen zum Werk Nikolai Lesskows', in Michael Opitz (ed.), *Walter Benjamin. Ein Lesebuch*, Frankfurt/M. 1996, pp.258–284. See Reinhart Koselleck on the disruption of continuity, in *Vergangene Zukunft. Zur Semantik geschichtlicher Zeiten*, Frankfurt/M. 1979.
21   Ernst Schulin, 'Absage und Wiederherstellung von Vergangenheit', in Moritz Csáky, Peter Stachel (eds.), *Speicher des Gedächtnisses: Bibliotheken, Museen, Archive*, I, Vienna 2000, pp.23–39.

Memory Politics and Cultural Identity

In our modern societies the much lamented cultural amnesia is coun-teracted by memory politics in which memories are purposefully used to form and stabilize social groups and their identities. Nevertheless 'it is important to recognize that although memory discourses appear to be global in one register, at their core they remain tied to the histories of specific nations and states'.[22] The creation and dissemination of narratives about the past arise out of identity politics.[23] Those narra-tives comprise foundation myths and are used to legitimate current or future aims of the group they define. In his contribution Lemmons points out that the decision to demolish the Ernst Thälmann Memorial in Berlin overlooked the fact that the monument can not be reduced to its function of legitimizing the GDR government by placing it in the tradition of anti-facist resistance, a dimension of the monument which could be described as 'top-down memory'. People living in the neigh-bourhood developed their own relations to and interpretations of the monument ('bottom-up memory'). By demolishing it, the officials would not only nullify the ideology in whose name it was erected but also those 'bottom-up memories'.

Over more than forty years of political division, opposing under-standings of German identity developed deep roots. This became especially evident in the months following the collapse of the GDR. In general, westerners, insisting that Soviet-style socialism had failed the German people completely, made a concerted effort to eliminate almost every trace of the former GDR's Marxist-Leninist past. In their eyes, to be German meant rejecting any manifestation of communism. Many citizens of the 'new states', however, insisted that 'real existing socialism' had not been a complete failure and wanted to maintain

---

22   Andreas Huyssen, *Present Pasts. Urban Palimpsests and the Politics of Me-mory*, Stanford, CA 2003, p.16.

23   See Allen Megill, 'History, Memory, Identity', *History of the Human Sciences*, 11/3 (1998): 37–62; Jeffrey K. Olick and Joyce Robbins, 'Social Memory Studies: From "Collective Memory" to the Historical Sociology of Mnemonic Practices', *American Review of Sociology* 24 (1998): 105–40.

many of the symbols of the defunct regime. As a result, much of the post-1989 discussion concerning German identity concentrated upon the memorials built to commemorate the socialist heroes of the GDR. Among the monuments about which there was a lengthy and heated debate was Prenzlauer Berg's Ernst Thälmann Memorial. Many westerners sought to tear down the fifty-ton bronze, maintaining that it was little more than a neo-Stalinist eyesore, while easterners sought to preserve it as a remnant of the socialist past commemorating the sacrifice of a Communist leader who had given his life in the fight against National Socialism. This case study provides an avenue for understanding the decision-making process in this debate as well as the ultimate triumph of practical considerations. In the end, the monument remained where it was because it was simply too expensive to remove. A careful examination of the debate surrounding this massive monument provides insight into the divergent understandings of 'Germanness' that became manifest in the debate.

The term 'national identity', which is implicit in any notion of 'Germanness', insinuates a continuity and coherence which can not be matched by a nation that was only founded in 1871 and in which what it means to belong to this nation and what it consists of was so often prone to changes. In its short history as a nation-state Germany was not only shaped by a sucession of political systems and ideologies, it is also a federal, regionalized and increasingly a multi-ethnic country. It had always incorporated a multiplicity of cultural identities – even before reunification. Therefore the term 'cultural identity' 'might provide a more useful perspective on shifting definitions of Germanness than the presumption of a "national character". Compared to an essential understanding of fixed traits, this flexible approach points to the constructed character, the contested nature, and the changing configurations of such a sense of self over time.'[24] The term also indicates that an individual identifies with the expections, values, practices and tacit knowledge of several groups simultaneously. Nationality might not be considered as the most formative or important factor for the understanding of one's social self. There

---

24   Konrad H. Jarausch and Michael Geyer, *Shattered Past. Reconstructing German Histories*, Princeton-Oxford 2003, p.223f.

might be a strong political interest in constructing a (normative) German 'national identity' in order to instrumentalize it as a tool of distinction and exclusion or to stabilize certain ideologies.[25] This volume is not a contribution to such a normative construction of 'German identity'. It rather aims to throw some light on identity discourses as communicative constructions, which, however unrealistic or manipulative they may be, still influence the way we perceive ourselves and the society we live in.

Rolf Parr's contribution shows that our daily conversation is coloured by symbols which, in their entirety, constitute a regular system of collective forms of concepts – however spontaneously they might be formed in daily life. This reservoir of 'images', which can be understood as a form of cultural memory, plays a vital role in the formation of symbolic ideas about the German 'national body' and German reunification. Focusing on this form of collective symbolism, the relatively fixed image of a nation can be seen as the effect of an abundance of frequently used symbols. Parr analyses what role collectively-used symbols play in the constitution of notions of national identity, what impact they have, and to which modifications they are subjected against the backdrop of political developments.

Friederike Eigler's article explores the relationship between German memory politics and the challenges facing post-unification Germany by looking at essays and speeches by Martin Walser and the German-Turkish author Zafer Şenocak. Though Walser has been labelled a renegade who switched from a liberal to a cultural-conservative position, Eigler maintains that both Walser and Şenocak represent positions that no longer fall neatly into the left/right paradigm. The main part of the article discusses Walser's and Şenocak's critiques of dominant forms of memory politics with reference to Şenocak's essays in *Atlas des tropischen Deutschland* (1992) and in *Zungenentfernung* (2001) on the one hand and Walser's 1998 Peace Prize speech and some of his essays dealing with the National Socialist past and with right-wing extremism in contemporary Germany

---

25 Jürgen Straub, 'Personale und kollektive Identität. Zur Analyse eines theoretischen Begriffs', in Aleida Assmann and Heidrun Friese (eds.), *Identitäten*, Frankfurt/M. 1998, pp.73–104: p.99.

(*Deutsche Sorgen*, 1997) on the other. Eigler examines their charges of moralism and ritualization concerning dominant discourses about cultural memory, charges that Walser and Şenocak articulate in a surprisingly similar manner but from which they draw very different conclusions. Comparing the alternative approaches to cultural memory Şenocak and Walser propose, Eigler argues that Walser's defense of the right to privacy concerning issues of memory and conscience is nostalgically oriented toward his own past. By contrast, Şenocak's call for linking cultural memory with issues in contemporary society, for example with Germany's transformation into a multi-ethnic society, indicates how the unproductive ideological battles of the period immediately before and after unification – conservatives calling for a 'closure' to the German past on the one hand and liberals defending ritualized practices of commemoration on the other – could be overcome in a constructive and forward-looking manner. Şenocak pleads for a revision of mono-cultural notions of 'German' memory and history. Cultural memory cannot be restricted to the history of one nation-state, but has to incorporate other perspectives on a history that has to be shared in more than one respect.

Memory Media

This volume aims to give its readers some insight into the impact of various memory media on our cultural memory. How we recall and envision the past is very much influenced by the media we use to extend the limited range of our individual memory. The metaphors we use to describe the workings of our memory, indicate that we imagine it according to our common 'memory devices', through which our memory emancipates itself from our mental restrictions. Each paradigm shift in modern media reflects on our memory theories, for example the discussion on 'outhoused memory' in response to the immense storage provided by the so-called digital revolution.[26]

Our belief in the ability of specific media to provide us with access to the past fluctuates. It is widely accepted, for example, that writing can transmit an extensive range of information in a more complex, differentiated and concentrated form than images, objects or the spoken word. We talk, for example, of something being 'inscribed' in our memory and, in the same way, envisage the mind of newborns as a blank page on which all future experiences will be written down. The idea that the written word is more durable than even large-scale, solid monuments and therefore represents the media of immortality is a *topos* from classical and Renaissance times.[27]

The first essays of the volume are concerned with the spoken and the written word, with Parr looking at the press, Eigler at public discussions in speeches, newspaper articles and essays, and Huber focusing on the impact of a family of famous authors on our political and cultural imagination. As mentioned above, memories are an aesthetic and imaginative recreation of the past. After all Mnemosyne, the Greek goddess of memory, is the mother of the muses. The muses acted as patron goddesses of the poets and indeed all fine arts, their modern temple being the museum (Greek *museion*, seat of the muses), our central institution for preserving, performing and transmitting the past. Literary texts are therefore at the centre of our cultural memory and this volume looks at the genres of prose, poetry and drama in order to find out how each genre places itself in the long tradition of commemorating and how it has established its own modes of commemoration.

Without denying the fictional status of those novels she analyses, Anne Friederike Müller highlights the overlapping of autobiographical, political, juridical and literary discourses through the narrative patterns and imagery they generate. Owen's contribution examines poetry of the *Wende*, distinguishing the generic possibilities of lyric

---

26   Götz-Lothar Darsow (ed.), *Metamorphosen. Gedächtnismedien im Computer-zeitalter*, Stuttgart-Bad Cannstatt 2000, p.7.
27   See Aleida Assmann, 'Text und Ruine', in Aleida Assmann, Monika Gomille and Gabriele Rippl (eds.), *Ruinenbilder*, Munich 2002, pp.151–163: p.151.

language to represent and understand such an historic shift. She argues that poets functionalize the ambiguity and openness of the poem to offer unusual and marginalized perspectives. They overwhelmingly write Germany's unification as a death – often a suicide – to be marked by obituary songs, which both celebrate and mourn. Identifying the sense of poets' commemorative task, it shows how their role in naming and imagining what is to endure becomes a matter of urgency. With reference to the 'Wall inside people's heads', Haas' essay deals with theatrical responses to reunification in both East and West against the backdrop of cultural images such as the 'marriage' of the two states, the *Wendehals* ('turncoat'), the 'colonizing' of the former GDR, and the theatricality of the gentle revolution.

In his contribution Bernhard Malkmus looks at W.G. Sebald's literary writings, which combine text and images, most of them photographs. The invention of the photographic image leading up to the medium film had a major influence on contemporary memory models. The photographic image seemed to guarantee an unmediated access to the past, reality having inscribed itself on the light-sensitive surface. The way modern technologies store and portray images of the past strongly influences how we imagine the workings of our memory. Sebald's texts make use of various forms of intermediality between text and image as a means of blurring the boundaries between fact and fiction, between collecting, recording and reconstructing historical data on the one hand and selecting, narrating and re-imagining history on the other. Malkmus' essay investigates the mutual illumination of textual and photographic strategies of stating and staging the past in Sebald. It argues that Sebald lays bare a paradoxical double-movement of the privatization of memory and simultaneous strategies of its conversion into cultural memory. He offers a 'mise en abîme' of the triangle of historical subject, historical fragments and voyeuristic historian-writer and thereby evokes a realm of constant translation between idiosyncratic condensations of historical memory and their return into a topicality of collective memory. Sebald aims at a language outside code, which establishes itself as a third space of constant re-formation between the poles stream-of-consciousness text and image, between signification and decodification. His technique of intermediality is analysed as symptomatic of a specific German post-1989 culture of remembrance which is marked by a rapid transformation of cultural memory of the traumata of twentieth century history due to demographic, geopolitical, social and psychological changes. Sebald's concept of intermediality facilitates a suspension of oblivion in a reunited Germany with its clashes of different cultures of collective memory.

Andreas Böhn's contribution looks at narratives, both in literature (Michael Kleeberg, *Ein Garten im Norden*, 1998) and in film (*Good Bye, Lenin!*, 2002), that centre around protagonists who succeed in creating an alternative history even though it is clearly marked as a fiction-within-the-fiction. These narratives reflect the need to distinguish between 'top-down' and 'bottom-up memories' on the one hand and authentic and artificially manufactured memories on the other hand, but at the same time they frustrate this need and confound strict boundaries. Even media which seem to guarantee a referential and historical truth – be it newscasts, documentary material or family photographs – are consciously or unconsciously portraying a version of our history that is made to fit prevailing demands.

And it is not only what we portray but also how we portray it that reflects the latest developments in storage techniques. With the invention of moving pictures we came to think of our memory as a flow of images; the German word 'Filmriß' describes both a jump in a film and a mental blackout. These metaphors clearly show how closely we connect memory to the medium of film. The film projector – a device which is able to capture time and make it available at any time – was invented in the same year which saw the publication of H.G. Wells' novel *The Time Machine* (1895).[28] Both devices respond to the same urge of not only visiting foreign places but also far-away times.[29]

---

28   The brothers August and Louis Lumière demonstrated their 'Cinematographe' at the Grand Café, 14 Blvd des Capucines in 1895. See Colin Sorensen, 'Theme Parks and Time Machines', in Peter Vergo (ed.), *The New Museology*, London 1989, pp.60–73: p.67.

29   Both devices are combined in the patent which British film pioneer Robert William Paul effected for his idea of a time machine, a performance of slide and film projections which was supposed to provide the illusion of time travel. See Hans-Arthur Marsiske, 'Zeitmaschinen – Alptraum oder Hoffnung der Geschichtswissenschaft? Über dieses Buch', in Hans-Arthur Marsiske (ed.), *Zeitmaschine Kino: Darstellungen von Geschichte im Film*, Marburg 1992, p.7.

Some metaphors concerning our memory reflect the most recent technological advancements in the electronic media: In the language of
digital data processing and its model of storage and retrieval we speak
of 'downloading' memories[30] and imagine a direct access to unchanged information that was simply put aside. But this should not
belie the fact that a medium such as the internet, widely used as an
alternative hightech library, works differently from the library, the
archive or the museum in that it does not involve the same conscious
selection criteria and voluntary forgetfulness, but stores simply anything that is posted on the Internet for a limited range of time.
Jonathan Bach's essay gives some insight into the virtual reconstruction of the memory of East Germany in the World Wide Web. The
Web has created a highly visible and complex network for the traces
of the GDR's afterlife. When the GDR vanished it seemed that its
physical traces would be mainly visible in pre-fabricated apartment
buildings and attics, official archives, the occasional museum exhibit,
and human memory. As the GDR disappeared into the pages of
history, however, it also reappeared in the pages of the Web. It
appears there today in the form of parody, nostalgia, memory and
history, as biting commentary on the present and as subtle digs at the
past. The chapter explores the Web as a technology of memory and
the modalities of memory this technology transmits or affords.
Through an analysis of this strange afterlife of the former German
Democratic Republic Bach seeks to explore the gray area where
nostalgia, memory and history coalesce. The blurred nature of these
categories is brought into stark relief by the Web's technology of
memory that has more in common with the 'memory palaces' of the
Renaissance than the linear trajectories of high modernity. The essay
extends the discussion of *Ostalgie* (nostalgia for the East) as expressed
through the material culture of consumption and takes *Alltagskultur*
(everyday life culture) as a starting point for understanding the question of German cultural identity. Bach raises the question of the 'virtual resurrection' of the GDR as part of a cultural survival strategy that

---

30   Peter Matussek, 'Erinnerung und Gedächtnis', in Hartmut Böhme, Peter
      Matussek and Lothar Müller (eds.), *Orientierung Kulturwissenschaft. Was sie
      kann, was sie will*, Reinbek bei Hamburg 2000, pp.147–164: p.148.

supplements and repositions the unification narrative and the role of German identity within it. A further aspect concerns the changing relation between exchange value and what Andreas Huyssen has called 'memory value' in regard to the GDR's appearance as a commodity and musealized object in the pages of the Web.

In times such as these, when the written word appears to depend on fickle fashions, nonliterary evidence gains in importance. Material traces are not only seen to encode messages from the past but also provide involuntary and therefore more truthful and authentic, even if more fragmented information.[31] Ward's and Lemmons' contributions show that unintended as well as intended monuments nevertheless change their memory value and their meaning over time. Sometimes these changes are caused by material alterations, as when the ruined church tower of the Kaiser Wilhelm-Gedächtniskirche comes to be seen as an anti-war memorial. Sometimes the interpretation is modified because the political and ideological framework and context in which the monument has acquired its meaning has changed, as is the case with the Ernst Thälmann Memorial in Berlin after reunification.

All these representations and materializations of memory are more or less based on negotiations between a range of people. Literary texts appear to be the solitary work of one person, but the decisions of the publisher and the expectations or anticipated reactions of the reading public also have to be taken into consideration. Monuments are commissioned by government officials based on open competitions, but the media and the communities claim to have a say in the matter. These materializations do not merely reproduce memories as dead signs, they form a cultural imagery, stimulate individual appropriations and provoke discussions in which we portray and recognize our past and draft our future.

Mannheim, January 2005[32]

---

31   See Aleida Assmann, 'Texts, Traces, Trash: The Changing Media of Cultural Memory', *Representations* 56 (1996), 123–34: 131.

32   I am grateful to the Herrmann-Weber-Stiftung (Mannheim University) for contributing to the funding of the volume. I would also like to thank David Midgley, Christian Emden and Antonio de Simine for their help and support.

Rolf Parr

National Symbols and the German Reunification

National Symbols

Because we subsume a very heterogeneous conglomeration of objects under the collective term 'national symbols', it seems reasonable to start with an overview of what this term can refer to. The spectrum ranges from national emblems such as national flags[1] and hymns,[2] heraldic animals, cockades, imperial and royal crowns, all of which assert the subject status of nations in contradistinction to others, to *national holidays* (14 July, Sedan Day, the Emperor's Birthday, 3 October), nineteenth-century national memorials (Valhalla, Monument of the Battle of Nations, Cologne Cathedral) and individual buildings, which are representative of historical and current political developments, such as the Reichstag, Brandenburg Gate and Berlin Wall. In addition, there are signs – often used as pars pro toto – such as the imprint 'Made in Germany' in the Fifties and Sixties, or the VW signet, the three Krupp rings and the Mercedes star. Another group includes personifications of national stereotypes in the sense of collective ideas about the different national characters: Germania, Michel for Germany,[3] Marianne for France, Uncle Sam, John Bull, Russian

---

1   See Martin Krampen, 'Zur Bedeutung nationaler Symbole und politischer Embleme in der visuellen Kommunikation', in Michael Titzmann (ed.), *Zeichen-(theorie) und Praxis. 6. Internationaler Kongreß der Deutschen Gesellschaft für Semiotik. 8.–11. Oktober 1990*, Passau 1993, pp.269–75.

2   See Eckhard Kuhn, *Nationale Symbole der Deutschen*, Bonn 1989; Bundeszentrale für politische Bildung (ed.), *Einigkeit und Recht und Freiheit. Nationale Symbole und nationale Identität*, Bonn 1985/1990.

3   See Karl Riha, 'Der deutsche Michel. Zur Ausprägung einer nationalen Allegorie im 19. Jahrhundert', in Jürgen Link and Wulf Wülfing (eds.), *Nationale*

Bear. A third group includes the pantheon of a culture's national heroes, that is the emblems of those historical or living persons who are well known, who are often used for analogies and who, moreover, can be said to be representatives of notions of nationality: Arminius, Luther, Siegfried, Queen Luise,[4] Bismarck;[5] Willy Brandt for some, Konrad Adenauer for others.

Now and again, the media point out that a politician has performed an important symbolic act. If these politicians are Federal Presidents or even Chancellors, these allegedly symbolic acts (such as Willy Brandt's kneeling before the Warsaw Ghetto Memorial for Polish victims of the Hitler regime and Helmut Kohl's striding through the Brandenburg Gate at Christmas 1989) come to be thought of as representative of the whole nation (and the politicians themselves). In a specific sense, they therefore become national symbolic acts.

Finally, however – and this is the most important area both quantitatively and qualitatively – our daily conversation is coloured by symbols in the form of images. We speak of 'engines of the economy', 'social safety nets', 'German and European houses', 'floods of asylum seekers', 'the ailing body' of the formerly so 'healthy' German economy, 'surgical operations' of military commandos, or – as in the case of the former German foreign minister Klaus Kinkel – a curiously out-of-place 'German Saint Bernard dog in a china shop':

> Deutschland ist nach der Wiedervereinigung so etwas wie ein ausgewachsener Bernhardiner in einem engen europäischen Wohnzimmer. Jedesmal, wenn er mit dem Schwanz wedelt, bedroht er das Kaffeegeschirr. Daran sollten alle denken, wenn sie die europäische Einigung mies machen.[6]

Mythen und Symbole in der zweiten Hälfte des 19. Jahhunderts. Strukturen und Funktionen von Konzepten nationaler Identität, Stuttgart 1991, pp.146–71.

4   See Wulf Wülfing, Karin Bruns and Rolf Parr, *Historische Mythologie der Deutschen 1798–1918*, Munich 1991.

5   See Rolf Parr, *'Zwei Seelen wohnen, ach! in meiner Brust!' Strukturen und Funktionen der Mythisierung Bismarcks (1860–1918)*, Munich 1992; Rolf Parr, 'Bismarck-Mythen – Bismarck-Analogien', *kultuRRevolution*, 24 (January 1991), 12–6; Rolf Parr, 'Diskursanalytische Betrachtungen zum Bismarck-Mythos', in Titzmann (ed.), *Zeichen(theorie)*, pp.283–91.

6   *Westdeutsche Allgemeine Zeitung* (17 February 1994), 2.

(Since reunification, Germany has become something of a fully grown Saint Bernard dog in a small European living room. Each time he wags his tail, he threatens the coffee set. Everyone should think about this, when they run down European unification.)

Upon closer inspection, it becomes evident that such symbols may be formed spontaneously in daily life and sometimes – as in the Kinkel example – seem a bit strange, but nonetheless, in their entirety, they constitute a regular system of collective ways of looking at things ('Anschauungsformen'). This reservoir of 'images', which we can understand as a form of cultural and occasionally also national memory, plays a vital role in the formation of symbolic ideas about the German 'national body'. Therefore, we ought to consider whether it does not make more sense to invert the perspective and enquire how a relatively fixed image of a nation can be seen as the effect of an abundance of frequently used symbols, what impact it has, and to which modifications it is subjected against the backdrop of political developments – rather than attempting to define the official status of national symbols. Hence, in the following, I would like to analyse what role collectively-used symbols play in the constitution of notions of national identity. To this end, I will first draw on a series of examples from the period of reunification, or *Wende*, during the years 1989–1992. In the second section, I will systematize in a schema the range of collective symbols which have frequently been deployed in our culture and especially in the media discourse. The third section concentrates on the relation between Germany and Europe and its related symbolic models. Finally, on the basis of the previously discussed material, I shall single out some important current political issues about disturbances and states of emergency affecting national bodies.

Symbols of Reunification – *Wende*

Without any doubt, the media discourse between 1989 and 1991 was quantitatively and empirically dominated by four nationally coloured configuration of signs: the talk about a 'common European' and then a 'common German house', the (Berlin) 'Wall' (or, as its pars pro toto, the 'Brandenburg Gate'), the East German 'Trabi' car, and last but not least the 'unstoppable train of German unification'.

'Common European'/'Common German House'

'The end of the schism between East and West'[7] first manifested itself symbolically, namely in the form of the 'common European house', an image which Mikhail Gorbachev borrowed from the western media discourse.[8] Like 'ship', 'plane', or 'car', 'house' symbols too serve as images for social and state systems and can be used to depict any conceivable form of solidarity with a system: just as we supposedly all sit in one 'boat' or (at least occasionally) pull together ('an einem Strang ziehen'), we also live in one 'house'. Besides, because of the many elements we might imagine in connection with it, the 'house' symbol can be used in a very flexible manner.[9] It caught on in the course of 1988, when a number of TV programmes and conferences made an issue of the 'European house'. In this phase, it was mostly about transferring the fourfold split (Berlin, German, European and

---

7   Jean François-Poncet, 'Deutschlands Einheit, Europas Chance?', *Die Zeit*, 8 (16 February 1990), 3.

8   See, for more detail, Rolf Parr, '"Was ist des Deutschen Vaterhaus?" – Kleines Belegstellenarchiv zum "Gemeinsamen europäischen Haus"', *kultuRRevolution*, 23 (June 1990), 74–9.

9   See Jürgen Link, *Die Struktur des Symbols in der Sprache des Journalismus. Zum Verhältnis literarischer und pragmatischer Symbole*, Munich 1978, pp.32, 115, 203f.

western/eastern) into an integrated 'European house'. The split – as a familiar abnormality – had to be moulded into an unfamiliar normality, the 'common European house', which sparked attempts to find the appropriate image to illustrate this. Dieter Schröder, editor of the *Süddeutsche Zeitung*, provided the right image for the problem. He suggested one should talk about 'a European double house'. It was, 'at the moment, less about the construction of a European house, but rather about the way in which the walls of the double house could be torn down, how one could organize neighbourly help and avoid confrontation'.[10]

'Wall', 'Brandenburg Gate'

As early as June 1989, the Berlin *tageszeitung* had referred to the 'wall' in the European house: 'Gorbachev's European house has a wall. Gorbachev tells Bonn press: Wall not greatest problem in the European house.'[11] The caricaturist Klaus Pielert visualized the partition vividly by splitting the European bull with a fire wall, of course *the* wall, into an eastern and a western part (Ill. 1).[12] At this point in time, against the backdrop of the emerging wave of refugees from the GDR, the wall and the division of Germany, and with it, the 'common German house', became the focus of interest.[13] 9 November 1989, the qualifying date for the economic de-facto reunification, finally established the change in symbols from 'European' to 'German house'. The opening of the Brandenburg Gate, a monument which had had a

10   Körber-Stiftung (ed.), *86. Bergedorfer Gesprächskreis am 3. und 4. Dezember 1988 in der Bad Godesberger Redoute. Das gemeinsame europäische Haus – aus der Sicht der Sowjetunion und der Bundesrepublik Deutschland*, Hamburg Bergedorf 1988, p.33.

11   *die tageszeitung* (16 June 1989), 1.

12   'Das europäische Haus muß noch zusammenwachsen' ('The European house still has to grow together'), *Westdeutsche Allgemeine Zeitung* (7 July 1989).

13   See also *Die Zeit*, 28 (7 July 1989), 12 (readers' letters about Theo Sommer's article 'Der Maurer und die Mauer' in No. 25).

particularly strong symbolic significance for decades, accelerated this development even more.[14] Klaus Hartung, in December 1989 in the *tageszeitung*, grasped the sense of what this opening meant much more effectively by using the 'house'-symbol, than any abstract description could have done: 'With the opening of the Brandenburg Gate', Berlin has 'become the small house in the European house – with rooms with a view to both sides'.[15] The development was no longer from the 'common European' to the 'common German house', but just the other way around, from the 'undivided Berlin house' to the 'all-German house', and from there to the 'European house'. Chancellor Kohl, when he visited Dresden on 19 December 1989, received 'cheering and acclamation' for uttering the sentence: 'The German house has to be built under a European roof'. Hence, the watchword 'German house' was employed also by the highest ranking German official. This statement, however, was then already understood as asserting the supremacy of the 'German' over the 'European house'. Spectators displayed a 'giant placard' which read 'First Germany, then Europe' and was equally greeted with acclaim.[16]

The 'Train of German Unification'

Another symbol was added to the 'German house' around January 1990, namely that of the unstoppable 'train of German unification'. 'Track' and 'timetable' fixed the direction and the destination, so that politics could only argue about the adequate 'speed'. This 'train' was nothing other than a 'German house'[17] which was put onto wheels and

14   See Rolf Parr and Siegfried Reinecke, 'Faszinationsenergie. Zur symbolischen Realität im neuen Deutschland', *medium. Zeitschrift für Hörfunk, Fernsehen, Film, Presse*, 22 (1992), 6–9.

15   Klaus Hartung, 'Öffnung zum Alltag', *die tageszeitung* (23 December 1989), 8.

16   'Nicht von heute auf morgen', *Der Spiegel*, 52 (25 December 1989), 16ff.

17   See Jürgen Link, 'Wie weich landen die Wendeturbulenzen des europäischen Hauses? Kollektivsymbole und aktuelle (De)Normalisierungsschübe', *kultuR-Revolution*, 23 (June 1990), 58–69: 65.

tracks. The European perspective also entered into this discussion, because the 'German train' corresponded to a 'European' one, and there were debates about which 'wagon' could be 'coupled up' where, and which could not, who was supposed to be the 'locomotive' and who the 'brakemen',[18] and who had to switch the 'points' in which direction.[19] The shift from the 'house' to the 'train' symbol highlights one of the most important structures of media discourse: individual symbols can be combined with one another and are partly interchangeable, so that they form chains of equivalence. 'House', 'train', 'ship', 'body' and 'family' can all equally be used as images for social systems, so that a tight net of interrelated symbols is produced.

The extent to which the 'train' symbols were, and still are, present in people's minds, was illustrated by reactions to the French Maastricht-referendum in September 1992, when the German Foreign Minister Klaus Kinkel showed delight that 'the German train keeps going'.[20] Kinkel thereby adapted the symbol 'train', which had proven so successful for the German unification, to the process of European unification. The following day, newspaper articles were dominated by the 'train' symbol: 'Bonn delighted: European train keeps going',[21] 'EU wants to stick to old timetable'.[22]

---

18   See the caricature 'SPD im Bremserhäuschen' ('SPD in the brake-house') in *Westdeutsche Allgemeine Zeitung* (28 June 1990).

19   See the caricature 'Weichensteller' ('Pointsman') in *Westdeutsche Allgemeine Zeitung* (28 June 1990).

20   *Westdeutsche Allgemeine Zeitung* (21 September 1992), 1; see also Werner A. Perger, 'Pandoras Büchse bleibt geschlossen', *Die Zeit*, 40 (25 September 1992), 2: 'Klaus Kinkel saw the 'European train' carry on going, now the Danes would have to see not to miss the connection'.

21   *Westdeutsche Allgemeine Zeitung* (21 September 1992), 1.

22   *die tageszeitung* (22 September 1992), 2.

Rules

Continuing with the interpretation of symbols, let us try to formulate some initial rules according to which such commonly used symbols are generated as configurations of signs with national dimensions.

First, there is a general tendency to symbolize historical events or issues. One example is the Brandenburg Gate as a symbol of the German division, as used on the well-known Berlin emergency stamp-duty in the early years of the Republic. This rule is manifest in the remark of the former German Federal President Richard von Weizsäcker, who maintained that the German question would remain open as long as the Brandenburg Gate remained closed.

Secondly, there is a tendency to subsume new events under already-established national symbols. On 2 October 1990, in its special edition on the German unification, the *Bild Zeitung* provided an example of this, when it showed the Potsdamer Platz – the symbolic German 'centre' or 'heart' of the new German national body – five times, and saw common meaning in all the following: the old Prussian Empire (1904), the Olympic Games in Berlin (1936), the German capitulation after the Second World War (1945), the legendary 'The Wall'-concert by Pink Floyd (1990) and the envisaged development of the site by Daimler-Benz and Sony. Hence, the realization of each individual element conjured up connotations of all the others – a mechanism which largely explains the much-quoted historical 'depth' of meaning that are attributed to national symbols.

Thirdly, there is a tendency to interpret new events by re-valuating symbols. For instance, since 1989, the 'wall' symbol 'Brandenburg Gate' has become the symbol of unity and freedom,[23] as illustrated by a caricature in the newspaper *Die Welt* of 3 October 1990 (Ill. 2), in diametrical contrast to its previous use in the media as

---

23 Only a few days after the construction of the Wall, a chronicle of events labelled the GDR – then still called SBZ (Soviet Zone of Occupation) – a 'KZ' (concentration camp). See Matthias Walden, *Die Mauer. Eine Dokumentation. Sender Freies Berlin* (August 1961), repeat *N III* (9 November 1990).

a symbol of division and incarceration.[24] This complete reversal of meaning, while referring to the same object, was made possible by linking several symbols and their meanings to create a complex texture. The necessary intermediate stage in this revaluation of the semantics of the Brandenburg Gate was that the symbolic Trabi car, (which stood for freedom, progress, individuality and, predominantly, private property, even though it was from a western perspective hopelessly primitive and technically unsophisticated),[25] broke both through the wall, which signified the precise opposite of freedom, and through the Brandenburg Gate, which was still closed (Ill. 3).[26] Subsequently, the entire media selected and favoured this particular linkage of symbols, never wearying of showing Trabis going straight through the Brandenburg Gate or, at least, the 'Wall'.

As a fourth rule, we can note the revaluation of existing symbols by connecting them with new symbols. Presented as a devotional object, toyshops offered a Trabi-model in a black-red-golden packaging with a transparent window for sale; in the background, one saw the Brandenburg Gate, the Wall, a cheering crowd and a sign which read 'Opening of the Berlin Wall 9 November 1989'. For an additional charge, this ensemble of national emblems was delivered together with an original piece of the wall and the slogan: 'The car with which

24　Strictly speaking, Berlin has always been a location symbolic of both division and connection at the same time (with special rights for a facilitated crossing of the border, for instance). The GDR-leadership, with their terminology 'capital of the GDR', always attempted to split 'the shared city of Berlin' into two different parts, and therefore to remove Berlin's symbolic dignity.

25　Due to the inevitable connotations of 'freedom' and 'self-determination', 'car' has always been a precarious symbol in the GDR; a large amount of GDR-literature testifies to this. On the *car*-symbol more generally see Siegfried Reinecke, *Autosymbolik in Journalismus und Film. Struktural-funktionale Analysen vom Beginn der Motorisierung bis zur Gegenwart*, Bochum 1992; GDR-literature on the topic: Gerd Katthage, Karl-Wilhelm Schmidt, *Langsame Autofahrten. Studien zu Texten ostdeutscher Schriftsteller*, Weimar-Cologne-Vienna 1997.

26　'Der neueste Hit' ('The latest hit'), *Westdeutsche Allgemeine Zeitung* (12 September 1989).

a whole nation set off to freedom.'[27] This multi-symbolic arrangement is also notable for its use of national colours, which were supposedly aimed at instructing people to grasp the national meaning of the objects on display (Ill. 4).[28] The linkage of 'freedom', as the 'content' which is delivered, and 'Brandenburg Gate' as a national symbol, could, however, also be deployed beyond the context of German reunification. In order to illustrate this, I would like to draw attention to a notice entitled 'Friendship in freedom', which was published during the time of the first Gulf War,[29] when protests made by the church met with the reproach of Anti-Americanism. Here, two symbols which are representative of their respective nations, are inter-connected (Ill. 5). This seems to work out well, since both the Bran-denburg Gate and the Statue of Liberty evoke ideas of freedom. Both guarantors of freedom become closely interlinked. The message is clear: whoever is against the United States, (it is implied) is against freedom. Taking this thinking one step further, Germans would para-doxically be against themselves if they were to take a stance against the United States.

Fifthly, these national symbols also offer ready models for social identification, that is, for the formation of a collective subject. The individual, practical realization of national symbols (Chancellor Kohl striding through the Brandenburg Gate at Christmas 1989, as many thousands of other German citizens and tourists have done since), as well as the collective realization (such as the 'occupation' of the Brandenburg Gate on the night of 9 November 1989 and in the night of New Year's Eve 1989/90) promoted strong feelings of community, and even mass enthusiasm.

---

27   See *Stadtspiegel Bochum* (23 January 1989): 'Mit ihm fuhr ein Volk in die Freiheit …' ('With this, a whole nation drove into freedom …'). The periodical *Die Zeit* used the title: 'Mit dem "Trabant" zur Sonne zur Freiheit' ('With the "Trabant" to the sun to freedom') (15 September 1989), *die tageszeitung*: 'Trabbi frei nach Westen' ('Trabbi free to travel west') (12 September 1989), *Die Welt*: 'Trabis: das Symbol der Freiheit' ('Trabis: the symbol of freedom') (3 October 1990).

28   Illustration from Parr and Reinecke, 'Faszinationsenergie', 7.

29   'Freundschaft in Freiheit' ('Friendship in freedom'), *Westdeutsche Allgemeine Zeitung* (20 December 1991).

National Signs – Approached from the Perspective of Discourse Theory

National identity is constituted only through the permanent use of symbols, and is therefore not prior to them, as is often presupposed. In this process, individuals associate themselves with the nation, which is in turn identified through symbols. They then apply the symbols to their own persona and their own choices of action, thereby realizing symbols in a very practical way. Individual and national identity thus reciprocally constitute one another in the same process.[30]

We can observe a shift in emphasis in national symbols from the nineteenth century to the media age. By associating random objects of daily life with national emblems, almost everything can be nationally (over)determined, as was the case between 1989 and 1991. And yet, it was not necessarily the national flag itself which attracted people's attention and made their bodies tremble with passion. When, in 1989, TV channels almost invariably broadcasted the signifier 'nation', often enough only the black, red and gold colours of the national flag were presented (but not the flag itself). This, however, applied to almost every advertisement in the print media and to all TV commercials, no matter whether they were about food, pencils, petrol stations, banks or insurances. By alluding to, or quoting, the national colours, any object could become a 'national' object. On the other hand, this was a very pragmatic process, in which firms and advertising managers associated themselves with, and thereby joined, the new German nation. There was no single outstanding symbol or unifying material symbol anymore, none which could have been regarded as sacrosanct, instead there was something like the following generative rule: associate each everyday object with the strong national overtones of the reunification process.[31] In order to realize this rule, it was easiest to equip daily objects, in particular commodities, with the colours com-

---

30 Jürgen Link elaborates on this context in 'Normalismus: Konturen eines Konzepts', *kultuRRevolution*, 27 (August 1992), 50–70: 69.
31 See the advertisement by the Volksbanken Raiffeisenbanken: 'Wir gratulieren: Deutschland!' ('We congratulate: Germany!'), *Die Welt* (3 October 1990), 5.

bination black, red and gold – often in a seemingly casual manner.[32]
This was also a way of celebrating the victory of the market economy.
Moreover, the colour triad 'black-red-gold' of the Federal Republic
could be conceived in opposition to the flag of the GDR with its
'tools': 'hammer and compasses'. The act of demonstrating affiliation
to the reunified Germany was therefore much more important than
the particular signs used for that purpose. In other words, in post-
modernism, symbols function in a different way than national emblems did in the nineteenth century. When all our aesthetic habits of
reading and seeing are trained to observe disparate and fluctuating
fragments of images, which recur in a variety of places, rather than
whole entities, then an extensively diversified national symbol corre-
sponds perfectly to this new aesthetic and is particularly apt at
integrating the most diverse social components under the heading of
'nationality'. Hence, in the end, telephone cards and advertisements
with illustrations of the Brandenburg Gate may be more important
than national anthems.

We occasionally encounter the complaint that it is regrettable
that national symbols no longer meet with broad approval. However,
in view of the general evolutionary processes that are taking place, we
have to ask whether old symbols can continue to exist. Perhaps this
loss of meaning, often deplored by politicians, finds an adequate
explanation in the shifts of our perception, rather than (just) in the
nation itself.

There are three arguments to support this suggestion. First, we
can point, in its support, to the fact that there were once broad-based
official discussions about national symbols. There were discussions
about how to name the new Germany, what the flag should look like,
and which national anthem, with which text, to choose. These debates
were at one time, for instance, led in the major weekly periodicals, but
having failed to arouse long-lasting public interest or achieve any
result, they have disappeared from the stage of public discussion.

Secondly, if in the past someone decorated their skis, yogurt
tubs or condom packaging with national colours, it would have been

---

32   See the advertisement by the Tengelmann Group: 'Wir freuen uns auf Deutsch-
      land' ('We look forward to Germany'), *Bild Zeitung* (2 October 1990).

seen, at least in some cases, as falling under the legal category of 'defamation', and would have provoked legal action. To my knowledge, in 1989, this was not even an issue.

Thirdly, I would like to point out the difficulties in dealing with traditional national symbols. For instance, 9 November would actually have been the appropriate day to become a national holiday. Since 1989, the media at least have celebrated it as the 'anniversary of the opening of the Wall'. However, it was not officially sanctioned due to past historical events associated with this day. It would be interesting to analyse whether the revolutionary 9 November 1918, the Hitler putsch on 9 November 1923, or the so-called 'Kristallnacht' on 9 November 1938 was the greatest obstacle to its being made a national bank holiday.[33] Furthermore, buildings which were, for instance, renovated in the former eastern part of Berlin (such as the Neue Wache and several building complexes which were supposed to host ministries), were discussed in terms of their historical 'depth' (one could also say, their contamination by 'historically dangerous waste'), in a twofold way: a) GDR-totalitarianism, especially associations with the Stasi, and b) National Socialism. Such historical 'depth', and the fear of it, resulted from oft-unspoken historical analogies such as: 'If the Ministry of Defence is accommodated in precisely the same building complex in which the SS or the infamous Mfs (Ministry of State Security) resided, then …'.

This symbolic value is particularly noticeable when comparing the *Palast der Republik* with the Internationales Congress Centrum (ICC) in West Berlin. The discovery that the building was contaminated with asbestos (which, connotatively, meant 'Stasi-contaminated', or even much more generally 'GDR-contaminated'), led to debates about its demolition. When the ICC in West Berlin, however, was also declared contaminated by asbestos, its possible destruction never even became an issue in public discussion.[34] Similar considerations apply to

---

33   On this issue, see Johannes Willms (ed.), *Der 9. November. Fünf Essays zur deutschen Geschichte*, Munich 1994.

34   In the case of Berlin, it was possible to abstract from the 'old historical depth' (Wilhelminian times and Hitler's reign), because its NS-history was eclipsed by the 'newer historical depth', its tale of woe beginning in 1945 and Ernst

other 'national events' which met with public disapproval: the transfer of Frederick the Great to Potsdam,[35] the plans to reconstruct the imperial 'Schloss' in Berlin, and the re-erection of the Kaiser-Wilhelm-Memorial at the Deutsches Eck in Koblenz.

The Systematic Character of Collective Symbols

If the images that keep occurring in daily life can be understood as a coherent network of symbols, which has a decisive impact both on political symbolic speech and the constitution of the 'nation', 'national feeling' and 'national signs', then it is well worth presenting the most crucial structural features of this system of symbols in an abstract way. Some years ago, Jürgen Link devised a basic diagram that constitutes 'the common "kernel" of the majority of symbolic statements in our culture'[36] (Ill. 6).[37] Central to this diagram is the 'right-left-axis' with 'heart/centre' and 'extremes', typically used to depict the topography of political parties,[38] an axis which favours the symbolic quality of the 'pair of scales', and accordingly the 'centre', which is very positively connoted due to its 'stability'.

Let us think back again to the divided Germany: the 'Wall' went right through the symbolic 'heart' of this national body, namely through Berlin. The 'vertical' axis, which is associated with a series of 'body'-symbols, forms the second constitutive dimension of this symbol system. The capital Berlin would constitute the symbolic heart on this axis. Correspondingly, a politician who represents Germany

---

Reuter's exclamation 'People, look at this city', together with Kennedy's declaration: 'I am a Berliner'.

35   See Ralf Lehmann, 'Schwere Symbole', *Westdeutsche Allgemeine Zeitung* (7 August 1991), 2.

36   Jürgen Link, 'Diskursive Rutschgefahren ins Vierte Reich? Rationales Rhizom', *kultuRRevolution*, 5 (February 1984), 12–20: 12.

37   Andreas Disselnkötter and Rolf Parr, 'Kollektivsymbolsystem – didaktisch aufbereitet', *kultuRRevolution*, 30 (October 1994), 52–65: 65.

38   See also *kultuRRevolution*, 6 (June 1984) and 26 (December 1991).

would have to take the place of the capital. Indeed, the satiric journal *titanic* realized this by incorporating Chancellor Kohl into the layout of a well-known series of street maps (Ill. 7: 'Helmut Kohl must remain [German] capital'). The third axis is dynamic and embraces the two opposing poles, 'progression' and 'retrogression', and the series of symbols that goes with them, namely 'light', 'sun', 'growth', 'forwards' and 'progression' versus 'backwards', retrogression', 'dark Medieval Ages' and 'Stone Age'. As a temporal axis, it can connect 'old' and 'new', thereby establishing continuity. It is obvious where an object has to be placed in order to achieve a balance of 'past' and 'present': namely in the 'centre', which is thus symbolic in a threefold sense. To use the example of Berlin again, all three axes together require its symbolic positioning in the middle.[39] Symbols create reality, as a simple experiment illustrates: asked to place Berlin on an empty map of Germany, almost every German citizen would locate Berlin in the 'centre' of Germany – quite contrary to its actual geographical position.

The symbolic social system now has to be extended beyond its home territory, taking into account the threat from outside – as illustrated for instance by the surrounding 'underground-chaos', which lacks the subject character of a nation. Again, the two grey-shaded squares include the symbols which are often used for 'system' and 'chaos'. Furthermore, there are two interfaces between 'system' and 'underground': the 'hole' in the outer frontier of the system, through which 'chaos' can penetrate into the home system, and the 'system enclave out there in hostile territory' (for instance 'our boys in Afghanistan'). Berlin, of course, constituted precisely such a 'system-enclave in hostile territory' during the entire period of the 'Cold War'. At the same time, Berlin was also a 'hole' for the 'infiltration' of foreign elements (for instance secret agents). An absurd situation occurred when, in 1986, more and more refugees came into the GDR via the Berlin-Schönefeld airport, subsequently entering the Federal

---

39   On the perception of the city through collective symbols see Rolf Parr, 'Kollektivsymbole als Medien in der Stadtwahrnehmung', in Bernd Henningsen (eds.), *Die inszenierte Stadt. Zur Praxis und Theorie kultureller Konstruktionen*, Berlin 2001, pp.19–42.

Republic of Germany via the frontier between the two Germanies and applying for asylum. At that time, western politicians bluntly called for the closure of the wall – an utterly ludicrous demand, given the fact that, for decades, these same politicians had demanded that the wall be opened. A second, very different threat to the system is posed by a counter-system, which, in contrast to the 'underground', also has subject status. Examples are implicit in the old opposing systems 'East/West', 'freedom/socialism', or 'democratic/totalitarian'.

I would like to take the systematization of this symbolic system one step further and enquire how exactly we should conceptualize the functioning of symbols as a system of interconnected perspectives. How do multiple relations between individual symbols come about? First, symbols from very diverse social domains can be combined to form a chain of image elements, while retaining the same meaning. In this way, we obtain a structural axis for the symbolic system, with chains of image-elements all with the same meaning – for instance, the German reunification is comparable to the construction of a common German 'house', like an unstoppable German 'train', like the 'victory' in the Football World Cup. 'Our' own system can figure sometimes as 'car', sometimes as 'body', or else as 'boat' or 'plane', and very different events, such as those involving sports, become equivalents of national identities. The threat to this system too adopts different shapes, from 'black floods of people' to 'explosions', 'terrorists' and 'Islamic fundamentalists'. Second, and contrary to what was said previously, different facts can be subsumed under one image, such as 'viruses', 'cars', 'the unemployed' and 'asylum seekers' under the single image 'flood'. Third, as a result of the interplay of both structural axes, collective symbols make up a complex synchronic system, which, although it consists of many individual symbols, ultimately comprises a finite number of such symbols which are set in relation to one another and can always be used to code political events and to compare them, symbolically, with one another. Fourth, we can understand the continuous misuse, or strained use of words (galloping catachresis) as the most decisive structure, which connects the two aforementioned axes. An impressive example from the *Die Welt am Sonntag* on 3 December 1989 concerned Chancellor Kohl's newly announced 'Germany plan' ('Deutschlandplan') and combined two completely different types of sport (football and mountaineering) with electrical engineering and psychology or medicine.

> Gezwungenermaßen, umständehalber steigt er [Kanzler Kohl, R.P.] die Stufe zum 'konföderativen Haus' empor, um sich von dort zum 'Bundesstaat Deutschland' zu seilen. Ob der Querpaß an die Steilwand gerät, hängt vom 'deutschen Volk' ab [...]. Der Deutschland-Plan erfüllt die Funktion eines Verstärkers, er destabilisiert die SED-Herrschaft im Zentralnervensystem.[40]

> (Circumstances compel him [Chancellor Kohl, R.P.] to climp the step to the 'confederative house', so that he can then swing across from there to the 'Federal German State'. Whether the cross meets a sheer rock-face, depents on the 'German people' [...]. The Germany-plan functions as an amplifier, it destabilizes the SED-regime in its central nervous system.)

New events and political decisions are invariably perceived through the 'lens' of the symbolic system, and also their media presentation is focused through the symbolic system.

This does not happen in an ideologically neutral way, but always from a particular evaluative perspective, which can be defined as the discourse position taken within the respective synchronic network of symbols. For instance, in the late summer of 1989, the 'floods' of GDR refugees were positively connoted (as 'fresh blood supply for the market economy',[41] 'injection for financing pensions', etc.), while those of refugees from southern countries were evaluated extremely negatively.

The 'lens' comprised by the symbolic system must, however, not be misunderstood as a sort of ideological 'veil', which only needs to be dropped for us to gain a true viewpoint onto the real facts. Rather, symbolic speech is required for a number of reasons and constitutes a culturally accessible framework of conceptions, which cannot simply be avoided. Collective symbols can, for instance, reduce the complex logic of questions regarding a certain issue to a simple logic of images, and thereby linking it to everyday experiences. This is extremely important for all forms of journalism.

---

40   *Welt am Sonntag* (3 December 1989).
41   See *die tageszeitung* (23 September 1989).

Mass-reproduced symbols and emotive words can be understood as a reservoir of models for convictions and attitudes, and consequently also for the formation of national subjectivities. If we remind ourselves, moreover, that we are continually exposed to the 'recycling of symbols on a massive scale (which begins in earliest childhood and ends only in death)',[42] we simply cannot overestimate its enormous impact, in particular on the formation of notions of national and supranational identities. The loss of orientation and of value regarding national identity can therefore also be understood as a disruption through frictions in the symbolic system. To conclude, I would like briefly to touch on a few examples.

a) Two symbolic systems: From the perspective outlined above, a first source of disruption at the time of the reunification lay in the fact that the collective symbolic system which was currently used in the GDR had a very different structure and function than that employed in the western media discourse of the Federal Republic.[43] Now, if both subjective as well as national identities are also generated and focused through the collective symbol system, then we would have to expect enormous challenges in the process of the 'growing together of what belongs together' (Willy Brandt).

b) Ambivalent counter-system: Before reunification, the shaping of West Germany's own national body in the symbolic system was done in direct comparison to, or in dissociation from, the counter-system 'eastern bloc'. After the dismantling of the GDR, the USSR took on a highly ambiguous image of both friend and enemy, which oscillated between 'capitalistic junior partner' and 'relapse into the old system', vacillating, as it were, between a 'good Yeltsin-Clinton' and a 'nasty Zhirinovsky-Hitler', with Putin recently taking a middle position. The collective symbolic system has permanently to redefine the object 'Russia', at times on a weekly basis, alternating between

---

42   Link, 'Normalismus', p.69.

43   Jürgen Link and Wilfried Korngiebel, 'Von einstürzenden Mauern, europä-
      ischen Zügen und deutschen Autos. Die Wiedervereinigung in Bildern und
      Sprachbildern der Medien', in Rainer Bohn, Knut Hickethier, and Eggo Müller
      (eds.), *Mauer-Show. Das Ende der DDR, die deutsche Einheit und die Medien*,
      Berlin 1992, pp.31–53.

'hostile system', 'friendly system' and 'underground-chaos'. National self-definitions vary accordingly.

c) Normalization as de-normalization: The normality attained as a result of reunification is often experienced as an immense and by now probably irreversible de-normalization, and therefore as a permanent state of emergency. This paradoxical discrepancy brings about enormous – and not exclusively symbolic – disruptions, which correspond to paradoxical statements such as the well known saying 'We have to overcome the division through sharing' ('die Teilung durch Teilen überwinden'). Similar to the previous example is the symbol of the 'social net', which is almost exclusively used in the context of 'absorbing the shock in the social net' ('abfedern im sozialen Netz'). In the past, there used to be talk about 'cushioning' or even 'lazing about in the social hammock'. Nowadays, however, 'crash' and 'impact' seem to have become inevitable, so that public discourse focuses on 'absorbing the shock' and the scope of the necessary 'interventions'.

National-German versus European Identity

The discussion about an economically unified Europe and the introduction of the Euro as a common currency was marked by permanent frictions between national and European identities. The symbol of the 'common European house' conjured up the image of a democratic community of inhabitants with equal rights, with the media regularly employing the image of the family. Yet, seen from a politically pragmatic viewpoint, there were of course distinctions, due to competition, between countries with differing economic power and, consequently, different 'classes of normality', as Jürgen Link put it in a series of essays, evoking a still more complex theoretical concept.[44]

The inhabitants of the 'European house', too, belong to a variety of classes of normality. Amongst the symbols previously introduced, it was easiest to extend that of the 'train' in the direction of the presen-

---

44   See, for instance, Jürgen Link, 'Normalismus'.

tation of different classes of normality, for instance by coupling wagons of different qualities to form a common vehicle. As the discussions and referendums on the Maastricht treaty and the lengthy process of the introduction of the Euro have illustrated, such differentiations made the identification of a 'European' communality difficult. In economic terms, Germany soon became, symbolically, a 'bastion' ('Trutzburg') within Europe. Theo Sommer, long-serving major political journalist for the periodical *Die Zeit*, addressed this problem in autumn 1992 as follows, using collective symbols:

> Ohne ein französisches Ja wäre alle europäische Liebesmühe vergebens gewesen. Dieses Ja reicht allerdings allein nicht aus, den EG-Dampfer wieder flottzumachen. Noch liegt das dänische Hindernis in der Fahrrinne. Vor allen Dingen steuert die britische Maastricht-Debatte in gefährliche Gewässer. Die Briten, die derzeit die Präsidentschaft innehaben und deren Aufgabe es eigentlich ware, das leckgeschlagene Schiff abzudichten, sind tief zerstritten. […] Ein angeschlagener John Major könnte schon im Unterhaus Schiffbruch erleiden. […] Von nun an wird in der Gemeinschaft, weit stärker als bisher, das Prinzip der variablen Geometrie herrschen. Es entsteht das Europa der zwei oder gar mehr Geschwindigkeiten. Jene, die den Willen dazu haben, werden voranschreiten; die nicht dazu bereit sind, bleiben zurück, ohne die anderen zu bremsen. Ausgeschlossen wird keiner, aufschließen zum Gros kann später jeder. Die langsamsten Schiffe bestimmen nicht länger das Tempo des Geleitzugs. Flexibilität ist das Gebot der Stunde.[45]

> (Without a French 'Yes', all European efforts would have been in vain. This 'Yes', however, is not sufficient to get the EU-steamer moving. The Danish obstacle still lies in its path. And above all, the British debate about Maastricht is steering into dangerous waters. The British, who have the presidency at the moment and whose task it would actually be to make the damaged ship seaworthy, are disunited. […] A tarnished John Major could already be shipwrecked in the House of Commons. […] From now on, the principle of variable geometry will reign in the community much more powerfully than before. A Europe of two or even more speeds is coming into being. Those who have the will to stride ahead will do so; those who are not prepared to do so will remain behind, without restricting the others. Nobody will be excluded, as everyone can catch up with the majority. The slowest ships do not define the speed of the convoy anymore. What is called for now is flexibility.)

---

45   Theo Sommer, 'Schwierigkeiten sind kein Scheitern', *Die Zeit*, 40 (25 September 1992), 1.

Hence, Sommer did nothing more than slightly adapt the 'train' symbol of German reunification. The figurative language revolving around the symbol 'train', which was discredited as a symbol for Europe, was replaced by that of 'ship'. On one hand, 'ship' stood for the EU as a whole: on the other, it stood for all individual member states, which together constituted a 'convoy', a super-'ship' consisting of many smaller 'ships'. Thus, the discussion about the 'speed', which (albeit only seemingly) made it possible to consider different positions (also because of the German reunification) could be split into many individual speeds, while the 'convoy' as well as the 'train' could continue to head for its preset destination. In order to complete the cycle back into politics, I would like to draw attention to the SPD (Social Democratic Party) spokeswoman on economic policy, Ingrid Matthäus-Meier, who, on 27 September 1992, called for a 'Europe of two speeds'.[46] However, when politicians wanted to emphasize European 'identity' while concurrently paying no heed to economic competition within Europe, Europe was presented – for instance in the question on asylum after the Schengen Agreement – ultimately as a closed fortress. This was adequately visualized in caricatures.[47]

Between 1991 and 1993, the crucial problem for the media was to maintain the concept of Europe and that of a global community of states with equal rights, while identifying elements through which nations were able to define themselves in political and economic terms. In the case of Germany, this included belonging to a higher class of normality.[48] To speak symbolically once again, it was about allowing streams of capital and commodities to circulate as freely as possible across frontiers, continents and classes of normality, together with streams of people. These were all symbolized in the media and political discourses by the well-known contrast between 'dyke' and 'flood'. It stands to reason, then, that the fact that Europe could seem-

---

46   'Helmut, wir brauchen ein Europa der zwei Geschwindigkeiten', *Westdeutsche Allgemeine Zeitung* (28 September 1992).

47   See, for instance, the caricatures 'Das Europa-Haus' ('The Europe-house'), *ZEITmagazin*, 37 (6 September 1991) and 'Lehrstunde an der Westgrenze' ('Teaching lesson at the Western border'), *ZEITmagazin*, 42 (15 October 1993).

48   See the statements of François Mitterrand and Hans-Dietrich Genscher on the evening of the French referendum.

ingly only be conceived in terms of an equivalent (namely as an 'either/or-equivalent') of the individual nations and their identities, was largely an effect of the media discourse and the collective symbolic system, which did not allow for conceptualizing two symbolic 'centres' for one entity, a national and a European.

Do we need National Symbols?

A question often asked is: 'Do we need national symbols?'[49] A possible answer on the basis of the collective symbolic system, which I have sketched here only roughly, could be as follows: without symbolic forms, communication across the borders of particular domains of knowledge would be extremely difficult in everyday life. Public and political speech in particular (the 'national' variant being only a special case) are largely dependent on symbols. To raise issues about the political 'situation of the nation' in historical or public-policy contexts, requires thematizing the symbolic political 'situation of the nation', since the symbols which help to constitute national identity cannot easily be excluded. It makes more sense, then, to acquire knowledge about the ways in which they function and about the collective symbolic systems of the European nations, in order to address critically the possibilities of dealing with them under changing historical and political conditions.

Translated from the German by Alexandra Kolb

---

49   See Brigitte Schlieben-Lange, 'Wozu brauchen wir nationale Symbole?', in Titzmann (ed.), *Zeichen(theorie)*, pp.265–8. See also articles by Hans Nicklas, Jochen Mecke, Winfried Nöth and Michael Titzmann in the same volume (pp.293–312).

Bibliography

Bundeszentrale für politische Bildung (ed.), *Einigkeit und Recht und Freiheit. Nationale Symbole und nationale Identität*, Bonn 1985/1990.

Disselnkötter, Andreas, and Rolf Parr, 'Kollektivsymbolsystem – didaktisch aufbereitet', *kulturRevolution*, 30 (October 1994), 52–65.

François-Poncet, Jean, 'Deutschlands Einheit, Europas Chance?', *Die Zeit*, 8, (16 February 1990).

Hartung, Klaus, 'Öffnung zum Alltag', *die tageszeitung* (23 December 1989), 8.

Körber-Stiftung (ed.), *86. Bergedorfer Gesprächskreis am 3. und 4. Dezember 1988 in der Bad Godesberger Redoute. Das gemeinsame europäische Haus – aus der Sicht der Sowjetunion und der Bundesrepublik Deutschland*, Hamburg Bergedorf 1988.

Krampen, Martin, 'Zur Bedeutung nationaler Symbole und politischer Embleme in der visuellen Kommunikation', in Titzmann (ed.), *Zeichen(theorie)*, pp.269–75.

Kuhn, Eckhard, *Nationale Symbole der Deutschen*, Bonn 1989.

Lehmann, Ralf, 'Schwere Symbole', *Westdeutsche Allgemeine Zeitung* (7 August 1991).

Link, Jürgen, *Die Struktur des Symbols in der Sprache des Journalismus. Zum Verhältnis literarischer und pragmatischer Symbole*, Munich 1978.

——, 'Diskursive Rutschgefahren ins Vierte Reich? Rationales Rhizom', *kulturRevolution*, 5 (February 1984), 12–20.

——, 'Wie weich landen die Wendeturbulenzen des europäischen Hauses? Kollektivsymbole und aktuelle (De)Normalisierungsschübe', *kulturRevolution*, 23 (June 1990), 58–69.

——, 'Normalismus: Konturen eines Konzepts', *kulturRevolution*, 27 (August 1992), 50–70.

——, and Wilfried Korngiebel, 'Von einstürzenden Mauern, europäischen Zügen und deutschen Autos. Die Wiedervereinigung in Bildern und Sprachbildern der Medien', in Rainer Bohn, Knut Hickethier, and Eggo Müller (eds.), *Mauer-Show. Das Ende der DDR, die deutsche Einheit und die Medien*, Berlin 1992, pp.31–53.

Parr, Rolf, '"Was ist des Deutschen Vaterhaus?" – Kleines Belegstellenarchiv zum "Gemeinsamen europäischen Haus"', *kulturRevolution*, 23 (June 1990), 74–9.

——, 'Bismarck-Mythen – Bismarck-Analogien', *kulturRevolution*, 24 (January 1991), 12–6.

——, *'Zwei Seelen wohnen, ach! in meiner Brust!' Strukturen und Funktionen der Mythisierung Bismarcks (1860–1918)*, Munich 1992.

——, 'Diskursanalytische Betrachtungen zum Bismarck-Mythos', in Titzmann (ed.), *Zeichen(theorie)*, pp.283–91.

——, 'Kollektivsymbole als Medien in der Stadtwahrnehmung', in Bernd Henningsen (eds.), *Die inszenierte Stadt. Zur Praxis und Theorie kultureller Konstruktionen*, Berlin 2001, pp.19–42.

——, and Siegfried Reinecke, 'Faszinationsenergie. Zur symbolischen Realität im neuen Deutschland', *medium. Zeitschrift für Hörfunk, Fernsehen, Film, Presse*, 22 (1992), 6–9.

Perger, Werner A., 'Pandoras Büchse bleibt geschlossen', *Die Zeit*, 40 (25 September 1992).

Riha, Karl, 'Der deutsche Michel. Zur Ausprägung einer nationalen Allegorie im 19. Jahrhundert', in Jürgen Link and Wulf Wülfing (eds.), *Nationale Mythen und Symbole in der zweiten Hälfte des 19. Jahhunderts. Strukturen und Funktionen von Konzepten nationaler Identität*, Stuttgart 1991.

Schlieben-Lange, Brigitte, 'Wozu brauchen wir nationale Symbole?', in Titzmann (ed.), *Zeichen(theorie)*, pp.265–8.

Sommer, Theo, 'Schwierigkeiten sind kein Scheitern', *Die Zeit*, 40 (25 September 1992).

Titzmann, Michael (ed.), *Zeichen(theorie) und Praxis*. 6. Internationaler Kongreß der Deutschen Gesellschaft für Semiotik. 8. – 11. Oktober 1990, Passau 1993.·

Willms, Johannes (ed.), *Der 9. November. Fünf Essays zur deutschen Geschichte*, Munich 1994.

Wülfing, Wulf, Karin Bruns, and Rolf Parr, *Historische Mythologie der Deutschen 1798–1918*, Munich 1991.

Illustrations

„Das Europäische Haus muß noch zusammenwachsen" waz-Zeichnung: Klaus Pielert

Ill. 1

Ill. 2

Der neueste Hit   waz-Zeichnung: Klaus Pielert

Ill. 3

Ill. 4

Laßt uns gemeinsam die Fackel der Freiheit weitertragen

Wenn Europäer und Amerikaner gemeinsam planen und handeln, wenn sie ihre geistigen und materiellen Kräfte im Atlantischen Bündnis zusammenfassen, dann werden sie aus den Umwälzungen, die unsere Welt erschüttern, gestärkt hervorgehen.

Wir bekräftigen deshalb den Willen, gemeinsam unsere Freiheit zu bewahren, um sie auch denen gewinnen und erhalten zu können, die zwischen Furcht und Hoffnung noch um sie ringen müssen. Die junge Generation drängt darauf, die Gelegenheit, welche die Geschichte vielleicht nur einmal bietet, jetzt zu nutzen und den Bau einer Friedensordnung zu versuchen.

FREUNDSCHAFT IN FREIHEIT
Eine deutsche Initiative
für europäisch-amerikanische Beziehungen e.V.

Gründer und Mitglieder der Initiative sind u.a.: Günter Diehl, Peter von der Heydt, Alphons Horten, Thomas Kielinger, Marie-Elisabeth Klee, Dieter Kronzucker, Dr. Tyll Necker, Friedhelm Ost, Botschafter Dr. Jürgen Ruhfus, General a.D. Johannes Steinhoff, Wolfgang Stresemann, Prof. Dr. Werner Weidenfeld, Admiral Dieter Wellershoff.

FREUNDSCHAFT IN FREIHEIT e.V.
Rheingasse 4, 5300 Bonn 1.

Ill. 5

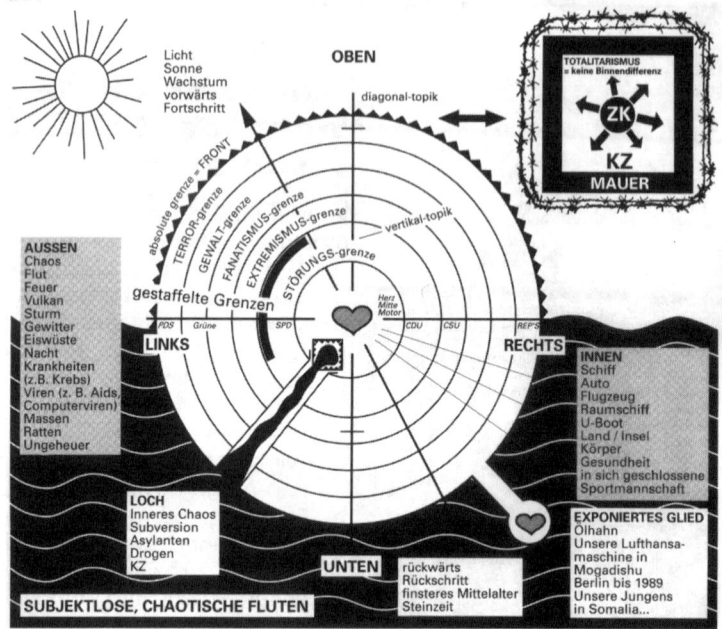

Ill. 6

Ill. 7

Friederike Eigler

Memory, Moralism, and Coming to Terms with the Present: Martin Walser and Zafer Şenocak

In his 1991 article, provocatively titled 'The Failure of German Intellectuals,' Andreas Huyssen argued that the political events of 1989/90 ushered in a 'paradigm shift' regarding 'the patterns of political and intellectual discourse in the unified Germany' but that most intellectuals failed to recognize the far-reaching implications of this shift. Huyssen specifically observed the 'unwillingness and inability of many left and liberal intellectuals to admit error, to analyze the nature of their delusions and political projections, and to admit that a thorough reorientation is the order of the day'.[1] An example is the debates about German unification and the literary legacies of East and West Germany. Instead of scrutinizing established positions, intellectuals fought the battles of the past: notions of *Kulturkonservatismus* (cultural conservatism), associated with the political right, were evoked against notions of *Gesinnungsästhetik* (art shaped by political and social engagement), associated with the political left. More generally, the debates of the early nineties were still marked by binary oppositions that had grown out of the Cold War era.[2]

In what ways, then, has the paradigm shift Huyssen described played out in the course of the 1990s? How have intellectuals in Germany responded to the dramatically changed political landscape of a post Cold-war world? A volume edited by the historian Michael

1   Andreas Huyssen, 'After the Wall: The Failure of German Intellectuals' (1991), in Huyssen (ed.), *Twilight Memories: Marking Time in a Culture of Amnesia*, New York 1995, pp.37–65.

2   See Gerd Gemünden, 'Nostalgia for the Nation. Intellectuals and National Identity in the Unified Germany', in Mieke Bal, Jonathan Crewe, and Leo Spitzer (eds.), *Acts of Memory: Cultural Recall in the Present*, Hanover-London 1999, pp.120–133: p.130.

Geyer, somewhat ironically entitled *The Power of Intellectuals* (2001), provides some insight into the course of discussions during the decade following the appearance of Huyssen's article. In the process of taking stock of East and West German traditions and of more recent developments, most contributors focus less on what Huyssen perceived as the 'failure' of individual intellectuals in the post-unification era than on the profound changes of the social, political, and economic conditions within which intellectual debates take place.[3] What makes the situation in post-unification Germany so intriguing is that the changes precipitated by the integration of the East into West German society coincided with the social and political upheavals and the economic restructuring that are associated with the effects of globalization.[4] What is at stake in the intellectual debates of the 1990s then is nothing less than the attempt to carve out new discursive territory by probing the possibilities and limitations of a civil society in a globalized world.

This process transcends national borders and is pertinent to other European countries and the U.S. as well, but it is being carried out in Germany with a particular urgency and with particular historical and ideological baggage. The terms of the debate are in flux and there is no guarantee for the continued importance of intellectuals. Yet despite declarations of the demise of the privileged public role of intellectuals in the 1990s[5] there is every indication that, in the German context, debates provoked by intellectuals or debates in which intellectuals play a central role are well and alive, and continue to draw public attention. Examples of major debates in the 1990s include: the contro-

---

3   The articles by Mitchell Ash, Andreas Huyssen, John Borneman and Michael Geyer (all in Michael Geyer (ed.), *The Power of Intellectuals in Contemporary Germany*, Chicago-London 2001) shift the focus from a reassessment of the past to the challenges of the present and future in the unified Germany. There is no talk about the 'failure of intellectuals', but a palpable sense of the 'crisis of intellectuals' (Michael Geyer, 'The Long Good-Bye: German Culture Wars in the 1990s.', in Geyer, *The Power of Intellectuals,* pp.355–80: p.366).

4   Geyer, *The Power of Intellectuals*, pp.1–3.

5   See Michael Geyer, 'The Politics of Memory in Contemporary Germany', in Joan Copjec (ed.), *Radical Evil*, New York 1996, pp.169–200; Russell Berman, 'Three Comments on Future Perspectives on German Cultural History', *New German Critique*, 65 (1995), 115–24; Huyssen, 'After the Wall'.

versy surrounding the publication of Botho Strauß's *Anschwellender Bocksgesang* (1993, *Impending tragedy*), the protracted debate about the role and design of the Holocaust memorial in Berlin, the responses to the controversial speech by Martin Walser at the occasion of receiving the 1998 Peace Prize of the German Book Trade, and the ongoing discussion about the role of German victims during the Second World War for cultural memory in contemporary Germany – triggered, among other things, by the publication of Günter Grass's novel *Im Krebsgang* (2002, *Crab Walk*).[6]

Stephen Brockmann has examined the role of these debates in the context of changing notions of national identity both in the divided Germany and the unified Germany. He reminds us that conservative positions, evoking nostalgic notions of a culturally coherent nation and heavily drawing on aesthetic modernism, were held long before 1989 by Karl Heinz Bohrer, Botho Strauß, Peter Handke, and others. But in the 1990s these positions gained new dominance while liberal and leftist positions, held by Günter Grass, Jürgen Habermas and others in the West lost ground or, as was the case for prominent intellectuals from East Germany like Christa Wolf and Heiner Müller, were discredited.[7] However, the number of writers and intellectuals that can no longer be easily grouped in either one of these two political/cultural factions is growing: Among these intellectuals who defy easy categorization are Peter Schneider, H.C. Buch, and others who have rethought part of the political belief system they helped shape in the student protest movement of the late 1960s; authors like Monika Maron and Kathrin Schmidt who were socialized in the GDR but never believed in the socialist utopia; as well as writers of non-German background like Emine Sevgi Özdamar or Zafer Şenocak who look at 'German' issues and traditions from vantage points that transcend right-left binaries.

---

6   These debates have attracted a lot of media attention and are indeed often spurred on by this attention; however, to discredit them as mere 'media events', reveals a reductive notion of the complex social role of the media.

7   Stephen Brockmann, *Literature and German Unification*, Cambridge 1999; Jay Julian Rosellini, *Literary Skinheads? Writing from the Right in Reunified Germany*, West Lafayette, IN 2000; Gemünden, 'Nostalgia for the Nation'.

Another example for the changes in the public discourse of the
1990s is the prominence gained by a young generation of writers,
proponents of the so-called 'Pop Literature.' In clear contradistinction
to earlier generations of writers in East and West, these 'Pop writers'
have broken with the traditions of aesthetic modernism (the strong-
hold of the 'conservative' intellectuals), while also turning away from
questions of moral, political, or historical weight (the focus of liberal
intellectuals of the previous generations).

There is one aspect that distinguishes all of these highly hetero-
genous groups of writers and intellectuals from both the traditional left
and the traditional right: in different ways and for different reasons,
they all question established ways of commemorating the 'German
past' (specifically, National Socialism and the Holocaust). The writers
Martin Walser and Zafer Şenocak are among those who have explicitly challenged the consensus regarding the importance and legitimacy
of the memory politics of the 1980s. Though Walser has been labelled
a renegade who switched from a liberal to a cultural conservative
position,[8] I maintain that both, Walser and Şenocak, represent positions that no longer fall neatly into the left/right paradigm. In this
article, I will examine the charges of moralism and ritualization concerning dominant discourses on cultural memory, charges that both
Walser and Şenocak articulate from two distinct discursive positions,
and charges from which they draw very different conclusions.

In order to contextualize and historicize Walser's and Şenocak's
criticism of ritualized and normative approaches to the 'German past',
it is helpful to turn to the historian Michael Geyer who examines the
role of memory politics in the pre- and post-1989 era. In his 1996 article
on 'The Politics of Memory in Contemporary Germany', he provides a
critical account of the history of *Erinnerungspolitik* (memory politics)
in West Germany following the Second World War. In the aftermath
of the 1960s that brought the opening of the educational system and a
generational shift, a new intellectual elite moved from the margins to
the center of public discourse on the German past. Intellectuals like

---

8   Among others Stuart Taberner, 'A Manifesto for Germany's "New Right"?
       Martin Walser, the Past, Transcendance, Aesthetics, and "Ein springender
       Brunnen."', *German Life and Letters*, 53/1 (2000), 136–41.

Heinrich Böll, Günter Grass, Christa Wolf,[9] and others worked on the premise that remembering the Nazi past would safeguard against similar evils in the present and future. Predicated on a 'cathartic effect' of reckoning with the past, German academics and intellectuals mobilized a 'politics of memory,' or what Geyer describes as 'the deliberate use of memory toward refashioning the German body politic'.[10] The commemorative events on the fortieth anniversary of the end of WWII in 1985 – in particular the often-quoted speech by Federal president Richard von Weizsäcker – illustrate the main streaming of this politics of memory. Public commemoration of Nazi Germany was thus no longer a marker of oppositional politics.[11]

After German reunification, the memory of National Socialism and the Holocaust did not suddenly fade or disappear, as some had feared; on the contrary, the 1990s saw a virtual 'memory boom'. Yet, Geyer argues, the 1990s demonstrated also that the public awareness of the past did not prevent the resurgence of neo-Nazism, racism, and anti-Semitism. Nor did this awareness provide any assistance in grappling with those problems and other challenges that faced contemporary Germany (for example, Germany's position vis-à-vis the war in former Yugoslavia). In the introduction to *The Power of Intellectuals*, Geyer highlights what he sees as the central challenge in contemporary Germany by employing the term *Gegenwartsbewältigung* (coming to terms with the present)[12] in variation and juxtaposition to the German *Vergangenheitsbewältigung* (coming to terms with the past).

Arguably, some of Geyer's arguments are rather sweeping but by thinking outside of the left/right 'box', he succeeds in challenging the efficacy of the dominant German memory politics without supporting a so-called *Schlussstrichmentalität*, that is the view that Germans have dealt with their past sufficiently and should put it behind them.

---

9   Geyer includes Wolf in his 2001 introduction to *The Power of Intellectuals*, p.12.

10 Geyer, 'The Politics of Memory', p.169.

11 Ibid., p.172.

12 To my knowledge, this term was first coined by Anna Kuhn in an article on Christa Wolf ('Rewriting GDR History', *GDR Bulletin*, 17/1 [Spring 1991], 7–11).

Indeed, Geyer asserts the continued importance of keeping the memory of the Holocaust as a 'rupture of civility' in twentieth-century history alive.[13] Yet it remains unclear what connections exist between coming to terms with the German past and coming to terms with the present. It is precisely this question regarding the relationship between German memory politics and challenges facing post-unification Germany, that is the point of departure for my discussion of Martin Walser and Zafer Şenocak.

My article considers some of Şenocak's essays in *Atlas des tropischen Deutschland* (1992)[14] and in *Zungenentfernung* (2001),[15] on the one hand, and Walser's 1998 Peace Prize speech and some of his essays dealing with the Nazi past and with right-wing extremism in contemporary Germany, on the other (*Deutsche Sorgen*. Frankfurt/M. 1997). I will discuss Walser's and Şenocak's arguments in the context of the diverging public positions they occupy. In other words, the 'cultural configurations in which intellectuals are capable of exerting palpable influence'[16] are part of the subject matter of this article.

Şenocak, born 1961 in Turkey and raised in Germany, is neither part of the young generation of 'Pop authors' (a label that some use for the German-Turkish author Feridun Zaimoglu), nor does he belong to any of the politically oriented groups of authors that emerged in the post-war period.[17] In Germany, Şenocak is known less as a poet and author of fiction than as an essayist and commentator on current

---

13   Presumably a translation of Dan Diner's term '*Zivilisationsbruch*.' See Geyer, 'The Long Good-Bye', p.374.

14   Zafer Şenocak, *Atlas des tropischen Deutschland. Essays*, Munich 1993. The English volume *Atlas of a Tropical Germany. Essays on Politics and Culture*, trans. and ed. Leslie Adelson, Lincoln, NE-London 2000 includes selected essays from the German volume and a number of more recent essays by Şenocak. Henceforth these volumes are quoted as '*Atlas* 1993' and '*Atlas* 2000' respectively with page number in brackets.

15   Zafer Şenocak, *Zungenentfernung. Essays*, Munich 2001. Henceforth quoted as '*Zungenentfernung*' with page number in brackets.

16   Geyer, 'The Long Good-Bye', p.366.

17   '"Einfach eine neue Form." Gespräch mit Tom Cheesman', in Tom Cheesman and Karin E. Yeşilada (eds.), *Contemporary German Writers: Zafer Şenocak*, Cardiff 2003, pp.19–30: p.20.

events.[18] He is co-founder of the international cultural journal *Sirene,* yet because of his Turkish background, he is seen as a spokesperson for the second generation of Turks living in Germany and, specifically, for the difficult relationship between Germans and Turks. His essays as well as his interviews regularly appear in major German newspapers (*die tageszeitung, Tagesspiegel, Süddeutsche Zeitung,* among others). Despite the media interest in Şenocak's views on German-Turkish issues, his literary writings and his collections of essays have received more attention abroad – in countries like the United States, France, and Great Britain – than in Germany.[19] Challenging this lack of public recognition, Leslie Adelson comments on the significance of Şenocak's essays: The essays 'write a new subject of remembrance into being. This is less about the dangers of forgetting the past than it is about new conditions for re-membering twentieth-century Germany in a present that Turks and Germans in the Federal Republic already share'.[20] It is worth taking this assessment as a point of departure in an examination of how Şenocak participates in the larger project of probing and expanding the parameters of 'German' cultural memory.[21]

In contrast to the partial and selective reception of Şenocak's writings, all of Walser's writings – literary and non-literary alike – receive a high degree of attention in the press, in particular in the *Feuilletons* (the style and art sections) of all major German news-

---

18 Matthias Konzett argues that the split into a relatively well received intellectual and a little-read author of fiction is symptomatic of the dilemma faced by writers of non-German background: as intellectuals they have to help bring about the kind of public awareness that is the precondition for an adequate reception of their literary writings. Matthias Konzett, 'Writing against the Grain: Zafer Şenocak as Public Intellectual and Writer', in Cheesman and Yeşilada, *Şenocak*, pp.43–60: p.45f.

19 See Leslie Adelson, 'Coordinates of Orientation. An Introduction', in *Atlas 2000*, pp.xi–xxxvii: p. xxxiv.

20 See Leslie Adelson, 'The Turkish Turn in Contemporary German Literature and Memory Work', *The Germanic Review*, 77/4 (2002), 326–38: 333 and Friederike Eigler, *Gedächtnis und Geschichte inGernerationsromanen seit der Wende,* Berlin 2005.

21 Adelson is the first to discuss Şenocak's essays in the larger context of post-unification Germany (see Introduction, *Atlas* 2000).

papers. Walser belongs to a generation of authors who emerged in the post-war era and who, in addition to their literary publications, have consistently commented on issues of societal and national importance. In many ways, Walser exemplifies the type of politically engaged liberal intellectual who assumed moral responsibility for the fledgling German post-war nation. Despite the changing public role of intellectuals in the post-unification era he continues to command consistent attention in the media and the public at large. The document stating the reasons for awarding Walser the prestigious Peace Prize of the German book trade (1998), stresses his central role as critical intellectual in the history of the Federal Republic of Germany.[22] Significantly, Walser's outspoken support for the reunification of Germany in the 1980s (before it became a political reality) was perceived by many liberal intellectuals as a form of betrayal of established leftist positions and as support for cultural conservatism.[23] His 1998 speech in which he attacks dominant forms of memory politics was widely perceived as a confirmation of this ideological shift from the left to the right.[24]

---

22   The official document (*Urkunde*) reads: 'Martin Walsers erzählerische und essayistische Kunst, die der "Gegenwehr gegen den Mangel" entspringt, hat den Deutschen das eigene Land und der Welt Deutschland erklärt und wieder nahegebracht. Mit seiner Kritik an der deutschen Teilung, die er schon früh als überwindbaren Zwischenzustand bezeichnete, hat Martin Walser eine Forderung vorweggenommen, deren Einlösung später von den Menschen der DDR erzwungen wurde.' ('Martin Walser's narrative and essayistic art, which originates from a "defense against lack", succeeded in explaining their own country to Germans and in bringing Germany closer to the world. With his critique of the division of Germany, which very early he characterized as a transitory state that could be overcome, Martin Walser anticipated a demand, whose fulfillment the people of the GDR later insisted upon.') Martin Walser, *Friedenspreis des Deutschen Buchhandels 1998: Ansprachen aus Anlass der Verleihung*, Frankfurt/M. 1998. Henceforth quoted as '*Friedenspreis*' with page number in brackets.
23   See Rosellini, *Literary Skinheads?*, pp.83f.
24   See Taberner, 'A Manifesto for Germany's "New Right"?'; Amir Eshel, 'Die Walser-Bubis Debatte und der Ort des Nationalsozialismus im Selbstbild der Bundesrepublik', *Deutsche Vierteljahrsschrift für Literaturwissenschaft und Geistesgeschichte*, 74/3 (2000), 333–60; Rosellini, *Literary Skinheads?* challenges this assessment, p.181–9.

For the purpose of this article, I am less interested in the controversies surrounding Walser's 1998 speech than I am in stressing the
diverging discursive contexts from which Walser and Şenocak speak
and within which they are being heard (or not heard, for that matter).
The rift separating the discursive positions which these two authors
occupy is symptomatic of the difficulties of transforming German
civil society to include active participants of non-German descent. The
participation of minorities in all segments of society has not yet
become the norm but remains the much-noted exception.[25] The flip
side to this exclusion from 'main-stream' public debates is the expertise a member of a minority is presumed to have about matters related
to his or her ethnic origins.[26]

The selective reception of Şenocak's social commentaries elides
his interest in what is generally considered to be a very 'German'
topic: Germany's relationship to its past, in particular the Second
World War and the Holocaust. It may therefore come as a surprise that
Şenocak's criticism of public forms of commemoration in Germany
shares a lot with Walser's commentaries on the subject. Both authors
bemoan the ritualization of public discourses on the past, with Walser
focusing on the adverse role of the media and Şenocak concentrating
on the tendency to insulate cultural memory from contemporary social
problems and political challenges.

Reading the social commentaries by Walser and Şenocak side by
side, I maintain, opens up new and productive perspectives on issues
that are too often being discussed along predictable lines. For instance,
Walser and Şenocak challenge the position of moral superiority
assumed by those who advocate the 'appropriate' way of dealing with
the German past. Şenocak, taking this argument a step further, sees a
similar tendency of taking the moral high ground when it comes to
embracing an 'enlightened' position vis-à-vis a multi-ethnic society
and to denouncing those who point at the difficulties of integration.
In both cases Walser and Şencoak challenge dominant discursive
positions which exclude critical self-examination either by distancing

---

25   See Konzett, 'Writing against the Grain', p.58.
26   Şenocak addresses this phenomenon critically in his essay 'Wann ist der
      Fremde zu Hause?' ('When is the Foreigner at Home?', *Atlas* 1993, 64–75: 66.)

oneself from the other (the 'bad' German of the Nazi-era) or by appropriating the other (the 'foreigner') according to one's own views of multiculturalism. Both authors contend that the tendency to quickly assign responsibility and guilt to others creates entrenched positions and precludes the critical analysis of one's own role.

In his 1998 Peace Prize speech, Walser did not criticize ritualized forms of cultural memory for the first time – yet his earlier comments did not receive much public attention.[27] The public attention his 1998 speech received, on the other hand, was largely due to the significance of the occasion, to the highly critical response by the late Ignatz Bubis – the leader of the Central Council of Jews in Germany – and to the ensuing controversy.[28] Amir Eshel has compared the significance of the Walser-Bubis debate with the historians' debate (*Historikerstreit*) in the 'old' Federal Republic during the mid-eighties. Eshel notes that in both cases the (re)positioning of the Federal Republic in the national and the international arena was at stake.[29] Rather than rehearsing the analysis of the entire speech and the subsequent controversy once again,[30] I want to foreground a central aspect of Walser's speech that was largely neglected in the course of the debate despite the fact that it has been a recurring theme in his essays and speeches over the last decade: Walser's critique of a particular kind of public discourse on guilt (*Schulddiskurs*) which dominates, according to Walser, the approach of the media and prominent intellectuals and writers to the German past and to major problems facing contemporary German society. Arguably, Walser's polemical and at times cynical rhetoric precluded a differentiated examination of this important aspect of his speech.[31]

---

27   See Dieter Borchmeyer, *Martin Walser und die Öffentlichkeit*, Frankfurt/M. 2001.

28   Frank Schirrmacher (ed.), *Die Walser-Bubis Debatte: Eine Dokumentation*, Frankfurt/M. 1999.

29   Eshel, 'Die Walser-Bubis Debatte', 340.

30   See Eshel, 'Die Walser-Bubis Debatte'; Rosellini, *Literary Skinheads?*; Taberner, 'A Manifesto for Germany's "New Right"?', among others.

31   Prümm observes this partial reception of Walser's critique of the media without discussing the reasons for this selective response. Karl Prümm, 'Selbstmächti-

Similar to Walser, Şenocak has investigated the moralistic dimension of Germany's approach to its past in his 1991 essay 'Schrebergärtner des Bewußtseins: über Schuld und Unschuld in Deutschland' ('Allotment-holders of the mind: on guilt and innocence in Germany'; *Atlas* 1993, 31–8). Şenocak's and Walser's arguments clearly overlap, yet they come to decidedly different conclusions. Both Walser and Şenocak are critical of the wholesale and easy assignment of guilt in public discourses. Both refer primarily to the ways the media represents and discusses the history of National Socialism and the Holocaust. Moreover, they also observe a similar dynamic of assigning guilt when it comes to public responses to current social and political issues, specifically public discourses on the history of East Germany and the complicity of East Germans with State Socialism, and media coverage of instances of racist violence and xenophobia.

Walser and Şenocak both criticize the position of moral superiority assumed by those who identify current societal problems and who, by assigning responsibility, position themselves as exterior to the problems they address. In his 1998 speech, Walser targets primarily the liberal press and liberal intellectuals when he states 'Sprachgrößen fühlen sich auch als Gewissensgrößen' ('the eloquent consider themselves moral giants'; *Friedenspreis*, 43).[32] According to Walser, the following mechanism is part and parcel of the public discourse on German guilt: intellectuals feel exonerated 'wenn sie wieder im grausamen Erinnerungsdienst gearbeitet haben' ('when they have laboured again in the cruel duty of commemoration'; *Friedenspreis*, 44). Şenocak's charge against public discourses on guilt and innocence coincides with Walser's in terms of substance but not in style. Though Şenocak employs irony and an occasional polemical aside as well, he refrains from the consistent use of hyperbole and polemic language that marks Walser's speech. Thus Şenocak's overall argument comes across as more compelling. In his essay 'Schrebergärtner des

---

ges und bilderloses Erinnern?', *Mitteilungen des Deutschen Germanistenverbandes*, 47/2 (2000), 452–61.

32   Unless otherwise noted, all translations are my own.

Bewußtseins' he argues, for instance, that the mechanism of prematurely assigning guilt closes down any further discussion:

> [D]urch die vereinfacht und identitätsbezogen gestellte Schuldfrage wird die Gegenwart totgeschlagen, zumindest aber in Vergangenheit verwandelt [...]. Schuld und Unschuld als Kategorien gesellschaftlicher Auseinandersetzung verleihen Immunität und Identität. Sie verhindern eine schonungslose, vielleicht aufwühlende oder düpierende Röntgenaufnahme, die Analyse festgefahrener Positionen (*Atlas* 1993, 32).

> (Posing the question of guilt in a simplistic and personalized manner has the effect of beating the present to death or, at the very least, turning the present into the past [...]. Employing guilt and innocence as categories in public debates endows [the speaker] with immunity and identity. They prevent an unconditional, perhaps disturbing or shocking examination; they prevent the analysis of entrenched positions.)

Specifically, Şenocak contends that the historical legacy of National Socialism is not explored in all its complexity and that current social challenges, like the transformation of Germany into a multi-ethnic society, do not receive the necessary attention (*Atlas* 1993, 35).

Whereas Şenocak and Walser share this critical diagnosis of the counter-productive effects of a rigidly circumscribed approach to the past and to contemporary social issues as well, they disagree concerning the alternative approaches they advocate. In his 1998 speech, Walser insists on his right to privacy when it comes to questions of conscience, and he rejects public discussions on issues of conscience and morality by drawing on aggressive, militaristic terminology: he speaks of 'Meinungsoldaten' ('soldiers of political correctness'), 'Moralpistolen' ('guns of morality'), 'in den Meinungsdienst nötigen' ('to coerce someone into espousing particular opinions'), and 'Gewissenswart' ('guard of conscience') (*Friedenspreis*, 50). By employing terms, some of which carry connotations of National Socialist ideology, Walser polemically reverses the oppositional terms of 'good' and 'evil' that structure debates of the German past. Linguistically, he associates those individuals and institutions (primarily the liberal press) who advocate particular forms of public commemoration of the victims of National Socialism with the perpetrators. At the same time, he portrays himself in the role of a 'victim' of today's 'Meinungssoldaten' ('soldiers of political correctness') who police the ways in which he is supposed to respond to past and present evils. It is in this context that Walser employs the term 'Moralkeule' ('moral stick') – the most controversial aspect of his speech – to articulate his rejection of the much-debated Berlin memorial for the murdered Jews of Europe.

This questionable use of the victim-perpetrator paradigm shapes the rhetorical structure of Walser's speech and is largely responsible, I argue, for the divisive nature of the controversy that ensued. Ironically, Walser's polemic and at times offensive rhetoric had the effect of distracting from the substance of his arguments and drawing attention, instead, to his personal convictions and moral beliefs. In other words, Walser provoked precisely the kind of debate he sought to avoid.[33]

Looking at Walser's 1998 speech in isolation, his main critic Ignatz Bubis (as well as others) charged that Walser rejected all attempts at coming to terms with National Socialism and that he promoted a brand of cultural conservatism that argues for closing this chapter of German history[34] or, at the very least, for adopting a new historical narrative that individualizes and thus relativizes the role of National Socialism and the Holocaust.[35] While I agree with critics who find the rhetoric of this speech highly problematic and inappropriate for a public event of this kind, I take issue with those who judge the author Martin Walser based on the rhetoric of this individual speech alone without engaging the substance of his arguments and without considering his earlier writings on related topics.

Placing Walser's speech in the larger context of his political essays and speeches prior to 1998 complicates any critical assessment of his Peace Prize speech. They demonstrate Walser's continuous grappling with the German past as well as with problems in contemporary German society.[36] Indeed in many of his essays, Walser

---

33   See Schirrmacher, *Die Walser-Bubis-Debatte.*
34   Taberner, 'A Manifesto for Germany's "New Right"?'
35   See Eshel, 'Die Walser-Bubis Debatte'; Aleida Assmann and Ute Frevert, *Geschichtsvergessenheit – Geschichtsversessenheit. Vom Umgang mit deutschen Vergangenheiten nach 1945*, Stuttgart 1999, pp.53–55 for a discussion of the history of the advocates of a 'Schlussstrich.'
36   See Borchmeyer, *Martin Walser.*

practices precisely the kind of approach to the past that Şenocak sees missing in dominant public discourses: Walser brings his own self into play instead of retreating into a position of moral superiority. For instance, in his 1993 essay 'Deutsche Sorgen II'[37] ('German concerns II'), Walser poses the following question regarding the way we deal with right-wing youth in the unified Germany:

> Könnte es nicht sein, dass wir durch diese peinliche Ausgrenzung die Rechts-tendenzen radikalisiert haben? Auf jeden Fall haben wir sie aus jedem Diskurs ausgeschlossen ('Sorgen', 458).
>
> (Could it be that we have radicalized the right-wing tendencies by taking em-barassingly careful measures of exclusion? In any case, we have excluded them from any discourse.)

Challenging what Walser claims are counter-productive strategies of exclusion and demonization, he speaks of the rigth-wing youth as 'our children' whom we need to accept as being part of us even when they develop intolerable traits.

It is perhaps no coincidence that the phrase 'our children' for right-wing radicals recalls Walser's 1965 essay entitled 'Unser Auschwitz' ('Our Auschwitz').[38] The recurring personal pronoun 'our' in his 1967 Auschwitz essay and in his 1993 essay on right-wing radicalism illustrates a continuity in Walser's approach, namely his willingness to bring into play himself and, by extension, his call on others to consider their own participatory role and their own responsi-bility for changing the situation, instead of adopting the moral high ground. Walser identifies a shortcoming in the way society in general and intellectuals in particular respond to right-wing extremism, yet he fails to fully recognize the limits of a politics of communication and

---

37 Henceforth quoted as 'Sorgen' with page number in brackets.
38 Walser wrote the essay 'Unser Auschwitz' in response to the 1967 Auschwitz trials in Frankfurt (*Sorgen*, 187–202). Walser challenges what he sees as the potential exonerating effect of these trials on average Germans (including himself) who may distance themselves too easily from the atrocities exposed at the trials instead of examining their own responsibility for the 'success' of National Socialist ideology.

understanding when it comes to acts of racist or xenophobic aggression.[39]

In his 1992 essay entitled 'Die verschwundenen Jahre der Deutschen' ('The lost years of the Germans'; *Atlas* 1993, 62f), Şenocak addresses the situation in the unified Germany from a different angle. Until 1990, he states in a somewhat flippant manner, Germans had disappeared into history; and instead of turning their attention to the present after German reunification in 1990, they merely expanded their sense of history by including East German history as well. This assessment, in its deliberate overstatement, articulates one of Şenocak's recurring concerns: that public forms of memory and commemoration tend to be detached from challenges of the present and, by extension, that Germany defines its national identity negatively through the commemoration of (and distancing from) an abhorrent past, in contrast to a positive affirmation of a future-oriented agenda (*Atlas* 1993, 63).[40] In ironic reversal of the well-known formula of Germany's 'unverarbeitete Vergangenheit' ('unresolved past'), Şenocak comments on the 'ungeklärte Gegenwart' ('unresolved present') claiming that precisely these unresolved issues of the present may have the effect that

---

39   Walser briefly discusses alternatives to the mechanism of attributing guilt and excluding the culprits from any further discourse. Instead of seeking public debates merely with like-minded people who affirm their repulsion toward right-wing radicalism, he asks us to find opportunities to talk to the youth itself, especially to those who have not yet turned to violence (*Sorgen*, 460f). Distancing himself from the role of the intellectual as conscience of the (German) nation, he has not primarily intellectuals in mind when it comes to addressing right-wing extremism; he attributes a far more important role to peer groups, grass root movements, churches and educational institutions (*Sorgen*, 460 and 466–7).

40   This assertion, when taken literally, does not hold up against research on cultural memory. Maurice Halbwachs, Aleida and Jan Assmann, among others have shown that all acts of memory have their point of reference in the present. Thus the politics of memory in post-unification Germany is of course closely linked to the new sense of national identity and self-representation of the Federal Republic of Germany. What is at stake in Şenocak's charge is precisely the linkage between national identity and a traumatic history at the expense of considering the ethnically diverse populace as integral part of the new German nation (see Huyssen, 'Diaspora and Nation', 162).

history catches up with the Germans ('dass die Geschichte die Deutschen einholt'). Here, Şenocak's argument recalls Geyer's point, mentioned at the outset of this article, that the politics of memory of the pre-unification era may have outlived the original purpose and risks becoming ineffective or, worse, turning into an obstacle to addressing pressing social or political problems in the present.

Employing a deliberately overstated binary opposition of the past and the present, Şenocak draws attention to a phenomenon that is also of concern to Walser: an approach to the German past that results in the affirmation of previously known positions and that, by ultimately avoiding a more sustained engagement with the 'other', may in fact accacerbate the deplored state of affairs instead of alleviating it. Şenocak's allegory of the *Schrebergärtner* (allotment-holder) refers to precisely this unwillingness to scrutinize or even challenge one's own patterns of thought and behaviour. Thus Şenocak concludes his essay: 'Dieses [das Bewusstsein] bleibt jener ordentlich gepflegte Schreber- garten, an dessen Pforte das uralte Schild hängt: "Unbefugten ist das Betreten verboten!"' ('This [the mind] remains a well kept garden with a sign hanging on its gate "No Trespassing!"'; *Atlas* 1993, 38).

Considering the extent to which Walser's and Şenocak's criti- cism of cultural memory in Germany coincide, it is perhaps surprising that their diagnoses have effected their literary writings in a markedly diverging manner. Walser's attack on what he sees as the 'instrumen- talization' of commemorating the Holocaust is closely linked to the poetic approach to memory he articulated, prior to his controversial speech, in his novel *Ein springender Brunnen* (1998). Employing the narrative perspective of a child and youth growing up in Nazi Germany, the novel insists on the validity of personal memory – exemplified by a protagonist largely unaware of the implications and effects Nazi ideology – as distinct from cultural memory. By contrast, Şenocak, similarly concerned with the loss of meaning in rituals of commemoration, calls for linking cultural memory to challenges of the present.[41] Şenocak, just like Walser, has used the realm of fiction,

---

41   For a critical discussion of Walser's novel, see Stephen Brockmann, 'Martin Walser and the Presence of the German Past', *The German Quarterly*, 75/2 (2002), 127–43; Friederike Eigler, 'Engendering Cultural Memory in Selected

specifically in his novel *Gefährliche Verwandtschaft* (1998, *Dangerous relations*) to imagine alternative ways of connecting the German past to the challenges of the present.[42]

But what exactly are the challenges of the present which, according to Şenocak's diagnosis, remain largely unaddressed because of an almost exclusive focus on commemorating the past? Similar to Walser, Şenocak comments on the xenophobic tendencies in post-unification Germany. But for Şenocak this problem is merely part of a much larger phenomenon, namely the transformation of the Federal Republic into a functioning multi-ethnic civil society. What is missing both on the individual and the public levels, according to Şenocak, are broad and sustained efforts to acknowledge and work through the multiple tensions and problems that are bound up with such a transformation.

This principal challenge of transforming German society should be faced, Şenocak argues, in full awareness of German history and, to some extent, Turkish history as well. Şenocak's critical assessment of the current state of affairs in Germany, a country that is *de facto* but not *de jure* a country of immigration is closely linked with his discussion of the politics of memory in Germany.[43] Specifically, Şenocak calls for revising dominant forms of cultural memory in Germany, a call he directs both at the German majority and at the Turkish minority living in Germany.[44] For instance, in his essay 'Die Heimat trägt der

---

Post-Wende Texts of the 1990s', *The German Quarterly*, 74/4 (2001), 392–406; Eshel, 'Die Walser-Bubis Debatte'; Taberner, 'A Manifesto for Germany's "New Right"?'.

42   Looking at the novel's main protagonist as a 'figure of history' (Leslie Adelson, *The Turkish Turn in Contemporary German Literature: Toward a New Critical Grammar of Migration*, New York 2005, p.68), one can read the entire novel as an ironic commentary on Germany's approach to its past (see also Şenocak 2003, 145–6). I provide an extensive analysis of both Şenocak's and Walser's novels in a forthcoming book-length study on cultural memory and family narratives of the 1990s.

43   Adelson, 'Coordinates of Orientation', p.xii.

44   I employ the terms of 'majority' versus 'minority' culture for heuristic reasons, following Şenocak's distinction between 'Germans' and 'Turks', a distinction that is more pronounced in his essays from the early 1990s. My use of these terms does not presuppose a static and dualistic relationship between two

Mensch in sich' ('Humans carry their home in themselves'; *Zungen-entfernung*, 22–24) he contends:

> Die deutsch-türkische Kultur ist eine Nischenkultur [...], deren Existenz besten-falls Subszenen schafft. Diese Szenen werden von schwachen Erinnerungen an die Herkunft und dünnen Verbindungslinien zur komplexen Gegenwart getra-gen. Das ist zu wenig, um auf der spannendsten Baustelle der Welt tragfähige Fundamente zu errichten (*Zungenentfernung*, 24).

> (The German-Turkish culture is a culture of niches [...], whose existence creates subcultures at best. These subcultures are marked by weak memories of the land of origin and thin lines of connection to the complex present. This is insufficient for building a stable foundation at the most exciting construction site of the world.)

If the second and third generations of Turks living in Germany wish to open up their largely closed communities within German society, Şenocak argues, they have to find a language for their own history without clinging to the phantasm of a lost homeland. According to Şenocak, this would involve the Turkish minority to acquire not only a better knowledge of Turkish history and Islamic traditions, but also developing a sustained interest in German history.

> Doesn't immigrating to Germany also mean immigrating to, entering into, the arena of German's recent past? The history of Jews in Germany – the history of the largest minority of another faith – and the creative influence that this history had (but also the effect of the Englightenment on Jews, with all its consequen-ces, including emancipation and assimilation), all this offers us an experiential background that we have not yet analyzed. Even the bitter experiences that led to the (near) annihilation of the Jewish minority in Europe must be reflected upon in the conception of a multicultural Europe.[45]

---

homogenous groups of people. In his essay 'Germany – Home for Turks?' (*Atlas* 2000, 1–9), Şenocak puts the onus on the Turkish communities in Germany, both on an individual and an institutional level. Furthermore he appeals to the responsibility of all Germans, especially of politicians, the cultural elite, and educators, to help revise mono-cultural notions of 'German' memory and history.

45   Şenocak wrote this essay entitled 'Deutschland – Heimat für Türken' together with Bülent Tulay in January of 1990. I quote here from the translated essay 'Germany – Home for Turks' (*Atlas* 2000, 6).

Conversely, Şenocak sees major flaws in the ways German majority society has dealt with the Turkish minority in their midst.[46] The consequences of a largely failed or missing politics of integration in Germany are well known and well documented.

Briefly put, these consequences involve on one hand the solidification of uniform and uninformed notions of Islam and of Turkey and, depending on one's political orientation, the tendency to either exoticize or demonize the Turkish 'other'. Even forty years after the first major influx of Turks into Germany, these stereotypes persist. Regardless of political orientation, Kolinksy and Horrocks observe, many Germans assume that 'Turk is like Turk, viewing the minority as a whole without internal differentiation and without its own history of social change'.[47]

On the other hand, the failed politics of integration has increased the influence of fundamentalist interpretations of Islam in some Turkish communities. Based on this critical assessment, Şencoak calls for revising dominant notions of cultural memory in the German majority society as well. He argues that homogenized representations of the Orient – as the dangerous or exotic other – have to be replaced by an awareness of the history of diverging Islamic traditions (*Atlas* 1993, 19). Closer to home, he calls for revising the very notion of 'intercultural dialog': instead of stabilizing one's own identity via the imagined (ethnic/racial/religious) 'other', instead of putting the onus of explaining identity on the 'other', he envisions forms of engage-

---

46   The best example for the lack of political vision, even after forty years of Turkish migration to Germany, were the highly divisive debates surrounding the proposed reform of the immigration laws in the spring of 2002. The use of the term *Zuwanderungsgesetz* (migration laws) exemplifies the ambivalence with which even fairly liberal politicians approach a debate that is really dealing with 'immigration laws', including issues of naturalization and citizenship.

47   Eva Kolinsky and David Horrocks (eds.), *Turkish Culture in German Society Today*, Oxford 1996, pp.xx–xxvi. There are some encouraging trends toward diversifying representations of Germans of Turkish descent, for example, the media attention surrounding the winner of the 2004 Berlin film festival, the director Fatih Akin. The publicity he and his prize-winning film received, however, also testifies to the fact that these cases are still seen very much as exceptions to the rule.

ment that bring into play everyone's notion of identity.[48] In his most recent essays, he goes even further and challenges the very idea of a dialog or clash 'between' distinct cultures, arguing instead that today more than ever each 'culture' and, by extension, every individual is the product of multiple cultural forces and competing traditions.[49]

In the aftermath of the terrorist attacks of September 11, Şenocak's calls for profound changes in attitude (based on an increased knowledge base) on the side of both majority and minority cultures have attained special urgency. Şenocak is well aware that such fundamental changes in the way we approach and conceptualize cultural memory cannot merely occur on the level of individual consciousness (as he seems to suggest in his article on 'Schrebergärtner') but that it would require comprehensive changes in all sectors of society, most importantly in the areas of political representation, education, and culture.[50] Concerning cultural memory of twentieth-century German history, new questions that could emerge are, for instance: what is the significance of the German past from the perspective of growing minority cultures in Germany? And, conversely,

---

48   See Şenocak, 'Orte zum Kennenlernen und Geniessen: Über den interkulturellen Dialog' ('Meeting places and places of enjoyment. On intercultural dialog'), in *Zungenentfernung*, pp.35–44, p.35.

49   Şenocak 'Orte zum Kennenlernen', in *Zungenentfernung*, pp.23–44. See also Adelson 'Against Between', in Cheesman and Yeşilada, *Şenocak*, pp.130–43 and James Jordan, 'Zafer Şenocak's Essays and Early Prose Fiction: From Collective Multiculturalism to Fragmented Cultural Identities', in Cheesman/ Yeşilada, *Şenocak*, pp.91–105: pp. 95f.

50   Calling for changes in the institutions responsible for forming and transmitting cultural memory leaves open the important question as to how and through what processes these changes should occur. In a comparative study of approaches to acculturation in European countries, Yasemin Soysal cautions against a top-down approach favoured in Germany: even when well-intended, attempts by the state to regulate acculturation tends to foster collective attitudes about 'foreigners' living in Germany. See Yasemin Nuhoglu Soysal, *Limits of Citizenship: Migrants and Postnational Membership in Europe*, Chicago 1994 and Konzett, 'Writing against the Grain', p.57.

how does a consideration of the histories of other ethnic groups living in Germany affect an exclusive focus on the German past?[51]

The significance of a modified approach to cultural memory in Germany becomes even clearer when one considers how closely cultural memory is linked to notions of national identity. In his essay 'Germany – Home for Turks?', written shortly after the opening of the Berlin wall and prior to German unification, Şenocak contends that the 'presence of a historical, cultural, and religious minority could prove to be an important corrective in the process of rediscovering new German national feeling' (*Atlas* 2000, 7). What Şenocak seems to suggest here and elsewhere, is that a sustained engagement with the historical and cultural traditions of the largest minority living in Germany could well have implications for revising ethnically-based notions of national identity. This linkage between cultural memory and national identity gives further weight to studies that challenge the long-standing disdain of liberal intellectuals for any notion of German national identity, a position that leaves the discourse on the nation up for grasps to conservative and right wing forces.[52] By contrast, working toward a modified approach to cultural memory in the unified Germany, one that is not exclusively focused on German national history would provide intellectuals (and others) the opportunity to challenge ethnically-based notions of the German nation and thus to help shape new notions of German national identity.[53]

Comparing the alternative approaches to cultural memory Şenocak and Walser propose, Walser's defense of the right to privacy concerning issues of memory and conscience comes across as nostalgically oriented toward his own past. Yet it remains open to debate if Walser's disdain for ritualized approaches to National Socialism and the Holocaust entails his rejection of all public forms of memory as

---

51 For a similar argument regarding the relationship of national and diasporic memory, see Huyssen, 'Diaspora and Nation', 154.

52 Gemünden, 'Nostalgia for the Nation', 120; Brockmann, *Literature and German Reunification*, pp.163–199; Huyssen, 'After the Wall', 77–84.

53 See Adelson, 'The Turkish Turn'; Andreas Huyssen, 'Diaspora and Nation: Migration Into Other Pasts', *New German Critique*, 88 (2003), 147–64.

always 'instrumentalized.'[54] Arguably, both Walser's speech and the
ensuing controversy suffered from a lack of differentation between
literary and political discourses.[55] Adopting an exclusive focus on
personal memory may be successful in the realm of literature, but
cannot be transfered into the socio-political realm without curtailing
public debate and social change: privileging individual memory in the
public arena would foreclose any consideration of the relationship
between competing forms of public and private memory and it would
thus also preclude the kind of fundamental change in the approach to
'German' cultural memory Şenocak demands. Şenocak's critical
assessment of the state of cultural memory in contemporary Germany
and the new approach he outlines exemplify how the unproductive
ideological battles of the pre- and immediate post-unification era –
conservatives calling for a 'closure' to the German past, on the one
hand, and liberals defending ritualized practices of commemoration,
on the other – could be overcome in a constructive and forward-
looking manner.

Bibliography

Adelson, Leslie, 'Coordinates of Orientation. An Introduction', in Zafer Şenocak,
    Atlas of a Tropical Germany. Essays on Politics and Culture, trans. and ed. L.
    Adelson, Lincoln, NE-London 2000, pp.xi–xxxvii.
——, 'The Turkish Turn in Contemporary German Literature and Memory Work',
    The Germanic Review, 77/4 (2002), 326–38.
——, 'Against Between', in Cheesman and Yeşilada, *Şenocak,* pp.130–43.

---

54   Challenging Walser's wholesale dismissal of the role of the media and
     discussing competing ways of media representation regarding the German past,
     Prümm's article is one of the few that responds to the substance of Walser's
     speech (Prümm, 'Selbstmächtiges und bilderloses Erinnern?', 459–61). That
     this kind of substantive debate never took place on a larger scale can be
     attributed both to Walser's polemic rhetoric and to ingrained forms of 'memory
     politics,' i.e., the very topic of Walser's speech.
55   See Brockmann, 'Martin Walser and the Presence of the German Past'.

——, *The Turkish Turn in Contemporary German Literature: Toward a New Critical Grammar of Migration*, New York 2005.

Assmann, Jan, 'Kollektives Gedächtnis und kulturelle Identität', in Jan Assmann and Tonio Hölscher (eds.), *Kultur und Gedächtnis*, Frankfurt/M. 1988, pp.9–19.

Assmann, Aleida, and Ute Frevert, *Geschichtsvergessenheit – Geschichtsversessenheit*, Stuttgart 1999.

Berman, Russell, 'Three Comments on Future Perspectives on German Cultural History', *New German Critique*, 65 (1995), 115–24.

Borchmeyer, Dieter, *Martin Walser und die Öffentlichkeit*, Frankfurt/M. 2001.

Brockmann, Stephen, *Literature and German Reunification*, Cambridge 1999.

——, 'Martin Walser and the Presence of the German Past', *The German Quarterly*, 75/2 (2002), 127–43.

Cheesman, Tom, and Karin E. Yeşilada (eds.), *Contemporary German Writers: Zafer Şenocak*, Cardiff 2003, pp.43–60.

Eigler, Friederike, 'Engendering Cultural Memory in Selected Post-Wende Texts of the 1990s', *The German Quarterly*, 74/4 (2001), 392–406.

——, *Gedächtnis und Geschichte in Generationsromanen seit der Wende*, Berlin 2005.

Eshel, Amir, 'Die Walser-Bubis Debatte und der Ort des Nationalsozialismus im Selbstbild der Bundesrepublik', *Deutsche Vierteljahrsschrift für Literaturwissenschaft und Geistesgeschichte*, 74/3 (2000), 333–60.

Gemünden, Gerd, 'Nostalgia for the Nation: Intellectuals and National Identity in the Unified Germany', in Mieke Bal, Jonathan Crewe, and Leo Spitzer (eds.), *Acts of Memory: Cultural Recall in the Present*, Hanover-London 1999, pp.120–133.

Geyer, Michael, 'The Politics of Memory in Contemporary Germany', in Joan Copjec (ed.), *Radical Evil*, New York 1996, pp.169–200.

—— (ed.), *The Power of Intellectuals in Contemporary Germany*, Chicago-London 2001.

——, 'The Long Good-Bye: German Culture Wars in the 1990s', in Geyer, *The Power of Intellectuals*, pp.355–80.

Halbwachs, Maurice, *On Collective Memory*, trans. Lewis A. Coser, Chicago 1992.

Huyssen, Andreas, 'After the Wall: The Failure of German Intellectuals' (1991), in Huyssen (ed.), *Twilight Memories: Marking Time in a Culture of Amnesia*, New York 1995, pp.37–65.

——, 'Diaspora and Nation: Migration Into Other Pasts', *New German Critique*, 88 (2003), 147–64.

Jordan, James, 'Zafer Şenocak's Essays and Early Prose Fiction: From Collective Multiculturalism to Fragmented Cultural Identities', in Cheesman and Yeşilada, *Şenocak*, pp.91–105.

Kolinsky, Eva, and David Horrocks (eds.), *Turkish Culture in German Society Today*, Oxford 1996.

Konzett, Matthias, 'Writing against the Grain: Zafer Şenocak as Public Intellectual and Writer', in Cheesman and Yeşilada, *Şenocak*, pp.43–60.

Kuhn, Anna, 'Rewriting GDR History', *GDR Bulletin*, 17/1 [Spring 1991], 7–11.

Prümm, Karl, 'Selbstmächtiges und bilderloses Erinnern?', *Mitteilungen des Deutschen Germanistenverbandes*, 47/2 (2000), 452–61.

Rosellini, Jay Julian, *Literary Skinheads? Writing from the Right in Reunified Germany*, West Lafayette, IN 2000.

Schirrmacher, Frank (ed.), *Die Walser-Bubis Debatte: Eine Dokumentation*, Frankfurt/M. 1999.

Şenocak, Zafer, *Gefährliche Verwandtschaft. Roman*, Munich 1998.

——, *Zungenentfernung. Essays*, Munich 2001.

——, *Atlas des tropischen Deutschland. Essays*, Munich 1993.

——, *Atlas of a Tropical Germany. Essays on Politics and Culture 1990–1998*, trans. and ed. Leslie Adelson, Lincoln, NE-London 2000.

——, '"Einfach eine neue Form." Gespräch mit Tom Cheesman', in Cheesman and Yeşilada, *Şenocak*, pp.19–30.

——, 'The Capital of the Fragment', trans. Tom Cheesman, *New German Critique*, 88 (2003), 147–164.

Soysal, Yasemin Nuhoglu, *Limits of Citizenship: Migrants and Postnational Membership in Europe*, Chicago 1994.

Taberner, Stuart, 'A Manifesto for Germany's "New Right"? Martin Walser, the Past, Transcendance, Aesthetics, and "Ein springender Brunnen"', *German Life and Letters*, 53/1 (2000), 136–41.

Walser, Martin. *Ein springender Brunnen. Roman*, Frankfurt/ M. 1998.

——, *Deutsche Sorgen*, Frankfurt/M. 1997.

——, *Friedenspreis des Deutschen Buchhandels 1998: Ansprachen aus Anlass der Verleihung*, Frankfurt/M. 1998.

Marc Oliver Huber

The Father and his Shadow:
The Mann Family in German Memory after 1989

Ich vermute, wie wir heute Fontane wieder lesen können, so werden unsere Enkel einmal ihren Thomas Mann wiederentdecken. Es wird dann, sagen wir im Jahr 2000, ein helles Entzücken sein, bei diesen. Bei uns bleibt Abwehr, Übersättigung.[1]

(Like we are able to enjoy reading Fontane again today, I guess our grandchildren will be able to rediscover their Thomas Mann some day. Then, let us say in 2000, it will fill them with great delight. We, however, remain defensive, surfeited.)

Today it seems that Horst Krüger's dictum of 1975 has come true. Together with the S. Fischer publishing house, a number of prominent scholars have already published the first volumes of the so-called Große kommentierte Frankfurter Ausgabe of Mann's works, diaries, and letters – an edition intended to comprise no less than fifty-eight volumes. What is more, the current interest in Thomas Mann clearly transcends the realm of expert culture. The great success of the three parts of the award-winning TV series *Die Manns: Ein Jahrhundertroman* by Heinrich Breloer (first broadcasted in December 2001), the positive media reports on the occasion of the centenary of *Buddenbrooks* (2001), as well as the high number of copies (more than 50,000 until mid-2003)[2] sold of Hermann Kurzke's highly readable biography

---

1   N.n., 'Deutsche Schriftsteller über Thomas Mann', in Heinz Ludwig Arnold (ed.), *Thomas Mann*, Munich 1982, pp.195–237: p.219.

2   See Hermann Kurzke, 'Das Leben als Kunstwerk: Geständnisse eines Thomas Mann-Biographen', *Kursbuch*, 148 (2002), 127–37: 128. This is all the more remarkable, given that the much discussed biographies on Thomas Mann by distinguished writers such as Klaus Harpprecht and Donald A. Prater had both been published only a couple of years earlier in 1995.

on Thomas Mann (*Das Leben als Kunstwerk*, 1999) seem to indicate a
Thomas Mann renaissance.

The current memory boom is not only about Thomas Mann, but
about the Mann family in general. A brief look at the non-fiction best-
seller chart of the German magazine *Der Spiegel* in summer 2003 as
well as in early 2004 provides first evidence for this. *Frau Thomas
Mann*, a biography on Thomas's wife Katia, essentially a potrait of the
whole family, written by Inge and Walter Jens, is ranked in the top ten,
trailing just behind Michael Moore's *Stupid White Men* and Hillary
Clinton's autobiography. Altogether, about twenty biographies about
the lives of Heinrich, Thomas, Katia, Erika, Klaus, Golo, and Elisabeth
have been published in Germany since 1990.[3] Other books about the
Mann family, most notably the interviews with relatives and friends of
the family that Breloer has made for his film (*Unterwegs zur Familie
Mann*, 2001), and Marianne Krüll's psychoanalytically inspired study
Im Netz der Zauberer (1991 and currently already in its tenth edition),
should also be mentioned. Moreover, a permanent exhibition on the
Manns has been set up in the Buddenbrookhaus in Lübeck. The building
itself, once home to Thomas Mann's father and grandfather, was bought
by the city of Lübeck in 1991. Since 1993 it has hosted the Heinrich-
und-Thomas-Mann-Zentrum. In Munich and Lübeck, the interested
public could also visit a temporary exhibition on the life of Klaus Mann
commemorating the fiftieth anniversary of his death in 1999 (*Ruhe gibt
es nicht bis zum Schluß*). Last, not least, we have to mention four films,
Ulrich Schwartz's documentary *Die Manns – Verfall einer Familie*
(1992), a documentary about Klaus and Erika by Andrea Weiss and
Wieland Speck (*Escape to Life*, 2000), a movie adaption of Klaus's
novel *Der Vulkan* by Ottokar Runze (1999), and the famous Brandauer
adaption of Thomas Mann's *Mario und der Zauberer* (1993; *Mario and
the Magician*).

---

3   On Heinrich (Willi Jasper, Stefan Ringel), on Thomas (Klaus Harpprecht,
     Donald A. Prater, Hermann Kurzke, Edo Reents), on Heinrich and Thomas
     (Klaus Schröter), on Katia (Inge and Walter Jens, Kirsten Jüngling and Brigitte
     Roßbeck), on Erika (Irmela von der Lühe), on Klaus (Harald Neumann, Marlis
     Thiel, Nicole Schaenzler, Armin Strohmeyr), on Erika and Klaus (Andrea
     Weiss, Armin Strohmeyr), on Golo (Jeroen Koch, Urs Bitterli), on Elisabeth
     (Kerstin Holzer), on the whole family (Hans Wißkirchen).

'Ist es schon so weit, gibt es die von manchen seit Jahren ge-
wünschte Thomas-Mann-Renaissance?' ('Has the time already come
for a renaissance of Thomas Mann that some people have been desiring
for years?').[4] This question was put up as early as in 1973 by Marcel
Reich-Ranicki, one of only a few prominent supporters of Mann in the
West German literary scene at that time. According to Reich-Ranicki, it
was the blind adoration of an idealized image of Thomas Mann in the
manner of nineteenth-century historicism that prevented a more intense
public discourse on his life and work.[5] In 1975, the year of Thomas
Mann's centenary, however, Reich-Ranicki's hopes were heavily
disappointed. In Reich-Ranicki's poll among writers for the *Frankfurter
Allgemeine Zeitung*, and in a similar poll arranged by Hanjo Kesting for
an anniversary radio programme, few authors went beyond expressing
respect or moderate admiration for Mann.[6] One of the exceptions was
the Kitsch-novelist Johannes Mario Simmel.

The author's idealization was not a major problem at all. In many
statements, the unease with Thomas Mann became crystallized in a
single attribute, Mann's *Bürgerlichkeit*, as it was examplified in descriptions of Mann as a 'Bürger'[7] ('bourgeois'), a 'bürgerlicher Künstler par
excellence'[8] ('bourgeois artist par excellence'), the representative of the
'Bildungsbürgertum'[9], a 'Buchhalter des deutschen Spätbürgertums'[10]
('bookkeeper of the late German bourgeoise'). The notion of the
bourgeois was followed quite regularly by the conclusion that Thomas

---

4   Marcel Reich-Ranicki, 'Die Geschäfte des Großschriftstellers' [1973], in
    Marcel Reich-Ranicki, *Thomas Mann und die Seinen*, Stuttgart 1987, pp.11–20:
    p.11.
5   See ibid., p.13.
6   See Marcel Reich-Ranicki (ed.), *Was halten Sie von Thomas Mann? Achtzehn
    Autoren antworten*, Frankfurt/M 1986; 'Deutsche Schriftsteller über Thomas
    Mann'; see also Eckhard Heftrich, 'Der gehaßte Kollege: Deutsche Schrift-
    steller über Thomas Mann', in Eckhard Heftrich and Hans Wysling (eds.),
    Internationales Thomas-Mann-Kolloquium 1986 in Lübeck, Bern 1987,
    pp.351–69.
7   Alfred Andersch in 'Deutsche Schriftsteller', p.198.
8   Heinz von Cramer in 'Deutsche Schriftsteller', p.198.
9   Gisela Elsner in 'Deutsche Schriftsteller', p.201.
10 Horst Krüger in 'Deutsche Schriftsteller', p.218.

Mann was a 'Relikt des vorigen Jahrhunderts'[11] ('relic of the last century'). Thus, he is assumed to belong to a social formation that has dominated the nineteenth century, yet has little contemporary relevance:

> Mein spezielles Desinteresse an Thomas Mann rührt daher, daß ich ihn für überwunden und ohne Zukunft halte. Die bei ihm sich ausdrückenden Denk- und Verhaltensformen des Bürgertums sind historisches Zeugnis, aber kein Vorbild.[12]

> (My particular lack of interest in Thomas Mann is due to the fact that I regard him as overcome and, thus, without any future. The bourgeois modes of thinking and behaving that he displays are historical evidence, but no ideal.)

This rejection of Thomas Mann, calling for a complete historicization of his literary achievements, often goes hand in hand with an admiration of his brother Heinrich, who was alleged to be politically and socially much more advanced.[13] In 1975, Thomas Mann seemed about to irrevocably lose his place in the functional part of Germany's cultural memory leading only an unexciting archival after-life.[14]

Roughly fifteen years later, however, the situation has decisively changed: The title of Willi Jasper's biography of Heinrich Mann gives a revealing hint: In it, Heinrich is *Der Bruder*, thus reduced to his pure

---

11   Reinhard Lettau in 'Deutsche Schriftsteller', p.219.

12   Uwe Herms in 'Deutsche Schriftsteller', p.211.

13   See Max von der Grün in 'Deutsche Schriftsteller', p.209: 'Wenn mancher Mann wüßte, wer Thomas Mann wär, gäb mancher Mann Heinrich Mann manchmal die Ehr.' ('If people really knew Thomas Mann, quite a few would pay honour to Heinrich Mann from time to time.') Von der Grün, at that time a well-known author with a deliberate working-class background, quotes a rhyme by John Höxter, Erich Mühsam, and Lotte Pritzel in the anarchic atmosphere of the famous *Café Größenwahn* in Berlin. See Gottfried Korff and Reinhard Rürup (eds.), *Berlin, Berlin: Die Ausstellung zur Geschichte der Stadt*, Berlin 1987, p.431. This statement highlights the continuities of left-wing polemics against Thomas Mann.

14   The distinction between a functional and an archival memory is made up by Aleida Assmann, 'Funktionsgedächtnis und Speichergedächtnis – zwei Modi der Erinnerung', in Aleida Assmann, *Erinnerungsräume: Formen und Wandlungen des kulturellen Gedächtnisses*, Munich 1999, pp.130–145.

family function vis-à-vis the now again widely acclaimed Thomas.[15] Like Thomas in the 1970s, Heinrich became in the 1990s 'mehr denn je zum Prügelknaben der Kritik'[16] ('more than ever the whipping boy of the critics'). Again, Reich-Ranicki was both indicator and initiator of this development when he announced his farewell to Heinrich in 1987: 'Es wird wohl Zeit, sich von Heinrich Mann zu verabschieden.' ('It is probably time to say goodbye to Heinrich Mann.')[17]

Against this background, a number of questions arise: which parameters of the discursive framework of the 1990s could be held responsible for this memory boom? How could both extremes of monumentalization and historicization be avoided in favour of a pluralist memory design? What kind of narrative could support this? What features made the Mann family attractive for renewed public interest? The first question points us to the unification debates about history, nation, and generation, the second to the mnemonic potential of family networks, the third to father-child relationships, the fourth to the discussion of a *neue Bürgerlichkeit,* or 'new bourgeoisie'.

In my essay, I would like to explore the Manns as a many-voiced site of German memory. By doing so, the decisive role of family constellations und generational patterns for the work of memory should become more obvious. In central points the Mann family romance parallels a national family romance with a firm place in the political imaginary of the Federal Republic – both offer narratives about a bourgeois, overwhelming, repressive father and his anti-bourgeois children struggling for an autonomous existence and, thereby, releasing the repressed. Nevertheless, the national family romance advanced by the generation of 1968 differs significantly from the account of history which the Mann family is able to provide. After 1989, the Manns develop into a prominent object of collective memory just because they function as a reminder of the achievements of the bourgeois way of life which the student revolution of 1968 has deliberately denied.

---

15   Willi Jasper, *Der Bruder: Heinrich Mann. Eine Biographie*, Munich-Vienna 1992.

16   Jasper, *Bruder*, p.9.

17   Marcel Reich-Ranicki, 'Ein Abschied nicht ohne Wehmut', in *Thomas Mann und die Seinen*, pp.109–51: p.151.

I.

The symbolic landmarks of recent German history such as 1945, 1968, and 1989 share a notion of *Wendezeit* or *Zeitenwende*,[18] that is a rupture in the continuous flow of time, that deeply affects perceptions of things past. Not surprisingly, the heated debates surrounding German unification in the aftermath of 1989 have widely been charged with semantics of new beginnings, overdue endings, conclusions, and re-evaluations, thus triggering diverse debates on memory, counter-memory, foundational narratives, and forgetting.[19] Stimulated by changing circumstances, new concepts enter the discursive arena, but old ones also find their way back from the dustbins of history. In 1989, it was, for instance, the concept of the 'nation' and the concern for national identity that re-entered the discussion as a major point of reference: 'Wie man sich auch dreht und wendet, ja windet, die Nation ist wieder da und der Nationalstaat mit ihr.' ('Whichever way you turn, the nation has come back again and so has the nation state.')[20]

In order to make conflicting positions more visible, and in order to mark a break in cultural continuity, it became popular again to talk about different 'generations' and the frictions between a 'younger' and an 'older' generation.[21] The modern development of this temporally, socially, and ideologically charged discursive unit in the late eighteenth

---

18 See Andreas Huyssen, 'On Rewritings and New Beginnings: W.G. Sebald and the Literature About the "Luftkrieg"', *Zeitschrift für Literaturwissenschaft und Linguistik*, 31 (2001), 72–90.

19 For an overview on the post-1989 debates see Brockmann, *Literature and German Reunification*, Cambridge 1999; Jan-Werner Müller, *Another Country: German Intellectuals, Unification, and National Identity*, New Haven, CT 2000.

20 Ralf Dahrendorf, 'Die Sache mit der Nation', *Merkur*, 44 (1990), 823–34: 823.

21 Special 'Literatur und Generation: Vom Jungsein und Älterwerden der Dichter', *neue deutsche literatur*, 48 (2000), 129–89; *Der Deutschunterricht: Sonderheft Generationenkonflikte*, 52 (2000); Thomas Anz, 'Epochenumbruch und Generationenwechsel? Zur Konjunktur von Generationenkonstruktionen seit 1989', in Gerhard Fischer and David Roberts (eds.), *Schreiben nach der Wende: Ein Jahrzehnt deutscher Literatur 1989–1999*, Tübingen 2001, pp.31–40. The entire construction of epochal turning points and generational replacements is, of course, a highly rhetorical strategy. It does not work without gross simplifications.

century and in the first half of the nineteenth century is strikingly embedded in a language of political upheaval.[22] Hence, it is hardly surprising that thinking in generational asymmetries has itself gained prominence in the intellectually heavily polarized 1920s,[23] as well as in the generational conflict that has become a foundation myth of the so-called movement of 1968. Heinz Bude has correctly pointed out, that this sense of belonging to a certain generation has been dominating public discourse in the Federal Republic after 1945, while alternative imagined communities like 'class' or 'nation' have lost status.[24] In 1989, whatever the allegedly young generation might have adopted as a self-definition, it had to draw on the differences from its supposed main opponent, the generation of 1968. German history could once again be told in terms of generational sequences organized around father-child relationships: a 'familiarisierte[r] Generationendiskurs'[25] ('familiarized discourse between the generations'), a national family romance.[26]

---

22   See Burghard Dedner, 'Der Begriff der Generation in der Literaturgeschichte', in Michael Ewert and Martin Vialon (eds.), *Konvergenzen: Studien zur deutschen und europäischen Literatur*, Würzburg 2000, pp.20–36. An overview on the history of generation formation in Germany is given in Mark Roseman (ed.), *Generations in Conflict: Youth Revolt and Generation Formation in Germany 1770–1968*, Cambridge 1995.

23   Hans Mommsen, 'Generationskonflikt und Jugendrevolte in der Weimarer Republik', in Thomas Koebner, Rolf-Peter Janz and Frank Trommler (eds.), *'Mit uns zieht die neue Zeit': Der Mythos Jugend*, Frankfurt/M. 1985, pp.50–67; Klaus-Michael Bogdal, 'Generationskonflikte in der Literatur', *Der Deutschunterricht*, 52 (2000), 3–12: 4ff; Walter Erhart, 'Generationen – zum Gebrauch eines alten Begriffes für die jüngste Geschichte der Literaturwissenschaft', *Zeitschrift für Literaturwissenschaft und Linguistik*, 30 (2000), 81–107: 85ff.

24   Heinz Bude, 'Das "übertriebene Wir" der Generation', *neue deutsche literatur*, 48 (2000), 136–143: 136ff.

25   Sigrid Weigel, 'Die "Generation" als symbolische Form. Zum genealogischen Diskurs im Gedächtnis nach 1945', *figurationen: gender literatur kultur*, 0 (1999), 158–73: 162.

26   Heinz Bude, 'Die Achtundsechziger-Generation im Familienroman der Bundesrepublik', in Helmut König, Wolfgang Kuhlmann and Klaus Schwabe (eds.), *Vertuschte Vergangenheit: Der Fall Schwerte und die NS-Vergangenheit der deutschen Hochschulen*, Munich 1997, pp.287–300 and pp.348–49.

The generation of 1968 was for good reasons identified as a generation of intellectuals with a predominantely negative stance towards
unification as well as towards feeling less embarrassed about German
identity.[27] They held the notion of a German *Sonderweg* against the
desire for 'normalization', which had its roots in the conservative milieu
of the 1980s and had met strong opposition in the *Historikerstreit*.[28] For
them, the nation itself had already lost any value as a frame of thought,
and, thus, came to be considered as a mere *lieu de mémoire*: 'It
[Germany] should […] serve as a reminder to all other nations of
the horrors of war and totalitarianism – and of the very concept
"nation".'[29] After 1989, claims were advanced from various sides
that this generation of intellectuals, sometimes portrayed as *the*
quintessential intellectuals, had failed to cope with the *Wende*.[30]
Such assessments were echoed by a considerable self-criticism among
renegades of the generation of 1968 such as Peter Schneider or Hans
Magnus Enzensberger.[31] In the *Literaturstreit*, the proponents of the
generation of 1968 came under heavy attack because of their so called
Gesinnungsästhetik, the fusion of political engagement and aesthetics.

In this intellectual atmosphere the interest in Thomas Mann could
grow. Unlike Böll or Grass, Mann has hardly ever been an outspoken
political writer or *Gesinnungsästhet* in his novels. Moreover, as the
centenary in 1975 had shown, he was far from popular with the
generation of 1968.[32] But what else could he offer? He certainly
profited from the fact that his anti-fascism – necessary for a positive
attitude towards him – had not coincided with a whole-hearted socialist

---

27   See Müller, *Another Country*, pp.64ff and pp.120ff; Brockmann, *Reunification*,
     pp.45ff and pp.165ff; Wolfgang Jäger and Ingeborg Villinger (eds.), *Die
     Intellektuellen und die deutsche Einheit*, Freiburg/B. 1997, pp.11ff and pp.179ff.
28   See Müller, *Another Country*, pp.56ff; Brockmann, *Reunification*, pp.13ff.
29   Brockmann, *Reunification*, p.191.
30   See Andreas Huyssen, 'After the Wall: The Failure of German Intellectuals',
     New German Critique, 52 (1991), 109–43.
31   Müller, *Another Country*, p.146f.
32   On the contrary, Peter Schütt (in 'Deutsche Schriftsteller', p.232) has named
     them a major obstacle for his own study of Thomas Mann: 'The radical stu-
     dents' movement, their disdain for the bourgeois-humanistic cultural heritage,
     has made it more difficult for me to get an unbiassed access to his work for
     several years. In 1967, I stopped studying Thomas Mann.'

commitment. Furthermore, Mann stood politically for a post-war balance between the Western and the Eastern part of Germany, and he was not willing to accept any permanent partition.[33] With his lifelong passion for Germany and the Germans, Thomas Mann came back into business not so much because of his conceptual strength (hardly any major thinker referred to him), let alone the content of his novels. Rather it was because of the biographical account of his life and the intellectual contexts in which it was embedded, one that was shaped in many respects by German history and, consequently, also mirrored German history:

> the tragic course that German culture has taken in the twentieth century becomes more clearly readable through the prism of Thomas Mann than through that of any other figure of German literary history.[34]

Along the concrete course of his life, one could again think through the complexities of German history from the Second Reich to the early Federal Republic. Mann provides the perspective of an at times politically naïve, but – unlike Hauptmann and others who chose to stay in Germany after 1933 – morally uncompromised contemporary.

In this respect, he offers possibilities for identification, especially among those who do not belong to the generation of 1968 and who are looking for positive integrative figures for a unified Germany. Commemorating Thomas Mann gives an opportunity to participate with a moderate voice in the renewed discourse on German identity. Referring to Mann, Hans Rudolf Vaget has uncovered a number of hidden continuities from discussions carried out in exile during the 1930s and 1940s to the current unification debates in Germany: 'Keine andere Gestalt vermag die verschüttete Kontinuität der Deutschland-Debatte klarer einsichtig zu machen als Thomas Mann.' ('No other figure is able to give a fuller insight into the hidden continuity of the debate on Germany

---

33   See Hans Rudolf Vaget, 'Deutsche Einheit und nationale Identität: zur Genealogie der gegenwärtigen Deutschland-Debatte am Beispiel von Thomas Mann', *Literaturwissenschaftliches Jahrbuch*, 33 (1992), 277–98: 289ff.

34   See Hans Rudolf Vaget, 'Mann and his Biographers', *Journal of English and Germanic Philology*, 96 (1997), 591–601: 592.

than Thomas Mann.')[35] It was notably the old claim that an 'other Germany' in opposition to the Nazi state existed that suited the interpretive patterns used by advocats for a newly attained normality. Thomas Mann has, at least temporarily, subscribed to this notion of an alternative Germany, and so have Klaus and Erika.[36]

II.

Now, how could a monumentalization as well as a complete historicization of Mann be avoided in favour of a more pluralist design of memory? For this, it is necessary not only to address the ambivalent traits in Mann but also to let further voices respond to this past. In both respects, the view of Thomas Mann as a family man – as a member and head of a rather extraordinary family which commentators have occasionally compared to the Windsors or the Kennedys[37] – opens up promising perspectives. Like the latter, the Mann family offers plenty of angles for more trivial concerns: the exclusive lifestyle and social contacts, family conflicts, the tragedies of gifted as well as less gifted children, creativity and its crises, love and renunciation, sexual turbulances, homosexuality, drug addiction, alcohol abuse, suicide, and, who knows, maybe even incest.

---

35   Vaget, *Deutschland-Debatte*, p.279.
36   See Herbert Lehnert, 'Bert Brecht und Thomas Mann im Streit über Deutschland', in John M. Spalek and Joseph Strelka (eds.), *Deutsche Exilliteratur seit 1933: I,1: Kalifornien*, Bern-Munich 1976, pp.62–88; Ehrhard Bahr, 'Die Kontroverse um "das andere Deutschland"', in John M. Spalek and Joseph Strelka (eds.), *Deutschsprachige Exilliteratur seit 1933: II,2: New York*, Bern 1989, pp.1493–1513; Volker Wehdeking, 'Zwischen Exil und "vorgeschobenem Posten" der Kulturnation: Thomas Mann als Projektionsfigur für die im Land gebliebenen Nichtfaschisten', in Günther Rüther (ed.), *Literatur in der Diktatur: Schreiben im Nationalsozialismus und DDR-Sozialismus*, Paderborn 1997, pp.145–62.
37   Irmela von der Lühe, 'Die Familie Mann', in Etienne François and Hagen Schulze (eds.), *Deutsche Erinnerungsorte*, I, Munich 2001, pp.254–71: p.254.

Derived from another context, Dorothea Dieckmann has named the receptional interests here at work:

> Die Kombination von Prominenz und Alltagsnähe garantiert eine quoten-fördernde Wirkung – den bekannten Regenbogen-Effekt. Er provoziert den Sozialneid des Massenpublikums und hebt ihn durch die Darstellung der Schattenseiten wieder auf.[38]

> (The combination of high society and everyday issues guarantees popularity with the viewers – the well-known rainbow-effect. It stimulates the social envy of the mass audience but at the same time it compensates this envy by showing the darker side of such a life.)

On a more complex level, we have to consider the dynamics of family constellations more closely. What kind of stories can be told about the Mann family that transcend the realm of that single family? that make the Mann family to count among the prominent *Deutsche[n] Erinne-rungsorte*?[39] Although hardly anyone happens to be a family member of a world-famous novelist and Nobel Prize-winner, many family features seem to be familiar to the observer. We can discover highly characteristic positions, relationships, and lines of conflict of modern western family life strongly developed in this unique family:[40] the unselfish mother as an emotional and organizational centre mediating between all members; the hard-working father being at the margin of the family's everyday life, yet structuring it both by his appearance and his authority; children struggling for parental love and/or opposing the former generation's values in their search for an autonomous

---

38   Dorothea Dieckmann, 'Eine schrecklich nette Familie: Vorschlag für eine TV-Vorabendserie', *Neue Rundschau*, 112 (2001), 100–109: 100f.

39   Etienne François and Hagen Schulze (eds.), *Deutsche Erinnerungsorte*, Munich 2001.

40   Introductory information on modern Western family life and family con-stellations in literature provide Andreas Gestrich, *Geschichte der Familie im 19. und 20. Jahrhundert*, Munich 1999; Christine Kanz and Thomas Anz, 'Familie und Geschlechterrollen in der neueren deutschen Literaturgeschichte: Frage-stellungen, Forschungsergebnisse und Untersuchungsperspektiven (Teil I)', *Jahrbuch für Internationale Germanistik*, 32 (2000), 19–44; Walter Erhart, *Familienmänner: Über den literarischen Ursprung moderner Männlichkeit*, Munich 2001; Peter von Matt, *Verkommene Söhne, mißratene Töchter: Fami-liendesaster in der Literatur*, Munich 2001.

identity of their own; finally brothers and sisters competing with each other and/or forming an undividable coalition among equals.

Even if our own family might differ notably from these patterns, the cultural imaginary we live by still draws on all this. The family romance has not come to an end yet. It integrates the paternal position into multi-faceted familial relationships of support, love, compromise, succession, rivalry, and guilt, thereby making the monument accessible to the recipient either in a critical or in an identificatory mode. The kind of memory that crystallizes around family networks has ceased to be monological in a Bakhtinian sense; it becomes dialogical.[41]

In a highly self-reflective manner, the members of the Mann family themselves have already given a symbolic meaning to their relationships within the clan. Irmela von der Lühe has noted

> in welchem Ausmaß in der Mann-Familie Epochenkonflikte als Geschwister-konstellationen und innerfamiliäre Gegensätze als allgemeine politische und geschichtsphilosophische Konflikte empfunden wurden.[42]
>
> (to what an extent members of the Mann family experienced epochal conflicts in terms of fraternal constellations, and differences within the family in terms of general conflicts in the realm of politics and the philosophy of history.)

This applies to the crude polemics of the monarchist Thomas against his democratic brother Heinrich during the First World War, but also to the level of father-child relationships with Klaus's essayistic and dramatic efforts during the 1920s outlining the young generation in contrast, though not open resistance, to the world of the father. Later on, during their exile in the 1930s and 1940s, Erika and Klaus portrayed their family as a model for a united fight against fascism.[43] From Thomas's reconciliation with Heinrich in 1922 onwards, family quarrels such as the argument about Thomas's official stance on the Third Reich in the first years after 1933, were rarely fought out in public, a policy that was continued well after 1955, the year of Thomas Mann's death. In her function as curator of Thomas's and Klaus's

---

41   Michail M. Bakhtin, 'Das Wort im Roman', in *Die Ästhetik des Wortes*, Frankfurt/M. 1979, pp.168ff and pp.219ff.

42   Von der Lühe, *Familie Mann*, p.259.

43   See ibid., pp.267f.

estate, Erika held back a number of documents of a more precarious nature, particularly in her edition of Thomas Mann's letters:

> Nicht die Brüche und Widersprüche, nicht die großen Konflikte und veritablen Tragödien [...] bestimmen die Darstellungsintentionen der innerfamiliären literarischen Erinnerungspolitik, sondern das Gegenteil von all dem. [...] Im Nachkriegsdeutschland [...] insbesondere im Kontext der 68er Bewegung war für ein solches Konzept, das Bürgerlichkeit auch um den Preis der privaten Wahrheit und der persönlichen Lebbarkeit hochhielt, gedanklich wenig Raum.[44]

> (The innerfamilial literary politics of remembrance are neither characterized by ruptures and contradictions nor by major conflicts and tragedies, but the opposite. [...] After the war, most notably in the context of the movement of 1968, there was mentally little room in Germany for a concept favouring bourgeois respectability even at the price of private truth and personal viability.)

It is a major merit of the edition of Thomas's diaries (1977–1995) – according to his own will, they remained sealed until twenty years after his death – that this is no longer the case. The supply of new material contributed to the rise of interest in Thomas Mann,[45] although it can hardly explain this interest in its entirety.

By the 1970s, family life had lost its innocence. The family became a place of conflict instead. Along the lines of Max Horkheimer's *Autorität und Familie in der Gegenwart* (1947/49), the generation of 1968 opposed the supposedly authoritarian family structure of the Wilhelmine Empire and its then still visible remnants. In a rather sensationalist pamphlet, David Cooper went as far as to pronounce *The Death of the Family* in 1971.[46] The way in which the generation of 1968 sought to come to terms with the Third Reich often took the shape of family romances, highly critical and personal accounts of the relationships between sons, or daughters, and their Nazi fathers, the so-called *Väterliteratur* published from 1975 onwards.[47] Along the father-child

---

44 Ibid., p.270.

45 See Hans Rudolf Vaget, 'Confession and Camouflage: The Diaries of Thomas Mann', *Journal of English and Germanic Philology*, 96 (1997), 567–590: 589.

46 David Cooper, *The Death of the Family*, London 1971.

47 See Michael Schneider, 'Väter und Söhne, posthum: Über die Väterliteratur der siebziger Jahre', in Heinz Ludwig Arnold (ed.), *Bestandsaufnahme Gegenwartsliteratur*, Munich 1988, pp.139–150, and Claudia Mauelshagen, *Der*

axis they forcefully defined themselves as a generation of rebellious or distraught children in opposition to the generation of their fathers whom they found silently caught up in guilt. More recently, this pattern was taken up by East German writers in their critical accounts of the totalitarian GDR.[48] In West Germany, however, the intellectual asymmetries that are assumed to exist between the generations following the *Wende* polemically turned the generation of 1968 into a scapegoat. Can the recent occupation with Thomas Mann and his family be said to reflect this situation?

III.

In his article on father literature, Michael Schneider analyzes the recurrent features of the Nazi father figures and later members of the *Wiederaufbau-Generation* such as they were painted by authors like Bernward Vesper, Christoph Meckel, Peter Härtling, and others. Illustrating the emotional constitution of the agents who had been involved in the moral, political, and ideological disaster of the Third Reich, the stereotypical image evoked by these authors is that of a father who forces structure on his and his family's life by strict rules; who intimidates by his authority; who either completely lacks feeling or who represses his affections, thus withholding his love from his children and rejecting the child's emotions towards him.[49] He is unable to deal with weakness or to show compassion; neither can he tolerate inner-familial opposition, since he depends on his family for his own inner stability.[50] Furthermore, he attempts to overcome his depressive inclination by an enhanced working discipline, a veritable

---

    Schatten des Vaters: Deutschsprachige Väterliteratur der siebziger und achtziger Jahre, Frankfurt/M. 1995.

48   See Brockmann, *Reunification*, pp.149ff.

49   See Schneider, 'Väter', p.144.

50   See ibid., p.146.

ethics of productivity – 'Arbeit als Verdrängungsarbeit'[51] ('work as the work of denial'). The critical focus in this family romance of the Federal Republic in 1968 is directed against an all too fragile bourgeois façade erected against an overwhelming feeling of guilt. Essentially bourgeois values, attitudes, and rituals came to be seen to support Nazism.

It is in strikingly similar terms that Thomas Mann, the family father, is being portrayed by his biographers, most notably when he comes to be characterized as a permanent shadow looming over the lives of his sons Klaus, Michael, and Golo. The latter even refused to be buried in the family's grave in Kilchberg because of the feared presence of his father.[52] In his autobiography *Erinnerungen und Gedanken* (1986), Golo Mann describes his father's terrifying temperament in the period of the First World War:

> Wohl konnte er noch Güte ausstrahlen, überwiegend aber Schweigen, Strenge, Nervosität oder Zorn. Nur zu genau erinnere ich mich an Szenen bei Tisch, Ausbrüche von Jähzorn und Brutalität, die sich gegen meinen Bruder Klaus richteten, mir selber aber Tränen entlockten.[53]

> (He could still communicate kindness, but mostly there was silence, severity, nervosity, and anger. Painstakingly exact I remember incidents when we had dinner, outbreaks of sudden rage and brutality directed towards my brother Klaus, which made me cry.)

In the view of the publicist Klaus Harpprecht, a former TV correspondent and speech writer of Willy Brandt, Thomas Mann has erected an almost impermeable barrier around himself: 'Sie [die Arbeit an seiner eigenen Größe] verzehrte sich in Ressentiments. Sie erstarrte in Kälte, von der die Frau, die Kinder, die Freunde Bitteres sagten und Schlimmeres hätten sagen können.' ('It [the work on his own greatness] consumed itself in resentment. It froze to a coldness for which his wife, his children, and his friends had bitter words, and could have had

---

51   Ibid., p.147.

52   See Heinrich Breloer, *Unterwegs zur Familie Mann: Begegnungen, Gespräche, Interviews*, Frankfurt/M. 2001, pp.21–198: p.190f.

53   Golo Mann, *Erinnerungen und Gedanken: Eine Jugend in Deutschland*, Frankfurt/M. 2001, p.41.

even worse ones').[54] Even in Hermann Kurzke's sympathetic view,[55] Mann resembles the negative father image of the generation of 1968: his strong wish for an orderly life structured by immutual regularities, especially in the domestic sphere,[56] the ascetic will to repress his emotions,[57] combined with his fear of a return of the repressed, the 'Zusammenbruch des Kunstbaus'[58] ('collapse of the artificial construction'), his relentless hard work,[59] his isolation even within the circle of his familiy:[60] 'Als Mensch war Thomas Mann versiegelt und ließ niemanden in sein Herz blicken. Mit virtuoser Disziplin hielt er eine Fassade aufrecht, ohne die zu leben er unerträglich gefunden hätte.' ('As an individual Thomas Mann remained sealed and let nobody have a look into his heart. With a masterly discipline he kept up a façade he would have found unbearable to live without').[61]

Behind the splendid bourgeois façade, the inner ambivalences, conflicts and tragedies in the relationships between Thomas Mann and his children, most notably Klaus, come into focus: 'Bei allen Aktivitäten und Reisen aber sehnten sich Erika und Klaus stets nach der Liebe und Anerkennung ihres entfernten und mächtigen Vaters.' ('Despite all their activities and travels Erika und Klaus constantly yearned for the

---

54   Klaus Harpprecht, *Thomas Mann: Eine Biographie*, Reinbek bei Hamburg 1995, p.28. Harpprecht speaks literally of an 'almost impermeable barrier' (p.21). In much the same way, Marianne Krüll talks about Thomas Mann's 'Versteinerung' ('emotional petrification') in *Im Netz der Zauberer: Eine andere Geschichte der Familie Mann*, Frankfurt/M. 2001, p.415. See also Kerstin Holzer, *Elisabeth Mann Borgese: Ein Lebensporträt*, Berlin 2001, p.28.

55   Kurzke, *Geständnisse*, p.132, emphatically claims a right to emphathize with his object: 'He [the biographer] describes what has moved him. I have tolerated that Thomas Mann's life is reflected in my own, that his experiences receive colour from mine whenever they could be compared to my own and remained untold whenever I had experienced nothing similar.' This method has already been applied by Emil Ludwig. See Hermann Kurzke, *Geschenke des Lebens: Ein Rückblick*, Berlin 1931, p.745.

56   See Hermann Kurzke, *Thomas Mann: Das Leben als Kunstwerk*, Munich 1999, pp.16f and pp.184f.

57   See ibid., pp.48f.

58   Ibid., pp.88ff.

59   See ibid., p.185.

60   See ibid., pp.305f.

61   Ibid., p.326.

love and acceptance of their remote and mighty father').[62] As a consequence of his demand for love being rejected, Krüll discovers in Klaus 'repressed feelings of hatred directed against his father' ('verdrängte Haßgefühle auf den Vater')[63], and invokes the hypothetical picture of a more personal communication between father and son:

> Was wäre geschehen, wenn Thomas nicht unnahbar und scheinbar unbeteiligt am Tisch gesessen hätte, sondern zusammen mit Katia dem Sohn von seinen eigenen Bedrängnissen in seiner Jugend oder in der Gegenwart gesprochen hätte [...]?[64]

> (What would have happened if Thomas had not been sitting at the table inaccessible and seemingly indifferent, but had been talking to his son together with Katia about his own troubles as a teenager or in the present?)

Furthermore, she accuses Thomas of not having realized Klaus's father complex:

> Thomas Mann lobt Klaus für die Verleugnung des 'Schattens', der von ihm, dem Vater, auf den Sohn fiel. Wieso sieht er nicht, dass gerade der Versuch, die Wirkung seines Schattens zu verleugnen, Klaus in den Selbstmord trieb?[65]

> (Thomas Mann praised Klaus for denying the 'shadow' that he, the father, was casting on his son. Why did he not realize that it was precisely the effort to deny the impact of his father's shadow that made Klaus to commit suicide?)

Nicole Schaenzler, too, seems to deeply sympathize with Klaus in her biography:

> dahinter verbirgt sich auch das Drama eines zutiefst bindungsängstlichen Menschen, der Zuneigung und Liebe vor allem ex negativo erlebt hat. [...] Gut möglich, daß diese (selbst-)zerstörerische Vermeidungsstrategie nicht zuletzt die Konsequenz frühkindlicher Erfahrungen und einer schwierigen Eltern-Sohn-Konstellation war.[66]

---

62   Andrea Weiss, *Flucht ins Leben: Die Erika und Klaus Mann-Story*, trans. Ernst-Georg Richter, Reinbek bei Hamburg 2000, p.7.

63   Krüll, *Netz*, p.401.

64   Ibid., p.296.

65   Ibid., p.18.

66   Nicole Schaenzler, *Klaus Mann. Eine Biographie*, Frankfurt/M.-New York 1999, p.112.

(Beneath the surface a drama is hidden of an individual deeply frightened of strong human bonds, who experiences love and affection primarily ex negativo. [...] It is well possible that this (self-)destructive strategy of avoidance has to be seen not at least as a consequence both of the experiences of his early childhood and as a difficult constellation between parents and son.)

In line with the general exposure of the bourgeois family idyll that the generation of 1968 pleaded for, the Mann family, too, came to be seen as a community overshadowed by private tragedies.

Thomas Mann is, however, far from being a Nazi father. For Hermann Kurzke, these well-known critical patterns gain new respectability by being transferred into a completely modified context: that of the inner and outer chaos which Thomas Mann, the problematic artist and disguised homosexual, had to face in a time marked by personal crises as well as political, social and economic upheaval. The bourgeois facts remain – but in the case of Thomas Mann the narrative has changed considerably. The old themes of Nazi commitment and repressed guilt are replaced by an interpretation which inquires the merit of having to come to grips with a difficult sexuality and external instabilities, including the illusory seductions of the Third Reich.[67] Kurzke defends in an outspoken manner the features named above as stabilizing factors crucial to the quality of Mann's work:

> Kein Leben kommt ohne Stabilisierungen gegen andrängendes Chaos aus. [...] Einen treuen Kunstbau zu errichten wie Thomas Mann, [...] mit festhaltendem Starrsinn die Ordnung aufrechtzuerhalten: es ist billig, das als Verdrängung zu brandmarken, es ist ergiebiger, die Kulturleistung darin zu sehen.[68]

> (Nobody is able to manage his life without putting up stabilizations against the pressing chaos. [...] To erect true-blue artificial structures in order to give his life a hold like Thomas Mann, [...] to keep up steadiness with a firmly held stubbornness: this could easily be denounced as repression but it would be far more productive to see the cultural achievement in it.)

---

67   This does not, however, rule out the possibility of a highly speculative narrative of individual guilt; Michael Maar, *Das Blaubartzimmer: Thomas Mann und die Schuld*, Frankfurt/M. 2000.

68   Kurzke, *Kunstwerk*, p.91.

Kurzke thus prepares the ground for a reconsideration of the bourgeois element in Thomas Mann in terms of both its cultural productivity and its powers of resistance against radical ideologies. With the title of one of Mann's essays, *Lübeck als geistige Lebensform* wins back some of the attraction that was once denied by the neo avant-garde attitude of the generation of 1968. Hence, the very same symptoms of a bourgeois family life can be read entirely differently in two distinct family romances: a narrative of achievement counterbalances a narrative of guilt.

In July 2003, the title story of the widely read magazine *Der Spiegel* was about *Die neuen Werte: Ordnung, Höflichkeit, Disziplin, Familie.*[69] The article suggested that the new values which have arisen in response to the ongoing economic crisis, the crisis of educational institutions (family, school), and the demise of the public sphere, are essentially old bourgeois ones: 'Vorwärts zurück in ein neues Biedermeier'[70] ('Forwards back into a new *Biedermeier*'). Following the trend-scouting *Spiegel*, a 'neue Bürgerlichkeit'[71] ('new bourgeois way of life') is about to be discovered:

> Möglich, dass vor allem die akute ökonomische Krise das Erstarken der Bürgerlichkeit fördert, die allmähliche Rückgewinnung von Tugenden wie Höflichkeit, Sauberkeit, Verlässlichkeit, den Mut zur Wiederbelebung althergebrachter Gebräuche, überhaupt die Wiederentdeckung der Form.[72]

> (Quite possibly it is primarily the burning economic crisis, which is supporting the strengthening of a bourgeois way of life, the gradual winning back of virtues such as politeness, cleanliness, reliability, the courage to revive time-honoured customs, generally the rediscovery of formality.)

Mirroring other debates already mentioned, the present relevance of the critical social concerns associated with the movement of 1968 is put into question:

---

69   'Die neuen Werte: Ordnung, Höflichkeit, Disziplin, Familie', *Der Spiegel* (7 July 2003), 124–137.

70   Ibid., p.137.

71   Ibid., p.124.

72   Ibid., p.125.

> Die aufrechten Kämpfer gegen alles gestrig Autoritäre, von der Jugendbewegung zu Beginn des vorigen Jahrhunderts bis zu den 68ern, haben sich [...] längst zu Tode gesiegt.[73]

> (The upright fighters against yesterday's authority from the youth movement at the beginning of the last century up to the 68ers have long ago been deadly victorious.)

The generation of 1968 is accused of having gone too far in its liberational fight against paternal authority:

> Bei der witzig-aggressiven Demontage der verlogenen Väter-Autorität ging um ein Haar auch das Verständnis für moderate, vernünftig begründbare Autorität [...] verloren.[74]

> (Along with the witty and aggressive dismantling of the hypocritical authority of their fathers they almost lost their sense for a moderate, reasonably justifiable authority.)

Now, on the contrary, an esteem for authority, discipline, steadiness, family life, good manners, and bourgeois rituals is said to re-emerge. Therefore, a reconstructive interest in bourgeois life is replacing former militant attitudes:

> 35 Jahre nach der pubertär auf 'Establishment' und 'Vater Staat' zielenden Parole 'Macht kaputt, was euch kaputtmacht!' heißt es nun offenbar: Rettet, was zu retten ist! Statt um Zerschlagung und Auflösung geht es jetzt um Rekonstruktion.[75]

> (35 years after the puberal slogan 'Destroy everything that is destroying you!' was aimed against the 'establishment' and 'father state', the motto now is: save everything that can be saved! The current focus is on reconstruction instead of destruction and disintegration.)

No doubt, the Mann family fits well into such an attempt to rediscover bourgeois values and paternal authority.

---

73   Ibid., p.126.
74   Ibid., p.129.
75   Ibid., p.136.

IV.

A site of reconstruction of a particular kind is Heinrich Breloer's semi-documentary TV production *Die Manns: Ein Jahrhundertroman* with Armin Mueller-Stahl playing Thomas Mann. Already at the beginning of the first part, the reconstructive effort is made visible. Old Elisabeth Mann Borgese, the only child of Thomas Mann to be still alive at the time of the film's realization, is shown as she walks from room to room in the now empty, once richly furnished family house at Poschingerstraße, Munich, where the Manns lived from 1914 to 1933. Here, like in the whole film, the verbal evocations of the past made by Breloer's interview partner intersect with fictional reality and documentary evidence such as photographs, original buildings and short film sequences of the real historical agents, but also much original film material of the Nazi era and the post-war years. The script is more or less accurately based on testimonial evidence, documents, and written comments by members of the Mann family. *Die Manns* was awarded a high budget according to German standards and it featured the *crème de la crème* of German actors and film staff. In the company of Elisabeth and of other witnesses of the past, Breloer visits Thomas Mann's houses or the places of his interim stays in Germany, Italy, France, Switzerland, and the United States: 'Über 60 Zeitzeugen wurden es auf der langen Reise zu den Geschichten der Familie Mann, die uns fast 140 Stunden Gespräche auf den Bändern eintrug' ('Over 60 contemporary witnesses have been interviewed on the long journey to the stories of the Mann family which added up to almost 140 hours of talk recorded on the tape').[76]

The four years of work on *Die Manns* were preceded by another TV project by Breloer and his partner Horst Königstein about Klaus Mann's exile novel *Treffpunkt im Unendlichen* (1984), linked to a film about Klaus's life *Treffpunkt im Unendlichen: Die Lebensreise des Klaus Mann* (1983). In a retrospective comment Breloer admits that, when they first started their work, they decidedly took sides with Klaus against his father: 'Interessiert hatte uns damals in erster Linie der Sohn;

---

76   Breloer, *Unterwegs*, p.13.

wir hatten eindeutig seine Partei ergriffen, der Vater war für uns noch der "kalte" Thomas Mann gewesen.' ('Back then we were primarily interested in the son; we took his side, and the father remained to us the "cold" Thomas Mann.')[77] By the time *Die Manns* was aired on TV, the perspective should change considerably. A similar swing of opinion may be observed in Hermann Kurzke's scholarly career. Kurzke's dissertation on Thomas Mann's conservatism (*Auf der Suche nach der verlorenen Irrationalität*, 1972) was inspired by Marxist views as well as terminology to such a considerable extent that the author felt obliged to revise his book in 1980.

What makes the cases of both Breloer and Kurzke particularly interesting is that their original view of Thomas Mann was rooted in the leftish background of the student revolution, which subsequently underwent a revision, whose results met an exceptionally high degree of public interest. Unlike Kurzke's biography, which pays attention primarily to Thomas Mann, Breloer's film introduces itself as nothing less ambitious than a 'Jahrhundertroman' centred on a family's course of life. Hence, it demands that twentieth-century history and the family story interact closely. In what sense, then, does Beloer's film – stretching from 1923 to 1955, and providing a more contemporaneous perspective through the numerous interviews – not only tell a pre-1968, but also a post-1968 family romance?

When we consider the Thomas-Klaus relationship more closely, parallels to the version of the family romance given in the *Väterliteratur* become immediately obvious. Breloer and Königstein took their path to Thomas Mann by starting out from the critical father image of 1968, and in particular from the disturbing effects that this dominant father had on his son. According to Schneider, the sons portrayed within this literary framework of highly asymmetrical family relationships have to be understood in reaction to their fathers' work of repression:

> Die depressive Disposition innerhalb der 'zweiten verlorenen Generation', für die die zeitgenössische Literatur und Kunst viele Belege liefert, legt den Schluß nahe, daß diese sich weniger mit dem offiziellen Wert- und Normsystem [...] der Wiederaufbau-Generation identifiziert hat als vielmehr mit deren emotiona-

---

77   Ibid., p.8. Compare a similar statement in Marianne Krüll, *Netz*, p.10.

ler Latenz, d. h. mit den verdeckten[,] unausgesprochenen, unausgelebten, apo-kryphen Seiten ihres Lebensgefühls.[78]

(The depressive inclination within the 'second lost generation', for which the currently produced literature and art shows many examples, suggests that they have to a lesser extent been identifying themselves with the official system of norms and values of the post-war generation concerned with rebuilding, but with the latters' emotional latency, i.e. with the hidden, unsaid, unlived, myste-rious aspects of their attitude to life.)

Switching from politics to sexual policy, this also sheds light on Klaus and Thomas, especially on their strictly divergent ways of handling their homosexuality, which Breloer follows in detail. In *Die Manns*, this leads to a sympathetic, sometimes even self-pitying portrait of Klaus (played by Sebastian Koch).

Like in the biographies on Klaus Mann, Breloer introduces Klaus as a man leading a restless, drug-induced, openly homosexual life alimented by his father throughout his career, changing his partners like his hotel rooms rather frequently. The unsettled son watches his father's steadfast life from a distance, with a bitter smile for the latter's need for a hold in bourgeois traditions. In a dialogue with his friend Fritz Landshoff, Klaus sums up his father's needs:

'Aber er ist treu in seinen Angelegenheiten. Er braucht die Sicherheit wie seinen Tagesablauf.' – 'Seine Familie.' – 'Ja, alle wie sie da sind.' – 'Und seinen Hund.' – 'Sein Haus.' – 'Weihnachten.' – 'Seine Geburtstage.' – 'Möbel.'[79]

('But he remains true in his personal matters. He is in need for security like he needs his daily routine.' – 'His family.' – 'Yes, all of us who are around.' – 'And his dog.' – 'His house.' – 'Christmas.' – 'His birthdays.' – 'Furniture.')

In what functions as the film's prologue, the original façades of the family house of Thomas Mann's grand-parents and parents in Lübeck are shown: an old 'Bürgerhaus' that for Mann represents a 'Symbol

---

78   Schneider, 'Väter', p.149. See also Bude, *Familienroman*, p.300, and Heinz Bude, 'The German *Kriegskinder*: Origins and Impact of the Generation of 1968', in *Generations in Conflict*, pp.290–305: p.304.

79   See the film-script by Heinrich Breloer and Horst Königstein, *Die Manns. Ein Jahrhundertroman*, Frankfurt/M. 2001, p.201.

der Überlieferung, aus der ich wirkte' ('symbol of the tradition that inspired me').[80]

Following a rather conventional gender typology, the narrator comments on the meaning and consequences of the marriage between the bourgeois father and the artistically inclined mother of exotic origins: 'Zwei Welten begegnen sich [...]. Der Ordnungssinn und die Leidenschaft, das wird das Erbe in dieser Familie.' ('Two worlds happen to meet [...]. The sense of order and passion, this is going to become the heritage of this family').[81] Shortly before the end, the plot returns to Mann's hometown when he became the town's honorary citizen in 1955, the year of his death. The last piece has fallen into place: regardless of how far away from Lübeck Thomas Mann might ever have been in geographical terms, his life and work remained rooted in the traditions of this Hanseatic town of bourgeois commerce and self-government. This sense of stability is demonstrated throughout the film, for instance, through the consistency with which Mann liked to furnish his working room and desk in always the same way, no matter whether he found himself in Munich, Princeton, Pacific Palisades, or Zurich. His achievements become clearer when put in contrast to his childrens' rather chaotic lives. *Die Manns* particularly draws attention to the differences between Thomas, on the one hand, and Erika (played by Sophie Rois) and Klaus, on the other. By presenting the father in his own right the film re-tells a father-child story that reshapes the generational account given by the self-righteous 'father literature' written by the generation of 1968. Breloer comments: 'Sie haben alle Recht, die Manns, jeder aus seiner Sicht und in der Entscheidung für seine Art zu leben' ('In the Mann family everyone is right in choosing to live his own particular way of life, everyone from his own point of view').[82] The intellectual background for Breloer's reassessment is provided by the critical eye casted over the generation of 1968 following the *Wende*.

---

80   Thomas Mann, *Deutsche Hörer!*, in *Gesammelte Werke*, Frankfurt/M. 1960, 1974, XI, 1035.

81   See Breloer and Königstein, *Die Manns*, p.9.

82   Breloer, *Unterwegs*, p.16.

Erika and Klaus found a sense in life not permanently, but during the years of their anti-fascist activism against Hitler when their anarchic, yet formerly rather unpolitical individualism resisted Nazism more decidedly than did Thomas. In the first years after 1933, the latter was more willing to compromise out of economic reasons. Before 1933, the occupation of *les enfants terribles*[83] was primarily with what could be called a carefree carnevalization of bourgeois values in art, life-style, sexual relationships, etc. Always good for a scandal, and without regular income, they spent their time travelling all over the world on a whim, thus expressing a desire to live life to the full. For good reasons they are introduced into the film at a turbulent post-war carnival party in 1923, the high point of inflation that made many people lose solid ground and fixed orientations. After the downfall of the Third Reich, they did not manage to find a new existence of their own; Klaus committed suicide in 1949, while Erika became Thomas Mann's assistant and, later on, the belligerent curator of his estate, full of animosities against Germany and the Germans. The argument she had with her father when she refused to visit Germany in 1949 is a case in point, and the film does not shy away from these developments.[84]

Thomas Mann's eldest children contribute to the Mann memory boom in a double sense: on the one hand, they integrate certain reservations, rejections and competing views into the memorization of Thomas Mann, thus constituting an interrogative kind of memory; on the other, they provide the background of ultimately failed lives on which the portrait of Thomas Mann gains a more positive shape. Although Erika and Klaus held no pronounced Marxist views, their political anti-fascism combined with their 'anti-anti-communist' convictions, their deeply skeptical stance towards post-war Germany as well as their anti-

---

83   Armin Strohmeyr, *Klaus und Erika Mann: Les enfants terribles*, Reinbek bei Hamburg 2000.

84   However, the film does not mention that Thomas Mann, too, viewed post-war Germany often with distaste and that he met strong reservations against his person there (e.g. his arguments with Walter von Molo and Frank Thiess). See Jost Hermand and Wigand Lange, *'Wollt ihr Thomas Mann wiederhaben?': Deutschland und die Emigranten*, Hamburg 1999, pp.23ff. This omission enables Breloer to view Thomas Mann's last visit in Lübeck as a celebrated home-coming to Germany.

bourgeois life-style can be said to be in accordance with central views of the generation of 1968. Therefore, Erika and Klaus can be given a representational function within the German family romance that would be incomplete without a figure taking up a post-1968 position.

V.

For Breloer, Thomas's favourite daughter Elisabeth Mann Borgese, born 1918, with her unambiguously positive image of her parents becomes her father's main spokeswoman. Unlike Katia, Erika, Golo, and, to a lesser extent, Michael, she was for most of her life rarely involved in representing her family in public. Unlike her brothers and sisters who largely remained in some way fixated on Thomas Mann, her life can be seen, like her biographer Kerstin Holzer notes, as one of a successful emancipation: she was a marine biologist by profession, who had made her own way outside the realm of art and literature. To express this, Holzer employs the metaphor of the fatherly shadow that apparently no biographer of Thomas Mann and his children is able to escape:

> Die jüngste Tochter von Thomas Mann hat früh ihren Weg aus dem Schatten des großen Vaters gefunden. [...] Als einzige hat sie es geschafft, sich ein Leben außerhalb des Bannkreises des 'Zauberers' aufzubauen. Das familiäre Erbe prägte sie, ohne sie zu lähmen.[85]

> (Thomas Mann's youngest daughter had found her way out of the great father's shadow early on. [...] She was the only one, who managed to set up a life beyond the spell of the 'magician'. The heritage of her family formed her without paralyzing her.)

In *Die Manns*, Elisabeth is seen in a similar light. Following Heinrich Breloer to the original scenes where the life of the Mann family took place, she reacts like a person who has finally gained a vital distance to this past, but enjoys the memory work of reconstruction. Her prag-

---

85   Holzer, *Elisabeth*, pp.8f.

matic, calm, and positive attitude towards the past, her refusal to blame her parents for all the misfortune of any single member of her family, goes along with a rather gentle critique directed against her brothers and sisters.[86] Nevertheless, Breloer's film fails to fully explain the development of her personality. There remains an unbridgeable gap between the story as it developed until 1955 (with Katharina Eckerfeld playing the young Elisabeth) and the time of 1998/99 when the interviews take place. For example, one does not really understand how Elisabeth managed to overcome her father's (and formerly her own) 'male chauvinist'[87] conviction that women are only people of minor importance in the intellectual, artistic, and professional field.

With Thomas Mann's youngest daughter a further discursive position is established within Breloer's film. It is one determined by a certain distance between the generations, yet at the same time characterized by peaceful coexistence. Interestingly, the lateborn Elisabeth has thought of her relationships with brother Klaus and sister Erika in terms of a generation gap: 'Das ist eben eine andere Generation.' ('This is simply a different generation').[88] Hence, Elisabeth can be said to represent a third, post-1968 position within the family romance, one that has already partially managed to overcome the latest generational gap of the years following the *Wende*. Her view is marked by indulgence towards the first generation (her parents) and by certain reservations against the second (Erika, Klaus). In a title story from 1999 with the heading *Die jungen Milden*, the magazine *Der Spiegel* judges this rather conciliatory attitude to be typical of the present youth culture rarely concerned with generational asymmetries.[89] Research on contemporary culture, too, leaves it in doubt whether the notion of generational antagonism is still fully valid for explaining the present:

---

86 Elisabeth could, for example, never understand 'that somebody of Erika's talent, beauty, and intelligence has finally managed to end up in such misery.' Breloer, *Unterwegs*, p.168.
87 Ibid., p.474.
88 Breloer, *Unterwegs*, p.40.
89 See *Der Spiegel* (12 July 1999), 94–103: 96f.

Auffällig ist, dass in der heutigen Inflationierung des Begriffs [Generation] etwas verloren ging, was damals [1968] für die Konstituierung einer Generation prägend war: der Generationenkonflikt.[90]

(It is remarkable that, along with the current inflationary use of the term [generation] something is being lost that had then [in 1968] been formative for the constitution of a whole generation: the generational conflict.)

Memory's familial imaginary is structured by generational sequence. Furthermore, cultural history suggests that this entails a gendered perspective. The notion of family life as it has been developed in the twentieth century comprises both the standard image of sons rebelling against paternal traditions and the less prominent image of daughters memorizing their fathers:

Das Bild des Vaters, auf das die Söhne seit Beginn des blutigen und konflikt-reichen zwanzigsten Jahrhunderts all ihre Bitterkeit und ihre Enttäuschung, auf das sie Fluch und Verwüstung gehäuft haben, wird von den Töchtern behutsam und sorgfältig und selbstlos von den Spuren der Verwüstung gereinigt.[91]

(Since the beginning of the bloody and conflict ridden twentieth century, the sons have projected all their bitterness and disappointment, malediction and devastation on the image of the father. The daughters, however, are cautiously, carefully and selflessly purging this image from the traces of devastation.)

---

90 Jörg Magenau, 'Literatur als Selbstverständigungsmedium einer Generation', *Zeitschrift für Literaturwissenschaft und Linguistik*, 31 (2001), 56–64: 60. Bogdal, *Generationskonflikte*, p.4, and Hans Oswald and Walter Boll, 'Das Ende des Generationenkonflikts? Zum Verhältnis von Jugendlichen zu ihren Eltern', *Zeitschrift für Sozialisationsforschung und Erziehungssoziologie*, 1 (1992), 30–51.

91 Wolfgang Frühwald, 'Väter und ihre Töchter: Ein vernachlässigtes Thema deutscher Literaturgeschichte', in Hans-Joachim Simm (ed.), *Europa, die Dichter und das Geld*, Frankfurt/M.-Leipzig 2001, pp.159–180: p.174. Früh-wald's somewhat one-sided point of view should be completed by Gisela Moffit, *Bonds and Bondage: Daughter-Father Relationships in the Father Memoirs of German Speaking Women Writers of the 1970s*, New York 1993; Frederick A. Lubich, 'Bester Vater – Bestie Vater: Familienromane der Töchter in der deutschsprachigen Gegenwartsliteratur', in Frederick A. Lubich (ed.), *Wendewelten: Paradigmenwechsel in der deutschen Literatur- und Kulturge-schichte nach 1945*, Würzburg 2002, pp.97–109.

In case of Elisabeth one shouldn't be troubled too much by the fact that she represents a discursive position that has come to be associated with teens and twens. Following Richard Herzinger,

> werden der Jugend heute paradoxerweise Eigenschaften zugeschrieben, die vormals als Merkmale reiferen Alters galten: Sie sei illusionslos, pragmatisch und praxisorientiert, anpassungsfähig und -bereiter als die Älteren. [...] Abgeklärtes, zielgerichtet nüchternes Zurechtfinden im Bestehenden [...] gilt als jung.[92]

> (Youth is nowadays paradoxically marked by characteristics that were formerly said to be traits of a more mature age: they are disillusioned, pragmatic and practice-oriented, flexible and more willing to adapt than the older ones. [...] Getting along with the existing circumstances in a balanced, purposeful, soberminded way is said to be young.)

Elisabeth's ability to adapt herself to the chaotic circumstances of the first thirty years of her life and, furthermore, her later unexcited acceptance of things past, make her appear rather 'young' in this respect.[93]

Bibliography

Anz, Thomas, 'Epochenumbruch und Generationenwechsel? Zur Konjunktur von Generationenkonstruktionen seit 1989', in Gerhard Fischer and David Roberts (eds.), *Schreiben nach der Wende: Ein Jahrzehnt deutscher Literatur 1989–1999*, Tübingen 2001, pp.31–40.

Assmann, Aleida, *Erinnerungsräume: Formen und Wandlungen des kulturellen Gedächtnisses*, Munich 1999.

Bahr, Ehrhard, 'Die Kontroverse um "das andere Deutschland"', in John M. Spalek and Joseph Strelka (eds.), *Deutschsprachige Exilliteratur seit 1933: II,2: New York*, Bern 1989, pp.1493–1513.

Bakhtin, Michail M., *Die Ästhetik des Wortes*, Frankfurt/M. 1979.

---

92   Richard Herzinger, 'Mythos, Stil und Simulation. "Generation" als kultureller Kampfbegriff und literarische Selbsterfindung', *neue deutsche literatur*, 48 (2000), 144–164: 155.

93   For advise and criticism I would like to thank Konstanze Baron (Konstanz), Kai Merten (Gießen), and Tobias Schulze-Cleven (Berkeley).

Bogdal, Klaus-Michael, 'Generationskonflikte in der Literatur', *Der Deutschunterricht*, 52 (2000), 3–12.

Breloer, Heinrich, *Unterwegs zur Familie Mann: Begegnungen, Gespräche, Interviews*, Frankfurt/M. 2001.

Brockmann, Stephen, *Literature and German Reunification*, Cambridge 1999.

Bude, Heinz, 'Die Achtundsechziger-Generation im Familienroman der Bundesrepublik', in Helmut König, Wolfgang Kuhlmann, and Klaus Schwabe (eds.), *Vertuschte Vergangenheit: Der Fall Schwerte und die NS-Vergangenheit der deutschen Hochschulen*, Munich 1997, pp.287–300.

——, 'Das "übertriebene Wir" der Generation', *neue deutsche literatur*, 48 (2000), 136–143.

Cooper, David, *The Death of the Family*, London 1971.

Dahrendorf, Ralf, 'Die Sache mit der Nation', *Merkur*, 44 (1990), 823–34.

Dedner, Burghard, 'Der Begriff der Generation in der Literaturgeschichte', in Michael Ewert and Martin Vialon (eds.), *Konvergenzen: Studien zur deutschen und europäischen Literatur*, Würzburg 2000, pp.20–36.

'Deutsche Schriftsteller über Thomas Mann', in Heinz Ludwig Arnold (ed.), *Thomas Mann*, Munich 1982, pp.195–237.

Der Deutschunterricht: Sonderheft Generationskonflikte, 52 (2000).

Dieckmann, Dorothea, 'Eine schrecklich nette Familie: Vorschlag für eine TV-Vorabendserie', *Neue Rundschau*, 112 (2001), 100–109.

Erhart, Walter, 'Generationen – zum Gebrauch eines alten Begriffes für die jüngste Geschichte der Literaturwissenschaft', *Zeitschrift für Literaturwissenschaft und Linguistik*, 30 (2000), 81–107.

——, *Familienmänner: Über den literarischen Ursprung moderner Männlichkeit*, Munich 2001.

François, Etienne, and Hagen Schulze (eds.), *Deutsche Erinnerungsorte*, Munich 2001.

Frühwald, Wolfgang, 'Väter und ihre Töchter: Ein vernachlässigtes Thema deutscher Literaturgeschichte', in Hans-Joachim Simm (ed.), *Europa, die Dichter und das Geld*, Frankfurt/M.-Leipzig 2001, pp.159–180.

Gestrich, Andreas, *Geschichte der Familie im 19. und 20. Jahrhundert*, Munich 1999.

Harpprecht, Klaus, *Thomas Mann: Eine Biographie*, Reinbek bei Hamburg 1995.

Heftrich, Eckhard, 'Der gehaßte Kollege: Deutsche Schriftsteller über Thomas Mann', in Eckhard Heftrich and Hans Wysling (eds.), *Internationales Thomas-Mann-Kolloquium 1986 in Lübeck*, Bern 1987, pp.351–69.

Hermand, Jost, and Wigand Lange, *'Wollt ihr Thomas Mann wiederhaben?': Deutschland und die Emigranten*, Hamburg 1999.

Herzinger, Richard, 'Mythos, Stil und Simulation. "Generation" als kultureller Kampfbegriff und literarische Selbsterfindung', *neue deutsche literatur*, 48 (2000), 144–164.

Holzer, Kerstin, *Elisabeth Mann Borgese: Ein Lebensporträt*, Berlin 2001.

Huyssen, Andreas, 'After the Wall: The Failure of German Intellectuals', *New German Critique*, 52 (1991), 109–43.

——, 'On Rewritings and New Beginnings: W.G. Sebald and the Literature About the "Luftkrieg"', *Zeitschrift für Literaturwissenschaft und Linguistik*, 31 (2001), 72–90.

Jäger, Wolfgang, and Ingeborg Villinger (eds.), *Die Intellektuellen und die deutsche Einheit*, Freiburg/B. 1997.

Jasper, Willi, *Der Bruder: Heinrich Mann. Eine Biographie*, Munich-Vienna 1992.

Kanz, Christine, and Thomas Anz, 'Familie und Geschlechterrollen in der neueren deutschen Literaturgeschichte: Fragestellungen, Forschungsergebnisse und Untersuchungsperspektiven (Teil I)', *Jahrbuch für Internationale Germanistik*, 32 (2000), 19–44.

Korff, Gottfried, and Reinhard Rürup (eds.), *Berlin, Berlin: Die Ausstellung zur Geschichte der Stadt*, Berlin 1987.

Krüll, Marianne, *Im Netz der Zauberer: Eine andere Geschichte der Familie Mann*, Frankfurt/M. 2001.

Kurzke, Hermann, 'Das Leben als Kunstwerk: Geständnisse eines Thomas Mann-Biographen', *Kursbuch*, 148 (2002), 127–37.

——, *Geschenke des Lebens: Ein Rückblick*, Berlin 1931.

——, *Thomas Mann: Das Leben als Kunstwerk*, Munich 1999.

Lehnert, Herbert, 'Bert Brecht und Thomas Mann im Streit über Deutschland', in John M. Spalek and Joseph Strelka (eds.), *Deutsche Exilliteratur seit 1933: I,1: Kalifornien*, Bern-Munich 1976, pp.62–88.

Lubich, Frederick A., 'Bester Vater – Bestie Vater: Familienromane der Töchter in der deutschsprachigen Gegenwartsliteratur', in Frederick A. Lubich (ed.), *Wendewelten: Paradigmenwechsel in der deutschen Literatur- und Kulturgeschichte nach 1945*, Würzburg 2002, pp.97–109.

Lühe, Irmela von der, 'Die Familie Mann', in Etienne François and Hagen Schulze (eds.), *Deutsche Erinnerungsorte*, I, Munich 2001, pp.254–271.

Maar, Michael, *Das Blaubartzimmer: Thomas Mann und die Schuld*, Frankfurt/M. 2000.

Magenau, Jörg, 'Literatur als Selbstverständigungsmedium einer Generation', *Zeitschrift für Literaturwissenschaft und Linguistik*, 31 (2001), 56–64.

Mann, Golo, *Erinnerungen und Gedanken: Eine Jugend in Deutschland*, Frankfurt/M 2001.

Mann, Thomas, *Deutsche Hörer!*, in *Gesammelte Werke*, Frankfurt/M. 1960, 1974, XI, 1035.

Matt, Peter von, *Verkommene Söhne, mißratene Töchter: Familiendesaster in der Literatur*, Munich 2001.

Mauelshagen, Claudia, *Der Schatten des Vaters: Deutschsprachige Väterliteratur der siebziger und achtziger Jahre*, Frankfurt/M. 1995.

Moffit, Gisela, *Bonds and Bondage: Daughter-Father Relationships in the Father Memoirs of German Speaking Women Writers of the 1970s*, New York 1993.

Mommsen, Hans, 'Generationskonflikt und Jugendrevolte in der Weimarer Republik', in Thomas Koebner, Rolf-Peter Janz, and Frank Trommler (eds.), '*Mit uns zieht die neue Zeit*': *Der Mythos Jugend*, Frankfurt/M. 1985, pp.50–67.

Müller, Jan-Werner, *Another Country: German Intellectuals, Unification, and National Identity*, New Haven, CT 2000.

Oswald, Hans, and Walter Boll, 'Das Ende des Generationenkonflikts? Zum Verhältnis von Jugendlichen zu ihren Eltern', *Zeitschrift für Sozialisationsforschung und Erziehungssoziologie*, 1 (1992), 30–51.

Reich-Ranicki, Marcel (ed.), *Was halten Sie von Thomas Mann? Achtzehn Autoren antworten*, Frankfurt/M 1986.

——, *Thomas Mann und die Seinen*, Stuttgart 1987.

Roseman, Mark (ed.), *Generations in Conflict: Youth Revolt and Generation Formation in Germany 1770–1968*, Cambridge 1995.

Schaenzler, Nicole, *Klaus Mann. Eine Biographie*, Frankfurt/M.-New York 1999.

Schneider, Michael, 'Väter und Söhne, posthum: Über die Väterliteratur der siebziger Jahre', in Heinz Ludwig Arnold (ed.), *Bestandsaufnahme Gegenwartsliteratur*, Munich 1988, pp.139–150.

Special 'Literatur und Generation: Vom Jungsein und Älterwerden der Dichter', *neue deutsche literatur*, 48 (2000).

Strohmeyr, Armin, *Klaus und Erika Mann: Les enfants terribles*, Reinbek bei Hamburg 2000.

Vaget, Hans Rudolf, 'Deutsche Einheit und nationale Identität: zur Genealogie der gegenwärtigen Deutschland-Debatte am Beispiel von Thomas Mann', *Literaturwissenschaftliches Jahrbuch*, 33 (1992), 277–98.

——, 'Mann and his Biographers', *Journal of English and Germanic Philology*, 96 (1997), 591–601.

——, 'Confession and Camouflage: The Diaries of Thomas Mann', *Journal of English and Germanic Philology*, 96 (1997), 567–590.

Wehdeking, Volker, 'Zwischen Exil und "vorgeschobenem Posten" der Kulturnation: Thomas Mann als Projektionsfigur für die im Land gebliebenen Nichtfaschisten', in Günther Rüther (ed.), *Literatur in der Diktatur: Schreiben im Nationalsozialismus und DDR-Sozialismus*, Paderborn 1997, pp.145–62.

Weigel, Sigrid, 'Die "Generation" als symbolische Form. Zum genealogischen Diskurs im Gedächtnis nach 1945', *figurationen: gender literatur kultur*, 0 (1999), 158–73.

Weiss, Andrea, *Flucht ins Leben: Die Erika und Klaus Mann-Story*, trans. Ernst-Georg Richter, Reinbek bei Hamburg 2000.

Anne Friederike Müller

Old Men and the Past: Personified Memories of German History after 1989

Taking their cue from Maurice Halbwachs's pioneering work on the social and historical aspects of memory, scholars have distinguished between two types of remembering: a more individual, autobiographical memory of events personally experienced in the past, and public or collective memories which are shared by members of a group or even a nation, and which shape their respective social, cultural, or national identities. Halbwachs insisted on the interconnectedness of both types of memory, and on the social construction of individual memory in particular: most memories are acquired and recalled in social settings, and language, one of the most important mediums of memory, is obviously a social phenomenon as it is usually shared by a group of language users.[1] If Halbwachs's prime objective was to reclaim the study of memory for the social sciences, instead of leaving it to psychologists investigating individual memory in isolation, later researchers have nuanced the articulation between the more individual and the more social kind of remembering.

Jan Assmann draws a distinction between communicative and cultural frames of memory.[2] Communicative memory includes recollections of the recent past which one shares with one's contemporaries. It is evoked in everyday interaction, and tends to be oral and informal. Cultural memory, by contrast, deals with a more distant, sometimes mythical past; it has an affinity to literary forms and rituals, and is perpetuated by particular experts (writers, priests, *griots*, historians).

---

1   Maurice Halbwachs, *Les cadres sociaux de la mémoire*, Paris 1925.
2   Jan Assmann, *Das kulturelle Gedächtnis: Schrift, Erinnerung und politische Identität in frühen Hochkulturen*, Munich 1997.

Communicative memory cannot reach further back than the individual memories of those living at a particular point in time. Drawing on evidence from African oral history as well as ancient and contemporary European history, Assmann estimates that, usually, communicative memory embraces the past forty years. When this threshold is reached, either ignorance and silence (the 'dark ages' phenomenon) or (formal, ritualized) cultural memory sets in.

In contemporary German history, an important forty-year threshold was reached in the 1980s. The fortieth anniversary of the end of the Second World War was accompanied by a (re-)assessment of the place that the war and Nazism were to hold in German history.[3] In West Germany, and to a lesser extent in the GDR, a renewed interest in history in general could be observed from about 1980 onwards, with a proliferation of local, regional, and national commemorations, with historical exhibitions attracting a large public, the foundation of new historical museums, and publishers vying for national history surveys.[4] The forty-year distance from that defining element of modern history, the Second World War, sparked similar phenomena in other countries, such as France, where the past decades have even been characterized as 'the age of memory'.[5] The new scholarly focus on memory and the history of memory, initiated by Pierre Nora's monumental *Lieux de mémoire* (1984–92), and recently replicated in Germany under the direction of Etienne François and Hagen Schulze (*Deutsche Erinnerungsorte*, 2001), testifies itself to fact that history and memory have come to the forefront of public attention to an unprecedented degree.

---

3   Assmann refers to Richard von Weizsäcker's speech on 8 May 1945 and the *Historikerstreit* of the late 1980s (Assmann, *Das kulturelle Gedächtnis*, p.51).

4   Etienne François, 'Von der wiedererlangten Nation zur "Nation wider Willen": Kann man eine deutsche Geschichte der "Erinnerungsorte" schreiben?' in Etienne François, Hannes Siegrist, and Jakob Vogel (eds.), *Nation und Emotion: Deutschland und Frankreich im Vergleich: 19. und 20. Jahrhundert*, Göttingen 1995, pp.93–107.

5   Pierre Nora, 'L'ère de la commémoration', in Pierre Nora (ed.), *Les lieux de mémoire*, III/3, *Les France: De l'archive à l'emblème*, Paris 1992, pp.977–1012: p.1012.

If, on account of the forty-year distance to the Second World War, the 1980s were a propitious period for remembering and re-assessing national history in many of the countries concerned, the German case is particular in that German national history took a decisive new turn precisely in this period. The fall of the GDR regime and the ensuing unification of the two German states committed the GDR and the first forty years of the Federal Republic to memory, so to speak. To apply Assmann's terminology: have pre-1945 recollec-tions become part of cultural memory, and have memories of the period from 1945 to 1989 been given more salience in communicative memory from 1989 onwards, as one might expect? In what ways are not only the National-Socialist period, but also the GDR and the 'Bonner Republik' remembered after 1989, and how do these memo-ries relate to German cultural identities?

In attempting to answer these questions, this essay looks at a series of selected literary texts in detail. Usually fixated in written form, sometimes symbolically encoded, and produced by a minority of 'specialists', literature would tend to fall into the category of 'cultural memory' in Assmann's scheme. However, I wish to argue that some contemporary literature can also be read as an indicator to 'communicative memory'. The author takes part in the community of his or her contemporaries who remember the recent past individually, but – as we know since Halbwachs – in ways that are mediated socially. Characters created by the author must at least to some extent share in particular, sometimes the same, communicative memories, if the aim is to evoke figures to which the reader can relate. It is obvious that this reasoning applies best to literary texts that are set in the present or in the very recent past, which are written in a realistic vein, and which contain autobiographical elements. The choice of texts for the purposes of this essay reflects these criteria throughout. However, the selection operates not only according to these formal characteris-tics, but also in relation to the specific content of the six texts discussed: all of them deal with old men, whether in the memory of the narrators, as characters, or in the person of the narrator himself. This specific interest results from the theories of memory discussed above. Old persons are the foremost bearers of communicative memo-ry. To be precise, it is only *their* individual memory which reaches back forty years approximately. With their death, communicative memory gives way to cultural memory (or nothingness). I wish to argue that, on account of this particular role for the memory of a community, old persons can come to stand as symbols or metonyms for the past of the community. Thus, they become markers, *topoi*, sites of memory themselves. This essay elucidates to which extent and in what ways this happened in Germany in the past two decades. What are the differences between the particular predicaments of East and West Germans, and what kind of changes occurred after 1989? What do these observations tell us about a potentially changing German cultural identity after 1989?

In order to be able to deal with these questions, the corpus discussed in this essay contains two texts written by West German authors before 1989: Ruth Rehmann's *Der Mann auf der Kanzel: Fragen an einen Vater* (1979; *The Man on the Pulpit: Questions for a Father*, 1997), and Christoph Meckel's *Suchbild: Über meinen Vater* (1980). The rest of the corpus dates from the post-1989 period, with two texts by East Germans (Monika Maron, *Stille Zeile Sechs* [1991; *Silent Close No. 6*, 1993], and Kurt Drawert, *Spiegelland* [1992]). Two further texts have been written by authors born in West Germany, namely Hanns-Josef Ortheil (*Abschied von den Kriegsteilnehmern* [1992]), and Uwe Timm (*Rot* [2001]), the lapse of time between the two permitting to have a relatively long-term perspective on post-1989 changes.[6]

The fact that this essay focuses on old *men*, to the almost complete exclusion of old *women*, is not related to a potential gender bias of the author. This emphasis has a particular cultural significance. In

---

6   The spatial limitation of this paper does not allow for a discussion of a larger corpus of texts. One might wish to challenge the implication that two texts are sufficient to illustrate each period and/or authorial perspective. The problem of a representative collection of evidence besets all qualitative research carried out by social and cultural scientists. When literary works are concerned, which at least in the mainstream Western tradition are conceived as springing from individual creation, it is particularly hard to see how one or two or even ten books could be said to 'represent' a class of literary texts. In this essay, they are treated as 'examples' and 'illustrations' for culturally possible attitudes towards old age in relation to communicative and cultural memory.

order to elucidate this, the first section of the essay deals with a completely different 'source' from the corpus of literary texts listed above: two prominent recent legal cases in which old men were on trial.[7]

The Past on Trial

The relation between law and memory becomes particularly evident in court cases. Both plaintiffs and defendants have to give their version of past facts, and the court decides which version of truth is authoritative. While this is true of court cases in general (logically, the judgement intervenes after the fact), some of them bear a special relation to the collective memory of a community. When fundamental values and/or political issues seem to be at stake, court cases are likely to attract heightened public attention.

These conditions come together when former political decision-makers are on trial. Post-war Germany saw a number of court cases in which high-profile and less well-known National-Socialist offenders were tried for their crimes, both in the West and in the East. However, these court cases were petering out by the 1980s and 1990s. With the

---

7   From the perspective of literary history and theory, law and literature may seem completely disconnected: law deals with 'facts', literature is 'fiction'. The profound differences between the two social/cultural domains are not at all to be negated in this essay. One does not have to subscribe to the extreme constructivist proposition that law is 'a species of social imagination' (Clifford Geertz, *Local Knowledge: Further Essays in Interpretative Anthropology*, New York 1983, p.232), which would indeed put it on the same plane as that other supreme instance of social imagination, literature. However, legal cases, and particularly those with a high media fallout, can tell us something about German cultural identity, just as literature can tell us other, or perhaps – and this is precisely the question – the same things. The new cultural history of Early Modern Europe has thrived precisely on such a non-legal, 'cultural' reading of court cases. It is perhaps surprising, but nonetheless legitimate, and – as this paper sets out to demonstrate – fruitful, to 'read' court cases and literature alongside each other in a more contemporary context.

demise of the GDR, a wave of trials of former state officials could have been expected. Contrary to suggestions that the political class of the GDR should answer to East Germans alone,[8] there were neither informal popular tribunals nor the equivalent of a truth-and-reconciliation commission. Openly political trials being excluded, former GDR officials could only be judged according to the rule of law for what in the view of the public did not necessarily seem their most significant offences.

One such trial which probably stirred most public attention was the proceedings initiated by the *Landgericht* (district court) of Berlin against six members of the National Defence Council of the GDR, including Erich Honecker, head of both the SED and the GDR from 1976 to 1989. The National Defence Council took the main decisions related to the construction and the military defence of the Berlin Wall, that is, from a West German perspective the supreme symbol of the East German regime. Six former members of the National Defence Council were accused of incitement to manslaughter in 1992.

From the start of the proceedings on 12 November 1992, it became clear that the defence lawyers had chosen as their main strategy to emphasize the frail physical condition of Erich Honecker. Most of the defendants were in advanced age (between 66 and 85 years old).[9] Honecker (b. 1912) already appeared exhausted on the second day of the proceedings (16 November 1992).[10] He had been diagnosed with a cancerous tumor in his liver earlier that year. A great deal of the time allotted to the hearings was spent discussing various medical reports on the exact size and development of the cancer.

---

8   Jacqueline Hénard, *Geschichte vor Gericht: Die Ratlosigkeit der Justiz*, Berlin 1993, p.20, and Peter Schneider, *Extreme Mittellage: Eine Reise durch das deutsche Nationalgefühl*, Reinbek bei Hamburg 1992, pp.101–5.

9   Willi Stoph (b. 1914) suffered a heart attack two days before the beginning of the hearings; the charges against him were dropped in July 1993 on account of his physical incapacity to stand trial. Erich Mielke (b. 1907) was not prosecuted for similar reasons (although he was later condemned in another trial on a different charge).

10   Uwe Wesel, *Ein Staat vor Gericht: Der Honecker-Prozeß*, Frankfurt/M. 1994, p.53.

The principle which was invoked time and again was the dignity of the human being, enshrined in the first article of the Basic Law. If it could be proved medically that Honecker would not live until the end of the trial, the charges would have to be dropped on humanitarian grounds according to a Federal Appeals Court decision in 1979. According to the line taken by the defence, the decision on this issue should be considered as a litmus test for the constitutional state – a particularly sensitive argument in a trial of the former East German leader by a West German court.[11]

The impression that Erich Honecker 'escaped justice' caused outrage for many Germans, perhaps because he, 'more than any other figure, seemed personally to embody the crimes of the GDR government'.[12] Honecker understood very well himself that his person was taken to symbolize the GDR. In his two-hour-long declaration in the courtroom on 3 December 1992, Honecker criticized the actor-centred view of history that seemed to underlie the charges brought against him:

Wie und warum es zum Bau der Mauer gekommen ist, interessiert die Staatsanwaltschaft nicht. Kein Wort steht darüber in der Anklage. Die Ursachen und Bedingungen werden unterschlagen, die Kette der historischen Ereignisse wird willkürlich zerrissen: Erich Honecker hat die Mauer gebaut und aufrechterhalten. Basta. So einfach vermag der bundesdeutsche Jurist die Geschichte zu sehen und darzustellen.[13]

(The prosecutor is not interested in learning how the construction of the Wall came about. No word about this is included in the bill of indictment. The causes and conditions are silenced, the chain of historical events is cut up arbitrarily:

---

11 The fact that the court understood the necessity of paying at least lip-service to 'human dignity' became obvious when Hansgeorg Bräutigam, the first presiding judge, suggested on 17 December 1992 that the details of the latest medical report should be discussed in private so as to protect Honecker's dignity – a proposal which the defence lawyers had to take up even if they had perhaps hoped to arouse compassion if the report was made public (Wesel, *Ein Staat vor Gericht*, p.93).

12 A. James McAdams, 'The Honecker Trial: The East German Past and the German Future', *The Review of Politics*, 58/1 (1996), 53–80: 68.

13 My translation, as for all other quotations, A.F.M. Quoted in Wesel, *Ein Staat vor Gericht*, p.72.

Erich Honecker built and maintained the Wall. That's it. The FRG lawyer can depict history as simply as that.)

Apparently, the new presiding judge, Josef Hoch, took Honecker's lesson on the history of the Cold War at least partly on board; in the final judgement rendered nine months later, he upheld the charge of the personal responsibility of GDR decision-makers such as Honecker for the shootings at the Wall, but argued that 'in favour of the defendants, the court had to consider the fact that they are prisoners of German history like all of us',[14] thus showing that the court did not take Honecker for an all-powerful representative of the GDR.

Despite its self-evident incapacity to render justice for Germany's political past, the present legal system distinguishes between old men emerging from the GDR past and those responsible for the worst National-Socialist crimes. Murder and, hence, genocide are not barred by the statute of limitations.[15] In Holocaust trials, the age of defendants is not a criterion taken into account by the courts.[16] Nonetheless, invoking old age has been a popular strategy for trying to escape justice for former National-Socialists as well. As recently as spring 2001, for example, Anton Malloth, who had organized killings in a police prison of Theresienstadt in his capacity as SS officer, told the judge that he 'was not able to follow properly' the remarks on victims 'who [in the words of the judge] suffered from unspeakable injustice, were tortured and murdered'.[17] Malloth, sentenced to death in the Czechoslovak Republic in 1948 and on the run for the following fifty years, was imprisoned for the short rest of his life.[18]

It is particularly intriguing to note that, according to a media report, 'the past itself appeared in court' in the person of the eighty-

---

14   Quoted in Wesel, *Ein Staat vor Gericht*, p.152.
15   Since a 1979 amendment of § 78 of the Criminal Code of the Federal Republic of Germany.
16   The prosecutor never established an analogy to this situation in the Honecker trial, thus implicitly recognizing that communist and National-Socialist injustices are not comparable (Hénard, *Geschichte vor Gericht*, pp.79–80).
17   Christian Habbe, 'Im Visier der Nazi-Jäger', *Der Spiegel* (3 September 2001).
18   Malloth died on 31 October 2003.

nine-year-old wheelchair user.[19] How is one to interpret the journalist's remark which equates the former SS officer with 'the past itself'? Arguably, both cases indicate that there is a widespread attitude in contemporary Germany according to which the past of the country can potentially be represented by certain old men.[20] Obviously, Honecker did not build the wall himself, nor did he take the decision to have it built and defended by military means in a political vacuum. A complex play of international and intra-German political forces conditioned that choice, as both the judge and the defendant stressed in different ways. There is, however, a widespread public tendency to focus on one single person when thinking of a (German) state. This attitude is certainly not unrelated to the fact that, historically, for centuries, the German state and/or nation has been represented by one person only, this person never being a woman in German history (apart from purely symbolic representations such as the virgin-like, maternal, or Valkyrian *Germania* of the nineteenth century). This male-biased tradition is maintained even in present-day Germany despite the fact that gender equality is inscribed in the constitution and in the programmes of most political parties.[21] Thus, one can conclude

---

19   Habbe, 'Im Visier der Nazi-Jäger'.

20   Naturally, I do not wish to argue that public opinion perceives the old men in question purely as symbols and has no interest in the actual facts of the case. It seems necessary to stress that, while tens of thousands of court cases take place in Germany each year without stirring any media interest at all, even if in some cases the facts discussed may be of public interest, the two cases in question moved public opinion to a high degree (Honecker more so than Malloth). As the media reports, other published accounts of the cases, and newspaper caricatures suggest, this is at least partly due to the spectacle of seeing an old, frail man being judged for actions linked to the exercise of power in former German states.

21   Election campaigns usually centre around one single person, rather than a party, or a set of ideas and programmes. More often than not this person is male, and almost certainly so when the highest levels of power are at stake. The candidate can be styled to express the 'force of the new', such as in the national election campaign of 1998 which brought the SPD to power and Gerhard Schröder to the chancellery, focussing on his masculinity (energy, dynamism) and youth (for an in-depth analysis of the historical dimensions of these phenomena, see Anne Friederike Müller, *'Strength' and 'Weakness' as Political Metaphors: An Ethnography of German Politics from 1871 to the Present*, Ph.D. thesis, University of Cambridge 2001, especially chapters 1–3 and 6).

in a more precise manner that high-profile defendants such as Honecker and Malloth do not just represent 'the past' *per se*, but the German state, German political power, in the past.

The specificity of these court cases lies in the fact that the men in question hardly embody anything like the 'force of the new', but rather the frailty of the aged. It is useful to distinguish between several aspects of this – at first sight purely physiological – fact. First, in legal terms, the physical decay of Honecker and some of his co-defendants simply means that they cannot be judged, while there is a special exception for NS perpetrators. Second, on the emotional level, the physical and/or mental decay of the defendants may arise pity, therefore emphasizing that it is an apt strategy for the defence in both cases.[22] Third, the old age of the defendants may have a symbolical dimension. As far as the former SS officer Malloth is concerned, the journalist quoted above implied that this specific part of the German past had aged. In 2001, the memory of the National-Socialist period, the journalist appears to suggest, may soon fade away like this frail old man.

The fact that in post-1989 Germany old men are put on trial so as to answer for actions committed in certain periods of German history, that there are open questions as to whether they should still be judged, and whether their physical state arouses pity, and if so, what the consequences are, the fact that in some contexts, their persons are taken to symbolize the state which they represent(ed),[23] constitute an important socio-cultural context for the representations of old men in contemporary German literature. Two questions need to be kept in mind when we turn away from the court cases towards literature. In the courtroom, as well as in literary texts, the old man may play a double role. He is a 'subject' of individual memory, and one has to ask what he himself remembers of his past. He is also an 'object' of

---

22   The legal and the emotional dimension are more connected than one might expect; they are linked by the notion of 'human dignity', which, although a legal term, has religious overtones and a subjective dimension, as jurisprudence admits.

23   On the double meaning of 'representation', see Pierre Bourdieu, *Language and Symbolic Power*, ed. John B. Thompson, trans. Gino Raymond and Matthew Adamson, Cambridge 1991, p.106.

communicative or cultural memory, and the question is then what others remember of his past.

Father Figures

Old age as a cultural category has certain elements in common with gender. Like gender, it is a social and cultural elaboration based on 'biological facts' (which one might chose to deconstruct). Like gender, it can be 'performed'. Unlike gender, however, old age is a dynamic category in the sense that one gradually moves towards old age in the course of one's life. This fluidity also implies that one applies the label 'old' primarily to those who are older than oneself,[24] be they aged 30, 60 or 90. 'Old age' is associated with certain external markers, but it is also situational. A typical situation in which 'old age' is attributed is within the family; saying that generations are defined by their age difference amounts to a tautology. An investigation into representations of old men in literature can therefore hardly do without looking at father figures.

A series of pre-1989 literary texts was particularly concerned with this topic. The writer Michael Schneider went as far as to identify an entire genre of *Väterromane* ('father novels'), a wave of literary biographies of authors' fathers. Schneider remarked that their date of publication coincided roughly with the broadcasting of the TV series *Holocaust* on German television in 1979 and the renewed interest in the National-Socialist past provoked by the television drama.[25] However, applying the forty-years 'rule' mentioned by Assmann, both the *Väterromane* and the reactions to *Holocaust* can be seen in a larger historical context, where the slowly beginning disappearance of the

---

24   Kathleen Woodward, *Aging and its Discontents: Freud and other Fictions*, Bloomington 1991, p.6.

25   Michael Schneider, 'Fathers and Sons, Retrospectively: The Damaged Relationship Between Two Generations', *New German Critique*, 31 (Winter 1984), 3–51.

war generation sparked a particular receptivity for the memory of the National-Socialist past. The analysis of the court cases has allowed us to differentiate the legal, emotional, and symbolical dimensions of judgements on old men. The 'father novels' can be examined with a particular view to the emotional reactions towards the old men they portray.

Two examples of father novels have been singled out for discussion: Christoph Meckel's *Suchbild: Über meinen Vater* (1980) and Ruth Rehmann's *Der Mann auf der Kanzel: Fragen an einen Vater* (1979; *The Man on the Pulpit: Questions for a Father*, 1997). Both figure in the usual lists of *Väterromane*. One is written by a male, one by a female author; they were published at about the same time; while set in different regional and professional contexts, the father figures are reasonably comparable.[26] In a typical way for a 1980s *Vaterroman*, Christoph Meckel is interested in the issue of fatherhood itself. Clearly, the narrator in Meckel's text suffered from the unloving behaviour of his father. At the age of four, the narrator was punished corporally on ten consecutive days for an unintended mistake; thus, the father drove him out of the 'paradise' of childhood.[27] *Suchbild* is an attempt to find an explanation for this key experience. The author suggests two interpretations for the father's emotional coldness. The narrator first looks at a trans-generational pattern for an explanation:

> Mein Vater litt unter chronischer Lieblosigkeit und stotterte früh. Was immer er tat, seinen Vater zu überzeugen, wurde knapp und kalt mit Verachtung belegt. [Des Großvaters] Erziehungsformel für seine Kinder hieß: du bist nichts, du kannst nichts, mach deine Schulaufgaben. Sie kehrte wörtlich bei meinem Vater wieder, als er meine ersten Gedichte las. Er fror im Schatten dieses frostigen Herrn. [...] Er verdankte ihm den Sinn für Prinzip und Strafe und den unbedingten Glauben an Autorität. (Meckel, 23).

---

26   The term 'father novel' is slightly misleading in this context because neither of the two authors chose to call their text a 'novel'. This may be due to the fact that both texts are relatively short; however, it is also important to note that both contain strong autobiographical elements. In the following discussion, 'narrator' and 'author' are distinguished. In practice, particularly in Meckel's text, the line between the two is sometimes difficult to draw.

27   Christoph Meckel, *Suchbild: Über meinen Vater*, Düsseldorf 1980, p.59. Henceforth quoted as 'Meckel' with page number in brackets.

(My father suffered from chronic unkindness and started to stammer early on. Whatever he did in order to convince his father was greeted quickly and coldly with contempt. [The grandfather's] pedagogical formula read: you are nothing, you can do nothing, do your homework. This formula returned word for word when my father read my first poems. He shivered with cold in the shade of this frosty master [*Herr*]. [...] Thanks to him, he developed a sense for principles and punishment and an unconditional belief in authority.)

The second explanation takes the particular historical circumstances into account. The narrator's father was a *Wehrmacht* officer and behaved accordingly inside the home as well. Eventually, one has to conclude that the narrator is condemned to reiterate the family pattern of emotional indifference. He watches his ageing father's physical decay and death with apparent coldness: 'Das Herz stand still. Der Schrittmacher klopfte weiter' ('His heart stopped. The pacemaker kept beating'; Meckel, 181). The father is portrayed as embodying both family memory and recent national memory which combine in a heightened lack of empathy for the following generation (which responds in kind).

If the narrator in Meckel's text is urged into writing by his painful childhood memories, and probably also by being puzzled about the signs of his own indifference towards his father, the stimulus of the narrator in Ruth Rehmann's text is her own children's inquiries about their grandfather. In this case, the narrator's father was born in 1875, son of a parson and later a parson himself. Both narrators have to come to terms with the memory of a politically compromised father. However, the tones of the account given of the fathers' lives differ dramatically. The parson did love and was loved by most members of his parish and his family. This text ends with a description of the aged father's death as well, but, unlike in *Suchbild*, this is presented as a sad event. The father lying on his deathbed is given the last word, which preserves the human dignity of the dying person, especially when one compares this passage to Meckel's choice of paying equal attention to the corpse and a machine (the cardiac pacemaker).

The emotions triggered by the sight of physical decay and death that are portrayed in these two texts range from condescending pity to empathic compassion. The anthropologists Catherine Lutz and Lila

Abu-Lughod suggest that emotions can be analyzed as 'vehicles for symbolizing and affecting social relations' or that they may be seen as 'practices that reveal the effects of power'.[28] The *Väterromane* discussed here suggest a correlation between the quality of intergenerational relations and the emotions felt towards the old men in question. In the case of the loveless father lacking of empathy for his children, the physical ageing and death are portrayed as provoking sentiments close to schadenfreude and satisfaction, whereas the dying of the – politically equally naive – other old man, who genuinely tried to build positive, understanding relations with most people of his entourage, is greeted with respect and sadness.

The description of different emotions correlates not only with different types of social relations, but also with political judgements of the fathers' actions. The emotional coldness of the father in Meckel's text is partly attributed to his experiences as a *Wehrmacht* officer. Meckel explores the political attitude of the father to a considerable extent. The father, who is clearly inspired by, if not identical with Meckel's memory of his own father (Eberhard Meckel, 1907–69), is presented as a writer of limited talent who enjoyed a certain regional renown in Southwest Germany. As a conservative, possibly a nationalist, an ostensibly apolitical *Bildungsbürger*, he kept aloof from the National-Socialist regime for what could be termed aesthetic reasons (Meckel, 45). He accepted the notion of collective guilt while held in a French prisoner of war camp, but refused to recognize any personal guilt (Meckel, 89–91). Apart from rare moments of insight (when he would describe himself as a 'Hyänenopfer, selbst Hyäne' ('a victim of hyenas, a hyena myself'); Meckel, 107), he was tempted to embellish his behaviour in the war once he was reunited with his family after 1945. The simple human gesture of sharing his bread ration with a Polish woman is glorified almost as an act of resistance; the son is invited to take it for the 'gute [...] Tat eines Deutschen'[29], for the expression of an unchanged positive cultural identity (Meckel, 129f).

---

28   Lila Abu-Lughod and Catherine A. Lutz, 'Introduction: Emotion, Discourse, and the Politics of Everyday Life', in Lila Abu-Lughod and Catherine A. Lutz (eds.), *Language and the Politics of Emotion*, Cambridge 1990, pp.1–23: p.12f.

29   'Good deed of a German', or rather the 'gesture of a good German'.

Consequently, the narrator's criticism of his father is summed up in the reproach of remaining 'immer derselbe' ('always the same'), of not being sufficiently self-incriminatory (Meckel, 164).[30]

The political posture of the father in *Suchbild* can be compared to the attitude of the narrator's father in Rehmann's text. Like him, the parson kept distant from the political regime. The narrator remembers that on one occasion, unlike everyone else including herself (a child at the time), he did not get up to watch the 'Führer' drive past on a ship on the Rhine. Like the other father discussed, the parson held on to *bildungsbürgerliche* values: 'Er glaubte an das Gute, Wahre, Schöne, auch wenn keine Spur davon zu erblicken war' ('He believed in the good, the beautiful, the true, even if nothing of this could be seen anywhere around');[31] in addition, he was led to obey not by painful educational experiences, but by his Protestant faith. In both cases, the fathers were 'weder Naziverbrecher noch Widerstandskämpfer' ('neither Nazi criminal[s] nor resistant fighter[s]'; Rehmann, 18).

In both texts, two different modes of remembering are confronted. It is most interesting to look at this in the light of anthropological work on individual and collective memory. Maurice Bloch identified two different 'ways of being in history', or 'folk theories of memory' (with the possibility of mixed types). As is customary in social anthropological thought, Bloch confronts ethnographical evidence from different parts of the world. The Sadah of Yemen (in a way that is exemplary for other Islamic societies) conceive of human beings as remembering an unchanged, ahistorical truth when acquiring religious and other knowledge, whereas the Bicolanos of the Philippines (in a typical way for other South-East Asian societies) see themselves as

---

30 An uncritical funeral speech which he wrote after the war for a fellow writer, a known National-Socialist, illustrates this clearly in the view of the narrator (Meckel, 163).

31 Ruth Rehmann, *Der Mann auf der Kanzel: Fragen an einen Vater*, Munich, Vienna 1979, p.122. Henceforth quoted as 'Rehmann' with page number in brackets.

constantly imprinted and changed by new knowledge and new historical experience.[32]

Both fathers in the texts discussed are described as seeing themselves in a long-standing, almost eternal, and certainly unchanging
tradition of Germanness, the defining components of which include
moral probity, cultural refinement, and respect for authority. The experience of the National-Socialist dictatorship and the truths about
German atrocities that were revealed after 1945 did not shake this
belief to the ground. By contrast, the following generation is portrayed
as subscribing to a more malleable concept of personal and historical
identity. The years between 1933 and 1945 are given crucial importance in their accounts. While the memory of the fathers embrace their
lives in the continuity of their national (as well as cultural and religious) tradition, the children of the *Väterromane* are committed to
digging up the memory of the Nazi years. It is implied that the fathers'
attitudes and actions during those years should have changed their
view of their personal-cum-historical/cultural identity, as, for the
younger generations, it is impossible to uphold the German cultural
tradition of their fathers uncritically. While the fathers remember the
Nazi years in the light of their previous and subsequent, unchanged
cultural identity as Germans, the children have a tendency to see their
fathers in the light of those twelve years only.

Social relations encoded in emotions impinge upon the political
assessment of both fathers respectively. The father who appears to
reproduce his behaviour as a 'bad German' perpetrator in the Nazi
years within the circle of his own family is judged harshly as a person
as well as politically. Arguably, when the younger generation identify
themselves with the victims of their fathers' politically compromised
past, the ageing process is shown to trigger negative emotions which
express the rejection of the period of German history for which they
are taken to stand as exemplars (1933–45 in this case), and the cultural
identity which they attributed to themselves (classic German *Bildung*,
moral goodness, and respect for authority). An analysis of post-1989

---

32   Maurice Bloch, 'Internal and External memory: Different Ways of Being in
      History. The Edward Westermarck Memorial Lecture, Helsinki, 31 January
      1992', *Suomen Antropologi*, 1 (1992), 3–15: 6–10.

literature written by East German authors will allow us to test the validity of this hypothesis, as well as to begin to explore the specificity of changing German cultural identity after 1989 as expressed through the literary portrayal of old men.

East German Reckonings with the Past

Again, two texts are chosen to investigate East German memories of old men, representations attached to them, and related cultural identities and 'ways of being in history' after 1989. Monika Maron's *Stille Zeile Sechs* was published in 1991 (*Silent Close No. 6*, 1993); however, the action takes place before the fall of the Wall, probably in the middle of the 1980s.[33] The novel relates the encounter of Rosa Polkowski, a woman in her forties who has just decided to give up her employment as a historian in the service of a state organization, and Herbert Beerenbaum, a retired university professor born in 1907. Rosa agrees to meet Beerenbaum twice a week in order to type his memoirs. This arrangement sets the scene for a series of debates about each generation's memories and outlook on life.

Old age and the relationship between generations are central to this novel, which illustrates the particular situation of the East German generation born during or shortly after the war vis-à-vis their elder fellow citizens. Herbert Beerenbaum belongs to the *Aufbaugeneration*, i.e. those Germans who shaped the German Democratic Republic from its beginnings and continued to wield influence in the 1980s. Rosa details a typical biography of such *Aufbaugeneration* Germans: working-class origins, membership of the Communist Party from age 17 or 18, imprisonment or emigration in 1933, liberation or return to Germany in 1945, and work in various state or Party functions since

---

33 Lothar Bluhm, '"Irgendwann, denken wir, muss ich das genau wissen": Der Erinnerungsdiskurs bei Monika Maron', in Volker Wehdeking (ed.), *Mentalitätswandel in der deutschen Literatur zur Einheit (1990–2000)*, Berlin 2000, pp.141–51: p.145.

then.[34] This description fits Beerenbaum's life course, but it corre-
sponds also to the biography of Rosa Polkowski's father, a school
director, and Monika Maron's step-father in real life, Paul Maron,
Interior Minister of the GDR from 1955 to 1963.[35]

The biographical pattern and the resulting behaviour is so typical
that Rosa can anticipate Beerenbaum's reactions. Rosa and her friends
have the impression that the generation of Beerenbaum and Rosa's
father (the reader might wish to add, of Honecker and Paul Maron)
have confiscated their entire life space, 'everything'. This is why the
younger ones avidly spot any signs of Beerenbaum's age-related
diseases and eventually long for his death (Maron, 156).

A parallel can be drawn to Christoph Meckel's text which also
alludes to the idea that the previous generation makes it difficult for
the younger one to live. However, if the impulse to attack the parents
and the ruling political class is similar, the moral situation of the
equivalent East German generation[36] is complicated by the fact that
the GDR *Aufbaugeneration* can successfully claim the status of victim
for itself. In the eyes of Beerenbaum and Rosa's father, the Nazi
persecution of Communists legitimated all political measures taken by
the Soviet Union, the Communist Party, and the GDR state.

The best strategy to undermine the older generation's 'way of
being in history' as well as their hold on political power is to elicit
subversive counter-memories. At one meeting, Rosa asks Beerenbaum
if he knew about the cruel elimination of fellow German exiles who
were lodged with him at the Hotel Lux in Moscow during the war.
His immediate answers are: 'Wir haben gegen Hitler gekämpft'
('we fought against Hitler'), and 'wir [haben] einen Staat aufgebaut'
('we built up a state'). The venerable achievements of his generation
are supposed to make one forget about any objectionable aspects of

---

34   Monika Maron, *Stille Zeile Sechs. Roman*, Frankfurt/M. 1991, p.27. Henceforth
      quoted in the text as 'Maron' with page number in brackets.
35   Most defendants in the Honecker trial follow this pattern as well. Erich
      Honecker, for example, was born in 1912 (the son of a miner), joined the KPD
      in 1930, fled to France and was caught by the Gestapo in 1935; the Red Army
      liberated him in April 1945, paving the way for his career in state and Party
      organizations.
36   Christoph Meckel was born in 1935, Monika Maron in 1941.

real-existing communism. When Rosa and Beerenbaum meet next, the old professor has prepared another argument:

> Am darauffolgenden Freitag diktierte er als ersten Satz: 'Meine Frau Grete wurde im Herbst 39 verhaftet.' Meine Finger wurden so steif, daß ich nicht schreiben konnte. Er sah mich an wie jemand, der zum Schlag ausholt und sein Ziel fixiert. 'Sie kam in das Konzentrationslager Ravensbrück.' Er stand auf, erregt, atemlos, ging zur Tür, wandte sich zu mir: 'Und das liegt nicht in Sibirien', schrie er und verließ das Zimmer. [...] Sie haben immer recht, dachte ich, was ich auch sage, alles Unglück gehört schon ihnen, den glücklichen Besitzern von Biografien. Kaum mach ich das Maul auf, um meine einzuklagen, stoßen sie mir einen Brocken wie Ravensbrück oder Buchenwald zwischen die Zähne. Friß oder stirb. Von Dienstag bis Freitag hat er diese eine Minute vorbereitet, diese drei Sätze, hat er sich vorgestellt, wie ich mit steifen Fingern und sprachlos von Scham dasitzen werde, unfähig, meine Frage nach dem Hotel Lux zu wiederholen, weil ich in meinem Leben nichts vorzuweisen hatte, was mich zu dieser Frage berechtigte. (Maron, 141f).

> (The following Friday, he started by dictating the following sentence: 'My wife Grete was imprisoned in the autumn of 1939.' My fingers became so stiff that I was not able to write. He looked at me like someone who swung back and fixed his eyes upon his target. 'She was brought into the concentration camp at Ravensbrück.' He rose, in a state of irritation, out of breath, went towards the door, turned back to me: 'And that is not in Siberia', he shouted and left the room. [...] They are always right, I thought, whatever I say, all misfortune is already theirs, they are fortunate possessors of biographies. As soon as I open my mouth so as to insist on mine, they shove a chunk like Ravensbrück or Buchenwald between my teeth. Eat this or die. He had prepared this moment from Tuesday to Friday, these three sentences, he had been imagining that I would sit there with stiff fingers and speechless because of the shame, incapable to repeat my question about the Hotel Lux, because there was nothing that I could show for in my life that gave me the right to ask this question.)

The memory of the persecution of communists is supposed to override any recollections that might endanger the moral prerogative of the *Aufbaugeneration*. Ravensbrück and Siberia are proclaimed to be incommensurable.

However, some time later, Rosa initiates a second attack on the dominant memory. At another meeting, she asks a further unpleasant question, this time about a sinologist, a friend of hers, who had to spend several years in prison because he knew about the plans of a fellow scholar who escaped to the West. Beerenbaum, his superior at the university, had agreed to this punishment. Rosa cross-examines the retired professor on this topic (Maron, 205), after which she has a vision of her more cruel self (which she calls Rosalind) killing Beerenbaum. In the reality of the narration, he suffers from heart trouble after this scene, and, when a few minutes have passed, Rosa decides to call for help. He will die in hospital a short time later.

The scene illustrates perfectly well the fact that the struggle for memory is a contest of power. Certain memories legitimate the power of the Communist Party, and anyone criticizing the Party's actions can be accused of 'forgetting'. Conversely, keeping the memory of communist wrongdoings alive (such as the Hotel Lux 'cleansing' or later persecutions of intellectuals) becomes an act of resistance. Political animosities are fought out in a contest about who can claim more legitimately to be a victim. The philosopher and historian Tzvetan Todorov noticed that the status of the victim is highly desirable as a political asset as one can derive claims for compensation from it; often there is an outright competition for victimhood.[37] In *Stille Zeile Sechs* (*Silent Close No. 6*), this contest opposes victims of National-Socialism (and their political inheritors) and victims of SED rule. In her private thoughts, Rosa works at subverting the ideological power of victimhood altogether, introducing a fine distinction between victimhood and innocence, and hence seeking to delegitimize any unreflected political exploitation of victimhood (Maron, 112).

In *Stille Zeile Sechs*, too, emotions towards the ageing person are an important vehicle for social relations and political attitudes. Four aspects of Rosa's sentiments towards Beerenbaum can be distinguished. First, the disgust instead of pity that Beerenbaum's ageing body inspires in her most of the time can partly be explained by her criticism of the glorification of victimhood. When Rosa asked the question about the fate of the Hotel Lux exiles, Beerenbaum's lips tremble, his face turns red, and then some blood drips from his nose.

Nicht Beerenbaums Blut, nicht, wie es sich zwischen den kaum sichtbaren Bartstoppeln auf der Haut verteilte, widerte mich an, sondern daß er mir statt einer Antwort sein altes, tablettenverseuchtes, gegen Thrombose künstlich verdünn-

---

37   Tzvetan Todorov, *Les abus de la mémoire*, Paris 1995, pp.55–7.

tes Blut anbot, daß er versuchte, sich durch diesen miesen Trick in ein Opfer zu verwandeln und mir das Fragen zu verbieten. Endlich fand er das Taschentuch. (Maron, 139).

(What disgusted me was not Beerenbaum's blood spreading on his skin between the hardly visible stubble, but the fact that, instead of an answer, he offered me his blood, which had been diluted artificially because of the risk of thrombosis, the fact that he tried to turn himself into a victim with this mean trick and to prohibit me from asking questions. At last he found his handkerchief.)

One is reminded of the strategy that Honecker's lawyers would adopt one year after the publication of *Stille Zeile Sechs*: emphasizing the physical frailty of old age so as to escape judgement. Implicitly, Rosa recognizes the parallel between the attempt to elicit admiration as a political victim and attempt to provoke pity as an ageing man, and she refuses both politico-sentimental tactics.

Second, Rosa proves to be self-reflexive about her emotional impulses. Rosa's fantasies about killing Beerenbaum (and perhaps earlier her death wishes concerning her father; Maron, 114) make her realize that there is a potential perpetrator hidden inside herself as well. Far from behaving in a self-righteous way like Beerenbaum, Rosa is able to adopt a self-critical stance towards her urges and sentiments. If she is a victim, this does not necessarily make her 'innocent'.

Third, and related to the second point, Rosa and Beerenbaum are locked into a power struggle which also has a gender dimension. When Rosa visits Beerenbaum one last time in hospital, he makes an attempt at sexual harassment (Maron, 164). In a fierce battle, the two antagonists humiliate each other by emphasizing biological features that are socially mostly negatively connoted: Rosa's being a woman and Beerenbaum's being an old man.

The complex love-hate relationship between Rosa and the professor echoes the ambiguous feelings that she harboured towards her father. Her father's main interest was in communist ideology; he only talked to his daughter in order to instruct or to punish her. The private and the public sphere were inextricably mixed; Rosa's father always used the artificial language of official ideology when talking to his daughter (Maron, 61–2). As a child, Rosa had to live with a representative of the State at her home – the father was the director of her school and thus wielded a double authority over her. As an adult, Rosa often feels helpless like a child in front of Beerenbaum, another representative of state power. This generational dimension is added to the gender dimension in the power struggle between the two protagonists.

Fourth, old age eventually proves to be a symbol for state power. When Beerenbaum is finally buried – scenes from his funeral punctuate the narrative again and again – Rosa realizes that she has not been liberated as she expected to be. Not only does the memory of Beerenbaum continue to haunt her in the form of the manuscript of his memoirs which he bequeathed to her, but also, and above all, the repressive political structures persist. Beerenbaum's own son is a younger state official, an army and Stasi officer with 'dead' eyes, a replica of the dead father in a different, chronologically younger guise. The death of the *Aufbaugeneration* does not result automatically in the demise of the GDR and the liberation of the younger generation. Young state officials can have 'dead' physical features, while chronologically old people without pretensions to power appear 'young'. It is only the simultaneously symbolical and real old age of 'powerholders' embodying the memory of the founders of the GDR state, which is greeted with negative feelings reaching up even to the wish to annihilate the other. The representatives of the two generations are locked in a struggle in which both memory and power are at stake.

While *Stille Zeile Sechs* exudes an atmosphere of resignation and inertia, Kurt Drawert's 'German monologue' *Spiegelland* (1992) is set in post-revolutionary East Germany. Like Rehmann, Kurt Drawert explored his own and his family's past for the sake of his children, as the dedication indicates.[38] The text deals with the narrator's childhood and adolescence in Dresden. The father of the protagonist works as a policeman. Like in *Stille Zeile Sechs*, the authority of the state thus reaches far into the private sphere. In this case as well, everyday language seems to be contaminated. The narrator develops a speech impediment early on:

---

38   'Meinen Söhnen Lars und Tilman im Sinne einer Erklärung' ('To my sons Lars
       and Tilman in guise of an explanation').

[E]s muß ein frühes und vielleicht gerade noch rechtzeitiges Gefühl dafür gewesen sein, daß das Sprechen ein von außen beobachtetes, beeinflußtes und beherrschtes Sprechen war. Ich spürte, sobald Vater (oder Großvater, beispielsweise) sprach, daß nicht tatsächlich Vater (oder beispielsweise Großvater) sprach, sondern daß etwas Fernes, Fremdes, Äußeres gesprochen hatte, etwas, das sich lediglich seiner (oder ihrer) Sprache bediente.[39]

([I]t must have been an early and perhaps just about timely sense for the fact that the language was a language observed, influenced and dominated from outside. I felt that as soon as father [or grand-father, for example] spoke, it was not really father [or grand-father for example] who spoke, but something far away, something strange and external had spoken, which only used his [or their] language.)

The change of regime in 1989 loosens the narrator's tongue, and the text of *Spiegelland* flows in a long stream of consciousness with virtually every sentence merging into the next.

In the two texts written by East German authors, the authoritarian, loveless fathers represent state power in a most direct way. As school director or policeman, they serve as transmission belts of Party and state in the workplace as well as in the family. On the one hand, their ageing and/or death provoke satisfaction, as their grip on their children's lives is weakened this way. On the other hand, the same physiological processes are described as causing also mixed feelings of guilt, pity, and love, because of the kinship bond, and because the anti-fascist ideology, the ideology of victimhood, is difficult to challenge for the younger generations.

Stille Zeile Sechs and *Spiegelland* illustrate clearly what Assmann identified as the 'alliance' between memory, or forgetting, and power, as well as the 'alliance' between memory and resistance.[40] The personal memory of Beerenbaum's generation has become the official memory of the GDR; Rosa's own personal memories would have the potential to become a subversive force if it was possible to make them public. In principle, the young East German generations represented here stand better chances to pose successfully as 'victims' than West German writers like Meckel who attacked their politically compro-

---

39   Kurt Drawert, *Spiegelland: Ein deutscher Monolog*, Frankfurt/M. 1992, p.25f. Henceforth quoted in the text as 'Drawert' with page number in brackets.

40   Assmann, *Das kulturelle Gedächtnis*, pp.70–3.

mised fathers. The younger East Germans in these texts are dominated
doubly by old men as loveless fathers and representatives of the state.
To resist the dominant ideology, it suffices for the protagonists and
narrators of these texts to mobilize their own memories of private and
political oppression instead of searching for lacunae and inconsisten-
cies in the memories of their fathers. Rosa and the narrator in
Drawert's text have not to identify with historically remote victims of
the German state in order to voice their resistance; as direct victims of
both state power and their fathers' emotional shortcomings, they
experience positive sentiments only in some rare moments when the
fathers or father figures are physically extremely weak and/or close to
death.

Again, the confrontation can be interpreted as one between two
'ways of being in history'. The older generations and 'powerholders'
cling to a stable version of the past, a memory 'frozen' in the late
1940s. The Nazi persecution of Communists is supposed to justify the
dominant position of the Party and the lack of individual and
intellectual freedom in the GDR. By contrast, Rosa militates for a
more malleable collective memory and identity, which takes the
wrongdoings of the supposed 'victims' into account. Drawert's text
reveals a third way of being in history. The memory and identity of
the grandfather are extremely malleable without his admitting it. In
the course of his life, he moves effortlessly from National-Socialism
to Communism to capitalism. This particular German cultural identity
(an unflinching allegiance to the powers-that-be) is based on the
denial of memory, on the 'alliance of forgetting and power', to use
Assmann's terms.

Post-1989 Germany from a Western Perspective

How do these 'ways of being in history' differ from those that appear
in post-1989 literature written by authors born in West Germany? Two
novels have been singled out so as to find an answer to this question.
Hanns-Josef Ortheil's *Abschied von den Kriegsteilnehmern* (1992)

begins with the funeral of the narrator's father. The latter, belonging to the same generation as the father in Meckel's text, and deeply connected to his home region, the Rhineland (just like the father in Rehmann's story), participated in the Second World War as a soldier and worked as a land surveyor in civilian life.

There are some typical elements of the *Vaterroman* in this novel. The son reckons with his father's past. The father served as a soldier in the Silesian town of Kattowitz and often travelled to Kraków, which makes the son think that he could not possibly not have noticed the extermination camp in nearby Auschwitz:

> Ich hatte aus meinem Vater [...] ein genaues Wissen über das Lager Auschwitz heraushören, ja, ich hatte ihn zwingen wollen, dieses Wissen zuzugeben, so als sei mein Vater mitschuldig an dem, was in Auschwitz geschehen war, und als sei ich der Richter, der über diese Schuld das Urteil zu sprechen hätte. Und so hatten wir uns wie der Angeklagte und der Richter gegenüber gesessen, und doch war ich mir in meiner richterlichen Rolle ganz fehl am Platz vorgekommen.[41]

> (I wanted to unearth some precise knowledge about the camp at Auschwitz, I wanted to force him to admit this knowledge, as if my father had been guilty for what happened at Auschwitz, as if I had been the judge who had to render a judgement about this guilt. And this is how we sat opposite each other like an accused and a judge, and still I felt completely out of place in my role as a judge.)

The son assesses the personal memory of his father as did the narrators in Meckel's and Rehmann's texts. However, in this novel, written ten years after the main wave of *Väterromane*, the narrator questions his right to sit in judgement on his father. He also analyses why, at a certain time of his life, he felt compelled to establish a relation (preferably of responsibility and guilt) between his father and the National-Socialist past. When, as a young man, the protagonist learned about Nazi crimes, he felt that the history of humanity should have stopped at that point in time. A new beginning after the horrible persecutions and exterminations seemed hypocritical and altogether impossible.

---

41   Hanns-Josef Ortheil, *Abschied von den Kriegsteilnehmern. Roman*, Munich-Zurich 1992, p.104. Henceforth quoted in the text as 'Ortheil' with page number in brackets.

And still his own birth after the war[42] proved that history moved on. The narrator finds life with the memory of National-Socialist atrocities difficult to bear:

> Und so war mein Haß auf meinen Vater, der mich immer wieder befallen hatte, ein Haß auf die Zeitzeugenschaft meines Vaters gewesen, ich hatte ihm keine persönliche Schuld unterstellen können, und doch hatte ich ihn als einen noch lebenden Zeitzeugen und als lebendes Überbleibsel der Vergangenheit gehasst (Ortheil, 107).

> (And therefore, the hatred for my father which seized me again and again, was a hatred for his contemporaneousness (*Zeitzeugenschaft*), I could not surmise that he was personally guilty, and still I hated him as a surviving contemporary and as a surviving remnant of the past.)

While the narrator sees himself as symbol of the (incomprehensible) historical continuity of Germany, the father becomes a symbol of the National-Socialist period. The author indicates that the temporary hateful feelings are due to the fact that father and son are locked into a historical constellation – to use the words of Honecker's judge Hoch in 1993, they are 'prisoners of German history'. It is important to note that the father considers himself to be a victim of the war (he and his wife lost all their elder sons while they were still infants), whereas, unlike the narrator of Meckel's text, the son cannot legitimately claim the status of victim apart from the fact that he was burdened with the terrible recent past of his fatherland. In addition, like in the case of Rehmann's text, a loving upbringing is shown to correlate with a more considerate political assessment of the father.[43] These factors combine to heighten self-awareness of the narrator, who lucidly analyses his propensity to judge.

---

42   Ortheil was born in 1951 himself. Unlike the pre-1989 *Väterromane* discussed above, *Abschied von den Kriegsteilnehmern* is a self-proclaimed novel. However, it is noteworthy that author and narrator belong to the same generation.

43   In this context, it is interesting to note that Ortheil's view of his own father has become more and more positive since 1979 (Volker Wehdeking, *Die deutsche Einheit und die Schriftsteller: Literarische Verarbeitung der Wende seit 1989*, Stuttgart 1995, p.71); with the course of time, the judgmental attitude pervading some *Väterromane* has become difficult to sustain.

Michael Schneider diagnosed that all 'father novels' illustrate the problem of growing up, which might have been typical of the West German youth in the 1960s and 1970s; the narrators of these novels, perhaps like their entire generation, are emotionally stuck in their childhood.[44] By contrast, Ortheil's novel can be interpreted as showing a way out of this prolonged childhood. On the level of the plot, the narrator remained in the posture of a child for a long time; he does not realize that his father was ageing physically (Ortheil, 87) and tries to deny the reality of his funeral. Shortly after the funeral, however, the son leaves the country, opposing the wishes of his mother who would have liked him to take his father's social role. In order to come to terms with the loss, the son embarks upon a long odyssey. He travels to the United States, lives through a period of surrogate fatherhood to a teenage girl, sinks into a weeklong alcoholic haze in New Orleans, and eventually flies to the Dominican Republic on a whim.[45] While living in a little village in the hinterland of the island, he eventually recognizes that he resembles his father at least externally (Ortheil, 294), which sets off a process of reconciliation with the father and with himself.[46]

Most interestingly, this process of mourning and growing up is completed in parallel to the process of German reunification. The narrator travels from the United States to Vienna, where he shares an apartment with an Austrian woman and a young East German couple who have just fled over the border, thus forming a sort of re-united German *Kulturnation in nuce* during the summer of 1989. Whereas, traumatized by the war experience and in particular by an epic journey

---

44   See Schneider, *Extreme Mittellage*, p.43. See also Stephen Brockmann, *Literature and German Reunification*, Cambridge 1999, p.140 on the figure of the child in post-war literature as a metaphor for post-war German society and culture more generally.

45   The same contrast between the *Heimat*-loving generation of the fathers and their globetrotting children escaping from the fatherland comes across in Christoph Meckel's text (Meckel, 150).

46   Ironically, on his way back, the protagonist has changed so much physically that the US border control finds that he does not resemble his passport photograph any more; a friend also notices his changed appearance (we do not learn whether the narrator resembles his father more or less after this change).

on foot from Berlin to his home region of the Rhineland in 1945, his father always insisted on travelling westwards when on holiday (and settled in the Rhineland in the very West of the West German state), the narrator now goes even further East. He meets friends of his new East German acquaintances who are still in the precinct of the West German embassy in Prague, waiting for the permission to emigrate to West Germany. The narrator hands over a letter to them saying that they are expected in Vienna.

Having accomplished this mission, he experiences a dreamlike sequence in which he carries his father and his dead brothers on his back from the Rhine over the Elbe to Berlin. The period of the Second World War and the present overlap – the son, his father and his brothers meet refugees streaming westwards and come under heavy shell-fire. Having arrived at his destination, the son drops the dead father and the brothers into a grave. He feels relieved from his burden, physically and emotionally. Thus the novel comes to its end. The scene reminds one of the myth of Aeneas carrying his father on his back when he escaped the sack of Troy; the founding of Rome would correspond to the new-found German unity. Reunification coincides with the completion of a long process of mourning for the father and the brothers, all victims of the war – it ushers in the *Abschied von den Kriegsteilnehmern*, the parting with those who took part in the war, and brings the haunting memory of a painful aspect of personal and national history to an end.

The inquiry into the lacunae of the father's memory (and, one might argue, the FRG's public memory) was limited to a certain period of time. In this novel published shortly after Germany's reunification, the narrator chooses to give the past a less prominent place in his future life. The fact that the protagonist of this novel becomes aware that he used to look at his father as a symbol for the Nazi years (only his *Zeitzeugenschaft* is said to provoke the son's hatred) testifies to a beginning historization of the judgmental stance that characterized the *Väterromane*. The narrator's own memory is fraught with both thoughts of his country's National-Socialist past and with recollections of his father which continue to haunt him after the death of the latter. The events of 1989 provide an opportunity to bury his father symbolically and to end the reckoning with the personal and national past. This evolution is portrayed as emotional maturity, a process of growing up which involves the recognition that the father is not necessarily a perpetrator whom one has to judge, but a victim as well. Can these changes in individual memory be indicative of an evolution of communicative/cultural memory in Germany after 1989?

A look at another novel written by a West German author after 1989, but almost ten years after *Abschied von den Kriegsteilnehmern*, allows us to formulate a tentative answer to this question. Uwe Timm's *Rot* (2001) is set in post-reunification Berlin. *Rot* has even less characteristics in common with the 1980s *Väterromane* than Ortheil's novel.

Uwe Timm was born in 1940, Thomas Linde, the protagonist of *Rot*, in 1945. Thus, Timm belongs to the 'middle generation'[47] of authors born in the early 1940s who entered a literary scene virtually monopolized by the writers of the *Gruppe 47*. Like Maron, Timm had to come to terms with a situation in which an older generation dominated cultural and political life. In *Rot*, Thomas Linde's father, an architect, had shaped the built environment of Northern Germany with his functional, ugly buildings in the 1950s.[48] Thomas actively took part in the student rebellion of 1968, joined the Communist Party for several years (until about 1976), and held various, rather less prestigious jobs. At the time when the events related in the novel take place, in the early 1990s, he writes funeral speeches and jazz music reviews for a living.

Like the narrator of Ortheil's *Abschied von den Kriegsteilnehmern*, Thomas comes to understand that he resembles his father in some respect. Similarly to the fathers in Meckel's and Rehmann's texts, Thomas's father is neither a convinced Nazi nor a resistance fighter. In the course of the novel, through comparing his own experience with the biography of his late friend Lüders/Aschenberger whose funeral speech he is to write, Thomas realizes that, like his father, he

---

47   Manfred Durzak, 'Ein Autor der mittleren Generation', in Manfred Durzak and Hartmut Steinecke (eds.), *Die Archäologie der Wünsche: Studien zum Werk von Uwe Timm*, Cologne 1995, pp.13–25: p.13.

48   His brothers, Thomas's uncles, are also typical members of the West German *Aufbaugeneration*; one of them worked as a corporate lawyer, the other built up a successful business producing floor-polish.

made a lot of compromises in his life. He did not act on his Marxist beliefs until the end, as Aschenberger did, but he has to admit that, apparently, the course of history has proved his former political adversaries right.

What distinguishes this novel crucially from the other texts discussed so far is the fact that Thomas, the protagonist, experiences the process of becoming old himself. Thomas does reckon with the past of his (dead) father like the other narrators discussed above, but this father-son relationship is viewed through the eyes of the next generation. Iris, Thomas's lover, a woman in her early 30s, twenty-one years younger than he is, wonders why he seems to be so obsessed with the memory of his father.[49]

The generation of 1968, characterized by the reckoning with the fathers, is shown to be part of the past. Faced with the reunification of Germany, this 'middle' generation, or at least its left-wing fraction, as portrayed by Timm, has entered into a phase of self-assessment. In a state of drunkenness and despair about the break-up of his marriage, Thomas's friend Edmond cries out that they are a 'Losergeneration' ('generation of losers') even though he has achieved at least economic success with a huge wine import and retail business, a capitalist venture which contradicts his former Marxist convictions (Timm, 207). The political outlook of the three former friends, Thomas, Edmond, and Aschenberger, appears hopelessly outmoded. Aschenberger's son makes derogatory remarks about his father's books – Marx, Marcuse, Benjamin, Adorno, Althusser, Bourdieu, Lukács etc. – none of which he wants to keep after his father's death; he even pays a specialized company for their disposal as waste (Timm, 47–53). By contrast, Thomas recognizes his own 'Lesevergangenheit' ('reading past') in these writings and saves at least one book dedicated to Aschenberger by Marcuse himself from destruction (Timm, 72). Aschenberger, the most politically radical of the three friends, dies at the age of 55, shortly after the fall of the Wall ('die Wende, das war für ihn das Ende. Reimt sich sogar', his son says – 'the "turn of events" [*Wende*] spelt his end'; Timm, 53).

---

49   Uwe Timm, *Rot. Roman*, Cologne 2001, p.136. Henceforth quoted in the text as 'Timm' with page number in brackets.

Thomas, on the other hand, has the opportunity to thoroughly assess the fate of his generation, through his acquaintance with some younger contemporaries (Iris, her partner Ben, and their Turkish-born friend Nilgün), as well as through the process of looking back on Aschenberger's life. He discovers physical signs of his own ageing. The everyday life of the generation of 1968 with its endless debates and utopian projects appears like an exotic world to Iris who is fascinated by Thomas's recollections which are so different from her conformist father's memories of the same time.

Rot historicizes the generation of the children of the 'Kriegsteilnehmer' even more than Orteil's novel sets out to do. This historicization opens up an unexpected ideological link. Thomas realizes the blind spots of his former political convictions when he assists at some public hearings of the Honecker trial. In the court-room, he meets an old woman who lost her job and was imprisoned in the GDR because she had wanted to visit her daughter in West Germany. Acknowledging the suffering caused by the practical application of an ideology which he used to share, Thomas starts to suffer from a splitting headache (Timm, 406). The old woman's ordeal in the name of 'equality' and 'justice' sparks off memories of 1968, when Thomas, perhaps naively, proclaimed similar slogans in Paris with his friend Edmond as exchange students ('liberté, égalité, fraternité').

While the memories of the 'middle' generation are sollicited and assessed in a new light after 1989, another cultural identity is shown to emerge. Ben and Iris, two representatives of the young generation, have no problem accepting the capitalist system in which they thrive. Their apartment reminds Thomas of Imperial German style. While Thomas lives in a minimalist, black and white apartment with as little furniture as possible, a far-away echo of his father's functionalist orientation, Iris has chosen a baroque, colourful, bombastic decoration for her living space (Timm, 113).

These different outlooks on life, and ways of being in history, converge on the symbol of the Berlin Victory Column (*Siegessäule*). Thomas discovers that Aschenberger had planned to blow up the *Siegessäule* on the exact day when the German government was going to move from Bonn to Berlin. According to him, the Column stood for everything that was reprehensible about recent German history:

militarism, wars, authoritarianism, the Nazi terror (Timm, 103f).
Thomas toys with the idea of carrying out his friend's plan himself,
but as with everything else, he does not manage to reach a clear-cut
decision and to take action. Iris, on the other hand, reminds him that,
in the new Germany, the *Siegessäule* is above all a landmark sign for
the *Loveparade*. As, implicitly, she embraces the German past with
the Wilheminian decoration of her apartment, she also has a different
idea about how to deal with the Victory Column. She imagines an
ephemeral work of art consisting of sayings by Bismarck, quotations
from letters by young men volunteering as soldiers, and extracts from
Hitler's *Mein Kampf* projected onto the column with laser light beams
(Timm, 112). The third, 'postmodern' generation plays ironically with
elements of pastiche.

There are hints in *Rot* indicating that self-critical members of the
second generation like Thomas could agree with this way of being in
history. On a tour through East Germany, Thomas exposes his views
about age to Iris. He contends that old things (like the East, like himself) should not be despised, but respected. To the present world
where constant marketing incites to the rapid disposal of things, he
opposes a vision of life with few chosen objects growing ever more
beautiful with age (Timm, 331f). Similarly, the author appears to
suggest that, rather than dismissing parts of the German past, different
layers of memory can be added to each other.

It is telling that *Rot* should be set in present-day Berlin where the
different historical layers of the German past have left their undeniable traces in the urban space. Prussian, Imperial, Nazi, and Socialist
buildings are preserved undiscriminately, with ministries being in-
stalled in former Nazi and Socialist government buildings alike, and
the Parliament having moved back into the *Reichstag* building (inau-
gurated in 1883) in which the last democratically elected representatives lost their power to Hitler in 1933. The almost playful and open-
minded attitude towards German history of the youngest generation
in Timm's novel reflects these practical urbanistic arrangements.
Arguably, it ushers in a new German cultural identity referring back to
nineteenth-century Germany with a hint of irony. In this context, it is
interesting to note that parallels between the 'Berliner Republik' and
the Kaiserreich appear also elsewhere in post-1989 German literature,

albeit in a much more critical vein, such as in Günter Grass's *Ein weites Feld* (1997; *Too Far Afield*, 2000).[50]

Political Debates about Literature after 1989

This essay began by establishing a link between the 'reality' of two court cases in the 1990s and a selection of literary works; in its concluding section, it seems appropriate to show how literary representations of old men as objects and subjects of memory spill over into the reality of post-1989 debates about the role of literature. Günter Grass, a man in his early sixties and thus slowly approaching old age himself, contended in February 1990 that reunification was unthinkable because of the atrocities committed by Germans at Auschwitz.[51] In this case, an (relatively) old man spoke out in favour of the preservation of memory, in particular the memory of the Nazi years. There were soon attempts to silence voices 'of the past' like this one with an argument *ad hominem*: old age. In 1989 and 1990, some influential literary critics would attack old men[52] like Walter Jens (b. 1923), Günter Grass (b. 1927), and Stefan Heym (1913–2001) for their

---

50   In this novel, Grass links the first and second German unifications (1871 and 1989).

51   Irene Heidelberger-Leonard, 'Der Literaturstreit – ein Historikerstreit im gesamtdeutschen Kostüm?', in Karl Deiritz and Hannes Krauss (eds.), *Der deutsch-deutsche Literaturstreit oder 'Freunde, es spricht sich schlecht mit gebundener Zunge': Analysen und Materialien*, Hamburg 1991, pp.69–77: p.76.

52   Old women were attacked likewise, such as Christa Wolf, who in 1990 was harshly criticized for her text *Was bleibt* (*What remains*). The debate about the moral and aesthetic assessment of this text and Wolf's role in the GDR received enormous media attention. Although Wolf belongs to the generation of Grass and Jens (she was born in 1929), in her case, gender rather than age connotations were used to devalue her person. See also Karoline von Oppen, *The Role of the Writer and the Press in the Unification of Germany, 1989–1990*, New York 2000, p.105, and literature indicated there.

critical opinions about the reunification process.[53] For instance, Walter
Jens, after calling for a dialogue between East and West German cultural traditions (rather than a westernization of the East), was
described as a '[müder] Olymp' ('tired Olympian') or as 'von sozialis-
tischem Leichengift angesteckt' ('contaminated by the poisonous
corpse of socialism') in the *Tagesspiegel* (8 December 1989) and the
Frankfurter Allgemeine Zeitung (16 June 1990).[54] Similarly, Karl
Heinz Bohrer judged that both Grass and Jens had been 'politisch und
intellektuell schon seit längerer Zeit überfordert' ('politically and
intellectually overstrained for a long time', *Merkur*, October/November
1990).[55] Stefan Heym, equally critical of the western-led unification
process and the blind adulation of capitalist consumer goods by East
Germans, was ridiculed as a nostalgic old man (*Frankfurter Allgemeine
Zeitung*, 13 December 1989).[56] Perhaps unsurprisingly, Monika Maron
became Heym's fiercest critic, accusing him (as Rosa did with
Beerenbaum) of arrogance and of a patriarchal attitude, his views
being only seemingly legitimated by his respectable biography (*Der
Spiegel*, 1 February 1990).[57]

From late 1990, the debate on German literature widened to an
assessment of writers and their work from 1945 until reunification.
It is intriguing that the arguments used most often referred to generational constellations like those outlined above. Frank Schirrmacher,
director of the culture section of the *Frankfurter Allgemeine Zeitung*,
argued that the literature of the Federal Republic was dominated by a
group of left-wing liberals born around 1930; this literature kept the
memory of the National-Socialist past alive while critically pointing at
continuities in German society and politics before and after 1945.

---

53   Keith Bullivant, *The Future of German Literature*, Oxford-Providence 1994,
      pp.3–4; Jennifer E. Michaels, 'Confronting the Nazi Past', in Keith Bullivant
      (ed.), *Beyond 1989: Re-reading German Literature since 1945*, Oxford-
      Providence 1997, pp.1–20.
54   Von Oppen, *The Role of the Writer*, p.148 and p.155.
55   Klaus-Michael Bogdal, 'Wer darf sprechen? Schriftsteller als moralische
      Instanz – Überlegungen zu einem Ende und einem Anfang', in Deiritz and
      Krauss (eds.), *Der deutsch-deutsche Literaturstreit*, p.145.
56   Von Oppen, *The Role of the Writer*, p.46.
57   See von Oppen, *The Role of the Writer*, p.48.

Schirrmacher's analysis results in a condemnation of the literary endeavours of left-wing West German authors and GDR intellectuals alike, both groups being primarily concerned with (belatedly) resisting fascism, pretending to have a critical attitude towards the GDR state, but, perhaps unbeknownst to themselves, actually colluding with it because of their ingrained authoritarian mindset (articles of 2 June and 2 October 1990). In an article in *Die Zeit* from 2 November 1990, Ulrich Greiner coined the term *Gesinnungsästhetik* for this moral (rather than aesthetic) orientation of East and West German literature.

Some commentators have detected a more or less hidden political agenda in these allegedly primarily aesthetic criticisms. GDR literature is devalued by attacking one of its most prominent authors, Christa Wolf,[58] and similar intentions may have lain behind the criticism of 'classical' post-war West German writers. The aim might be to prevent the emergence of critical literature in the new re-unified Germany.[59] Intellectuals with conservative leanings such as Karl Heinz Bohrer might want to further a new national consciousness and cultural identity renewing the traditions of Romanticism and Nietzscheanism.[60] In other words, when certain left-wing, critical authors are disparaged on grounds of their 'old age', it is in fact the memory of Nazi atrocities and unpleasant continuities in modern German history, which their writings keep alive, that is targeted. Thus, the fall of the Wall and German reunification gave a new impetus to attempts at reformulating a more positive German cultural identity, oblivious of the Nazi past, which were underway since the 1980s (the *Historikerstreit* their most visible sign). The historical turn of 1989 also encouraged parallel orientations in literature emerging in East *and* West Germany from the late 1970s onwards with – primarily – young authors creating rather apolitical works focused on 'entertainment' or

---

58 Heidelberger-Leonard, *Der Literaturstreit*, p.70.

59 Jochen Vogt, 'Langer Abschied von der Nachkriegsliteratur? Ein Kommentar zur letzten westdeutschen Literaturdebatte', in Deiritz and Krauss (eds.), *Der deutsch-deutsche Literaturstreit*, pp.53–68: pp.61–2.

60 Andreas Huyssen, 'Das Versagen der deutschen Intellektuellen: Verschiebebahnhof Literaturstreit', in Deiritz and Krauss (eds.), *Der deutsch-deutsche Literaturstreit*, pp.78–94.

celebrating the medium of language as such.[61] Ironically, the 'old' generation, authors born around 1930 who could not possibly have taken an active part in politics before 1945, are equated with the unpleasant memory of National Socialism, their works and political orientations being rejected on these grounds.

The court cases discussed at the beginning of this essay have made it possible to grasp some of the relevant cultural meanings of old men in post-1989 Germany: the public is used to seeing old men on trial in their capacity as former high-ranking state officials. These old men are often taken to symbolize the German state in the past. Their physical frailty and their impending death may provoke pity and thus a less harsh judgement of their past actions; at least their defence lawyers hope that this association becomes effective. An analysis of the literary portrayal of typical emotional reactions towards politically compromised fathers in pre-1989 father novels showed that the sentiments described are encodings of both social relations and political judgements. The old men in question conceive their 'being in history' as unchanging (as cultured Germans respectful of state authority) and remember the Nazi years in this long-term perspective, while the younger generation probes critically into the memory of those years in particular, aiming to unsettle the fathers' version of past facts, their authoritarianism, their disregard for victims of National-Socialist persecution, and their seemingly self-righteous way of being in history.

In the East German texts discussed, the association between fathers and state power is even more salient. The *Aufbaugeneration* bases its alleged moral superiority and its political domination on the memory of former persecution and suffering. Again, the young generation attacks this memory; there are attempts to question the pertinence of the ideology of victimhood. Post-1989 novels written by authors born in West Germany indicate that the accusatory stance of the previous *Väterromane*, and the tendency to take fathers for symbols of German history, are in the process of becoming parts of the past. The 'middle' generation approaches old age itself, and this argument is exploited in debates on literature so as to lessen the

---

61   Vogt, 'Langer Abschied', p.60, and Brockmann, *Literature and German Reunification*, p.13.

influence of the critical, left-wing perspective on German history attached to keep the memory of National-Socialist atrocities alive.

The literary texts, the court cases, and the debates discussed are permeated by a multiplicity of different 'German cultural identities': first, a way of being in history which takes classical German *Bildung* and (Protestant) obedience to authority as its reference points; the importance of National Socialism for the course of German history tends to be underplayed, which is precisely the weak point which the second cultural identity sets out to attack. This identity became salient in left-leaning West German circles, particularly from the 1960s. It is characterized by an identification or at least a strong empathy with the victims of National Socialist persecution. The memory of Nazi perse-cution served also to legitimize the firm hold on power of the ruling class in the GDR. This way of being in history amounts to a stance of permanent victimhood, as in Honecker's comparison between the judges of National-Socialist and re-unified Germany; both had him detained in Moabit prison.[62] Third, an extremely flexible way of being in history appears in Drawert's *Spiegelland*: adapation to the changing dominant ideologies without any self-critical reflection or permanent cultural ideals; personal interests provide the only orientation.

A fourth cultural identity emerges after 1989. This 'post-modern' way of being in history acknowledges all recent periods of German history; it links the 'Berliner Republik' back to Imperial Germany with a hint of self-irony. This new identity embraces the second per-spective on the German past mentioned with a certain curiosity and open-mindedness, as in Timm's novel. By contrast, the second per-spective may also be attacked as in recent debates on literature; critics such as Bohrer may even hark back to the first way of being in history described. The literary texts, the court cases, the debate analysed show that, since 1989, the National Socialist past is in the process of being relegated to cultural memory; the (left-wing) stance that keeps the memory of the Nazi years alive in communicative memory becomes itself a layer of history superseded by more recent developments.

---

62   Wesel, *Ein Staat vor Gericht*, p.66.

These reflections confirm Halbwachs's early insights on collective memory: firstly, in principle, each social group has its own memory, so that in a multi-faceted society like the re-unified Germany, one has to talk of social memories and concomitant cultural identities in the plural; secondly, new readings of the present reshape the view of the past – the events of 1989 and their aftermath did indeed bring about a significant shift in the way in which the German past is remembered.

Bibliography

Abu-Lughod, Lila, and Catherine A. Lutz, 'Introduction: Emotion, Discourse, and the Politics of Everyday Life', in Lila Abu-Lughod and Catherine A. Lutz (eds.), *Language and the Politics of Emotion*, Cambridge 1990, pp.1–23.

Assmann, Jan, *Das kulturelle Gedächtnis: Schrift, Erinnerung und politische Identität in frühen Hochkulturen*, Munich 1997.

Bloch, Maurice, 'Internal and External Memory: Different Ways of Being in History. The Edward Westermarck Memorial Lecture, Helsinki, 31 January 1992', *Suomen Antropologi*, 1 (1992), 3–15.

Bluhm, Lothar, '"Irgendwann, denken wir, muss ich das genau wissen": Der Erinnerungsdiskurs bei Monika Maron', in Volker Wehdeking (ed.), *Mentalitätswandel in der deutschen Literatur zur Einheit (1990–2000)*, Berlin 2000, pp.141–51.

Bogdal, Klaus-Michael, 'Wer darf sprechen? Schriftsteller als moralische Instanz – Überlegungen zu einem Ende und einem Anfang', in Deiritz and Krauss (eds.), *Der deutsch-deutsche Literaturstreit*, pp.40–9.

Bourdieu, Pierre, *Language and Symbolic Power*, ed. John B. Thompson, trans. Gino Raymond and Matthew Adamson, Cambridge 1991.

Brockmann, Stephen, *Literature and German Reunification*, Cambridge 1999.

Bullivant, Keith, *The Future of German Literature*, Oxford-Providence 1994.

Deiritz, Karl, and Hannes Krauss (eds.), *Der deutsch-deutsche Literaturstreit oder 'Freunde, es spricht sich schlecht mit gebundener Zunge': Analysen und Materialien*, Hamburg 1991.

Drawert, Kurt, *Spiegelland: Ein deutscher Monolog*, Frankfurt/M. 1992.

Durzak, Manfred, 'Ein Autor der mittleren Generation', in Manfred Durzak and Hartmut Steinecke (eds.), *Die Archäologie der Wünsche: Studien zum Werk von Uwe Timm*, Cologne 1995, pp.13–25.

François, Etienne, 'Von der wiedererlangten Nation zur "Nation wider Willen": Kann man eine deutsche Geschichte der "Erinnerungsorte" schreiben?', in Etienne François, Hannes Siegrist, and Jakob Vogel (eds.), *Nation und Emotion: Deutschland und Frankreich im Vergleich: 19. und 20. Jahrhundert*, Göttingen 1995, pp.93–107.

Geertz, Clifford, *Local Knowledge: Further Essays in Interpretative Anthropology*, New York 1983.

Grass, Günter, *Ein weites Feld. Roman*, Munich 1997.

Habbe, Christian, 'Im Visier der Nazi-Jäger', *Der Spiegel* (3 September 2001).

Halbwachs, Maurice, *Les cadres sociaux de la mémoire*, Paris 1925.

Heidelberger-Leonard, Irene, 'Der Literaturstreit – ein Historikerstreit im gesamtdeutschen Kostüm?', in Deiritz and Krauss (eds.), *Der deutsch-deutsche Literaturstreit*, pp.69–77.

Hénard, Jacqueline, *Geschichte vor Gericht: Die Ratlosigkeit der Justiz*, Berlin 1993.

Huyssen, Andreas, 'Das Versagen der deutschen Intellektuellen: Verschiebebahnhof Literaturstreit', in Deiritz and Krauss (eds.), *Der deutsch-deutsche Literaturstreit*, pp.78–94.

Maron, Monika, *Stille Zeile Sechs. Roman*, Frankfurt/M. 1991.

McAdams, A. James, 'The Honecker Trial: The East German Past and the German Future', *The Review of Politics*, 58/1 (1996), 53–80.

Meckel, Christoph, *Suchbild. Über meinen Vater*, Düsseldorf 1980.

Michaels, Jennifer E., 'Confronting the Nazi Past', in Keith Bullivant (ed.), *Beyond 1989: Re-reading German Literature since 1945*, Oxford-Providence 1997, pp.1–20.

Müller, Anne Friederike, *'Strength' and 'Weakness' as Political Metaphors: An Ethnography of German Politics from 1871 to the Present*, Ph.D. thesis, University of Cambridge 2001.

Nora, Pierre, 'L'ère de la commémoration', in Pierre Nora (ed.), *Les lieux de mémoire, III/3, Les France: De l'archive à l'emblème*, Paris 1992, pp.977–1012.

Oppen, Karoline von, *The Role of the Writer and the Press in the Unification of Germany, 1989–1990*, New York 2000.

Ortheil, Hanns-Josef, *Abschied von den Kriegsteilnehmern. Roman*, Munich-Zurich 1992.

Rehmann, Ruth, *Der Mann auf der Kanzel. Fragen an einen Vater*, Munich-Vienna 1979.

Schneider, Michael, 'Fathers and Sons, Retrospectively: The Damaged Relationship Between Two Generations', *New German Critique*, 31 (Winter 1984), 3–51.

Schneider, Peter, *Extreme Mittellage: Eine Reise durch das deutsche Nationalgefühl*, Reinbek 1992.

Timm, Uwe, *Rot. Roman*, Cologne 2001.

Todorov, Tzvetan, *Les abus de la mémoire*, Paris 1995.

Vogt, Jochen, 'Langer Abschied von der Nachkriegsliteratur? Ein Kommentar zur letzten westdeutschen Literaturdebatte', in Deiritz and Krauss (eds.), *Der deutsch-deutsche Literaturstreit*, pp.53–68.

Wehdeking, Volker, *Die deutsche Einheit und die Schriftsteller: Literarische Verarbeitung der Wende seit 1989*, Stuttgart 1995.

Wesel, Uwe, *Ein Staat vor Gericht: Der Honecker-Prozeß*, Frankfurt/M. 1994.

Woodward, Kathleen, *Aging and its Discontents: Freud and other Fictions*, Bloomington 1991.

Ruth J. Owen

'wenn ein staat ins gras beißt, singen die dichter': The *Wende* in Poetry[1]

In the way it approaches a revolution like the German *Wende*, poetry differs from other literary genres, as well as differing from the accounts constructed by journalists, historians, psychologists and political scientists. Lyric responses to the revolutionary changes initiated in 1989/90 demonstrate the possibilities poetry offers that these other types of text do not. Prose histories tend to see the *Wende* as a broadly linear process from Soviet-led change throughout eastern Europe, whereas the short form of poetry favours flashpoints that have struck the imagination and summary images, which capture a feeling about the whole. Roulette, for example, is a metaphor for German history in *Wende* titles by Barbara Köhler and Gabriele Stötzer and in Steffen Mensching's Berlin elegy 'Rot hat verloren':[2] it exposes how social change feels like a game of chance, bringing winners and losers, even perhaps (by analogy with Russian roulette) suicide. Poems offer viewpoints like this that are unusual and may be highly ambiguous. Concerned with a proliferation of representations, they hold open the paradoxes and resist imposing closure on their object of study.

1   I am grateful to the Alexander-von-Humboldt Stiftung for funding the research fellowship at the Humboldt-Universität Berlin, during which I wrote this essay. I would also like to thank Roland Bleiker for reading a draft and Anna Linton for resolving a bibliographical matter. The German poems in this chapter are not translated because most of the poetic effects under discussion are lost in English versions.
2   Barbara Köhler, *Deutsches Roulette*, Frankfurt/M. 1991; Gabriele Stötzer, *Erfurter Roulette*, Munich 1995; Steffen Mensching, *Berliner Elegien*, Leipzig 1995, p.43.

Poetry works 'against the grain of the manifest and, because of that requirement, *good* poems about historical crises speak a different language from historical record and historical myth'.[3] In the essay appended to his anthology of *Wende* poems, Karl Otto Conrady identifies this different language as the special language of poetry.[4] Unlike analytical or descriptive prose, lyric language pulls away from the manifest, opening up additional dimensions of meaning in the marginal areas of non-systemic perspectives. In seeking to represent and understand any historic shift, it does not privilege statistical generalities or the agency of states and political leaders, but rather is often fascinated by minority and marginalized voices. So, in his *Wende* poem 'Gestörte Verhältnisse', Heinz Czechowski alludes to the personal conscience perceived amid the excess of news information.[5] Where this 'inner voice' ('innere Stimme') is being discounted and denied general importance, poetry becomes restorative. At the same time, poetry can still command social resonance precisely where it opens up perspectives beyond the limits of news media: this was evident at the *Wende*, for example, in the case of Volker Braun's signal poem 'Das Eigentum'.[6]

Instead of forming an end-directed proposition, poetry draws attention to the phrases along the way, each of which competes for a dominance ultimately withheld. Since it is constitutively metaphorical, it inevitably eschews a single object and approaches events obliquely rather than head-on, so challenging established notions of what has significance. In Reiner Kunze's *Wende* poem 'Demonstranten' and in

---

3   Frank Kermode, *Poetry, Narrative, History*, Oxford 1990, p.67.

4   ('die besondere Sprache des Gedichts'). Karl Otto Conrady (ed.), *Von einem Land und vom anderen. Gedichte zur deutschen Wende 1989/1990*, Leipzig 1993, p.175.

5   Heinz Czechowski, *Nachtspur. Ein Lesebuch aus der deutschen Gegenwart. Gedichte und Prosa 1987–1992*, Zurich 1993, pp.177–79: p.179: 'Mein schlechtes Gewissen / Richtet sich auf. Im Überfluß / Aller Nachrichten hör ich auf meine innere Stimme. Dies, / Wie fast alles, hat keine / Allgemeine Bedeutung'.

6   See description in Dieter Schlenstedt, 'Ein Gedicht als Provokation', *neue deutsche literatur*, 40/12 (1992), 124–32. Volker Braun, 'Das Eigentum', *Neues Deutschland* (4–5 August 1990), p.1.

Kathrin Schmidt's 'vierzigster und einundvierzigster oktober',[7] the otherwise commonplace candle motif is 'made new'. Kunze sets political coup beside individual cautiousness:

> In der faust
> eine kerze
> Für den sturz!
>
> Bedacht,
> daß aufs straßenpflaster
> kein wachs tropft
>
> Niemand
> soll stürzen

This very short poem uses the relatedness of a noun and a verb to assert and then retract the notion of a courageous opposition set on toppling the government; from the word 'Bedacht' onwards, it installs a conflicting modesty of purpose. Schmidt relocates the candle motif:

> oktober wars ich hatte am rande der arena mir platz genommen wo das getümmel mich nicht wirklich erreichen konnte ich hatte eine kerze in meine stirn gestellt es tropfte ein wenig wachs ins angsthaben

Rhythm and enjambment anticipate the drips of candle-wax, before the image comes into focus; when it does, the candle in the *Wende*-demonstrator's head is also an attitude. As in this case, poetry often stems from emotional responses and imaginative connections, where the dominant discourse excludes these possibilities. It does not have the duration of a novel or drama, but in its concentration and distillation lies the potential for creative ambiguity. The placing of each word, the sound patterns it completes, the subverting play with commonplaces, the conjunction of images which rub up against one another in awkward ways – these things create a web of allusion, of hazarded statements and their retraction, which hold open paradoxes and complexities, and allow the poem to achieve a functional ambiguity which expands the bounds of what has been sayable.

---

7   Kathrin Schmidt, *Flußbild mit Engel. Gedichte*, Frankfurt/M. 1995, p.17, and Reiner Kunze, *ein tag auf dieser erde. gedichte*, Frankfurt/M. 1998, p.59.

Successful poems are made of words that zing, each a small surprise, attention-grabbing and memorable, needing no propping up with piles of extra words. Durs Grünbein has eloquently described memorability as the key poetological principle (a very traditional idea of course): 'Erst die Emphase der Dichtung hat aus dem Gemurmel, dem lebensbegleitenden Singsang von Emotionen und Erkenntnis etwas Erinnerbares heraufgeholt und zu Kieseln gehärtet'.[8] These pebbles of the memorable represent the opposite of 'die sanften vergeßlichen Technologien'. Whilst other poets are not as confident of such recouping after the latest caesura in German history, Grünbein designates the poem a 'Gedächtnismaschine, präzis wie ein Insektenauge, eine Maschine zum Wiederfinden gelebter Zeit'.[9]

Lyric expression becomes memorable by breaking the rules of writing; it does not have to make concessions to clarity, simplicity or rationality. It is not simply an abridgement of journalistic summaries or evocative narrative; as Wolfgang Ertl states, of the *Wende* poems, '[e]inige der Gedichte schürfen auf knappem Raum tiefer als die so aufregenden Berichte in der Presse und die notgedrungen langatmigeren Prosastücke, die inzwischen zum Thema erschienen sind'[10] ('some of the poems go deeper in a short space than the exciting reports in the press and the necessarily lengthy prose texts which have been published on that topic'). Depth comes precisely with concentration, because it highlights semantic slippage and the treachery of language; thus lyric concentration makes words slip from the most easily taken meaning and reform around another, without losing vestiges of the first. Even where poems cite historical utterances, they tend to transform in this way: Volker Braun's poem 'Der 9. November' ironizes Bürgermeister Momper's comment 'Berlin, nun freue dich', for example;[11] the

---

8   Durs Grünbein, *Galilei vermißt Dantes Hölle und bleibt an den Maßen hängen. Aufsätze 1989–1995*, Frankfurt/M. 1996, p.23.
9   Ibid., p.19.
10   Wolfgang Ertl, 'Grenzfallgedichte', *Germanic Review*, 67 (1992), 183.
11   Volker Braun, in Conrady (ed.), *Von einem Land*, p.21.

     Das Brackwasser stachellippig, aufgeschnittene Drähte
     Lautlos, wie im Traum, driften die Tellerminen
     Zurück in den Geschirrschrank. Ein surrealer Moment:

conjunction of this *Wende* comment with Hölderlin (not to mention Braun's images of floating mines and a splitting bandage) shows it in a different light from that in which it originated. It shakes the imperative, breaking the public manipulation and showing up the habits of power. Kurt Drawert's 'Politisches Gedicht, Januar 1990' re-casts the words of another prominent *Wende* figure, Egon Krenz.[12] Drawert not only preserves Krenz's comments, but employs Rolf Dieter Brinkmann's technique to expose their irony:[13] set in the poem, they suddenly refer tangentially to the dissolution of the SED, to unemployment in the new federal states and to creative writing becoming the last resort of failed politicians.

> Krenz erklärte abschließend,
> er habe 'wieder von unten
> in der Partei anfangen' wollen.
>
> 'Das geht jetzt auch nicht
> mehr. Andere Arbeit zu finden,
> ist sehr schwierig. Ich werde
>
> wohl Schriftsteller.'

Speech marks frame the entire poem, emphasizing its status as a found or overhead text. This points to the poet as a documenter not only of the patently historic but also of telling throwaway lines. Once in the poem, language reclaimed from politicians mocks their linguistic impotence and counters the propagandistic.

Besides being alert to poetry's genre-specific possibilities, it remains crucial to consider how we identify a *Wende* poem. Poets are

---

Mit spitzem Fuß auf dem Weltriß, und kein Schuß fällt.
Die gehetzte Vernunft, unendlich müde, greift
Nach dem erstbesten Irrtum... der Dreckverband platzt.
Leuchtschriften wandern okkupantenhaft bis Mitte. BERLIN
NUN FREUE DICH, zu früh. Wehe, harter Nordost.

12   Kurt Drawert, 'Politisches Gedicht, Januar 1990', in Anna Chiarloni (ed.), 'Die Dichter und die Wende', *GDR Monitor*, 23 (1990), 1–12: 6.

13   Compare Rolf Dieter Brinkmann, 'Politisches Gedicht 13. Nov. 74', in Rolf Dieter Brinkmann, *Westwärts 1&2. Gedichte*, Reinbek bei Hamburg 1975, pp.160–7.

themselves sensitive to the fact that a poem is always about many things at once, that its fundamental nature is expansively metaphorical. Many append dates to their *Wende* poems, which function as revealing final lines. Titles may also locate the text temporally (November, October, 1989, 1990, autumn) and geographically (Berlin, *Heldenstadt*), whilst containing other allusions (*Montagsdemonstrationen* or *Grenzfall*) to *Wende* thematics. Sometimes these indications are missing yet one is tempted, because of the use of certain imagery (of duality amid unity, say) and the timing of the poem's first publication, to draw connections that are hard to legitimate except as a *Wende*-reading.[14] Some such texts are included here, but in the main I have taken pragmatic decisions to focus on those that declare themselves to be *Wende* poems.

The *Wende* gave rise to an extensive corpus of poems, some of them merely for the moment, but others genuinely moving and memorable, startling in their evocation of the situation, incisive in their use of imagery and aesthetically satisfying. *Occasio* as a muse, the inspiration and focus of a poem, has a long poetic tradition: in antiquity the *occasio* was usually a significant death, marriage or birth. The events of the *Wende* have been variously designated as all three – the death of the GDR, the marriage of East and West (with the East usually the bride) and the birth of a New Germany. In poetry, however, death predominates, rather than the marriage metaphors popular with newspaper cartoonists of the time,[15] or optimistic birth metaphors (although Durs Grünbein's two 'In utero' poems could be read as such *Wende* poems).[16]

Poets overwhelmingly evoke unification as a demise marked by the presence of obituaries, tombs and funerary urns. Thus Gisela Kraft's unification-day poem moves from a deathbed to a corpse on the floor to the shovelling of ashes.[17] Braun's title 'Nachruf' (used above the text that became famous as 'Das Eigentum') and Grünbein's 'Posthume

14   See for example the Siamese twin poem in Brigitte Oleschinski, *Your Passport is Not Guilty. Gedichte*, Reinbek bei Hamburg 1997, p.11.
15   See Susan S. Morrison, 'The Feminisation of the German Democratic Republic in Political Cartoons 1989–1990', *Journal of Popular Culture*, 25/4 (1992), 35–51.
16   Durs Grünbein, *Falten und Fallen. Gedichte*, Frankfurt/M. 1994, pp.50–1.
17   Gisela Kraft, 'Am dritten Tag des Oktobers', *West-östliche Couch. Zweierlei Leidensweisen der Deutschen*, Berlin 1991, p.142.

Innenstimmen' pinpoint the sense of writing after the death of the GDR: both the public obituary and private voices from within are posthumous texts.[18] The death of the GDR is a drowning recalled in Kurt Drawert's poem 'In dieser Lage',[19] where the repetition of 'kein' suggests irrevocable disappearance:

> Keine störenden Zeichen
> drangen nach oben und bewegten
> das friedliche Wasser. Keine Reste
> von Luft und von Gasen. Kein letzter Befehl,
> der uns drohend als hilfloses Blubbern erreichte.

A new absence of 'Zeichen' may be especially resonant for a writer, of course, however disruptive their presence has been in the past. Elsewhere, signs of the death which has occurred do not vanish: in Braun's 1999 collection *Tumulus*,[20] unification is a massacre, which has resulted not only in the ancient barrow of the title, but further graves, a death mask and another burial mound; the tomb seems to become a metaphor for the post-*Wende* poem. In Steffen Mensching's first epigram of 'Berliner Elegien 2', the 'Urne' is both ballot box and cremation jar; Annerose Kirchner's poem 'Halbzeit' uses the same word to link funeral rites to voting for unification, concluding: 'Mein Körper stirbt / bedeckt von Sand der Urnen'.[21] Death allows these poets to convey how uncomfortable they are with unification, to declare its vastness, significance and saddening finality. Poets know that their literary predecessors have been negotiating death since time immemorial: B.K. Tragelehn takes up the 1848 'Song' by Christina Rossetti,[22] his translation foregrounding history's ability to recast an extant poem. In the *Wende* version, the lyric voice becomes that of a

---

18   Volker Braun, in Anna Chiarloni and Helga Pankoke (eds.), *Grenzfallgedichte. Eine deutsche Anthologie*, Berlin-Weimar 1991, p.109, and Durs Grünbein, *Schädelbasislektion. Gedichte*, Frankfurt/M. 1991, p.16.

19   Kurt Drawert, *Wo es war. Gedichte*, Frankfurt/M. 1996, p.12.

20   Volker Baun, *Tumulus. Gedichte*, Frankfurt/M. 1999.

21   Mensching, *Berliner Elegien*, p.21, and Annerose Kirchner, in Conrady (ed.), *Von einem Land*, p.151.

22   B.K. Tragelehn, 'Beim Abschied zu singen, nach C.G. Rosetti [*sic*]', *neue deutsche literatur*, 43/5 (1995), 6.

GDR projecting its own death: 'Wenn ich tot bin, seid so gut / Singt mir nicht Lieder nach'. These lines reject obituary songs for socialism though this poem is exactly that. Apostrophizing a you-plural becomes an address to the German people: 'Und wenn ihr wollt, dann denkt an mich / Und wenn ihr nicht wollt, vergeßt'. Tragelehn's version reveals that the *Wende*, a shift political, geographical, economic and cultural, also brings a shift in how texts are read – even how a foreign-language poem from a distant era is read: the national event moves to the centre of readers' consciousness and subsumes other concerns.

   Wende poems seldom address forgetting with the equivocation expressed in the Rossetti-Tragelehn lines above. Thomas Böhme's 1991 poem 'Die Entfernung des Herbstes' takes careful measure of the dispersing *Wende*-November. A horizon or 'ritze' between past and present becomes an audible scratch in the assonating ending of 'nicht', 'ritze' and 'vergißt':[23]

> der lichteinfall ist hart ohne beispiel
> die volks seele himmelt sich bis an den horizont
> was gestern stimmte ist heut unauffindbar
> dazwischen aktenzeichen, XY ungelöst
>
> tage die nur aus sperrstunden bestehen
> wechseln mit tagen blauer erwartung
> strenggenommen hat es dich nicht überrascht
> im rauchfang krepiert ein sturm nach dem andern
>
> bestenfalls wird dir die scham gestundet
> die landschaften schwitzen abschiede aus
> der november hat sich über die jahre verteilt
> ein solider staub der nicht eine ritze vergisst

Repeated use of the simplest syntax and the casual facility of line 7 with its unspecified 'es' are part of an unpretentiousness, from which spring the fugitive effects of GDR words like 'beispiel', 'volk' and 'akten'. Euphemisms for dying proliferate to include the heaven-bound soul, closing time, and goodbyes. They trace the disappearance of the *Wende* autumn into a dusty distance, whilst borrowing the ZDF

---

23   Thomas Böhme, *Und an Bahnhöfe denken. Gedichte*, Aschersleben 2000, p.13.

programme title 'Aktenzeichen XY... ungelöst' creates an allusion to unsolved crime. Thus, for all its measured tone (almost every line of verse is a complete and simple syntactic unit), this poem makes unsettling allusions, such as that to unreleased pressure, which emerges in the ideas of 'sperrstunden', of storms caught in a chimney, and of sweating landscapes.

Elsewhere in the early 1990s, the receding past is met with urgent references to 'was bleibt' (not least around Christa Wolf's story of that title). Texts take up Hölderlin's concluding line 'Was bleibet aber, stiften die Dichter',[24] recompleting the phrase in ways which undermine the poets' commemorative task, while still silently referring to it. In Heinz Czechowski's poem 'Verkommen',[25] for instance, what remains seems insubstantial and the task hesitantly posited, without direct mention of 'Dichter':

> Was bleibt,
> Ist das Gedenken
> An eine Zeit,
> Die es niemals gab.

These lines capture a typical sense of impossibility and double loss (which appears in Braun's 'Nachruf' as missing a life never lived). In the poem 'Bauernsterben', Czechowski thematizes a search for solace in a childhood place now deserted and desolate.[26] Here no reconciliation with the lost past can be found and the lyric 'wir' leave again, 'ungetröstet'. The site of past events is also the focus of the final poem in Harald Gerlach's collection *Nirgends und zu keiner Stunde*,[27] which closes with another 'was bleibt':

---

24   Friedrich Hölderlin, 'Andenken', in Friedrich Hölderlin, *Gedichte*, Frankfurt/M. 1992, pp.360–2: p.362.

25   Heinz Czechowski, *Mein westfälischer Frieden. Ein Zyklus 1996–1998*, Cologne 1998, p.71.

26   Czechowski, *Nachtspur*, pp.255–6.

27   Harald Gerlach, 'Stunden', in Harald Gerlach, *Nirgends und zu keiner Stunde. Gedichte*, Berlin 1998, p.103.

> Was bleibt: der Ort,
> an dem es
> geschah.

This unspecified 'es', like that of Kurt Drawert's *Wende* title 'Wo es war', reflects a more widespread suspicion of terminology.[28] But echoing the Freudian 'Wo Es war, soll Ich werden' suggests that identity will form on the vacated site,[29] although it has not yet emerged. Drawert's poem 'Zustandsbeschreibung Zwischenbericht' (a title which itself points to this provisional stage) employs a neat conflation of biblical and sanitary euphemisms, so that death becomes the 'Weg / aller Dinge von gestern / in die Entsorgung'.[30] Here 'was bleibt' is a name and a disabled foot, which leaves a trail of broken steps: together these may allude to a poem (which invariably appears with its writer's name and is traditionally the striding of metrical feet), thus revisiting Hölderlin's belief that literature survives.

Personal names anchor the ethics of memory, for without them individuals' memories cannot be honoured; their erasure becomes an acute concern in post-*Wende* poetry. Grünbein's untitled poem beginning 'Und nachher' thematizes the problem of where to record the names of the dead.[31] Graveyard listing is judged misplaced, because the people's bodies are no longer there (let alone their souls):

> Jedes Jahr wieder, im Sommer,
> Im Winter, wird Platz gemacht
>
> Für die nächsten, wird ausgefegt.
> Eingeholt werden die Knochen,
> Die Schädel verbrannt. Asche
>
> Ist was noch übrigbleibt, bald
> Verstreut, eine Tafel mit Namen
> Und Zahlen, ein Memento mori
>
> Am falschen Ort.

---

28   Drawert, *Wo es war*, p.80.
29   Sigmund Freud, *Studienausgabe*, Frankfurt/M. 1969, I, 516.
30   Kurt Drawert, *Haus ohne Menschen. Zeitmitschriften*, Leipzig 1993, pp.118–9: p.118.
31   Durs Grünbein, *Den teuren Toten. 33 Epitaphe*, Frankfurt/M. 1994, p.31.

Hardly anything at all remains here. At its close, the poem invites the question of whether the right place for a *memento mori* would better be in poetry. Communities' memorial activity is deficient according to many *Wende* poems. In the Roman empire, *damnatio memoriae* meant the removal of condemned traitors' statues and the deletion of their names from inscriptions. This Latin phrase forms the title of Grünbein's poem evoking a sinister GDR-Rome.[32] Namelessness recurs in Drawert's *Wo es war* in the figure of the anonymous lover.[33] Within this collection, names are also lost from gravestones, from a data bank, by orphans, and by an inner self.[34]

The issue of commemoration in 'Elegie XIX' by Günter Kunert invokes L'Inconnu, the nameless girl drowned in the Seine, whose death mask was a cult object in the Weimar Republic.[35] Kunert compares her with a raped and murdered Snow White on the TV screen. These two female images commemorating beauty and death pinpoint the distinction between yesterday and today:

> Äonen vergingen
> bis gestern,
> da hingen wir noch Masken von Verstorbenen
> an Wände: 'L'Inconnu'.
> Heute reichen die Wände
> nicht mehr aus
> für all die unbekannten Gesichter
> der Toten.

This poem shows how nostalgia is less about the past than about felt absences in the present – specifically a post-*Wende* absence of walls.[36] As the insufficient graveyard in Grünbein's poem above implied poetry's greater memorial possibilities, so the limits on death-mask

---

32 Grünbein, *Falten und Fallen*, p.105.
33 Drawert, *Wo es war*, p.66 and pp.67f.
34 Drawert, *Wo es war*, pp.26f, p.28, pp.103–10, and p.101.
35 Günter Kunert, *Mein Golem*, Munich-Vienna 1996, p.85.
36 Obviously the primary fallen wall was 'Mauer' not 'Wand', but lyric extrapolation from the 'house' of socialism and the fall of the Berlin Wall also produces images of collapsing houses and other buildings reduced to ruins.

memorials in Kunert's poem also beg the estimation of obituary songs.

Suicide is a recurring version of the death motif in *Wende* poetry. It is not always treated with the solemnity that characterizes the poems discussed so far, however. Matthias Holst composes a satirical Loreley poem in response to the *Wende*, which links suicide with dissidence, and which illustrates well his use of words that seem right, though loosely in touch with reason:[37]

> ich weiss nicht was soll es bedeuten dass ich so
> glasnost bin ich küsse auf der strasse schon jedes
> doppelkinn
> ich höre auf zu schreiben denn fühl mich viel zu frei
> was gestern deutlich unrecht schluck heut wie süßen brei
> und all die toten tanzen wer toter noch
> der träumt die knuten bluten frohsinn
> bei uns wird aufgeräumt
> pardon wird nicht gegeben
> gib pfötchen dissident!
> vergessen all die jahre
> ins offne messer rennt
> ein jeder frisch beseelt

Flippancy is an effective means to address demoralizing developments without whining: thus Holst replaces the word 'traurig' in Heine's famous 'Lore-Ley' line with Mikhail Gorbachev's reformist principle of political transparency. The continuation of Heine's lines seems to be implicit in the *Wende* poem, namely 'Ein Märchen aus alten Zeiten / Das kommt mir nicht aus dem Sinn';[38] the fairytale referred to is the writer's GDR role as a dissident who identified injustice. Holst's poem represents *Wende* euphoria as a 'Totentanz', ironizing such resurrection by the impossible comparative 'toter noch' and by the happy rushing into a suicide bid: enjambment and a lurching between satirical rhymes reinforce the idea of joyfully lurching into fatal social change.

---

37   'matthias' BAADER holst, 'ich weiss nicht was soll es bedeuten', in 'matthias' BAADER holst, *Temperamente*, 33/1 (1990).

38   Heinrich Heine, 'Die Heimkehr II', in Heinrich Heine, *Buch der Lieder*, Munich 1975, p.107.

Durs Grünbein's 1994 collection of epitaph poems *Den teuren Toten* makes a witty nod to memorial activity in a society of the disposable. Some of these poems articulate a sarcastic *memento mori*: deaths undignified and unlikely are here presented as amusingly, if uncomfortably, ludicrous. Grünbein treats the dead with tender contempt. People do not normally find death funny, and the incongruity of humour in *Wende*-death poems alerts the reader to the unspoken emotion, namely anger. In Heinz Kahlau's 1990 poem 'Zeitbegriffe', the 'Genossen' climb into a deep-freeze, in order to wait out the current era.[39] Thematizing the long-term survival of socialism by means of cryonics makes a quirky, playful poem, but the absurdity is also more effective than an explicit statement of anger.

Anger likewise occupies the gap between irreverent humour and a death out-of-the-blue in Bert Papenfuß's poem 'mors ex nihilo'.[40] This long text, which is structured by funerary motifs, spools through lists of individual deaths. An opening address to comrades and colleagues can be read as referring to writers and the death of a literature (especially in references to 'drucksachen' and 'literarischer nachlaß'), another 'death of the author' as it were:

> genossen, unterdruß im unterschlupf,
> kameraden, verrat ist unaufhaltbar; kollegen,
> lassen wir uns nicht lumpen: alles wird teurer,
> wir aber, im einklang mit unserer zielgruppe,
> senken unsere preise: das kapital ist machbar,
> herr nachbar, 'big bank take little bank':
> bekannt durch fresse, buschfunk, rundflunk &
> teleflax: sarg-discount christburger bietet an:
> selbstbestattungen aller arten, erledigung
> aller formalitäten, sämtliche pietätsartikel,
> drucksachen, blumendekoration, heraldische
> elemente, überurnen, memoiren, literarischer
> nachlaß, copyright-probleme, auf wunsch
> hausbesuche: sargmodelle für feuerbestattung

---

39   Heinz Kahlau, *Kaspers Waage*, Berlin 1992, p.46.
40   Bert Papenfuss, *mors ex nihilo*, Berlin 1994.

Through the bumps and stumbles, these lines convey pain and mimic the way memory emerges before it is sterilized with syntax. Indulgent obscurity is evaded by a focus on the death of the state:

> wenn ein staat ins gras beißt, singen die dichter
> wenn er zu langsam stirbt, zündeln sie die lichter

Stylistically, this long poem marks a departure for Papenfuß: a return to the semantic. Enjoyment in the deferral of meaning through word-play cannot be sustained now; history seems too pressing, the need to write (and thus counter) the new deathliness too urgent for tail-chasing aesthetic games.

The first section of Papenfuß's tripartite text is entitled 'prolog auf dem schirm', reworking Goethe's 'Prolog im Himmel': the screen has replaced both the heaven of *Faust* and also the post-war division epitomized by Christa Wolf's 'geteilter Himmel'.[41] More generally, poets set matters of memory and memorial beside the fleeting televisual and advertising images felt to be defining products of united Germany. Jens Reich's idea that 'billions of people experienced history as a video clip' ('Milliarden erleben Geschichte als Videoclip') is reflected in Grünbein's poem 'Vorm Fernseher die Toten', where the dead are watching and hearing the *Wende* exodus on the TV screen:[42]

> Es war wie ein Film
>
> Der Das Ende des Wartens hieß. Amigo, erleichtert
> Sah ich, es war vorbei, die Geduld verbraucht.
> 'Wir wollen raus hier, hört ihr. Wir wollen raus.'

The lyric 'ich' is a passive observer, importing into the poem the over-heard cry of the *Volk* and apprehending history as a film. 1989 demon-strations are another film, 'einen Stummfilm mit dem Titel *Volk*', in

---

41   Johann Wolfgang von Goethe, *Faust. Eine Tragödie*, Munich 1978, pp.156–9, and Christa Wolf, *Der geteilte Himmel. Erzählung*, Halle 1963.

42   Jens Reich quoted in Klaus Hartung, *Neunzehnhundertneunundachtzig. Ortsbe-sichtigungen nach einer Epochenwende*, Frankfurt/M. 1990, p.22 and Grünbein, *Schädelbasislektion*, pp.36–37.

Grünbein's second poem in the cycle 'Die leeren Zeichen'.[43] Whilst elsewhere the screen appears as a source of rival memorial activity, this silent film does not encroach on the poet's business of speaking and naming.

Even as writers at the *Wende* rallies declared a liberation of language, literary participation was being overtaken by poems of passive spectatorship and a proliferation of references to screen images, which suspected the redundancy of writer and text. Intellectual alienation is already implied by the mediation of the television screen in Heiner Müller's early *Wende* poem 'Fernsehen':[44] Müller sets Brecht's 1938 poem 'An die Nachgeborenen',[45] cited in capitals, beside images of death by torture:

> 2 DAILY NEWS NACH BRECHT 1989
> Die ausgerissenen Fingernägel des Janos Kadar
> Der die Panzer gegen sein Volk rief als es anfing
> Seine Genossen Folterer an den Füßen aufzuhängen
> Sein Sterben als der verratene Imre Nagy
> Ausgegraben wurde oder der Rest von ihm
> BONES AND SHOES das Fernsehn war dabei
> Verscharrt mit dem Gesicht zur Erde 1956
> WIR DIE DEN BODEN BEREITEN WOLLTEN
> FÜR FREUNDLICHKEIT
> Wieviel Erde werden wir fressen müssen
> Mit dem Blutgeschmack unserer Opfer

The funeral-service notion of bodies as 'Erde zu Erde' is stripped of all comfort where the ground is mixed with the remains of victims, and the poem's emergent 'wir' is the voice of maggots. Television witnesses Nagy's exhumation; 'das Fernsehn war dabei' becomes part of that sense of personal failure developed beneath the subtitle 'SELBSTKRITIK':

---

43   Grünbein, *Schädelbasislektion*, p.70.
44   Heiner Müller, *Die Gedichte*, Frankfurt/M. 1998, pp.232–3. This poem was read out by Müller in the Berliner Ensemble at the height of the exodus and demonstrations in October 1989.
45   Bertolt Brecht, *Gesammelte Werke*, Frankfurt/M. 1967, IX, 722–5.

> Auf dem Bildschirm sehe ich meine Landsleute
> Mit Händen und Füßen abstimmen gegen die Wahrheit
> Die vor vierzig Jahren mein Besitz war

The onlooker, who does not participate in voting for unification, articulates dispossession. Television has become a medium of truth, correcting the delusions of intellectuals. In Hanns Cibulka's *Wende* poem 'Ohne Titel' another despondent lyric subject can only watch and shrug:[46]

> Ich sehe wie die Menschen
> von einem Land ins andere gehen,
> die Luft ist kalt geworden,
> die Krähen kehren heim in Scharen,
> wo ist der Ort
> um niederzuschreiben was wahr ist?

This open ending reflects uncertainty about writing because, even in the brief, doomed interval between exodus and inevitable unification, writing is contingent upon 'Land' and 'Ort'. As these poems by Müller and Cibulka suggest, truth is a key category at the *Wende* and writers' ability to contest it suddenly becomes problematized anew.

The role of writers, especially those with 'Dichter'-status, becomes a matter of urgency in poetry after the *Wende*. In the last two stanzas of Harald Gerlach's poem 'Der Neckar',[47] the 'Dichter' have been occupied with preservation:

> Gestern wars uns, als hätten wir irgendwann
> eine Wahrheit gewußt, durch furchtsame Zeiten
> Worte bewahrt, die jetzt auszusprechen wären.
>
> Aber nun sind sie vergessen. Und wir hüten uns
> sorgsam, sie zu erinnern. Wissend, daß niemand
> zuhören würde.

---

46   Hanns Cibulka, in Stefan Heym and Werner Heiduczek (eds.), *Die sanfte Revolution: Prosa, Lyrik, Protokolle, Erlebnisberichte, Reden*, Leipzig-Weimar 1990, p.296.
47   Gerlach, *Nirgends und zu keiner Stunde*, p.56.

Three aspects to being a 'Dichter' are presented: knowing truth, remembering, and being listened to. Each is threatened by the *Wende*. Setting subjunctive suppositions against present actualities captures a sense of futility here, which in the first seven lines of Günter Kunert's 'Bekennerbrief' lies in the awful ambiguity of 'entriegelte Türe'.[48] Rhythmic and syntactic reversals convey mixed feelings, whilst full stops in these lines create pauses, in which an emotional emptiness is inscribed:

> Durch die leeren Häuser
> der Dichter tappen erblindete Gorgonen.
> Vor den entriegelten
> Türen die Polizisten
> haben ihre Posten verlassen.
> Kein Wort lohnt mehr
> die Bewachung.

Assonance linking 'tappen', 'verlassen' and 'Bewachung', also links the loss of (in)sight to the loss of surveillance. The seers or poets have been superseded by blinded gorgons, quite harmless.

After the initial *Wende* had been claimed for truth and language,[49] much of the later poetry responding to Germany's unification was preoccupied with absences. Poets write the *Wende* as a vacating of spaces: the untenanted houses of Kunert's 'Bekennerbrief' are empty cattle sheds in Kerstin Hensel's 'Trauer Arbeit' and empty rooms in Wolfgang Hilbig's 'prosa meiner heimatstraße'.[50] Hensel's poem portrays mourning the *Wende*-death as scrubbing out the stalls of slaughtered cows. In Michael Wüstefeld's equally unsettling 1990 poem

---

48   Günter Kunert, 'Bekennerbrief', 'Durch die leeren Häuser der Dichter: Vier neue Gedichte', *Neue Rundschau*, 104 (1993), 147–50: 149.

49   See the speeches made by writers at the 4 November 1989 demonstration at Alexanderplatz, East Berlin.

50   Kerstin Hensel, *Freistoß. Gedichte*, Leipzig 1995, p.11, and Wolfgang Hilbig, 'prosa meiner heimatstraße', *Neue Rundschau*, 101 (1990), 81–99, continued *Sprache im technischen Zeitalter* (1991), 99–102.

'Gegenwärtige Vergangenheit' exodus produces a 'Raum ohne Volk', inverting the Nazi formulation 'Volk ohne Raum':[51]

> 1)
> Am Elbhang die Lichter
> vergrößern den Käfig der Nacht
> in der Stadt und den AbSteigen
> Im Dürrholz der Bäume
> das KrähenVolk wacht
> ein schwarzer Flügelreigen
>
> Das ElbTal voll Ahnung
> zu viele haben weggewollt
> aus der Stadt unter dem Schweigen
> Der Tag fragt: Sind wir schon
> ein Raum ohne Volk
> wollen die Krähen noch bleiben
>
> 2)
> Auf allen Bäumen kahlen Landes
> blühen die Krähen
>
> Mit schwarzen Mänteln hängen sie
> im Wind und rufen
>
> Wir sind das Volk
> Wir sind ein Volk

Although the *Wende* demonstrations took place during winter months when days were short, darkness is rendered ominous here: crows, the cage of night, black wings and black coats seem threatening, even funereal. The text also locates the most famous slogans of the *Wende* and unification in a natural landscape, as though they were the voice of Nature itself.

B.K. Tragelehn's poem 'Die Losungen des Jahres' mounts the same slogans from the demonstrations.[52] The capitalized cries of the

---

51   Michael Wüstefeld, *Deutsche Anatomie. Gedichte*, Dülmen-Hiddingsel 1996, p.59, and Hans Grimm, *Volk ohne Raum*, Munich 1928.

52   B.K. Tragelehn, 'Die Losungen des Jahres', *neue deutsche literatur*, 43/5 (1995), 5.

Volk interrupt the lyric voice, but the poem also preserves these mottoes after the placards have gone, aware that revolutionary sentiments soon become invalid.[53]

> Eben hat er noch um sich geschlagen der Staat
> Obwohl versprochen war und er immer gewußt hat
> Er soll verschwinden, wuchert und wuchert er bis
> WIR SIND DAS VOLK
> Er beim Wort genommen und endlich enteignet gleich
> WIR SIND EIN VOLK
> Über die eigene Grenze springt. Und wie bereits
> Stalin gesagt hat: Die Honecker kommen und gehen
> Denn alles hat ein Ende nur die Wurst hat zwei
> Und ICH BIN VOLKER
> 1989

Here the state is personified as a figure finally leaping over its own border, essentially Erich Honecker himself. Delaying the first subject, relentless reiteration of the conjunction 'und', and piling up subordinate clauses create changes of direction, so that the poem emulates the state's lashing-out and leaping. Tragelehn links 1989 to 1945 and Honecker to Hitler by means of a play on Stalin's slogan.[54] Making an opposition of the old identity between state and *Volk*, it is a case of 'das Volk / Ohne Staat'.[55]

Holger Teschke's poem 'Berliner November' imports and preserves further street slogans (line 3), but speaks directly and unproblematically for a 'wir'.[56] Run-over lines and omission of punctuation convey the breathlessness of change:

> Alles auf einmal brüllten wir heraus
> Auf unsern Straßen Unter diesem Himmel
> Sägt Bonzen ab statt Bäume Stasi raus
> Aufriß der Himmel wie in alten Filmen

---

53   'Viel zu schnell verschwanden die originellen Losungen, die wunderbaren Demo-Bilder', *Leipziger Andere Zeitung* (1 March 1990), p.1.

54   The Stalin quotation was originally displayed in 1945 in the Soviet zone of occupation and actually ran: 'Die Hitler kommen und gehen, das deutsche Volk, der deutsche Staat bleibt'.

55   Czechowski, 'Gestörte Verhältnisse', in Heinz Czechowski, *Nachtspur*, pp.177ff.

56   Holger Teschke, in Conrady (ed.), *Von einem Land*, p.13.

> Im ungarischen Herbst Im Prager Frühling
> Und keine Panzer kamen von Karlshorst
> Aber als sich einer auf die Barrikade ging
> Das Holzgerüst am Alexanderplatz
> Auslachte unsern Kindertraum Tapetentanz
> Anstatt den Hunderttausenden zum Maul zu reden
> Aussprach was Herren aller Länder fürchten Streik
> Da gellten Pfiffe War der Spaß zu Ende

Here the *Wende* is likened to other revolutionary impulses: the 1956 Hungarian Uprising, the 1968 Prague Spring, the GDR uprising of 17 June 1953 (when the tanks came from Karlshorst) and the barricades of the 1789 French Revolution. This poem epitomizes deflation and a sense of failure; it ends as abruptly as the 'Spaß', exemplifying the fact that poetry readers will struggle to find documents of an exhilarating freedom.

One of the remarkable things about these poems is that they tend not to offer images of unification at all in the sense of a coming together or union, but rather focus on ending and disappearance – of a country, a context, and of writing itself. The 'opening up' of 1989/90 is written as a liberation only in the deeply sceptical sense of releasing everything known and familiar into a void. Wilhelm Bartsch's poem 'Gen Ginnungagap' presents barbarians travelling into a bottomless ravine as an image of the New Germany.[57] This title poem of Bartsch's 1994 collection draws on the apocalyptic verses of the *Edda* to name the void or magic gorge. It fits beside lyric evocations of collapsing time and collapsing distances, cosmic irregularities like Lutz Rathenow's *Verirrte Sterne*,[58] lines crossed, bounds broken, and rules disregarded. Time is non-linear and reversible, for instance, in Grünbein's post-*Wende* dawn-song 'Alba':[59]

> In den Zweigen hängen Erinnerungen,
> Genaue Szenen aus einem künftigen Tag.

---

57   Wilhelm Bartsch, *Gen Ginnungagap. Gedichte*, Halle 1994, p.6.
58   Lutz Rathenow, *Verirrte Sterne oder Wenn alles wieder ganz anders kommt. Gedichte*, Gifkendorf 1994.
59   Grünbein, *Falten und Fallen*, p.95.

Überall Atem und Sprünge rückwärts
Durchs Dunkel von Urne zu Uterus.

Und das Neue, gefährlich und über Nacht
Ist es Welt geworden.

The *Minnesang* title, which suggests a lovers' parting brought by day-break, understates the caesura: 'Welt werden' is all-embracing (quite different in scope from 'zur Welt kommen'). This new world renders categories suddenly fluid and alternatives no longer mutually exclusive. Wolfgang Hilbig's *Wende* poem 'berlin. sublunar', written in 1994, evokes the new world as another night-side:[60]

dic zeit ist wieder eingekehrt in berlin
und die hochstapler defilieren in der oranienburger straße
um mitternacht gen himmel deutend: die zeit
ist retour aus dem exil.

die ganze stadt in den fesseln silbergrauer magie
der vollmond rollt

This moonlit Berlin of celestial portents, where fraudsters parade at midnight, conveys the eeriness of change. Hilbig uses the conceit of time itself returning from exile, along with the incoming developers, thereby combining two established ideas of the GDR – namely of its internal stagnation and its practices of expatriation.

Barbara Köhler's poem 'Berlin, November 94' writes the *Wende* city as an alternative landscape of geometrical terms: it is a matter of lines and distances.[61] Prefixes cut off from word-stems by line breaks ('er-innerung', for example) and the pairing of antonyms ('ab' and 'zu', or 'außen' and 'innen') contribute to the theme of binary division, which the highly united visual block of the poem on the page undercuts. Hence the form of the poem both makes a delicate interrogation of medium, and reflects the theme of a binary unity:

---

60 Wolfgang Hilbig, 'berlin. sublunar', *neue deutsche literatur*, 42/5 (1994), 7. Hilbig himself designated this poem a 'Wendegedicht' during his reading at the *Literarisches Colloquium Berlin* on 30 July 2003.
61 Barbara Köhler, 'Berlin, November 94', in Michael Speirs (ed.), *Berlin, mit deinen frechen Feuern. 100 Berlin-Gedichte*, Stuttgart 1997, pp.100f.

> die andere seite der grenze
> war bunt: eine entfernte er
> innerung weiß von vergessen
> frisch gestrichene häuser &
> namen genommene abstände an
> genommener ausnahmezustände
> die blicke sind nahverkehrt
> ins leere wird abgesehen von
> den umgebenden außenseiten
> nichts wahrgenommen es geht
> vorbei die andere seite der
> grenze war fremd es gab ein
> innen ein leben eine grenze
> die sich überschreiten ließ
> & es geht doch weiter danke
> es geht hier jeder tritt zu
>   nah

Representation and interpretation are this poem's primary concerns. It plays with 'ein' meaning one (as opposed to 'the other' or as opposed to 'two') and 'ein' meaning 'in' (as opposed to 'out' or 'away'), sets distance against proximity, and runs the echoing participles 'genommen', 'angenommen' and 'wahrgenommen' into the nouns 'ausnahme' and 'name'. Köhler takes the reader behind the scenes, as it were, to examine the machinery by which textual meaning is produced. Gaps she opens up by breaking prefixes and suffixes from stems kibosh the monolithic and reveal the material language. The transgression theme at the centre of this poem also refers back to a GDR tradition that was powerful in the 1980s (and was picked up as definitive in the scholarship which canonized the underground poetry, such as Karen Leeder's work on boundaries and 'Entgrenzung').[62]

Various versions of binary representation occur in response to the *Wende*, not all as complex and stimulating as Köhler's. Some poems return to the Cold-War idea of a contest. Unification becomes constructed as an unexpected defeat: a loss of the concrete (land) and the abstract (truth); a defeat for one side (as against an alien, victorious side) within which the position of the lyric subject is typically

---

62   See Karen Leeder, *Breaking Boundaries: A New Generation of Poets in the GDR*, Oxford 1996.

ambiguous or confused. Such oppositions between the victorious and the defeated recall Brecht's famous line 'Denn die Besiegten von heute sind die Sieger von morgen',[63] as well as the status of victory as a watchword of 1950s poetry in the GDR and an enduring cliché of GDR officialese (as evidenced by 'Von den Sowjetmenschen lernen heißt siegen lernen' or 'Der Sozialismus siegt, weil er wahr ist'). They convey a sense of *déjà vu*. The danger of seeking sanctuary in these over-familiar categories is offset in some poems by nuanced considerations of the poet's role. Steffen Mensching's portrait 'Rimbaud 2' in effect describes poetry itself as 'der Spleen der Verlierer', but at its end, the nineteenth-century French poet has become 'ein verlorner Mann / Der in der Haut des Siegers tanzen kann'.[64] The motif of losers returns more stridently in Mensching's 1999 cycle 'New York Lines', especially in the overheard poem 'Milano's Bar' which gives voice to a self-appointed victor who equates losing with not believing in America.[65] In Heiner Müller's 'Fremder Blick: Abschied von Berlin' of 1994,[66] victors are deaf to opponents or other marginalized voices, a context in which the overheard poem then reclaims a special function, as the voice of the defeated who cannot write.

In addition to such taking-up of inherited GDR categories for understanding history, a sense of *déjà vu* can also be invoked through imagery. Symbols of fallen dictatorship such as toppled statues are clichés, not only of the *Wende* throughout the Communist bloc but of regime change in general. Fallen statues in Gisela Kraft's poem 'Bitte des Karlmarxkopfes an das rotliegende Chemnitz' and Armin Richter's 'Ein Monument', as well as Grünbein's 'Ozymandias' translation, function in this way.[67] They suggest the necessity of removing old monuments before society can proceed with new memorials. In these instances, poetry crystallizes around an old-familiar image so as

---

63   Brecht, 'Lob der Dialektik', *Gesammelte Werke*, IX, 467f.
64   Mensching, *Berliner Elegien*, p.49.
65   Steffen Mensching, 'New York Lines', *neue deutsche literatur*, 47/3 (1999), 46–52: 50.
66   Müller, *Die Gedichte*, p.287.
67   Gisela Kraft in Chiarloni (ed.), 'Die Dichter und die Wende', p.5; Arnim Richter, *Die kleinen mecklenburgischen Meere*, Frankfurt/M. 1991, p.86; Grünbein, 'Transsibirischer Ozymandias', *Schädelbasislektion*, p.58.

to convey weariness with history and the never-ending vanities of power. Similarly, whilst Lutz Rathenow declares 'Neuer Staat, neues Gedicht' and Jan Faktor, 'wir brauchen eine neue lyrik',[68] there is a more prevalent concern with hand-me-down antiquity. Cultural memory becomes crucial to negotiate a time of turmoil and uncertainty: parallels between the present and antiquity, re-accessing ancient traditions, are a major element of the lyric response to the *Wende* (and demonstrate the contribution of a perspective rare in non-literary texts).

Günter Kunert writes the breaching of the Berlin Wall as the biblical fall of the walls of Jericho, in his poem 'Jericho, kürzlich', labelled '19.11.1990' (later undated and entitled 'Jericho 1989'). Dating such as this becomes crucial to poets who wish to mark their texts as *Wende* poems. For Kunert, history personified and embodied, strides and cries out:

> Anschwellender Ton
> aus Mündern gleichgestimmter
> Schall
> Stachel Lebenssucht
> Glücklicher Wahn
> Menschen verkörpern eine Menge
> Massenhaftes Geschiebe
> Leibliche Lava sprengt
> alle Regeln alle Bande
> Gitter wie Mauerwerk
> Und erst zum Morgendämmer hin
> im Schleppschritt der Geschichte
> kehrt zage
> ein Befremden heim.

---

68   Lutz Rathenow, 'Deutschland', in Chiarloni (ed.), *Grenzfallgedichte*, p.112. Jan
      Faktor, *Litfass* 16/54 (1992), 4–9. Faktor's demand for new poetry in any case
      bears formal resemblance to his earlier 'Manifeste der Trivialpoesie', in Jan
      Faktor, *Georgs Versuche an einem Gedicht und andere positive Texte aus
      den Dichtergraben des Grauens*, Berlin/East-Weimar 1989, pp.87–102, and
      Rathenow published countless prose essays in the post-unification period, rather
      than new poetry.

This *Wende* is an eruption of united sound from a trumpeting and marching *Volk*. The poem follows from the imperative in Kunert's GDR poem 'Schofar' to remember Jericho:[69] the *Wende* thus becomes a long-sought re-enactment of the mass-action led by Joshua. However, there seems to be a disjunction between the biblical story and the *Wende* poem: the GDR border's barbs may be replaced by a barb of 'Lebenssucht', but the biblical exemplar was not, of course, a liberation at all, but rather a conquest and a massacre.[70]

The *Wende*-death is a Roman crucifixion in Christa Wolf's poem 'Prinzip Hoffnung'.[71] In earnestly equating the cross with history and the body dying on it with the principle of hope, Wolf focuses on agonizing death, rather than the salvation which crucifixion primarily represents in Christianity. Yet associations with martyrdom and a final victory over death persist. Stoicism and centuries of repute attach to various deaths revisited in *Wende* poems. The Roman philosopher Seneca, in Heiner Müller's conception, becomes a *Wende* suicide. In 'Senecas Tod', the most resonant line is capitalized: 'MEINE SCHMERZEN SIND MEIN EIGENTUM'.[72] Nero's former educator, who committed a tortuous suicide, hacking at his veins with defiance when forced by Nero to commit suicide, becomes a figure of identification in the post-*Wende* period (when the writer as educator becomes an untenable role). Forced suicide also constitutes an element in Holger Teschke's vision of fallen civilization in 'Elegie nach Vergil':[73]

> Kaum stürzten die Säulen Kaum hat der Rauch sich verzogen
> Da ziehn übers Forum salbadernd die neuen Augurn
> Sehn dem Adlerflug nach überm Fluß Stochern in Därmen
> Aufsteht aus seinen Trümmern der alte Senat
> Der Wolf bleibt Bote im Tempel der Juno Moneta
> Bald fallen die Römer still in ihr herbstliches Schwert

Like Kunert's 'Jericho', this poem uses an ancient exemplum: Rome as a fallen empire, site of ruins, superstition, deified commercialism

---

69   Günter Kunert, *Unterwegs nach Utopia*, Munich-Vienna 1977, p.47.
70   See *Josua* 6.1, 6.20f.
71   Christa Wolf, in Conrady (ed.), *Von einem Land*, p.134
72   Müller, *Die Gedichte*, pp.250–251: p.250.
73   Holger Teschke, in Conrady (ed.), *Von einem Land*, p.64.

and imminent suicide. Reference to augurs ironizes the commentators on Germany's future, to Juno Moneta the worship of money, and the eagle is a Nazi as well as Roman imperial emblem. By paralleling the fall of Rome with the fall of the Soviet empire, poets not only convey the scale of the upheavals they have witnessed. They are also invoking a culture and a civilization, which enjoy cornerstone status in the contemporary western world. Down through the centuries the words of Seneca and Virgil have survived to be known today. This seems to be important for ex-GDR writers coming to terms with a crisis of purpose.

Privileging public objects of myth and history, rather than fore-grounding private objects, is exemplified by a fascination with Roman sayings, such as that of Cato the Elder, who ended his senatorial speeches declaring his conviction that Carthage must be destroyed ('ceterum censeo Carthaginem esse delendam'). His wish was fulfilled in 146 AD when Carthage was hit by an earthquake. In the poem 'Reiseleiter',[74] Kerstin Hensel takes up Cato's famous statement of attack:

> Im übrigen bin ich der Meinung daß Karthago
> Zerstört werden muß.

Carthage (read: the American empire) represented a dangerous rival to Rome (read: the Soviet empire). The effect of the legendary formulation is to problematize the contemporary sentiment, holding it at arm's length, as it were. Braun, on the other hand, juxtaposes Carthage with New York in his *Wende* poem 'Das Theater der Toten',[75] but closes on an even more ambiguous note:

> Und das Spiel ist gelaufen. Im übrigen bin ich der Meinung
> Daß der Sozialismus zerstört werden muß, und
> Mir gefällt die Sache der Besiegten.

This seems to be an expression of satisfaction with the end of the GDR, but the echoing presence of Cato's and Brecht's famous

---

74   Hensel, *Freistoß*, p.39.
75   Volker Braun, *Die Zickzackbrücke. Ein Abrißkalendar*, Halle 1992, p.91.

declarations ushers in a sarcastic tone; after all, the 'Spiel' is a performance by the dead. An additional effect of recourse to phrasing inherited from a dead Roman senator is to foreground the contemporary poet as ventriloquist, perhaps feeling otherwise lost for weighty words with which to confront history.

Within the poetry staging the ancients, historiographical reflections proliferate in poems by Heiner Müller and Günter Kunert. In 'Klage des Geschichtsschreibers', Müller draws on Tacitus's contribution to the annals of history, in order to celebrate turmoil as literary 'Stoff'.[76] Bloody history is judged by its usefulness to contemporary writers, rather than by ethical standards, a provocative perspective, which also implicates the new social configurations (in so far as history has ceased to be a dialectical course to utopia and is once again the recurrence of uprisings and mammoth wars). Kunert's 'An Clio' poem evokes an oneiric wander through annals and museums.[77] History-writing is set here against dreams, which are a source of truths other than those rationally acquired:

> Brandzeichen
> die Zäsuren der Geschichte.
> Glorifiziert die Namen
> der Cäsaren. Zum Wohle der Völker
> gewaltige Kriege. Du
> hast sie alle überlebt. Du hast die Erde
> mit Blut getränkt, mit Leichen gedüngt
> und bloßes Erinnern geerntet.
> Ich bin deiner Spur gefolgt
> durch die Annalen, durch die Museen
> den Tätern, den Opfern
> bis hinter der letzten Tür
> keiner mehr da war. Vergebliche Umschau.
> Begegnet bin ich nur
> einem kleinen Tier
> angstvoll und momentweise
> wie aus Träumen erschaffen
> die man besser vorm Erwachen
> vergißt.

---

76   Müller, *Die Gedichte*, p.246.
77   Kunert, *Mein Golem*, p.35.

This poem addresses Clio, muse of history, its accusation (in lines 6–8) more compelling for being directed to a 'du'. Following characteristic concerns with 'Zeichen', names and vacated spaces, the final lines posit a human beyond history: he or she is just a little animal. History equates with glory, war and bloodshed, and, of course, the ubiquitous post-war German dichotomy of *Täter* and *Opfer*; but ultimately these fall away to leave the frightened human-animal. An elusiveness in the closing simile formally reinforces leaving the official record behind, to instead access something fearful and feral.

After 1989, poets take issue with how memory is organized, with naming and imaging the newly historic, and with what is to endure. They predominantly memorialize the German *Wende* as a death, besides dedicating their work to the dear departed (Grünbein's *Den teuren Toten*) and discerning posthumous actors on stage (Braun's 'Theater der Toten'). Obituarists in a broad sense, obsessively returning to explore death euphemisms, they employ poetic technique to expose tired binary thinking on German unity and reveal startling conceptions of agentless history. It may be Rathenow's 'Hokuspokus ohne Hexerei' or Grünbein's impromptu magic-trick: 'Was für ein Trick: Eins zwei drei...n, / Schon war das Kollektiv verschwunden'.[78] Kunert's post-*Wende* golem figures the past as a stalking colossus, magically raised to artificial life.[79] As these references to magic forces exemplify, poems invite reassessment of familiar events, by forging unorthodox comparisons. Of poems complicating the contemporary with the ancient, making bold, often disturbing leaps across a museum of the mind, many depict memorial activity with respect to ancient models of verbal durability. Poets of the *Wende* sing the death of the GDR state, and its unrealized ideals, in obituary songs, which both celebrate and mourn. They show events equivocally and thereby press back against the mainstream and the propagandistic. Their diverse literary record of the *Wende* also reveals a community of memory, constituted and sustained by poetry since the end of the GDR.

---

78   Lutz Rathenow, 'Dezember 89', in Conrady (ed.), *Von einem Land*, p.29, and
       Grünbein, *Schädelbasislektion*, p.74.
79   Kunert, 'Mein Golem', *Mein Golem*, p.24.

Bibliography

Bartsch, Wilhelm, *Gen Ginnungagap. Gedichte*, Halle 1994.

Böhme, Thomas, *Und an Bahnhöfe denken. Gedichte*, Aschersleben 2000.

Braun, Volker, 'Das Eigentum', *Neues Deutschland* (4–5 August 1990).

——, *Die Zickzackbrücke. Ein Abrißkalendar*, Halle 1992.

——, *Tumulus. Gedichte*, Frankfurt/M. 1999.

Brecht, Bertolt, *Gesammelte Werke*, Frankfurt/M. 1967, IX.

Brinkmann, Rolf Dieter, 'Politisches Gedicht 13. Nov. 74', in Rolf Dieter Brinkmann, *Westwärts 1&2. Gedichte*, Reinbek bei Hamburg 1975, pp.160–7.

Chiarloni, Anna (ed.), 'Die Dichter und die Wende', *GDR Monitor*, 23 (1990), 1–12.

——, and Helga Pankoke (eds.), *Grenzfallgedichte. Eine deutsche Anthologie*, Berlin-Weimar 1991.

Conrady, Karl Otto (ed.), *Von einem Land und vom anderen. Gedichte zur deutschen Wende 1989/1990*, Leipzig 1993.

Czechowski, Heinz, *Nachtspur. Ein Lesebuch aus der deutschen Gegenwart. Gedichte und Prosa 1987–1992*, Zurich 1993.

——, *Mein westfälischer Frieden. Ein Zyklus 1996–1998*, Cologne 1998.

Drawert, Kurt, 'Politisches Gedicht, Januar 1990', in Anna Chiarloni (ed.), 'Die Dichter und die Wende', *GDR Monitor*, 23 (1990), 1–12.

——, *Haus ohne Menschen. Zeitmitschriften*, Leipzig 1993.

——, *Wo es war. Gedichte*, Frankfurt/M. 1996.

Ertl, Wolfgang, 'Grenzfallgedichte', *Germanic Review*, 67 (1992), 183.

Faktor, Jan, *Litfass* 16/54 (1992), 4–9.

——, 'Manifeste der Trivialpoesie', in Jan Faktor, *Georgs Versuche an einem Gedicht und andere positive Texte aus den Dichtergraben des Grauens*, Berlin/East-Weimar 1989, pp.87–102

Freud, Sigmund, *Studienausgabe*, Frankfurt/M. 1969, I.

Gerlach, Harald, *Nirgends und zu keiner Stunde: Gedichte*, Berlin 1998.

Goethe, Johann Wolfgang von, *Faust. Eine Tragödie*, Munich 1978.

Grimm, Hans, *Volk ohne Raum*, Munich 1928.

Grünbein, Durs, *Schädelbasislektion. Gedichte*, Frankfurt/M. 1991.

——, *Falten und Fallen. Gedichte*, Frankfurt/M. 1994.

——, *Den teuren Toten. 33 Epitaphe*, Frankfurt/M. 1994.

——, *Galilei vermißt Dantes Hölle und bleibt an den Maßen hängen. Aufsätze 1989–1995*, Frankfurt/M. 1996.

Hartung, Klaus, *Neunzehnhundertneunundachtzig. Ortsbesichtigungen nach einer Epochenwende*, Frankfurt/M. 1990.

Heine, Heinrich, 'Die Heimkehr II', in Heinrich Heine, *Buch der Lieder*, Munich 1975.

Hensel, Kerstin, *Freistoß. Gedichte*, Leipzig 1995.

Heym, Stefan, and Werner Heiduczek (eds.), *Die sanfte Revolution: Prosa, Lyrik, Protokolle, Erlebnisberichte, Reden*, Leipzig-Weimar 1990.

Hilbig, Wolfgang, 'prosa meiner heimatstraße', *Neue Rundschau* 101 (1990), 81–99.

——, 'berlin. sublunar', *neue deutsche literatur*, 42/5 (1994), 7.

Hölderlin, Friedrich, 'Andenken', in Friedrich Hölderlin, *Gedichte*, Frankfurt/M. 1992.

Holst, 'matthias' BAADER, 'ich weiss nicht was soll es bedeuten', in 'matthias' BAADER holst, *Temperamente*, 1 (1990), 33.

Kahlau, Heinz, *Kaspers Waage*, Berlin 1992.

Kermode, Frank, *Poetry, Narrative, History*, Oxford 1990.

Köhler, Barbara, *Deutsches Roulette*, Frankfurt/M. 1991.

——, 'Berlin, November 94', in Michael Speirs (ed.), *Berlin, mit deinen frechen Feuern. 100 Berlin-Gedichte*, Stuttgart 1997, pp.100–1.

Kraft, Gisela, 'Am dritten Tag des Oktobers', in Gisela Kraft, *West-östliche Couch. Zweierlei Leidensweisen der Deustchen*, Berlin 1991.

Kunert, Günter, *Unterwegs nach Utopia*, Munich-Vienna 1977.

——, 'Bekennerbrief', 'Durch die leeren Häuser der Dichter: Vier neue Gedichte', *Neue Rundschau*, 104 (1993), 147–50.

——, *Mein Golem*, Munich-Vienna 1996.

Kunze, Reiner, *ein tag auf dieser erde. gedichte*, Frankfurt/M. 1998.

Leeder, Karen, *Breaking Boundaries: A New Generation of Poets in the GDR*, Oxford 1996.

Mensching, Steffen, *Berliner Elegien*, Leipzig 1995.

——, 'New York Lines', *neue deutsche literatur*, 47/3 (1999), 46–52.

Morrison, Susan S., 'The Feminisation of the German Democratic Republic in Political Cartoons 1989–1990', *Journal of Popular Culture*, 25/4 (1992), 35–51.

Müller, Heiner, *Die Gedichte*, Frankfurt/M. 1998.

Oleschinski, Brigitte, *Your Passport is Not Guilty. Gedichte*, Reinbek bei Hamburg 1997.

Papenfuss, Bert, *mors ex nihilo*, Berlin 1994.

Rathenow, Lutz, *Verirrte Sterne oder Wenn alles wieder ganz anders kommt: Gedichte*, Gifkendorf 1994.

Richter, Arnim, *Die kleinen mecklenburgischen Meere*, Frankfurt/M. 1991.

Schlenstedt, Dieter, 'Ein Gedicht als Provokation', *neue deutsche literatur*, 40/12 (1992), 124–32.

Schmidt, Kathrin, *Flußbild mit Engel. Gedichte*, Frankfurt/M. 1995.

Stötzer, Gabriele, *Erfurter Roulette*, Munich 1995.

Tragelehn, B.K., 'Beim Abschied zu singen, nach C.G. Rosetti [*sic*]', *neue deutsche literatur*, 43/5 (1995), 6.

——, 'Die Losungen des Jahres', *neue deustche literatur*, 43/5 (1995), 5.

Wolf, Christa, *Der geteilte Himmel*, Halle 1963.

Wüstefeld, Michael, *Deutsche Anatomie. Gedichte*, Dülmen-Hiddingsel 1996.

Birgit Haas

Wendedramen

Introduction

While German poetry and prose after 1989 have been at the centre of heated debates,[1] the development of drama is often regarded as a marginal issue, if not entirely ignored. The so-called *Literaturstreit*, however fiercely fought out, hardly ever touched on dramatic issues, and dramatists' responses to the gentle revolution scarcely feature in recent publications.[2] This is probably due to the fact that, since the mid-1980s, both theatre and drama were believed to hover in a permanent state of crisis which was by and large an offshoot of another even more familiar phenomenon, namely 'Der Tod der Literatur', proudly announced by Hans-Magnus Enzensberger as early as 1968. Following the highly theatrical political events in Germany during the *Wende*, however, playwrights have seized the chance to resculpt the theatrical landscape and, particularly during the second half of the decade, young playwrights have entered the scene and made their voices heard.

1   See Thomas Anz (ed.), *Es geht nicht um Christa Wolf. Der Literaturstreit im vereinten Deutschland*, Frankfurt/M. 1995.

2   Arthur Williams, Stuart Parkes, and Roland Smith (eds.), *German Literature at a Time of Change 1989–1990*, Frankfurt/M. 1991; Arthur Williams, Stuart Parkes, and Julian Preece (eds.), *'Whose Story?' – Continuities in contemporary German-language Literature*, Frankfurt/M. 1998; Gerhard Fischer and David Roberts (eds.), *Schreiben nach der Wende. Ein Jahrzehnt deutscher Literatur 1989–1999*, Tübingen 2001; Robert Weninger and Brigitte Rosenbacher (eds.), *Wendezeiten – Zeitenwenden. Positionsbestimmungen zur deutschsprachigen Literatur 1945–1995*, Tübingen 1997.

As the post-1989 drama has been overshadowed by the *Literatur-streit*, Christoph Hein's pre-*Wende* drama *Die Ritter der Tafelrunde* (1985) remains the last widely performed and well-received contemporary play. Hein's attack on the senile Politbüro was to be the last contemporary 'hit' for years to come.[3] Against the backdrop of the *Literaturstreit*, which can be seen as a type of theatre in itself, the post-1989 drama played only a minor role, causing the playwright Elfriede Müller to state that 'Wendedramen' were merely a kind of 'disposable crockery' ('Einweggeschirr').[4] Whilst classics such as *Wilhelm Tell* or *Fidelio* played to full houses,[5] the public did not take much notice of contemporary plays.

Due to the fact that the *Literaturstreit* was acted out in public, in newspaper articles and talk shows on television, it became a political 'spectacle' which reflected the rift between East and West. The debate served as a release for the tensions which politicians liked to ignore. Instead, the official line was to emphasize the notion of a unified people, yet the concept of a 'Gemeinschaftsmythos' ('communal myth') was regarded to be higly problematic.[6] The political drama of these years took the conflict from the feuilletons and put it on stage in order to shed light on the cracks in the thin veneer of the shiny unified country.

The culture clash between East and West Germans after the velvet revolution of 1989 and a set of cultural images, such as the 'overbearing western capitalist' and the 'feminized East German victim', immediately found their way into the plays written at the time. As the years 1989 and 1990 marked a fundamental change for Germans both East and West, the social, economic, and psychological consequences form the background of a considerable number of political plays. Particularly during

---

3   Terrance Albrecht, *Rezeption und Zeitlichkeit des Werkes Christoph Heins*, Frankfurt/M. 2000, pp.104–7.

4   Elfriede Müller, 'Warum flutscht das alles so gut durch?', *Theater Heute Jahr-buch* (1995), 152–3: 153.

5   Moray McGowan, 'Beating time? *Fidelio* in Dresden, 7–8 October 1989', in Mark Ward (ed.), *Proceedings of the Scottish Conference of University Teachers* 2003.

6   See Lothar Probst, 'Ost-West Unterschiede und das kommunitäre Erbe der DDR', in Lothar Probst (ed.), *Differenz in der Einheit. Über die kulturellen Unterschiede der Deutschen in Ost und West*, Berlin 1999, pp.15–27: pp.15–7.

the first years of reunification, playwrights responded vividly to the altered shape of Germany, yet the fact that plays written in 1999 address the 'Wall inside people's heads' says something about the impact of the merger of the two states. The most common stereotypes emerging during the 'Mauershow'[7] of 1989 were the 'raping' and 'colonizing' of the GDR by the potent West; the calling into question of the revolutionary character of the events before the collapse of the GDR; the longing for the GDR (*Ostalgie*); and the dubious role of East German opportunists.

As nations are defined by more than just a set of common values,[8] the bonds of individuals within a community are characterized by 'phantasms', as Anderson puts it, and are therefore imaginary.[9] The period after 1989 is thus particularly interesting in terms of the German nation, as the cultural images which developed in those years expressed the inter-German rift. As East and West insisted on their own social practices, the mechanisms of rejection resulted in a set of cultural images which a journalist commented on as follows: 'Der Ost-West-Vergleich ist deshalb weiterhin ein Wettstreit von Phantomen.' ('The comparison between East and West thus continues to be a competition of phantoms.')[10] Christa Wolf referred to a wave of cultural myths and images which also found their way into contemporary drama.[11] In relation to the common symbols surrounding the 'Wall inside people's heads',[12] the alleged weakness of post-1989 drama – its focus on contemporary issues – can be seen as its strength. The dramas offer an interesting kaleidoscope of images which tell the story of the German-German 'psychodrama'.

---

7   See Rainer Bohn (ed.), *Mauer-Show: Das Ende der DDR, die deutsche Einheit und die Medien*, Berlin 1992.

8   Slavoj Zizek, 'Eastern Europe's Republic of Gilead', *New Left Review*, 183 (1990), 50–63.

9   Benedict Anderson, *Imagined Communities: Reflections on the Origin and Spread of Nationalism*, London 1983, pp.15–6.

10   Stefan Berg, 'Die neue deutsche Sippenhaft', *Der Spiegel* 39 (23 September 1996), 51–3: 53.

11   Christa Wolf, 'Die Rede vom Auslöffeln – Zur Sache: Deutschland', *Wochenpost Extra* (3 March 1994).

12   See Jürgen Link, *Die Struktur des Symbols in der Sprache des Journalismus. Zum Verhältnis literarischer und pragmatischer Symbole*, Munich 1978.

Harking back to the idea of a 'collective symbolism' ('Kollektiv-symbolik'),[13] the plays allow a reconstruction of the so-called 'linguistic images' (*Sprachbilder*), which can be regarded as typical of the German-German culture clash after 1990. Wilfried Korngiebel and Jürgen Link define the tendency to express the inner German conflict through symbols as follows:

> Wir bezeichnen die Gesamtheit erläuternder Sprachbilder in der modernen Politik und in den Massenmedien als 'Kollektivsymbolik'. 'Kollektiv' deshalb, weil solche Bilder eben nicht zum Expertenwissen gehören, sondern kulturell weit verbreitet und allgemein bekannt sind sowie in alltäglichen Reden, Handlungen und Ritualen immer wieder appliziert werden. [...] Als Symbole bezeichnen wir also all jene Sprachbilder, durch die ein komplexes Wissen schematisch und ggf. ideologisch perspektiviert veranschaulicht werden kann. [...] Dieses vage Bild fungiert imaginär als Subjekt aller Vorgänge, mit dem sich Individuen 'identifizieren' und so einen gemeinsamen Sozialkörper ausbilden können.[14]

> (We refer to the entirety of explanatory images in language, be they used in modern politics or in the mass media, as 'collective symbols'. 'Collective' because such images are not used by experts but are well-known and widely-used in speeches, everyday practices and rituals. [...] Symbols are those images in language, which can be schematically and ideologically exemplified through complex knowledge. [...] This vague image functions as an imaginary subject of all processes with which the individuals can 'identify' and which enables them to form a common social body.)

The most prominent examples are the 'Zug zur Einheit', the term 'Wende', and the 'europäische Haus'. Whilst the plays written shortly after 1989 mainly focus on the symbolism of the *theatrum mundi*, i.e. the 'Mauershow' and the influence of the media, other images were soon to emerge, such as 'Wendehals' ('turncoat'), 'Hochzeit' ('wedding'), and 'Kolonisierung' ('colonization'). Particularly during the *Literaturstreit*, journalists attacked East German writers using the

---

13   On the 'Kollektivsymbolik' of the Wende see Jürgen Link, 'Wie weich landen die Wendeturbulenzen des Europäischen Hauses? Kollektivsymbolik und aktuelle (De)Normalisierungsschübe', *kulturRevolution*, 23 (1990), 58–69.

14   Wilfried Korngiebel and Jürgen Link, 'Von einstürzenden Mauern, europäischen Zügen und deutschen Autos. Die Wiedervereinigung in Bildern und Sprachbildern der Medien', in Bohn (ed.), *Mauer-Show*, pp.31–54: p.33f.

terms 'Kollaboration' ('collaboration'), 'Scheinheiligkeit' ('hypocrisy') and 'Feigheit' ('cowardice').[15] In other words: a normal relationship between East and West seemed out of reach. As a consequence, both East and West Germans resorted to clichés and stereotypes, such as the 'marriage' between the two states. Wolf Biermann summarizes the unequal relationship with the following words: 'Der Wohlstands-Michel, ein häßlicher Beau, heiratet sein elendes, verprügeltes Cousinchen aus dem Armenhaus.' ('The affluent "Michel", an ugly beau, marries his down-trodden and beaten little cousin from the almshouse.')[16] It is particularly in the early unification plays that this cultural image is taken up and criticized. Besides, the economic gap between East and West Germany disgruntled many writers, not only from the former GDR, since it was felt the West Germans had taken advantage of the East Germans' ignorance in economic matters. The East Germans felt duped and ripped off by their 'colonisers', which led Günter Grass to speak of the 'Schnäppchen namens DDR'.[17] In view of the sudden collapse of the socialist state that left East German intellectuals without an intellectual 'home', Heiner Müller stated:

Das Gespenstische ist das Vakuum. Die Utopie ist weg, ein Feindbild ist weg, und jetzt gibt es eine verzweifelte Suche nicht nach Utopien, sondern nach neuen Feindbildern. Das führt zu Süffisanz und Häme. Nicht nur gegen den Osten.[18]

(The uncanny thing is the vacuum. The utopia is gone, the mental image of the enemy is gone, and now there is a desperate search not for alternative utopias, but for new images of the enemy. This leads to smugness and malice. Not only towards the East.)

---

15 Compare Wolfgang Ullmann, 'Die triste Kumpanei der Kollaboration', *Freitag* (20 August 1993); Wolfgang Templin, 'Erst die Wahrheit!', *Die Woche* (22 December 1994); Helmut Böttiger, 'Ostmoral', *Frankfurter Rundschau* (12 January 1995); Joachim Gauck, 'Wut und Schmerz der Opfer', *Die Zeit* (10 January 1995).

16 Wolf Biermann, 'Duftmarke setzen', in *Klartexte im Getümmel*, Cologne 1990, pp.316–32: p.321.

17 Günter Grass, *Ein Schnäppchen namens DDR. Letzte Reden vor dem Glockengeläut*, Frankfurt/M. 1990.

18 '"Die Wahrheit, leise und unerträglich": Ein Gespräch mit Heiner Müller, von Peter von Becker', *Theater heute Jahrbuch* (1995), 9–30: 14.

It is therefore not surprising that the void was filled with a set of vexed projections, freezing the images of 'Besserwessi' – the West German know-it-all – and 'Jammerossi' – the whining East German. The gap between East and West perpetuated the state of mind of the cold war era, resulting in two apparently neatly distinctive strands of literature. In his essay on the state of German literature after unification, Weck writes:

> Nun verfallen viele wieder in die ziel- und ortlose Wehmut des enttäuschten Idealisten einer 'tragischen' Gesellschaft, wie sie die DDR einmal war. Dies ist der Boden, auf dem die Ressentiments gegen den 'satten' Westen wachsen, dem die Schuld am Unbehagen in der neuen Kultur gegeben wird. [...] Deshalb wirken die 'Wessis alle so 'kalt' und 'profitsüchtig', und deshalb scheinen die 'Ossis' immer zu 'jammern'. Der eine erscheint dem andern als Unmensch: konsumistisch 'korrumpiert' oder kommunistisch 'verdorben'. Damit nähern sich die wechselseitigen Einschätzungen wieder den Feindbildern des 'kalten Krieges', wie sie die staatlichen Zentren in der Phase der Systemkonfrontation gezeichnet haben.[19]

> (Once again many lapse into an aimless melancholy so typical of the disappointed idealist of a 'tragic' society such as the GDR had been. This prepares the ground for so many resentments against the 'well fed' West, which is blamed for the unease which many feel in this new culture. [...] This is the reason why all 'Wessis' seem to be so 'cold' and eager for profit and why the 'Ossis' appear to 'complain' all the time. They see each other as brutes, as the 'deformed' consumer or the 'corrupted' communist. These reciprocal assessments start to resemble the 'cold war' images again as they were depicted by the two opposing systems.)

It is debatable, however, whether the view of the two literatures can be maintained. Tracing back and comparing cultural images in East and West German drama, this essay will answer the question: Can the post-1989 plays all be divided into the 'ironic West' and the 'tragic East'?

---

19   Michael Weck, 'Der ironische Westen und der tragische Osten', *Kursbuch*, 109 (1992), 133–148: 139f.

Mauershow

From the start, the *Wende* was perceived as a spectacle on television.[20] This view is maintained by Helga Königsdorf, for example, who compares the *Wende* to a drama performed on the political stage:

> Aber, verführt vom schönen Anfang unserer Revolution, verführt vom Glauben an die Möglichkeit großer Inszenierungen, wollten wir endlich Regisseure sein, nachdem wir überall die Spuren der Demütigung gefunden hatten.[21]
>
> (Seduced by the encouraging beginnings of our revolution, seduced by the belief that great productions were possible, we finally wanted to be the directors, after we had found traces of humiliation everywhere.)

It is common knowledge that the expectations were soon to be dashed, and Wolf Biermann summarized the situation as follows: 'Ich erlebe die Wiedervereinigung wie ein brutales Rührstück' ('I experience reunification as a brutal type of sentimental drama').[22]

Manfred Karge's *Mauer-Stücke* (1990) adopts an ironic attitude towards the events of 1989. In the last scene of *Mauer-Stücke*, the pathos of the gentle revolution is mocked in a parody of Goethe's *Faust II*. Due to the fact that, firstly, Karge's characters are mere clichés, and, secondly, the events of 1989 did not change the world in the same way as, for example, the French Revolution did. The contrast between the grand gesture and the lack of content leaves the pseudo-revolutionaries with an empty bubble that is likely to burst into laughter any time:

---

20   Vgl. Monika Lindgens and Susanne Mahle, 'Vom Medienboom zur Medien-barriere. Massenmedien und Bürgerbewegungen im gesellschaftlichen Um-bruch in der DDR und im vereinten Deutschland', in Bohn (ed.), *Mauer-Show*, pp.95–112.

21   Helga Königsdorf, *1989 oder ein Moment der Schönheit. Eine Collage aus Briefen, Gedichten, Texten*, Berlin-Weimar 1991, p.9.

22   Wolf Biermann, 'Duftmarke setzen', in *Klartexte im Getümmel*, p.317.

SCHAUSPIELER
Ach, sie standen nicht mehr
Die Mauern
Aber die Glut zog
Schon, vom Nachbarn
Zum Nachbarn sich
Verbreitend
Hier und dort her
Über das Land.
Flüchtend sah ich
Durch Glut und Rauch
Wundergestalten
In dem düstern
Feuerumleuchteten Qualm.[23]

Alluding to the description of the fall of Troy in *Faust*,[24] Pohl presents us with a caricature of the revolution. The 'colonizing' of the former GDR becomes ludicrous when compared to the battle of Troy. Through the contrast between 1989 and the pseudo-mythological background, the conflict between East and West becomes ridiculous. In a farcical manner, Karge deconstructs the pathos of the so-called 'revolution' of 1989; the parody of the eighteenth-century verse results in a comedic pastiche. As opposed to those in Goethe's drama, the actors here are rather self-conscious indeed and one thus exclaims pathetically: 'Mein Gott, dies Theater kurz vor unserm End. Nun, da

---

23   Manfred Karge, *Mauer-Stücke*, in *Die Eroberung des Südpols*, Berlin 1996, pp.129–208: p.206. We have refrained from translating the quotations from the German plays into English because their poetic quality and the way they play with language and allusions is often untranslatable.

24   Die Stelle lautet im Original: 'Durch das umwölkte, staubende Tosen / Drängender Krieger hört' ich die Götter / Fürchterlich rufen, hört' ich der Zwietracht/ Eherne Stimme schallen durchs Feld, / Mauerwärts.
Ach! sie standen noch, Ilios' / Mauern, aber die Flammenglut / Zog vom Nachbar zum Nachbar schon, / Sich verbreitend von hier und dort / Mit des eignen Sturmes Wehn / Über die nächtliche Stadt hin.
Flüchtend sah ich durch Rauch und Glut / Und der züngelnden Flamme Loh'n / Gräßlich zürnender Götter Nahn, / Schreitend Wundergestalten / Riesengroß, durch düsteren / Feuerumleuchteten Qualm hin.' Johann Wolfgang von Goethe, *Faust. Eine Tragödie*, in *Werke. Hamburger Ausgabe*, ed. Erich Trunz, Hamburg 1959, III, 262f.

uns stürzend die Zeit überrennt.'[25] Karge alludes to the style of the drama of the eighteenth century, but through the contrast with the ridiculous self-importance of the characters the revolutionaries appear laughable.

East-West stereotypes and projections can be found in Botho Strauß's farcical play *Schlußchor* (1991), which emphasizes the spectacular character of the *Wende*, yet at the same time renders this stereotypical view ridiculous. The first act mocks people's desperate attempts to become immortal through a photograph, taken while the Wall comes down. Ironically, the group fails to pay attention at the critical moment, despite the fact that the whole point of their gathering was to prove that they were present at the crucial moment, i.e. the fall of the Wall. What is more important than the act of taking the picture is the fact that they will be able to show it to others afterwards. They display a keen awareness of their own 'historical importance,' a phrase used so often by the then chancellor of the Federal Republic, Helmut Kohl, that the 'historical importance' of 1989 became a running joke at the time. In the first few lines of the play, Strauß subtly picks up on this complacency:

> M 8 brüllt
> Deutschland!
> Stille. Der FOTOGRAF unterbricht seine Arbeit.
> M 5
> Sie wissen, wie das gemeint ist?
> FOTOGRAF
> Nein?
> M 5
> Sie wissen nicht, was das zu bedeuten hat?
> FOTOGRAF
> Ich wüßte nicht...
> M 5
> Ach? Das wundert mich nun wieder.
> FOTOGRAF
> Tja. Damit hatte ich nicht gerechnet.
> M 5
> Damit hatte n i e m a n d von uns gerechnet.

---

25   Karge, *Mauer-Stücke*, p.206.

F 1
Mit anderen Worten: Sie haben gar nicht abgedrückt?
M 9
Und gerade in d e r Sekunde hätte man sich später gern gesehen![26]

Strauß freezes the German-German sensitivities in a highly symbolic *tableau* which expresses not only a general inertia, but also a loss of identity. The photograph is thus an attempt to merge East and West into one, albeit artificially and against people's will, and the photographer threatens the group with the words: 'Ich fotografiere euch so lange, bis ihr ein Antlitz seid. Ein Kopf – ein Mund – ein Blick. Ein Antlitz.'[27] Through this, he reduces the group to an anonymous chorus that witnesses the fall of the Wall, yet is unable to critically comment on this event in the way the theatrical chorus of antiquity would. In *Schlußchor*, the masses do not actively shape the course of history. On the contrary, the people are formed by history, which in turn appears to be only a marginal part of their lives. History is therefore not something that people are interested in because of its political dimension; all that counts is the sensational and representational aspect of history which is transformed into a media event at the very moment it takes place.

'Colonizing' the GDR

The cultural shock that followed reunification[28] had a deep impact on writers such as Volker Braun and Heiner Müller. Both suffered from the fact that Socialism – a system in which they had always believed no matter how harshly they had criticized it – had been disposed of so swiftly after 1990. As far as the 'gentle' revolution and the victory of capitalism were concerned, however, Müller's hopes for a better future came to an end, as unified Germany was ruled by money, or, in

---

26   Botho Strauß, *Schlußchor*, Munich 1991, p.15.
27   Ibid., p.28.
28   Wolf Wagner, *Kulturschock Deutschland. Der zweite Blick*, Hamburg 1999.

his words, the 'principle Auschwitz.'[29] This negative view is shared
by Rolf Hochhuth, whose play *Wessis in Weimar* (1993) criticizes the
actions of the Treuhandanstalt, the federal institution that was re-
organizing the economic infrastructure in East Germany. As early as
the first scene, Karsten Rohwedder, the boss of the Treuhand at the
time, is accused of dubious transactions:

> Die werden nun zum zweitenmal beraubt; vor vierzig Jahren, bei Kriegsende
> durch deutsche Kommunisten im Solde des Kremls – jetzt durch ihre Treuhand,
> deren Beamte den Einheimischen gnädigst gestatten, eine Vorortkneipe an der
> Ausfallstraße Rixdorf-Ost zu erwerben, – nie aber die Ecke Friedrichstraße/
> Untern Linden![30]

Despite the fact that Hochhuth presents us with a long conversation
between a lawyer and Rohwedder, the play is not a genuine platform
for an exchange of ideas. Instead of offering room for thought, Hochhuth persuades the audience of his central hypothesis, namely that
Ossis are good, and *Wessis* are bad. This black and white portrayal of
East and West reduces the play into a mere vehicle of information,
and thus the characters become mouthpieces of Hochhuth's views. For
this reason, and for its lack of controversy, it has been argued that the
play becomes little more than propaganda.[31]

In all thirteen scenes, Hochhuth expands on the greed and the
ruthlessness of the West Germans, who merely came to the East in
order to make profit. In his view it is therefore not surprising that
Karsten Rohwedder – in reality and in the first scene of the play –
becomes the victim of political murder. In an interview Hochhuth
maintains:

---

29   'Was wird aus dem größeren Deutschland? Ein Gespräch mit Alexander Weigel
      für *Sinn und Form*, 4 (1991)', in Heiner Müller, *Gesammelte Irrtümer 3*,
      Frankfurt/M. 1994, pp.123–8, p.125.
30   Rolf Hochhuth, *Wessis in Weimar*, Munich 1994, p.25.
31   David Barnett, 'Tactical Realisms: Rolf Hochhuth's *Wessis in Weimar* and
      Franz Xaver Kroetz's *Ich bin das Volk*', in Williams, Parkes, and Preece (eds.),
      'Whose story?', Bern 1998, pp.181–96: pp.182–7.

Daher bleibt ein Meuchelmord zwar ethisch unhaltbar, aber er mußte voraus-
gesehen werden von jedem, der Geschichte kennt. Wer so etwas wie Rohwedder tut, der mußte wissen, was auf ihn zukommen könnte.[32]

(An assassination may be ethically indefensible, but it had to be foreseen by
anyone who knows history. Anybody who does what Rohwedder did ought to
know what is in store for him.)

Whilst Hochhuth indirectly calls for revenge on the part of the East
Germans, the attitude of one of the most famous East German playwrights, Volker Braun, is rather plaintive and passive. Shortly after
the *Wende*, the East German playwright expressed his culture shock in
view of the reunited Germany with his play *Iphigenie in Freiheit*
(1990),[33] which depicts how Iphigenie becomes the victim of the post-
socialist era. In contrast to Goethe's drama *Iphigenie auf Tauris*
(1779), for example, Iphigenie is quickly subjected to the rules of
capitalism. Braun summarizes this with a simple 'equation':
'ELEKTRIFIZIERUNG MINUS SOWJETMACHT / Gleich Kapita-
lismus'.[34] The audience is presented with a couple of bodiless voices
that are echoing inside Iphigenie's head, thus becoming a skullscape
that mirrors Braun's own thoughts, namely the feeling of isolation
which beset many East Germans after the immediate euphoria which
followed the demolition of the Berlin Wall. Even the sky begins to
look like an iron wall, merely echoing the words which are spoken.
Harking back to the notion of the iron age in ancient mythology, this
dark image anticipates an age of war and destruction. The Cold War
period of the 'Iron Curtain' is therefore superseded by another era of
hostility and ignorance. In his *Büchner-Preis* speech, Volker Braun
addresses the events of 1989 from the viewpoint of the duped and
overpowered East German:

Der Abbruch der Alternativen zur bürgerlichen Gesellschaft im Augenblick, da
diese selbst verschwindet, bewirkt die Spannung, das Drama, den kopflosen

---

32   Rolf Hochhuth, 'Das Bekenntnis. Im *manager magazin* Interview: Die
      kalkulierten Provokationen eines professionellen Dramatikers', in *Wessis in
      Weimar*, Munich 1994, pp.263–71: p.264.
33   Volker Braun, *Iphigenie in Freiheit*, Frankfurt/M. 1990.
34   Braun, *Iphigenie*, p.27.

Kampf unserer gegenwärtigen Aufführung, durch die, Sie hören es, Büchners Figuren wie lauter Planeten ihre Fragen schleppen.[35]

(The lack of alternatives to bourgeois society at that very moment when bourgeois society itself is disappearing, triggers the tension, the drama, the headless battle of our current production, through which, you can hear, Büchner's figures drag their questions as if they were planets.)

According to Braun, the victory of capitalism entails the complete destruction of his East German homeland. As the former GDR was rapidly transformed into an offshoot of the West German state, its authenticity seemed to be erased from the face of the earth. The painful loss of the socialist utopia is also depicted in Braun's play *Böhmen am Meer* (1992).[36] It takes place in a dystopian setting, a polluted island in the middle of nowhere, in which the Czech idealist Pavel – a follower of the Prague Spring of 1968 – is eventually overpowered by the capitalist Bardolph and the former communist Michail. After the collapse of the East-West divide, Bardolph and Michail become friends. The play ends with a triumphant Bardolph walking away and announcing that the new capitalist 'paradise' is about to begin. During an uprising on the island, Pavel is shot dead, and finally dies in a world which is devoid of positive features and reigned only by money. Just like Iphigenie, Pavel can be regarded as an alias for the writer Braun, who after the *Wende* faced a major crisis that threatened to stifle his creativity. This crisis becomes apparent in Pavel's last monologue:

Die Julischen Alpen. Ich war, im Traum, vom Weg abgewichen und sofort, in einem Taumel, aus der Straße geweht, das Geräusch der Panzerketten erlosch im Dröhnen des Autoverkehrs, eine fremde, große Landschaft, der Luftstrom riß meine Taschen und Koffer auf und verstreute meine Sachen, alles was mir gehört hatte, und auch die Gedanken flogen mir aus dem Kopf und zerklirrten auf dem Asphalt, [...] es mußte schnell jaja oder nein gesagt werden, und ich konnte doch immer erst nach einer Umarmung einen Gedanken fassen, es blieb mir nur in der Hast, mich selbst zu umarmen und auch das durfte ich nicht merken lassen – all das, was man sagen möchte und nie sagt, was man

---

35   Volker Braun, *Die Verhältnisse zerbrechen. Rede zur Verleihung des Georg-Büchner-Preises 2000*, Frankfurt/M., 2000, p.28.
36   Volker Braun, *Böhmen am Meer*, Frankfurt/M. 1992.

empfinden möchte ... den Sturm, in der harten Geometrie der Geschichte die
hellen, getünchten Schluchten, und ich sah den Fanatismus ihrer Faltungen, die
Deckgebirge, Schlacke, eine Gebrauchsanweisung PROSPERITÄT, die Waren-
halde von Milano, in die sich Lastwagen gruben, ARIEL IN DEN HAUPT-
WASCHGANG, ah DIE LUFT UND DIE WELT, DIE ICH NICHT SUCHTE,
ein Verbrechen, rasch, daß ich ins Nichts falle, ich kannte doch etwas Wildes,
Regelloses in meinen Regungen, das keine Form annehmen wollte, eine Freiheit, die aus einer festen Tiefe kam, aus einem Massiv, das ich in mir spürte.[37]

This passage takes up the topos of the wandering poet, like for
example the self in Schiller's poem *Der Spaziergang*, where the poet
seeks inspiration on a long walk up the mountains. In a similar manner
to the wanderer in Schiller's poem, Pavel walks into the mountains,
yet he is far from inspired by the landscape surrounding him. Unlike
Schiller's enlightened self, Pavel is blown away and his thoughts are
shattered. He is hardly able to decipher the message contained in the
crevices of the blasted mountains, which is obviously a symbol for
Braun's own traumatic experience of loss after 1989.

The haste with which the events around Pavel follow one another
leaves him dizzy and confused, so that he can only embrace himself.
The course of history is like a storm raging across bleak, rugged
mountains. To the susceptible self, history becomes visible, its twisted
course lies open to the eye of the wanderer. The landscape unfolds its
palimpsest, yet the layers of memory are cut to pieces, which renders
them practically illegible. The strata of memory contained in the
layers of rock is hardly accessible to the analytic mind. Bedazzled, the
wanderer can just about decipher the hidden message of the scenery:
all he sees is fanaticism lurking in the crevices, barely glossed over by
cheap paint. The self, or Pavel, voices fears in view of an estranged
environment. If the past had been difficult because of the restraints of
dictatorship, the present is even worse. The swift changes in history
destroy traditions and values: Prospero becomes prosperity, and Ariel
is associated with a well-known brand of washing-powder. After the
capitalists captured the East, life lacks freedom, and freedom equals a
free fall through existence (*freier Fall*). As this fear invaded many

---

37   Ibid., pp.55–7.

East German intellectuals after reunification,[38] it is not surprising that Pavel commits suicide by exposing himself to the crossfire of revolution (also a symbol of his intellectual position). Pavel remains intellectually grounded in the spring of 1968 and can neither comprehend the victory of capitalism, nor the idea that, according to Bardolph, the East will finally arrive at the materialist 'paradise' of the West. Socialism is nothing more but an absurd joke, a contradiction in terms, or as Michail puts it, an 'Aberwitz.'[39]

The *Wende* as a Wrecked Marriage

Shortly after 1990, the image of the marriage of the two German states became popular. Many caricatures feature East Germany as a weak and meagre bride, whilst the West is usually depicted as the wealthy groom.[40] The cartoonists express what the philosopher Peter Sloterdijk referred to as a 'Machokratie' – reunification as a result of an uncompromising and ruthless implementation of the West German model.[41]

Two ironic plays are Manfred Karge's *Mauer-Stücke* (1990) and Botho Strauß's *Schlußchor* (1990). The second act of Botho Strauß's *Schlußchor* presents us with an encounter between the East German Delia, who rejects the love of the western architect Lorenz after he surprised her in the bathroom. In a similar manner to Delia, who refuses both Lorenz's love and also physical reunion, the 'Neue Bundesländer', the new federal states, strongly opposed the swiftness and boldness of the reunification process, which was perceived as ignoring the feelings of East Germans. The intended parallel to the

---

38   Wolfgang Bialas, *Vom unfreien Schweben zum freien Fall. Ostdeutsche Intellektuelle im gesellschaftlichen Umbruch*, Frankfurt/M. 1996, pp.106–8.

39   Braun, *Böhmen am Meer*, p.60.

40   Compare Susan S. Morrison, 'The Feminisation of the German Democratic Republic in Political Cartoons 1989–1990', *Journal of Popular Culture*, 52 (1991), 35–51.

41   Peter Sloterdijk, *Versprechen auf Deutsch. Rede über das eigene Land*, Frankfurt/M. 1990, p.9.

Greek myth of Actaion is compounded with mythical imagery, identifying the naked Delia with the Greek goddess. Yet the mythic theme is slightly modified, because after realizing that he will never win her love again, Lorenz shoots himself in front of a mirror during a banquet. The glimpse he caught of her, 'das Versehen,' turns into a pessimistic self-consciousness, induced by his hour-long staring into the mirror.[42] To judge from the slightly exaggerated reaction by Lorenz, it can be concluded that Strauß implicitly mocks the architect's self-critical attitude adopted by many West Germans after the *Wende*.

In Karge's *Mauer-Stücke*, the stereotype of the 'rape' of the GDR is mocked in the scene 'Ostfotze' ('Eastern cunt'), where he playfully picks up on the Nibelungen myth, re-reading it as a parody on the so-called occupation and colonization of the GDR. The scene begins with the West Germans' takeover:

> Wie Gunter, Gernot und Giselher vom Niederrhein mit ihrer
> Schwester Kriemhild nach dem Fall der Mauer in Ostberlin einritten.
> GUNTHER Das Ganze halt. Was diese Straßen im Osten, Brüder, so
> schreckliche Schlaglöcher haben.
> GISELHER Ja, warum ist dem so, sagt an?
> GERNOT Warum Giselher? Na, weil man die nicht exportieren kann.[43]

The reason for their visit to threadbare East Germany is, hardly surprisingly, Gunther's courting of Brunhilde, here an East German waitress. Like his forerunner, the modern Gunther is incapable of satisfying her sexual needs, and asks Sigi, the eastern 'Held der Arbeit' who happens to come along, for assistance. He is easily persuaded to help out, 'UND WÄHREND SIEGFRIED SCHUFTET WIE EIN BULLE VERZEHRT GUNTHER IN DER KÜCHE EINE BUTTERSTULLE.'[44] It is however ironic that, metaphorically speaking, the East helps to rape itself.

---

42   Thomas Oberender suggests that Strauß regards the 'gentle revolution' to be an error, a 'Versehen', something that happened by mistake and cannot be taken back. See Thomas Oberender, 'Die Wiedererrichtung des Himmels: Die "Wende" in den Texten von Botho Strauß', *text & kritik*, 81 (1998), 76–99: 84.
43   Karge, *Mauer-Stücke*, p.165.
44   Ibid., p.174.

In his play *Iphigenie in Freiheit* (1992), Volker Braun presents the 'Anschluss' from the viewpoint of a victim. The protagonist Iphigenie falls prey to her capitalist brother, as after the fall of the wall, he comes to humiliate her a second time:

> Komm an die Kasse, Schwester. An mein Herz.
> Sie ist noch schön, Orest.
> Wenn auch nicht klug.
> In unsere Schule wird die Schöne gehen
> Und rechnen Lernen.
> Mit den Knien, Orest.
> Will ich befreit sein so von einem Bruder.
> ein Bruder der mich ausführt in die Welt.
> Geschminkt gekleidet Iphigenie.
> Iphigenie im Supermarkt.
> Schaufensterpuppe Iphigenie.[45]

In this passage, capitalism is blamed for the disregard of humanity, as Iphigenie is forced to become a prostitute. The free market economy destroys emotional relationships between people, replacing them by trade and money. Iphigenie can thus be seen as a powerful symbol for the duped East Germans as a whole. Braun shows that she is set free by her brother only to be put under the yoke of money. However, the postmodern style underlines that Iphigenie is no longer an individual in the traditional sense, because her mind is divided into a din of voices. The dramatic form of the postmodern pastiche, successfully opposes the principles of consumerism, because the play is not marketable. Moreover, the pastiche dissolves history and resists a logical interpretation of the fall of the Wall. Through a long stream of consciousness, in which several viewpoints are at times discernible, yet cannot be attributed to any one character in particular, the outside world turns into a blurred speech. Statements, quotations, and thoughts are intertwined until they resemble an incoherent babble. *Iphigenie in Freiheit* thus negates the idea of a logical flow of historical events which unfold one after the other; in Braun's play, history becomes incomprehensible.

---

45   Braun, *Iphigenie in Freiheit*, p.19.

Wendehals and Stasi

Even before the heated debates on 'Gesinnungsästhetik'[46] came to the fore, Christa Wolf herself touched on the issue of the opportunist in a speech in 1989. It was she who coined the famous term *Wendehals* ('turncoat'):

> Verblüfft beobachten wir die Wendigen, im Volksmund 'Wendehälse' genannt, die, laut Lexikon, sich 'rasch und leicht einer gegebenen Situation anpassen, sich in ihr geschickt bewegen, sie zu nutzen verstehen.' *Sie* am meisten blockieren die Glaubwürdigkeit der neuen Politik.[47]

> (We watched with amazement those contortionists, in the vernacular 'Wendehälse', who, according to the dictionary, are able 'to adapt quickly and easily to a given situation, handle it cleverly and make good use of it.' It is they who inhibit the credibility of the new politics.)

Whilst some writers reacted to the Stasi accusations with stunned silence, others such as Sascha Anderson tried to restore their reputation, albeit in vain.[48] The public repentance and theatrical self-assertion of writers such as Anderson is criticized in *Autorenschlachten* (1993), a play by the East German dissident Lutz Rathenow. In this play, Anderson's efforts are hardly more than a cheap way of attracting media attention. In the second scene, we find a writer called Ronald Schinsk who strongly resembles Rainer Schedlinski. Together with a theatre director, Schinsk rehearses a public confession which he plans to present 'spontaneously' in front of the press. The advice of his drama teacher is:

---

46   See Ulrich Greiner, 'Mangel an Feingefühl', *Die Zeit* (1 June 1990).

47   Christa Wolf, 'Sprache der Wende. Rede auf dem Alexanderplatz', in *Auf dem Weg nach Tabou,* Munich 1996, pp.11–3: p.12.

48   Compare Paul Cooke, 'Die volkseigene Opposition? The Stasi and the Alternative Culture in the GDR', *German Politics*, 6/2 (1997), 117–38.

Deine Sätze nicht zu lang, Verschachtelungen meiden. Richte dich nach der Dramaturgie von diesem, ich komme nicht auf den Namen.[49] Sein Geständnis ist Spitze. Bühnenreif: 'Manchmal wußte ich im nachhinein gar nicht, was die eigentlich wollten. Irgendeiner mußte doch auch mit denen reden. Mir war, als ob die, wirklich, gerade nichts besseres zu tun hatten und einfach mal vorbeischauen wollten, was es so Neues gibt.' Atemtechnik! Nicht an der falschen Stelle pausieren.[50]

Here, Rathenow vents his anger about those writers whose allegedly honest speeches only served one purpose: to secure enough media attention that would enable them to sell their memoirs. In an interview, Rathenow explicitly criticizes this hypocrisy:

Sie versuchen ihre Vergangenheit, als Oppositioneller zum Beispiel, auszuschlachten. Dabei bleibt unklar, inwieweit sie sich, um sich in den Medien gut verkaufen zu können, verstellen.[51]

(They try to gain from their past, for instance, as a dissident. But it remains unclear how much they have to disguise themselves in order to sell themselves efficiently to the media.)

As Rathenow criticizes his own fellow citizens, his views expressed in *Autorenschlachten* contradict the simple East-West scheme mentioned earlier. The play of the former dissident shows that East German playwrights cannot simply be dismissed as self-pitying and tragic; Volker Braun is therefore not typical of the East German point of view, but has to be regarded as an exception.

Even more so, ten years into reunification, Christoph Hein also adopts an ironic attitude towards his fellow citizens. In his drama *In Acht und Bann* (1999), Hein revives the knights of the round table of his famous pre-1989 play *Die Ritter der Tafelrunde* (1985).[52] A

---

49   In the manuscript that Rathenow sent me he had crossed out the name 'Rainer Schedlinski' and replaced it by 'ich komme nicht auf den Namen' ('I cannot think of the name').

50   Lutz Rathenow, *Autorenschlachten* (1993), unpublished manuscript, p.9. Quoted by consent of the author.

51   Quoted in 'Sich von den Verhältnissen freischreiben: Der Schriftsteller Lutz Rathenow über die Beziehungen von DDR-Literatur und Staatssicherheit', in *Berliner Zeitung* (10 June 1993).

52   Christoph Hein, 'Die Ritter der Tafelrunde', *Theater Heute*, 7 (1989), 27–35.

decade into reunification, however, things look quite different. The knights are now locked up in a mental asylum, yet refuse to acknowledge that they are no longer in power. Despite this, Keie, Orilus and Lanzelot still work on a new constitution that bears the traits of a dictatorship masked by a democratic cloak. Hein thus mocks the *Ostalgie* of the political hardliners who lost their influence. The character of Parzival remains central to the play, but unlike in *Die Ritter der Tafelrunde*, he has now changed his mind and developed into an uncritical West German capitalist. Whilst he had once criticized Socialism as an unachievable chimera,[53] he now denies any responsibility for his actions, and refuses to acknowledge that he even compromised at the time. As Parzival intends to become a top floor manager in a big West German firm, he distances himself from the dissidents in the GDR, and desperately tries to appear as an unpolitical person:

> ARTUS Aber wir haben doch alles in der Tafelrunde besprochen, jede Maßnahme. [...]
> PARZIVAL Ich kannte die Details wirklich nicht, Artus. Wenn ich nur ein Wort davon erfahren hätte, das hätte ich nie zugelassen. Das hat doch mein Anwalt sehr überzeugend beweisen können, nicht wahr? Während der Gerichtsverhandlung sind mir ja die Tränen gekommen, als ich von diesen Details hörte. Hast du das nicht bemerkt? [...]
> Ich konnte ja nichts tun gegen euch. Weil ich nichts wusste. Und in der Artus-Runde war ich im Grunde in der inneren Emigration. Ich gehörte nicht zum Widerstand, aber zur inneren Emigration.
> ARTUS Ihr wart alle dagegen, wie? Ich merke schon, ich habe das alles alleine gemacht. Nun, zumindest muß ich damals sehr fleißig gewesen sein.[54]

With biting irony, Hein unmasks the self-pity of Parzival as the bad acting of a traitor who wants to escape punishment. After the *Wende*, he does not want to be involved with anything to do with the old regime since this could tarnish his reputation. As a model citizen of the new Germany, Parzival quickly adapts to the new circumstances and after his release from prison he intends to become a top-level manager. He is thus a prime example of those intellectuals who immediately after the fall of the Wall turned their backs on the ideals of the

---

53   Hein, 'Tafelrunde', 30.
54   Christoph Hein, 'In Acht und Bann', in *Stücke*, Berlin 1999, pp.85–128: pp.100f.

revolutionaries. Moreover, Hein hints at the fact that many collabo-
rators refused to own up to the crimes against humanity which they
tolerated, even if they did not actively commit them; similar to
Honecker, Artus obviously did not commit all the crimes on his own.

The intellectual turncoat aside, the *Wendehals* often features as a
member of the police. It is therefore hardly surprising that this cliché
is taken up by three playwrights: in Herbert Achternbusch's *Auf
verlorenem Posten*, in Manfred Karge's *Mauer-Stücke,* and in Einar
Schleef's *Deutsche Sprache schwere Sprache* (2000). In all three
plays, the opportunist appears to be a harmless idiot, far from being a
responsible member of a social movement.

Achternbusch's *Auf verlorenem Posten* (1989) implicitly accuses
the East Germans of not really having staged a revolution at all,
presenting them as useless and braindead. Written in four days over
Christmas 1989, the farce is a montage of a wrecked marriage,
pseudo-philosophical talk about politics, news reports about the
uprising in Romania, the massacre of Temesvar, and the Nativity. It
opens with the monologue of a disorientated East German soldier. A
former artillery general, who is not even able to pronounce his
military rank correctly, is cuckolded by his wife, undertakes a joyless
trip to Italy in order to rid himself of his claustrophobia after forty
years of Socialism, and finally marries a character which is referred to
as 'Das Glück'. Despite the artificially constructed happy ending, the
play focuses on the downsides of this sudden freedom, since the
former general seems unable to take life into his own hands.

According to Achternbusch, who wrote his play as an immediate
response to the 'gentle' revolution, the term 'revolution' is not an
inappropriate description of what really happened. Although the
former general is now free, he cannot get used to it, and instead,
freedom turns out to be rather frightening. He complains, for instance,
that he cannot seem to put the correct 'Akzent' on the things he
encounters, because old accents whirl through his body until they
resemble a Swastika. It is quite telling that he is unable to get rid of

the party symbols in him, a metaphor for the fact that the GDR
allegedly failed to really enlighten its populace about their Nazi past.[55]

> Mein Gefühl ist marod, so marod – Ein Knattern geht durch meinen Leib. Und
> wenn das Knattern laut genug ist – von vorne, und wenn ich hinten ein leises
> Knattern höre wie von ferne, denke ich: Ich bin zwei. Zwei Artillengenerale aus
> der DDR. Macht zwei Begrüßungsgelder – oh mein Bauch! Ich krümmte mich
> zu lange in der DDR.[56]

Here we encounter a ridiculous man, who misses out on the importance of the political events around him because he is mainly concerned with his stomach. As his illness is seen as the direct result of
his cringing under the GDR authorities, Achternbusch depicts him as a
man, who does not really understand what is happening around him.
Although the general finds himself in the midst of a revolution, he is
neither able to take part nor to comprehend it. The events of 1989 are
thus merely a backdrop for the identity crisis of a man who is everything but a revolutionary. *Auf verlorenem Posten* thus employs common stereotypes to mock the East German turncoat.

A similarly ridiculous character is presented in Karge's *Mauer-
Stücke*. During the fall of the Wall, an East German border guard slips
through a hole in the wall and quickly dresses himself in the uniform
of the West, only too ready to change his allegiance. This opportunistic
behaviour is criticized by his dog, and in a typically farcical dialogue,
the man and his dog start to squabble over ethical matters. In view of
the fact that Karge mocks the dramatic style of the eighteenth century,
it is telling that Karge uses silly rhymes instead of sophisticated style
to depict this conflict. The pathos of Schiller's drama, especially his
Wilhelm Tell, is mocked. The famous scene concerning Geßler's hat
and the peoples' refusal to greet it is turned into a mock debate about
ethical behaviour:

---

55   In the GDR, the Wall was perceived as the anti-fascist shield, and anti-fascism
      was used to legitimize the political system, although it was acted out rather
      superficially. This unsatisfactory approach to the Nazi past is perceived to have
      caused a dramatic rise in right-wing extremism in East Germany after reunifica-
      tion. See Marcus Neureiter, *Rechtsextremismus im vereinten Deutschland*,
      Marburg 1996, pp.36–8.
56   Achternbusch, *Auf verlorenem Posten*, p.15.

> DER HUND Ich warn dich, Soldat, laß diesen Scheiß.
> Herunter den Hut, oder ich beiß.
> DER SOLDAT Sind Sie von Sinnen, Gefreiter Fritz.
> Ich sag, Gehorsamsverweigerer sitz.
> *Der Hund pariert.*
> DER SOLDAT Hut oder Nichthut, das ist die Frage.
> Was ists, was ich auf dem Kopfe trage?[57]

By means of a caricature of the eighteenth-century drama *Wilhelm Tell*, Karge unmasks the self-conscious attitude of many contemporaries. The soldier here is a far cry from the idealized Tell who refuses to succumb to Geßler's power. In contrast, he cannot seem to change his beliefs fast enough. It is ironic, however, that the dog – normally the classic symbol of an oppressed existence – rebels against the turncoat attitude of his owner. Tell's call for freedom of thought is echoed by the words of an animal.

The mockery of *Wilhelm Tell*, the striving for freedom, has its equivalent in Karge's farcical style. The mixture of allusions to, and altered quotations from, Schiller's text are merged into a parody of the blank verse. In *Mauer-Stücke*, the playwright combines a comedic replica of eighteenth-century verse with a rather clownesque situation, namely the chat between a human being and a dog. It is only a small step from the sublime to the laughable, and Karge thus depicts the events of 1989 as a cheap comedy, in which actors simply swapped sides without changing their minds.

Einar Schleef's *Deutsche Sprache schwere Sprache* (2000) also presents us with a former policeman, Herr Meyer. Whilst the fall of the Wall is showing on television, Meyer has already rid himself of his SED party-membership in order to switch to the West German police force:

> TRUDE, ELLY, LOTTE Genosse Meyer!
> MEYER Herr Oberamtmann, wenn ich bitten darf.
> TRUDE, ELLY, LOTTE Genosse sind wir gewesen.
> MEYER Ich bin das Aushängeschild unseres Kreises, der aktive Widerstand.

---

57   Karge, *Mauer-Stücke*, p.159.

TRUDE, ELLY, LOTTE Wir gratulieren, was ehemals ein Genosse war.
[...]
MEYER [...] Bin pünktlichst aus der Partei ausgeschieden auf eigenen
Antrag, noch die Kurve gekriegt [...].[58]

Meyer has no qualms about changing his political beliefs overnight,
leaving the three old women completely flabbergasted. The sceptical
attitude towards Meyer is expressed in a chorus-like style which is
typical of Schleef's theatre work. Schleef merges the three voices into
one, so that the women practically form a chorus that critically comments on Meyer's behaviour. This results in an anti-realistic dialogue,
in which the actual events appear distanced and take on a deliberately
artificial air. Here, language as a medium is emphasized by means of
an unnaturally shortened, often ungrammatical sentence structure. As
Schleef does not depict a realistically polished dialogue, he emphasizes the contradictions and oddities of the year 1989 through a highly
artificial dialogue. He opposes the 'Nationalrausch'[59] displayed by
politicians through his own artistic resistance which refuses easy consumption. *Deutsche Sprache schwere Sprache* is not an easily marketable product. The role of Schleef's dramatic art is thus to engender
artistic alternatives to consumerism, and to call the perceived reality,
the 'Mauershow', into question. In the same vein, the three women
remain truthful to their name 'Totentrompeten', that is, 'the trumpets
of the dead', which is the German name of the 'black chanterelle', a
mushroom that grows in the dark, also known as *craterellus cornu-
copioides*. Despite the euphoria around the three women, they stay
distanced and critical towards the historical events. As they refuse to
participate in the celebrations, the audience is encouraged to view the
fall of the Wall as a media-generated 'spectacle'.

---

58   Einar Schleef, *Deutsche Sprache schwere Sprache. Totentrompeten 3*, in
     Totentrompeten 1–4, Frankfurt/M. 2002, pp.171–225: p.222.
59   Compare Wolfgang Herles, *Nationalrausch*, Munich 1990.

Conclusion

Where does the post-1989 drama stand with respect to the two German identities? Are the terms 'Ostidentität' and 'Westidentität' merely a handy excuse to retire to the 'Schmollwinkel' ('sulking corner') of the intellectuals, as Günter Kunert once phrased it?[60] Is the *Wendedrama* another brick in the 'Wall inside people's heads'? Is it really true that German literature can be separated neatly in two strands, thus confirming the negative verdict by Iris Radisch:

> Ironie, Indifferenz und Konsum im Westen. Ideale, Ernst und Seele im Osten. Das war der vergröberte Schattenriß der neuen deutschen Selbstbilder, wie er in den Werken der jüngeren ostdeutschen Autoren in der ersten Hälfte der 90er Jahre nachzulesen war.[61]
>
> (Irony, indifference and consumerism in the West. Ideals, seriousness and soulfulness in the East. That was the rough silhouette of the new self-image as it could be encountered in the texts of the younger East German authors in the first half of the 1990s.)

At first, the judgement which Radisch herself called a 'Milchbubenrechnung' ('naïve fallacy') sounds convincing. Particularly in view of the failed attempts to create a united 'Kulturnation'; according to Roberts, cultural life tends to split into an eastern, more literary culture, on the one hand, and a shallow western media culture, on the other.[62] This division is apparent in the cultural images of the *Wendehals* and the colonizing of the GDR. As regards ironic West German dramas by Achternbusch and Strauß, which depict the *Wende* in terms of a farcical event, and the existential crisis expressed in Braun's plays, the East-West distinction seems to hold true. Whilst the first two depict the ridiculous side of the gentle revolution, Braun portrays

---

60   Günter Kunert, 'Unsere Identität', in *Der Sturz vom Sockel*, Munich 1992, pp.10–13: p.13.

61   Iris Radisch, 'Es gibt zwei deutsche Gegenwartsliteraturen in Ost und West!', in Gerhard Fischer and David Roberts (eds.), *Schreiben nach der Wende*, Tübingen 2001, pp.1–14: p.5.

62   David Roberts, 'Schreiben nach der Wende', in Fischer and Roberts (eds.), *Schreiben nach der Wende*, pp.xi–xvi: p.xii.

his characters, especially Iphigenie, as victims of history twice over. He shows how the East Germans were liberated from the socialist regime only to be subjected to capitalism. However, the more plays one considers, the more the East-West scheme becomes questionable.

Comparing Braun's despair to the mockery that is at the core of Karge's and Strauß's farces, it looks indeed as if the division into the tragical East and ironic West could be maintained. Yet it must not be forgotten that both Strauß and Karge were also born in the GDR, and can thus serve as a prime example of former East Germans who distance themselves from the self-pitying perspective of the East. The cliché is further weakened by West German authors such as Hochhuth, who takes the economic consequences of reunification seriously. Placing himself in the position of an advocate for the deprived East, Hochhuth takes the West Germans to court, as it were, and presents the audience with meticulously researched cases that prove the injustice inflicted on the East Germans. By contrast, Braun does not adopt a superior viewpoint, but presents himself and his characters as the victims of reunification. Nevertheless, Braun is probably the only East German playwright who fits the cliché of the 'tragic' East German. He casts himself as a defender of the suppressed East Germans, and exhibits the injustice inflicted on the East in his play *Wessis in Weimar*. Just as Hochhuth does not fit the pattern of the ironic West, some East German writers do not match the cliché of the tragic East.

In view of the plays discussed here, it can be concluded that the post-1989 plays cannot be subsumed under the simple East-West divide. The plays do not match the stereotype of the self-pitying East Germans. In their typically ironic fashion, Rathenow and Hein are overtly critical of the goings-on in the East after reunification: Both *Autorenschlachten* and *In Acht und Bann* mock the *Ostalgie*, the nostalgic lament for the past. The plays by Hein and Rathenow are examples of East German texts that do take an ironic stance on such issues as the opportunist or the concept of *Ostalgie*. In *In Acht und Bann*, Hein presents the *Wendehälse* as inmates of a mental asylum who are unable to understand that the world around them has changed fundamentally. Rathenow's *Autorenschlachten* points at the hypocritical attitude of writers, who now try to become successful in the West despite the fact that they had worked as informal helpers of the Stasi.

As far as the plays by Achternbusch, Karge und Schleef are concerned, the cultural clash of East and West Germany is presented through an artificially construed language that also emphasizes the media-orientated elements of the velvet revolution, exhibiting it as the caricature of an entertaining media event. *Auf verlorenem Posten*, *Deutsche Sprache schwere Sprache*, and *Mauer-Stücke* present the year 1989 through the distorting lens of comedy and farce. The emigrated East German whose heart always beats for his 'Heimat', Einar Schleef, retains a distanced view of the *Wende* by presenting it as an artificial spectacle. By means of a concise language, he portrays the years 1989 as an artificial event, the causes and effects of which are dissected on the stage.

No sharp line between East and West German playwriting can be drawn. To sum up, the gap is smaller than commonly thought, at least as far as dramatic texts are concerned. Although this is not an attempt to ignore existing differences, this essay nevertheless demonstrates that the Germans are probably a little less 'vernagelt'[63] than is generally believed today.

Bibliography

Albrecht, Terrance, *Rezeption und Zeitlichkeit des Werkes Christoph Heins*, Frankfurt/M. 2000.

Anderson, Benedict, *Imagined Communities: Reflections on the Origin and Spread of Nationalism*, London 1983.

Anz, Thomas (ed.), *Es geht nicht um Christa Wolf. Der Literaturstreit im vereinten Deutschland*, Frankfurt/M. 1995.

---

63   Laurence Mc Falls, '"Ein Brett vor dem Kopf". Zur politischen Kultur der deutschen Teilung', in Claudia Mayer-Iswandy (ed.), *Die Nation. Transatlantische Perspektiven zur Geschichte eines Problems,* Tübingen 1994, pp.223–30: p.224: 'Die Mauer im Kopf existiert. Dies allerdings wäre an sich kein weiteres Problem, wenn das Brett vor dem Kopf ihr Abbauen nicht verhindern würde.' ('The wall in the mind exists. That would not be a major problem, if people's obsessions were not to prevent the wall being torn down.')

Barnett, David, 'Tactical Realisms: Rolf Hochhuth's Wessis in Weimar and Franz Xaver Kroetz's Ich bin das Volk', in Williams, Parkes, and Preece (eds.), *Whose story?*, pp.181–196.

Becker, Peter von, '"Die Wahrheit, leise und unerträglich." Ein Gespräch mit Heiner Müller, von Peter von Becker', *Theater heute* Jahrbuch (1995), 9–30.

Berg, Stefan, 'Die neue deutsche Sippenhaft', *Der Spiegel*, 39 (23 September 1996), 51–3.

Bialas, Wolfgang, *Vom unfreien Schweben zum freien Fall. Ostdeutsche Intellektuelle im gesellschaftlichen Umbruch*, Frankfurt/M. 1996.

Biermann, Wolf, 'Duftmarke setzen', in *Klartexte im Getümmel*, Cologne 1990, pp.316–32

Böttiger, Helmut, 'Ostmoral', *Frankfurter Rundschau* (12 January 1995).

Bohn, Rainer (ed.), *Mauer-Show: Das Ende der DDR, die deutsche Einheit und die Medien*, Berlin 1992.

Braun, Volker, *Iphigenie in Freiheit*, Frankfurt/M. 1990.

——, *Böhmen am Meer*, Frankfurt/M. 1992.

——, *Die Verhältnisse zerbrechen. Rede zur Verleihung des Georg-Büchner-Preises 2000*, Frankfurt/M. 2000.

Cooke, Paul, 'Die volkseigene Opposition? The Stasi and the Alternative Culture in the GDR', *German Politics*, 6/2 (1997), 117–38.

Fischer, Gerhard, and David Roberts (eds.), *Schreiben nach der Wende. Ein Jahrzehnt deutscher Literatur 1989–1999*, Tübingen 2001.

Gauck, Joachim, 'Wut und Schmerz der Opfer', *Die Zeit* (10 January 1995).

Goethe, Johann Wolfgang von, Faust. *Eine Tragödie, in Werke. Hamburger Ausgabe*, ed. Erich Trunz, Hamburg 1959, III.

Grass, Günter, *Ein Schnäppchen namens DDR. Letzte Reden vor dem Glockengeläut*, Frankfurt/M. 1990.

Greiner, Ulrich, 'Mangel an Feingefühl', *Die Zeit* (1 June 1990).

Hein, Christoph, 'Die Ritter der Tafelrunde', *Theater Heute*, 7 (1989), 27–35.

——, 'In Acht und Bann', in *Stücke*, Berlin 1999, pp.85–128.

Herles, Wolfgang, *Nationalrausch*, Munich 1990.

Hochhuth, Rolf, *Wessis in Weimar*, Munich 1994.

Karge, Manfred, Mauer-Stücke, in *Die Eroberung des Südpols*, Berlin 1996, pp.129–208.

Königsdorf, Helga, *1989 oder ein Moment der Schönheit. Eine Collage aus Briefen, Gedichten, Texten*, Berlin-Weimar 1991.

Korngiebel, Wilfried, and Jürgen Link, 'Von einstürzenden Mauern, europäischen Zügen und deutschen Autos. Die Wiedervereinigung in Bildern und Sprachbildern der Medien', in Bohn (ed.), *Mauer-Show*, pp.31–54.

Kunert, Günter, 'Unsere Identität', in *Der Sturz vom Sockel*, Munich 1992, pp.10–13.

Lindgens, Monika, and Susanne Mahle, 'Vom Medienboom zur Medienbarriere. Massenmedien und Bürgerbewegungen im gesellschaftlichen Umbruch in der DDR und im vereinten Deutschland', in Bohn (ed.), *Mauer-Show*, pp.95–112.

Link, Jürgen, *Die Struktur des Symbols in der Sprache des Journalismus. Zum Verhältnis literarischer und pragmatischer Symbole*, Munich 1978.

——, 'Wie weich landen die Wendeturbulenzen des Europäischen Hauses? Kollektivsymbolik und aktuelle (De)Normalisierungsschübe', *kulturRevolution*, 23 (1990), 58–69.

McFalls, Laurence, '"Ein Brett vor dem Kopf". Zur politischen Kultur der deutschen Teilung', in Claudia Mayer-Iswandy (ed.), *Die Nation. Transatlantische Perspektiven zur Geschichte eines Problems*, Tübingen 1994, pp.223–30.

McGowan, Moray, 'Beating time? Fidelio in Dresden, 7–8 October 1989', in Mark Ward (ed.), *Proceedings of the Scottish Conference of University Teachers 2003.*

Morrison, Susan S., 'The Feminisation of the German Democratic Republic in Political Cartoons 1989–1990', *Journal of Popular Culture*, 52 (1991), 35–51.

Müller, Elfriede, 'Warum flutscht das alles so gut durch?', *Theater Heute* Jahrbuch (1995), 152–3.

Müller, Heiner, *Gesammelte Irrtümer 3*, Frankfurt/M. 1994.

Neureiter, Marcus, *Rechtsextremismus im vereinten Deutschland*, Marburg 1996.

Oberender, Thomas, 'Die Wiedererrichtung des Himmels. Die "Wende" in den Texten von Botho Strauß', text & kritik, 81 (1998), 76–99.

Probst, Lothar, 'Ost-West Unterschiede und das kommunitäre Erbe der DDR', in Lothar Probst (ed.), *Differenz in der Einheit, Über die kulturellen Unterschiede der Deutschen in Ost und West*, Berlin 1999, pp.15–27.

Radisch, Iris, 'Es gibt zwei deutsche Gegenwartsliteraturen in Ost und West!', in Fischer and Roberts (eds.), *Schreiben nach der Wende*, pp.1–14.

Roberts, David, 'Schreiben nach der Wende', in Fischer and Roberts (eds.), *Schreiben nach der Wende*, pp.xi–xvi.

Schleef, Einar, *Deutsche Sprache schwere Sprache*. Totentrompeten 3, Totentrompeten 1–4, Frankfurt/M. 2002, pp.171–225.

Sloterdijk, Peter, *Versprechen auf Deutsch. Rede über das eigene Land*, Frankfurt/M. 1990.

Strauß, Botho, *Schlußchor*, Munich 1991.

Templin, Wolfgang, 'Erst die Wahrheit!', *Die Woche* (22 December 1994).

Ullmann, Wolfgang, 'Die triste Kumpanei der Kollaboration', *Freitag* (20 August 1993).

Wagner, Wolf, *Kulturschock Deutschland. Der zweite Blick*, Hamburg 1999.

Weck, Michael, 'Der ironische Westen und der tragische Osten', *Kursbuch*, 109 (1992), 133–48.

Weninger, Robert, and Brigitte Rosenbacher (eds.), *Wendezeiten – Zeitenwenden. Positionsbestimmungen zur deutschsprachigen Literatur 1945–1995*, Tübingen 1997.

Williams, Arthur, Stuart Parkes, and Roland Smith (eds.), *German Literature at a Time of Change 1989–1990*, Frankfurt/M. 1991.

Williams, Arthur, Stuart Parkes, and Julian Preece (eds.), *'Whose Story?' – Continu-ities in contemporary German-language Literature*, Frankfurt/M. 1998.

Wolf, Christa, 'Die Rede vom Auslöffeln. Zur Sache: Deutschland', *Wochenpost Extra* (3 March 1994).

——, 'Sprache der Wende. Rede auf dem Alexanderplatz', in *Auf dem Weg nach Tabou*, Munich 1996, pp.11–3.

Zizek, Slavoj, 'Eastern Europe's Republic of Gilead', *New Left Review*, 183 (1990), 50–63.

Bernhard Malkmus

'All of them Signs and Characters from the Type-Case of Forgotten Things'[1] – Intermedia Configurations of History in W.G. Sebald

זָכוֹר
Remember what Amalek did to you on your way out of Egypt.
(Deuteronomy 25:17)

I. The Curse of Kronos

In his travelogue *Die Ringe des Saturn. Eine englische Wallfahrt* (1995; *The Rings of Saturn*, 1998), W.G. Sebald uses the leitmotifs of *peregrinatio* and peripatetic rumination as spatial vectors to migrate through various realms and layers of the historical imagination. During his seemingly aimless wandering through the county of Suffolk he witnesses his impressions and figments of imagination turning the fens of East Anglia into a palimpsest of history and histories. The boundary between a very personal stream of consciousness and a collective dimension of history is blurred, the two voices intermingle and are inextricably intertwined. A certain uncanny effect ensuing from this balance is also due to the clairvoyant way in which Sebald moves from one association to the next, partly guided by his own idiosyncratic taste, partly mysteriously guided by the fields of gravity that history imposed upon topography long ago. The use of photographs

---

1   W.G. Sebald, *Austerlitz*, trans. Anthea Bell, Harmondsworth 2001, p.214. 'lauter Buchstaben und Zeichen aus dem Setzkasten der vergessenen Dinge', W.G. Sebald, *Austerlitz*, Frankfurt/M. 2003, p.222.

and images as integral parts of the text underlines this effect of uncanny linkage and mysterious guidance. It is often impossible to determine whether the images function as a trigger of memory or whether
they serve as a subsequent condensation of the rhizome of linguistic
associations governing the stream of consciousness in the text. They
are points of reference within a mnemoscape, and yet they often add
an ambiguous character to the surface structure of the narrative.

Many of these visual inlays in the literary texture simultaneously
condense and render opaque the wide range of references they imply.
At one point, for example, the reader is caught up in a reflection
on the malaise of the increasing rationalization and acceleration of
modern life:

> Gleich ob man über Neufundland fliegt oder bei Einbruch der Nacht über das
> von Boston bis Philadelphia reichende Lichtergewimmel, über die wie Perlmutt
> schimmernden Wüsten Arabiens, über das Ruhrgebiet oder den Frankfurter
> Raum, es ist immer als gäbe es keine Menschen, als gäbe es nur das, was sie
> geschaffen haben und worin sie sich verbergen.[2]

> (No matter whether one is flying over Newfoundland or the sea of lights that
> stretches from Boston to Philadelphia after nightfall, over the Arabian deserts
> which gleam like mother-of-pearl, over the Ruhr or the city of Frankfurt, it is as
> though there were no people, only the things they have made in which they are
> hiding.)

This passage is followed by an indefinable photograph showing a
mess of gleaming wires spun around an agglomeration of rocks (Ill.
1). A cobweb of telephone wires and electric cables serves as an
abstract image of the complexity and interrelatedness of modern
times. The reader cannot possibly establish a reference to any concrete
passage in the text except for a very general idea of complexity. The
image derives its haunting effect from the very fact that the reader
intuitively knows that it both refers to something concrete and at the
same time functions as an abstract representation of something beyond
human grasp, of an 'abacus designed to calculate infinity'.[3] At the top

---

2   W.G. Sebald, *Die Ringe des Saturn. Eine englische Wallfahrt*, Frankfurt/M.
     1995, p.113; *Rings of Saturn*, trans. Michael Hulse, London 1995, p.91.
3   'zur Berechnung der Unendlichkeit erfundenen Abakus', ibid., p.112; p.90.

of the following page[4] the reader is given a clue as to what is represented in the photograph. In a whole series of comparisons the increasing complexity of modernity is likened to 'thousands of hoists and winches'[5] in a South African diamond mine. This is also rendered in the stilted intricacies of phrases like 'tied into the networks of a complexity that goes far beyond the power of any one individual to imagine'.[6]

The interesting aspect of this oscillation between a concrete and an abstract dimension of photographs from the viewpoint of reader-response criticism is the fact that it is made part and parcel of an intricate structure of anticipated reactions of the reader. In this case the reader is first tempted to latch on to the abstract level when seeing the picture, although the concrete character of the image is obvious, yet not decipherable. Consequently images never function as mere illustrations, but they also entangle the reader in a subtext of interpretation and anticipation. Images are both trigger and residua of memory; they transcend and undermine temporal (narrative) categories and simultaneously establish an idiosyncratic mnemoscape from where the reader's act of remembering can depart.

The Janus-faced abstract-concrete quality of the photograph analyzed above epitomizes Sebald's concept of historical imagination. His text-image configurations are conceptually new. They are not primarily attempting to defamiliarize conventional modes of perception in the wake of the Russian formalists, DADA experimentalism or the Beat generation and their German followers like Rolf Brinkmann,[7] nor are they structured dialectically like Alexander Kluge's literary work in the 1960s and 1970s. They are intermedial in the proper sense of

---

4   As Sebald's publisher Michael Krüger pointed out in a conference discussion in Brighton (June 2003), Sebald always took pains to have images placed in exactly the position where he wanted them to be. This does not necessarily hold for the English translations of his books.

5   'Tausende von Seilzügen und Winden', Sebald, *Die Ringe des Saturn*, p.114; Sebald, *Rings of Saturn*, p.91.

6   'eingespannt in Netzwerke von einer das Vorstellungsvermögen eines jeden einzelnen bei weitem übersteigenden Kompliziertheit', ibid., pp.113f; p.91.

7   See *Rom, Blicke*; *Schnitte*.

the word as 'a differentiating form of an in-between.'[8] The reader is caught up in the interstices between narrative text and visual subtext. It is often impossible to disentangle these two dimensions in Sebald because he is aiming at a *topos* which arises in the in-between, in the mutual illustration, anticipation and undermining of text and image.

The aim of this essay is to show that this imaginary third space of intermedia can be seen as representative of current ways of perceiving history. The year 1989 marks a major shift in German self-awareness and its subsequent reflection in literature. It suddenly rendered the notion of *posthistoire*, which had loomed large in the 1970s and 1980s, very problematic, if not anachronistic,[9] and roughly coincides with the passing away of that generation that was actively involved in the Second World War. I shall argue that Sebald's work participates in both developments: he is writing against the notion of *posthistoire* and he is trying to develop a sustainable mnemoscape by rooting narratives in images and vice versa, thereby creating a dialogue between fragments of individual and collective forms of memory. For Sebald, imagining history means thinking of humans as living in 'Zeitrissen', 'rifts of time', exposed to the wrath of time, as his colleague Alexander Kluge famously put it:

> [a] Teil Lebendiger [...], auch Vaterländer und Gemeinwesen, werden wie durch Blitz der Götter ausgesondert aus dem Wirklichen und kommen doch im Möglichen nicht an. Das ist der Fluch des Kronos [...], eines ungezähmten Monstrums, das wir für die Zeit halten.[10]

> ([a] part of the living [...], and also fatherlands and communities, will be separated from the realm of the real as if struck by the lightning bolt of the

---

8   See Joachim Paech, 'Intermedialität. Mediales Differenzial und transformative Figurationen', in Jörg Helbig (ed.), *Intermedialität*, Berlin 1998, pp.14–30: p.16. (Unless otherwise noted, all translations are my own.)

9   See Lutz Niethammer, *Posthistoire. Has History Come to an End?*, London 1992, p.148: 'The posthistory diagnosis sees the social formation as marked to its core by an objective, power-structured process of standardisation, which no longer promises any qualitative movement but is moving towards petrification. Whatever deviates from it is a hangover from prehistory or a posthistorical, aesthetic "as if".'

10 Alexander Kluge, *Chronik der Gefühle*, Frankfurt/M. 2000, I, 126.

Gods – and yet they do not arrive in the realm of the possible. That is the curse of Kronos [...], of an untamed monster which we consider to be time.)

That is what Sebald is up against in his work. History is nesting between what a community agrees upon as a basic vertebra of facts and the multitudes of individual approximations. Sebald creates a literary and visual texture that reflects the complexity of this interface.

Sebald's concept of interspersing his texts with visual material owes a lot to Benjamin's concept of memory as medium of, rather than instrument for, the exploration of the past: 'It is the medium of that which is experienced, just as the earth is the medium in which ancient cities lie buried.'[11] In his work on the Paris arcades, Benjamin also conceived of the archive of history as a medium, as a third space between fragments. The medium character of what Benjamin terms 'archive' and 'memory' tie in with his concept of epistemology and the fact that the perception of reality and the past is always already shot through with contexts that have to be reconstructed. This process of reconstruction is always tinged by the medium, i.e. the archive of collected objects and fragments into which it is inserted, the realm of individual and collective memory within which it is discovered. To a substantial degree this is based on the principles of contiguity and elective affinities. Like Benjamin's historian, who is brought into a dialectic process of thinking about the past in the light of the present situation and vice versa by ordering fragments, Sebald enacts his 'recherche à la temps perdu' by spelling out a series of photographic *tableaux* as a form of resistance to mimetic voyeurism. He creates a realm of translatability and convertibility between non-sensory and sensory correspondences, text and image, context and object. The author becomes a voyeur, who detects idiosyncratic correspondences he can textually process as allegories of cultural memory. Sebald offers a mise en abîme of this triangle of historical subject, present

---

11   'Es ist das Medium des Erlebten wie das Erdreich das Medium ist, in dem die alten Städte verschüttet liegen.' Walter Benjamin, *Ausgraben und Erinnern*, in Walter Benjamin, *Gesammelte Schriften*, IV/1, ed. Rolf Tiedemann and Hermann Schweppenhäuser, Frankfurt/M. 1984, p.400; Walter Benjamin, *Selected Writings II (1927–1934)*, trans. Rodney Livingstone et al., ed. M.W. Jennings, H. Eiland and G. Smith, Cambridge, MA 1999, p.576.

historian-writer and the historical fragments. He evokes stories of re-contextualization as a constant realm of translation between idiosyn-cratic condensations of historical memory and its return into collective topicality. In *Austerlitz* (2001) the reader is confronted with the blurred picture of a porcelain rider on horseback who is just rescuing a female figure; this little sculpture is behind a shop window which faintly reflects the face of Austerlitz or the author taking the photo-graph.[12] The border between the documentary character of the photo-graph and its translation into a discursive code testifying to its genealogy is blurred. The photograph anticipates both the preservation of the historical moment and the mortality of the photographed object.

A meta-reflection on this blurring is the picture of the Nazi book burning in front of the Episcopal residence in Würzburg in Sebald's *Die Ausgewanderten* (1992; *The Emigrants*, 1996, Ill. 2).[13] This photograph encompasses different levels. First, it is a fake, Nazi propaganda material; the picture actually shows a different public gathering and the smoke of the book burning is retouched into the photograph. In a Sebaldian context, this should be read as a demon-stration of how quickly an image becomes part and parcel of a code system. Second, although it is a fake, it is historically true, not in a mimetic sense, of course – the picture probably shows a political rally or a Franconian wine feast –, but in a historical sense: it shows some-thing that actually happened, as written record shows it, without pic-turing it. Third, the narrator cannot disentangle the historical, perso-nal, uncoded direct association from the self-reflexive awareness of the mediality of history in its archival records. By creating this aware-ness the narrator stages himself as the Benjaminian historian ordering fragments of history. These dimensions play into Sebald's text-image configurations of history which cast 'memory' into profile as medium rather than method or instrument. This becomes particularly evident in his last work, *Austerlitz*, which deals with the so-called Kindertrans-porte as a Shoah-related experience.

---

12   Sebald, *Austerlitz*, p.284.
13   W.G. Sebald, *Die Ausgewanderten. Vier lange Erzählungen*, Frankfurt/M. 1994, p.275.

II. *Austerlitz*: Retrieving the Irretrievable

Between the pogrom of November 1938 ('Reichskristallnacht') and the outbreak of the Second World War, 10,000 children aged between three and sixteen from Germany, Austria, the Czech lands and Poland, mostly of Jewish extraction, were issued special visas by the British government and sent off to households all over their new home country, where they often faced a complete change of cultural and social environment and related difficulties. They were supposed to stay only for a couple of months. The outbreak of the Second World War, however, changed the situation completely. Many of the children lost their parents in the following extermination warfare and the Shoah. After the war, some of them returned to their homeland and faced the difficult challenge of reintegrating themselves into a culture and a language they felt largely alienated from; many more stayed in the United Kingdom or moved on to relatives in the United States. For more than forty years their voice was marked by silence, and it was not until 1989 that they started organizing reunions.[14] Only since then have the 'Kinder' – as they proudly call themselves – begun to create a voice for themselves. The 'Reunion of Kindertransporte' in Britain has been meeting since 1989, the American 'Kindertransport Association' since 1990.

There are many reasons for these late reunions, one of them being a very complex psychological situation dominated by survivor guilt. Only after their parents' generation had mostly died (their actual parents often having perished in the Shoah) did they start talking about their traumata in public. Another reason is their increasing exposure to questions of their children and grandchildren, who were less influenced by resentments towards Germany within British or US-American societies. The younger generations were both more detached from the historical events and had a different sense of historicity.

---

14   The most detailed account of the so-called Kindertransporte to date can be found in Rebekka Göpfert, *Der jüdische Kindertransport von Deutschland nach England 1938/9*, Frankfurt/M. 1999.

In Germany this development became particularly prominent after the caesura of 1989. Especially in eastern Germany the overall effect of the generational shift was exacerbated by the sudden drastic change of daily life routines, which seemed to have created a profound sense of transitoriness: 'Warum ich das erzähle? Weil man so schnell vergisst' (Why am I telling this? Because you forget things so quickly), writes Ingo Schulze in his novel *Simple Storys* (1995). 'Dabei ist es gar nicht lange her, dass Ernst und ich noch an dasselbe gedacht und in einer schwarzrot karierten Tasche Konserven mit uns herumgeschleppt haben.' ('But it isn't long since the two of us had still the same thoughts and carried around canned food in a bag with a black and red check pattern.')[15] This short passage about the ephemeral character of memory, of remembrances of things past in the former GDR, epitomizes the cult of memory in the 1990s and the profound awareness of the historicity of a daily life that had changed radically in the course of a few years. The coincidence of the historical breakdown of the ideological polarity between two political systems and the demographic fact that the second post-war generation came of age, triggered a deep awareness of the historicity of the present.

The psychological urge of 'because you forget things so quickly' among both the young generation and the ageing eye witnesses[16] contributed to a paradigmatic shift in conceiving of German history. This moment is exacerbated by the fact that it also marks a first threshold between what Jan Assmann termed 'communicative memory' (referring to Maurice Halbwachs's terminology) and 'cultural memory'. As opposed to the kind of memory and personal historical knowledge that is still communicated and circulated within a certain group or society, 'cultural memory' according to Assmann relies on cultural canons, rites, institutional condensations of expression. The latter form a 'stock of recyclable texts, pictures and rites characteristic of each

---

15   Ingo Schulze, *Simple Storys. Ein Roman aus der ostdeutschen Provinz*, Munich 1999, p.22.

16   The theory that the historical awareness of the historical loss of contemporary witnesses creates a major threshold between communicative and cultural memory, is expressed by the German term 'Letztmaligkeitsthese'.

society and each epoch, a stock by which each society "cultivates" and thereby stabilizes and conveys an image of itself.'[17]

Communicative memory can be likened to the short-term memory of society. '[Es] kennt keine Fixpunkte, die es an eine sich mit fort-schreitender Gegenwart immer weiter ausdehnende Vergangenheit binden würden.' ([It] does not know any vantage points which would bind it to a past that is increasingly expanding within a progressing present.)[18] There are certain generational shifts that change communi-cative memory, the first major one after the death of the contemporary witnesses (after 40–50 years, two generations), the final one after three or four generations, when petrified cultural practices and codes replace the rootedness of historical experience in first-hand experien-ces. The first shift characterizes commemorative culture with regard to the Shoah, the latter marks the situation of the Armenian communities across the world with regard to the genocide inflicted upon the Armenians by the Turks during the First World War. The inflationary interest in the problems of memory in literature and the humanities in Germany and elsewhere can be attributed to these major shifts from a history whose stories are part and parcel of the communicative nexus of a society to a history which does not translate as easily into stories any more, but relies on cultural rituals and institutions in order to remain in the public realm.

With regard to the development of memory culture in post-war West Germany, Aleida Assmann[19] suggests the following categoriza-tion: First, a form of political engineering of the past ('Vergangen-heitspolitik'; 1945–57), which revolved around the key issues of reparations and the amnesty of former NS officials and which was

---

17   '[...] jeder Gesellschaft und jeder Epoche eigentümliche[n] Bestand an Wieder-gebrauchs-Texten, -Bildern und -Riten [...], in deren "Pflege" sie ihr Selbstbild stabilisiert und vermittelt.' Jan Assmann, 'Kollektives Gedächtnis und kulturel-le Identität', in Jan Assmann and Toni Hölscher (eds.), *Kultur und Gedächtnis*, Frankfurt/M. 1988, pp.9–19: p.15.

18   Ibid., p.11.

19   Aleida Assmann and Ute Frevert, *Geschichtsvergessenheit – Geschichtsver-sessenheit. Vom Umgang mit deutschen Vergangenheiten nach 1945*, Stuttgart 1999, pp.140–7.

also marked by a revival of humanistic and religious ways of self-assertion ('Kulturnation'). Second, a critique of these preceding forms of *Vergangenheitsbewältigung* ('coming to terms with the past') in a period which was marked by a more systematic approach to the Nazi past both in terms of the legal system (Auschwitz trial, Eichmann trial) and in terms of academic approaches (critical theory, Frankfurt School), both of which changed the public perception of the past (1958–85). Third, the increasing importance of public commemoration in a time marked by the psychological shifts outlined above (from 1985 onwards). Within this last period, Assmann distinguishes two major trends, namely the political attempt to finally 'come to grips with the past' represented by chancellor Helmut Kohl's symbolic rituals of forgiving and forgetting on the one hand and a commemoration culture concerned with the conservation of the past ('Vergangenheitsbewahrung') associated with the Federal President Richard von Weizsäcker on the other hand. In his speech on the occasion of the fortieth anniversary of the end of the Second World War,[20] Weizsäcker related the German situation to the Chassidic wisdom of seeking reconciliation and salvation through memory and commemoration, through solidarity in memory.

These later changes and shifts in awareness, however, only really took effect in the wake of 1989 and the radical changes it triggered with regard to collective perceptions of the past. While the 1980s were still largely marked by a sense of moving beyond history that was facilitated by the impasse of the Cold War, the sudden historical caesura of 1989 forced official cultures of commemoration to confront each other and mutually question the foundations they were built on.[21] It was only the spark of this collective awareness of living in a historically shaped moment that rekindled a sense of history, historical

---

20   See Peter Reichel, *Politik mit der Erinnerung. Gedächtnisorte im Streit um die nationalsozialistische Vergangenheit*, Munich-Vienna 1995, pp.290–6 for contextualization.

21   See ibid., pp.34–47, for a concise account of historical ideology in the two German states. See also Assmann and Frevert, *Geschichtsvergessenheit*, pp.151–72, pp.234–57. With regard to the psychology of Holocaust survivors narrating experiences and traumata in the two different German states, see Friedhelm Boll, *Sprechen als Last und Befreiung*, Bonn 2003.

legacy and historical responsibility that facilitated the culture of 'Erinnerung' that Weizsäcker had postulated in his speech.

One of the principal features of this idea of a solidarity in memory is the principle of dialogue, of a constant exchange with the past and the way it shapes the present, a principle that can be observed, for example, in the Jewish Museum in Berlin or in the plans for the Holocaust Memorial in Berlin, both of which try to establish a dialogical form of conversing with the past by means of topography and architecture. More than ten years after that decisive caesura, W.G. Sebald wrote a novel in which he described various encounters between a Jewish émigré and a German. The novel is a stream of consciousness, but it is also the product of the conversations between these two characters and it paradigmatically demonstrates a conception of commemoration and memory typical for intellectual discourses on the past in the reunified Germany. One might call the novel the literary embodiment of a certain culture of 'Erinnerung' characteristic of the post-Cold-War era – with the reception of a wider range of voices speaking on the Shoah,[22] with a more pronounced articulation and self-thematization of a German voice within historical discourses, with a sense that certain cultures of dialogical commemoration are the only way out of the predicament of rapid oblivion or petrified rituals:

> Gerade den fiktionalen Darstellungen wird immer mehr Bedeutung zufallen
> […]. Ohne diese persönlichen und durch Gefühle stabilisierten Bezüge aber
> bricht individuelle Erinnerung zusammen. Übrig bleiben dann nur die expressiven Formen des kollektiven Gedächtnisses, die unter solchen Bedingungen
> schlimmstenfalls zur 'Zwangsarbeit' (Wolf Lepenies), bestenfalls zu sinnentleerten Ritualen gerinnen.[23]

> (It is exactly fictional descriptions which will increasingly loom large. […]
> Without these personal references stabilized by feelings, however, individual
> memory collapses. What remains in this case are only the expressive forms of
> collective memory, which under these conditions function as 'forced labour'

---

22   A prime example would be Imre Kértész's novel *Novel of a Man Without Destiny*, which was first published and immediately disregarded in 1975 in Hungary. It only received wider acclaim in the 1990s after its translation into German as *Roman eines Schicksallosen* in 1990 and finally earned him the Nobel Prize.

23   Assmann and Frevert, *Geschichtsvergessenheit*, p.286.

[Wolf Lepenies], if the worst comes to the worst, or at best turn into ritual bereft of any meaning.)

Austerlitz was inspired by the Kindertransporte movement in Britain, in particular by a BBC documentary featuring Susi Bechhöfer's search for her past.[24] In his book Sebald creates a text-image configuration of the Kindertransporte which constitutes both the narrator and the implied reader in a way characteristic of the shift outlined above. The narrative situation is marked by an ageing Kind named Austerlitz who keeps on meeting an exile German (Sebald barely disguises himself) in railway stations across Europe. During the course of their random and coincidental encounters a narrative evolves through the double voice of Austerlitz/narrator which is accompanied, glossed and undermined by the insertion of pictures. Without really ever taking on the form of an actual dialogue, the novel presents a stream of consciousness, which does not allow the two voices to be separated from each other; the novel is in its very fabric the product of two voices merged together.

As much as the narrator is lending Austerlitz his style – the novel's diction is the very opposite of 'oral history' –, Austerlitz is lending the narrator his story as a topography of the past. Towards the end the two figures increasingly merge into each other – in particular when Austerlitz narrates his trip to Terezín. By then it is clear to every reader that the trip to Prague and Terezín and its photographic documentation was done by no other than Sebald himself. This fact is highlighted by a diction that simultaneously expresses the emotional involvement and consternation of both partners in their dialogical exploration of the past. Scrutinizing the items in the ghetto museum in Terezín, Austerlitz/narrator/Sebald ruminates:

> Das alles begriff ich nun und begriff es auch nicht, denn jede Einzelheit, die sich mir, dem, wie ich fürchtete, aus eigener Schuld unwissend Gewesenen, eröffnete auf meinem Weg durch das Museum aus einem Raum in den nächsten und wieder zurück, überstieg bei weitem mein Fassungsvermögen.

---

24   'Whatever happened to Susi' (1991). See also Jeremy Josephs and Susi Bechhöfer, *Rosa's Child. One Woman's Search for her Past*, London 1998.

(I understood it all now, yet I did not understand it, for every detail that was revealed to me as I went through the museum from room to room and back again, ignorant as I feared I had been through my own fault, far exceeded my comprehension.)[25]

Apart from struggling to give back a voice to Austerlitz and his long suppressed traumatic childhood experiences via this specific dia-logical situation and its reduplication in the interlacing of moments of collective and individual memory in the visual dimension of the book, *Austerlitz* also renders a specific German voice appropriating the past as a peripatetic pilgrim in a scarred and raped land- and cityscape. The phrase 'ignorant through your own fault' applies to both the 'Kind', tortured by survivor guilt, and to the German troubled by the perman-ent call of the past. The painstaking diligence with which the narrator/ Sebald reassembles Austerlitz's story and redesigns his historical mnemoscape of wartime Europe can be read as the voice of a German deeply affected by the omnipresence of history, a person who knows that oblivion is stronger and has largely covered up all the historical evidence.

The melancholic strain in Sebald's novel that many critics latched on to, as well as Sebald's art of a mutual illumination of a narrative stream of consciousness and the visual moments of conden-sation and ambiguity, are both representative of a new culture of com-memorating the Shoah and related experiences in Germany at a point in time when a surge of national reassertion in the wake of re-unification, and the clash of two very different official cultures of commemoration in former East and the West Germany, seem to have profoundly changed the ways Germans reflect on recent history:

Die Vielfarbigkeit individueller Erinnerungen verschwindet, das kollektive Ge-dächtnis wird endgültig monochrom und konsolidiert sich als Täter-Gedächtnis. Darin liegt die Chance, dass sich die einzelnen in ihrem persönlichen Umgang mit der Vergangenheit an diesem Kollektivgedächtnis orientieren und seine Botschaften übernehmen.[26]

---

25   Sebald, *Austerlitz*, p.287; *Austerlitz*, trans. Anthea Bell, p.279.
26   Assmann and Frevert, *Geschichtsvergessenheit*, p.187.

(The diversity of individual memory vanishes, the collective memory finally becomes monochrome and consolidates itself as the memory of the perpetrators. This provides an opportunity for the individual and the way he or she takes a personal stance on the past, an opportunity to choose collective memory as an orientation and accept its messages.)

The dissolution of heterogeneous communities tied together by certain modes of commemoration, so-called 'Erinnerungsgemeinschaften', in East and West gives way to a more unified and abstract collective memory. Its counterbalance can be found in a profound interest in daily life and the life of the common people and soldiers, as can be seen in the interest in Victor Klemperer's diaries, the Goldhagen debate and the Wehrmacht exhibition with their focus on the role of the average citizen or soldier within the NS system.[27]

Sebald's art of memory as a perpetual process of intellectual effort is an art of memory which resists any temptation to be petrified in an epitaph in the common sense, an art of commemoration which can be appropriated by ideological superstructures. He creates epitaphs in the original Greek sense of λογος επιταφιος, which stands for the annual 'funeral oration' spoken in Athens over the citizens who had fallen in battle. It is the both frightening and tempting power of oblivion that forms the strongest undercurrent of Sebald's melancholy, and against which he establishes an art of commemoration that engages collective and individual dimensions of memory in a dialogue. In order to understand these processes, it is crucial to investigate how Sebald uses the dimensions of individual and collective memory and demonstrates their mechanisms in the third space between image and text. It is through the dialogues negotiated in these very intermedial openings that the trauma of displacement and loss is addressed and dealt with.

---

27   Victor Klemperer, *Ich will Zeugnis abgeben bis zum letzten. Tagebücher 1933–1945*, Berlin 1995 and Daniel Goldhagen, *Hitler's Willing Executioners. Ordinary Germans and the Holocaust*, New York 1996.

1. The Double Concept of 'Trauma'

One of the key concepts in *Austerlitz* is the notion of trauma and the traces of its scars on physical, psychological, social, political and topographical bodies. In his essay *Heidegger and 'the jews'* Jean-Francois Lyotard postulates 'traumatization' as the only adequate reaction and reference to the Shoah and related experiences. It is a semiotic rather than psychological argument based on the conviction that as soon as experience enters a symbolic code, it will inevitably enter an infinite chain of potential interpretations. A sign can be paradigmatically exchanged or syntagmatically reshuffled, it inevitably draws attention away from what it signifies to how it signifies, from experience to medium. Lyotard's point is that we have to prevent the Shoah from entering the closure of an archive, a narrative or an iconic image. This is utopian in an etymological sense: it signifies an ου–τοπος, the 'non-place', 'nowhere', a place without representation or signification.

This notion of the traumatic event as being extrinsic to signification draws upon the psychology of Jacques Lacan. In his *Four Fundamental Concepts of Psycho-Analysis* Lacan generalizes the strictly clinical notion of 'trauma' in Freud's *Beyond the Pleasure Principle*. It is only from this general notion that we can understand Lyotard's specific one. For Lacan, humans are constantly concerned with evading the encounter with reality. This potential encounter he calls *tuche*, derived from Greek τυχη: fate, chance, luck, gift of the Gods. Instead, humans want to reach back past the mirror stage, during which they recognize themselves as subjects by entering a symbolic system, which allows them to detach themselves from themselves: 'This split constitutes the characteristic dimension of analytic discovery and experience; it enables us to apprehend the real, in its dialectical effects, as originally unwelcome.'[28] Lacan calls this primal rift 'traumatic', metaphorically, so to speak, anticipating what later was to become termed Post-Traumatic Stress Syndrome with its typi-

---

28   Jacques Lacan, *Four Fundamental Concepts of Psycho-Analysis*, Harmondsworth 1986, p.69.

cal symptoms of freezing, panic inaction and paralysis of initiative. For Lacan, the primal rift poses a permanent danger to the Ego. The Ego is always affected by the trace of its primordial non-Ego. For Lacan, concrete psychiatric traumatic syndromes are a reinforcement of this rift of the holistic stage that took place during the mirror stage.

Lyotard draws on both the Lacanian and the psychiatric notion of 'trauma'. He wants to situate the historical trauma in the faults of the primordial stages of human development. He is not playing down the psychological traumata of the victims; he is rather talking about how people not directly affected by the Shoah should make this caesura in human consciousness unforgettable. His answer is: by putting it 'nowhere', by denying it a *topos* in the human systems of representation, by localizing it metaphorically in the interface of the 'traumatic' encounter of the human being with its pre-symbolic holistic state: '[the Shoah] cannot be represented without being missed, being forgotten anew, since it defies images and words. Representing "Auschwitz" in images and words is a way of making us forget this.'[29]

Lyotard does not allow for a *topos* of memory of the Shoah, a representative place to be revisited. He does not allow for the ancient notion of *ars memorativa* as a technique but focuses on the notion of *memoria* as *vis*, as psychological strength. The following chapters will investigate how photography and its use in Sebald's text conceptualize and render this specific notion of trauma.

2. Photography and Memory

Traditionally photography has been linked to its preserving qualities as a trigger of memory and as a mimetic tool for recreating the past. In an address to the Harvard Camera Club a hundred years ago, the philosopher George Santayana characterized photography as preserving

---

29   Jean-François Lyotard, *Heidegger and 'the jews'*, Minneapolis 1992, p.26.

transitory moments of experience und irrevocable spiritual images.[30] The perception of photography since has been subject to many changes, the most paradigmatic one being its Janus-faced character as preservation and displacement of memory through visualization. Photography is also perceived as a surrogate of experience, an aesthetics of disappearance[31], the fixation of a moment and its exposure to both preservation as matter and death as experience. It is the trace of the irretrievability of the irretrievable and opens up a minute time frame, within which the viewer can experience the singularity of the past. Hubertus von Amelunxen tries to capture this in the following remark:

> Das photographische Bild ist eine 'Emanation des Referenten' und beerbt unweigerlich auch die Zeit des Referenten. Somit ist in jeder Übersetzung, d.h. in jeder sprachlichen Inbezugnahme auf das Photographische dieser noematische zeitliche Charakter der Photographie als ein Verlust markiert.[32]

> (The photographic image is an 'emanation of the referent' and necessarily inherits the time of the referent. Thus in every translation, i.e. in every linguistic reference to photography, this noematic temporal character of photography is marked as a loss.)

In his essay *La Chambre Claire* Roland Barthes elaborates on this particular character of photography: 'it is the absolute Particular, the sovereign Contingency, [...] the *This* (this photograph, not Photography), in short, what Lacan calls the Tuche, the Occasion, the Encounter, the Real, in its indefatigable expression.'[33] He develops a semiotics without a sign. His fundamental assumption is that photographs cannot be separated from their referent and its historicity, they are an enunciation of that very historicity. That makes the photograph

---

30   George Santayana, *Animal faith and Spiritual life*, previously unpublished and uncollected writings by George Santayana with critical essays on his thought, ed. John Lachs, New York 1967, pp.391–403.

31   See Paul Virilio, *Esthétique de la disparition*, Paris 1980.

32   Hubertus von Amelunxen, 'Photographie und Literatur. Prolegomena zu einer Theoriegeschichte der Photographie', in Peter V. Zima (ed.), *Literatur Intermedial. Musik – Malerei – Photographie – Film,* Darmstadt 1995, pp.209–35: p.218.

33   Roland Barthes, *Camera Lucida. Reflections on Photography*, London 1982, p.4.

hover between subject and object as a 'micro-version of death.'[34] The photograph anticipates its objectified return as a dead object in the moment of it being taken, it anticipates and frames memory. It is the very lack of a symbolic code that allows photography to just state history and testify to mortality. Photography has become what I call the gaze of history, constantly whispering: 'Faithful departed. As you are now so once were we.' Photographs are a 'memento mori', as Susan Sontag writes in her essays *On Photography*: 'To take a photograph is to participate in another person's (or thing's) mortality, vulnerability, mutability. Precisely by slicing out this moment and freezing it, all photographs testify to time's relentless melt.'[35]

Barthes introduces the notion of *punctum* by which he means one or several details in a photograph, which shed a sudden light on the situation, the setting, the historical or social context. It resembles an epiphanic, sudden, unforeseeable moment, which turns the 'memento mori' into an epigraph of a certain time. The *punctum* can be a very personal and idiosyncratic connection. It is a 'blind field', the silent, uncoded discourse in a photograph. It is from the angle of this *punctum* that the spectator revitalizes the whole photograph. It triggers a *mémoire involontaire*, an empathy with history that allows a re-entry into history through a revealing moment captured in a second. The fulguration of a *punctum* is tantamount to the coalescence of different time layers. It makes the spectator adopt a gaze which is already anticipated in the picture, 'it is what I add to the photograph and *what is nonetheless already there.*'[36] The magical moment of opening up a space of insight is an encounter with the Real, with the predisposition of a particular episteme of historicity before its discursive encoding – a *tuche* in the Lacanian sense. How does this character of photography relate to Sebald's *ars memorativa* in *Austerlitz*?

---

34 Ibid., p.14.
35 Susan Sontag, *On Photography*, Harmondsworth 1973, p.15.
36 Barthes, *Camera Lucida*, p.55.

3. *Ars memorativa* in *Austerlitz*

In Sebald's *Austerlitz* the stream of consciousness of a fully-fledged life-story encounters the palimpsest of images that are deposited in collective memory. This encounter is acted out between Jacques Austerlitz and the narrator in Sebald's novel: the photographic leitmotif of bunker buildings and railway stations records a private obsession of Austerlitz related to his traumatic loss. This marks him as a typical traumatic person according to a standard psychiatric definition of the term:

> The pathology consists [...] in the structure of its experience or reception: the event is not assimilated or experienced fully at the time, but only belatedly, in its repeated possession of the one who experiences it. To be traumatised is precisely to be possessed by an image or event.[37]

The recurrence of the trauma in these pictures is tantamount to a return of the event in a non-discursive and non-symbolic form. The *punctum* of all these pictures of buildings is that they do not show any people. Austerlitz' individual *loci* of memory touch on a collective dimension in the narrator's imagination, for whom this *mémoire involontaire* means an uncanny encounter with a collective dimension within himself. The bunker buildings and railway stations are coalescing images of Austerlitz's personal mnemonic topography and the German narrator's pool of diffuse, submerged collective images of the wartime and Nazi-past. For Austerlitz they form an *ars memorativa*, an idiosyncratic way of orientation in the maze of the past, an obsessive codification of the past, the localization of the trauma in an *ars combinatoria* of signification.

For the narrator this mnemonic topography is reminiscent of a collective trauma of loss. He is spelling out and gives voice to Austerlitz's submerged stream of consciousness and simultaneously gets entangled in his own submerged historical consciousness and detects that it is working according to a comparable pattern of trauma, albeit

---

37   Cathy Caruth (ed.), *Trauma. Explorations in Memory,* Baltimore-London 1995, p.4f.

on a completely different level (victimhood vs. self-inflicted traumatic loss). Aleida Assmann elaborates on this parallel, though not symmetrical pattern: 'While the victims suffer from their memories because they confront them with the most torturous experiences again and again, the perpetrators suffer from the compulsion to remember.'[38]

a. *Punctum*

Austerlitz remembers his foster father showing him some pictures of his own home village, which was flooded to give way to a reservoir. His favourite photograph is one that shows a little girl with a dog on her lap (Ill. 3). The photograph is literally framed by the enigmatic sentence

> [Ich habe die Photographien] immer wieder von neuem angeschaut, bis die Personen, die mir aus ihnen entgegensahen, [...] vor allem das Mädchen, das mit seinem kleinen Hund auf dem Schoss auf einem Sessel im Garten sitzt, so vertraut wurden, als lebte ich bei ihnen auf dem Grund des Sees.
>
> (I leafed again and again through these few photographs [...] until the people looking out of them [...], most of all the girl sitting in a chair in the garden with her little dog on her lap, became as familiar to me as if I were living with them down at the bottom of the lake.)[39]

Austerlitz describes the process of acquainting himself with a second-hand experience of home. He is using the medium of photography to inscribe himself into surrogate family roots, to create for himself the aura of belonging somewhere without really belonging anywhere.

A closer look at the picture reveals a double *tableau*: besides the little girl and her dog it also shows a white doll playing with another white doll or toy pet. The little sub-*tableau* automatically draws attention to itself, forming the *punctum*, the angle through which the reader enters the picture and through which the whole picture appears in a new light. Without the dolls the picture would only reveal a setting within a certain time frame – a mixture of natural and artificial pose.

---

38   'Während die Opfer an ihren Erinnerungen leiden, weil sie ihnen immer wieder die quälendsten Erlebnisse vor Augen führen, leiden die Täter am Druck, sich erinnern zu müssen.' Assmann and Frevert, *Geschichtsvergessenheit*, p.114.

39   Sebald, *Austerlitz*, p.81; *Austerlitz*, trans. Anthea Bell, p.73f.

The dolls as a child's arrangement do not copy this pose, the girl's pose appears to be rather modelled on the dolls. They express this indescribable poise of self-consciousness, self-awareness and oblivion of the self that creates the aura of childhood.

The picture epitomizes Austerlitz' peculiar Kindertransport childhood as a second-hand experience. He is locked from his original child memory, which is doubly traumatized by the separation from his parents and the later news that his parents had been deported. He is also barred from any kind of family roots in the Calvinist household of his foster parents.

b. *Ekphrasis*

Some twenty pages into the book we read the following passage which describes the painting of a Dutch master showing a lady who lost her balance on skates:

> als sei der von Lucas van Valckenborch dargestellte Augenblick niemals vergangen, […] als geschähe das kleine von den meisten Betrachtern gewiss übersehene Unglück immer wieder von neuem, als höre es nie mehr auf und als sei es durch nichts mehr gutzumachen.

> (as if the moment depicted by Lucas van Valckenborch had never come to an end, […] as if the little accident, which no doubt goes unnoticed by most viewers, were always happening over and over again, and nothing and no one could ever remedy it.)[40]

This passage underscores and exposes the leitmotif of trauma as a repetitive ocurrence. It reads literally like a description of the typical mechanical recurrence of traumatic pictures: 'never come to an end', 'always happening again', 'no one could ever remedy'. The picture is set in the so called 'Little Ice Age', a geological term used to explain the period of exceptional cold in the 1500s, which in this context is a subtle and unobtrusive metaphor for the persistence of trauma. It highlights what Assmann analyzes as the most characteristic feature of the black-out effect of trauma:

---

40   Ibid., p.24; p.16.

> Das Pathologische des Traumas kann [...] weder in dem verursachenden Ereignis noch in der Entstellung dieses Ereignisses gesucht werden, sondern betrifft die Struktur seiner Erfahrung, oder besser gesagt: seiner Nicht-Erfahrung. Es geht um ein Ereignis, das zum Zeitpunkt seines Geschehens nicht wahrgenommen werden kann, weil es sich der geltenden Ökonomie des Bewusstseins versperrt.[41]

> (The pathological nature of trauma can [...] neither be found in the causing event nor in the distortion of this very event [in memory]; it is rather concerned with the structure of experience, or more precisely: non-experience. It is about an event which cannot be apprehended at the time of its occurrence, because it is refused subjection to the extant economy of consciousness.)

A later scene in the book shows the traumatic speechlessness and the impossibility of finding the correct words for the 'flicker of fire' of experience. Austerlitz is standing in front of a picture in the Rijks-museum in Amsterdam,

> das, der Beschriftung zufolge, die Flucht nach Ägypten darstellte, auf dem er aber weder das hochheilige Paar noch das Jesuskind, noch das Saumtier habe erkennen können, sondern nur, mitten in dem schwarzglänzenden Firnis der Finsternis, einen winzigen, vor meinen Augen, so sagte Austerlitz, bis heute nicht vergangenen Feuerfleck.[42]

> (which according to its label showed the Flight to Egypt, although he could make out neither Mary and Joseph, nor the child Jesus, nor the ass, but only a tiny flicker of fire in the middle of the gleaming black varnish of the darkness which, said Austerlitz, he could see in his mind's eye.)

Austerlitz only seems capable of an indirect expression of his self, be it in these examples of ekphrasis or in the *ars memorativa* of his study of architecture. This trait of Austerlitz is also reflected in the intricate structure of indirect speech, which is one of the most memorable linguistic characteristics of the book. While the literary character 'Austerlitz' is capable of the most intricate sentence structures when he wishes to convey his expertise in architecture, he has to rely on another person to tell his own story by combining its fictitious visual and discursive manifestations. Most of the time, we cannot be sure

---

41   Assmann and Frevert, *Geschichtsvergessenheit*, p.115.
42   Sebald, *Austerlitz*, p.177; *Austerlitz*, trans. Anthea Bell, p.169.

who is speaking, but the overall impression is that at the core of the eloquent and nostalgic flow of stream of consciousness there is the speechlessness of trauma.

c. Metareflexivity

One of the leitmotifs of the novel is the gaze of history, which inverts active and passive. It makes the one who remembers the one who is remembered by history. During Austerlitz' journey from Prague to Marienbad his attention is captured by a small detail:

> Was mich beunruhigte [...] war [...] die an sich unsinnige Vorstellung, dass diese durch die Verschuppung ihrer Oberfläche gewissermassen ans Lebendige heranreichende gusseiserne Säule sich erinnerte an mich und, wenn man so sagen kann, sagte Austerlitz, Zeugnis ablegte von dem, was ich selbst nicht mehr wusste.

> (What made me uneasy at the sight of it was [...] the idea, ridiculous in itself, that this cast-iron column, which with its scaly surface seemed almost to approach the nature of a living being, might remember me and was, if I may put it, said Austerlitz, a witness to what I could no longer recollect myself.)[43]

The whole book is haunted by this feeling of being subject to observation. It is a double effect encompassing the uncanny and the familiar.

On the third page of the novel the reader is confronted with a set of four pairs of eyes gazing at him: two animals and two humans (Ill. 4). This exposition has multiple textual and visual reverberations throughout the text. The nocturnal animals with their big eyes can be taken as a metaphor for human beings piercing the darkness of history. They can also be taken as the uncanny-familiar gaze of history out of the dark.

The pairing of this metaphorical uncanny-familiar gaze of history with a painter and a philosopher representing 'pure contemplation' and 'pure reflection' is again a meta-reflexive device. The second pair of eyes belongs to Wittgenstein, who is later likened to Austerlitz 'in the makeshift organisation of their lives'.[44] The author and with him

---

43 Ibid., pp.319f; p.311.
44 'in ihrem nur provisorisch eingerichteten Leben', Sebald, *Austerlitz*, p.64; *Austerlitz*, trans. Anthea Bell, p.56.

the reader are actually being watched by Austerlitz-Wittgenstein rather than watching him. It is the aura of not being premeditated which makes the photograph seem as if it was watching us. It is the 'status of a found object',[45] the primordial quality of something real, outside systems of representation, which makes us believe that the photograph anticipated our reaction.

The familiar part of the gaze of history through photography is that the photograph makes us rediscover parts of our memory; the uncanny part is that it gives us the feeling that it already had rediscovered it for us. Sebald finds haunting words for this inversion:

> Man habe den Eindruck [...], es rühre sich etwas in ihnen [den Fotographien], als vernehme man kleine Verzweiflungsseufzer, gémissements de désespoir, so sagte sie [Austerlitz' Kindermädchen], sagte Austerlitz, als hätten die Bilder selbst ein Gedächtnis und erinnerten sich an uns, daran, wie wir, die Über-lebenden, und diejenigen, die nicht mehr unter uns weilen, vordem gewesen sind.

> (One has the impression, she said, of something stirring in them [the photo-graphs], as if one caught small sighs of despair, gémissements de désespoir was her [Austerlitz's nanny] expression, said Austerlitz, as if the pictures had a memory of their own and remembered us, remembered the roles that we, the survivors, and those no longer among us had played in our former lives.)[46]

This is reminiscent of Paul Virilio's characterization of photography as an art of disappearance. It renders the person recalling the past incapable of governing and structuring the past. The photograph works as a trigger of memory to shuttle one back into the past, but it also blurs the character of past experience by dissecting it into visual segments.

---

45   Sontag, *On Photography*, p.69.
46   Sebald, *Austerlitz*, p.266; *Austerlitz*, trans. Anthea Bell, p.258.

III. Conclusion

Sebald neither confirms nor refutes Lyotard in his conviction that the Shoah should not be ascribed to any mode of representation. His rendition of the Kindertransport trauma is in constant danger of collapsing as a narrative, because the inserted pictures tell their own story, a subplot of the Lacanian *tuche*. Simultaneously, however, they inspire the opening-up of an intermedial third space as a dialogical counter-concept to Lyotard's idea of a perpetual 'traumatization'. This third space shows modes of representation in permanent tension between signification/decodification and their potential implosion.

First of all, it is necessary to note that Sebald creates a dialogical narrative situation which merges and mutually reinforces individual and collective memories. The mutual interlacing of these modes of memory can be illustrated by the narrator's footnote on Austerlitz's association of the railway stations of Antwerp with the one in Luzern (Ill. 5). The latter was destroyed by a fire in 1971 – shortly after the narrator had visited the city. The dome of Antwerp, symbol of imperial power, and the burning dome of Luzern railway station are juxtaposed in a way which suggests the rise and fall of power. The fire of domes or cupolas during night-time may be connoted with two historical incidents: the burning of the Reichstag in 1933[47] and the Pogrom in 1938.

The narrator remembers – triggered by Austerlitz's architectural comparison – that the pictures he saw in the papers after the fire in Luzern incited 'unease and anxiety' within him; they reminded him of something 'which crystallised into the idea that I had been to blame, or at least one of those to blame, for the Lucerne fire'.[48] This is like a

---

47   Hitler used the fire as a pretext to systematically erode the Weimar constitution in the 'Ermächtigungsgesetze'.

48   Sebald, *Austerlitz*, trans. Anthea Bell, pp.11f; 'Von den Bildern […] ist für mich etwas Beunruhigendes und Beängstigendes ausgegangen, das sich in der Vorstellung verdichtete, daß ich der Schuldige oder doch zumindest einer der Mitschuldigen sei an dem Luzerner Brand.', *Austerlitz*, p.20.

flashlight of the collective memory and associated emotions of guilt and shame in the midst of highly idiosyncratic associations.

On a second level, Sebald opens up an intermedial, simultaneously discursive and non-discursive space in which 'trauma' is acted out as an ongoing process of 'traumatization.' Intermediality in Austerlitz functions as a suspension of oblivion. A passage which illustrates the perpetual character of trauma, is the story of Moses.[49] Describing one of the illustrations showing the exodus from Egypt in a Welsh children's Bible, Austerlitz ponders:

> Ich [...] versenkte mich, alles um mich her vergessend, in eine ganzseitige Illustration, in der die Wüste Sinai mit ihren kahlen, ineinander verschobenen Bergrücken und dem grau gestrichelten Hintergrund [...] ganz der Gegend glich, in der ich aufgewachsen bin. Tatsächlich wusste ich mich [...] an meinem richtigen Ort. Jeden Quadratzoll der mir gerade in ihrer Vertrautheit unheimlich erscheinenden Abbildung habe ich durchforscht.

> (I immersed myself, forgetting all around me, in a full-page illustration showing the desert of Sinai looking just like the part of Wales were I grew up, with bare mountains crowding close together and grey-hatched background [...] I knew that my proper place was among the tiny figures populating the camp. I examined every square inch of the illustration, which seemed to me uncannily familiar.)[50]

This is a rather kitschy use of an epitome of Jewish collective memory, the child literally remembering the exodus of his people in ancient history. In the preceding ekphrasis of this illustration, the focus is directed to the picture, but the fact that Austerlitz had to learn the story by heart and recite it 'correctly and with good expression'[51] suggests that it is also the Biblical texts, which are reminiscent of his early childhood in Prague and kept him in touch with the 'Schmerzensspuren' ('traces of pain') of the Jewish exodus.[52]

The trauma of abandonment is metaphorically encompassed in the leitmotif scenes of waiting in a station and in scenes of rescue. Embedded into these two circles of textual and visual leitmotifs the

---

49   Sebald, *Austerlitz*, p.85.
50   Ibid.; *Austerlitz*, trans. Anthea Bell, pp.77 and 80.
51   Ibid., p.76.
52   Sebald, *Austerlitz*, p.24; *Austerlitz*, trans. Anthea Bell, p.20.

reader can find one of the central images of the whole book already referred to above. During his research in Teresienstadt/Terezín Auster-litz/Sebald takes a photograph of a little porcelain statue (Ill. 6). The silhouette of the photographer can be seen on the shop window pane. The statue is a rider on horseback rescuing a woman. Austerlitz' mother was not among those who experienced the new exodus herself, she was killed in the death camps. Austerlitz is still waiting for her in railway stations all across Europe.

On a third level, Sebald creates both an individual *ars* and a collective *vis memorativa* of one of the neglected chapters of German-Jewish history. 'All the occurrences of the past are equidistant from our present existence,'[53] Sebald once stated. The mnemonic topography of *Austerlitz* is an illustration of this sentence and its ramifications. It is an *ars memorativa* which is situated between text and image and derives its strength from the 'unsinnliche Ähnlichkeit'[54] ('nonsensuous similarities') between the participating media. That allows for 'a constellation in which similarities between things become apparent in a flashlight, a shape that is only recognisable as difference in a quick fleeting glance, as similarity which does not lie in things themselves but emerge from what is in between them.'[55] In the baroque emblem, for instance, there is no principal explicatory predominance of either *pictura* or *subscriptio*. Likewise, Walter Benjamin's notion of mutual resemblence is based on a concept of mimesis which stresses the common rootedness of text and image in one realm of imagination and demiurgic creativity.

---

53   W.G. Sebald in an interview with Uwe Pralle, *Süddeutsche Zeitung* (22 December 2001).

54   Walter Benjamin, *Lehre vom Ähnlichen*, in *Gesammelte Schriften*, II/1, ed. Rolf Tiedemann and Hermann Schweppenhäuser, Frankfurt/M. 1977, pp.204–10: p.208.

55   'eine Konstellation, in der "blitzartig Ähnliches" zum Vorschein kommt, eine Gestalt, die nur im Moment als Differenz im schnellen, flüchtigen Hinsehen erkennbar ist und als Ähnlichkeit, die nicht in den Dingen selbst, sondern nur zwischen ihnen aufscheint.' Joachim Paech, 'Das Bild zwischen den Bildern', in Joachim Paech (ed.), *Film, Fernsehen, Video und die Künste. Strategien der Intermedialität*, Stuttgart 1994, pp.163–78: p.167, with reference to Benjamin's *Lehre vom Ähnlichen* (1933).

There is no mimetic shortcut to history. Photography only delimits past events as lost events; language only translates the past into a symbolic code. In their mutual 'nonsensuous similarities' they reconstruct their demiurgic power and are bound together in a matrix of mutual decodification and mimetic approximation. Sebald opens up an intermedial space in which trauma is not signified but kept in a process of translatability and constant re-encounter. He creates a literary stage on which the present is mirrored in the past, the symbolic code in silence and vice versa, and he dramatizes the impulse of an idiosyncratic traumatized *ars memorativa* as a *vis memorativa*, by which our collective memory is endowed with a new topicality of memory.

Austerlitz can also be read as a reflection on German identity in a reunified Germany, a reflection which moves away from the battle of the entrenched parties of the 1980s torn between 'Sonderweg' options (alternative political movements), national reassertion (conservatives), avoidance of the issue of national identity (liberals, social democrats)[56] towards a mode of appropriating history in a productive approach of dialogue.[57] Sebald's art of memory avoids the pitfalls of *Vergangenheitsbewältigung* (coming to terms with the past) and *Erinnerungspolitik* (memory politics) and creates a mnemoscape which allows for encounters with the past and dialogue with collective memory. In this sense Sebald is an invitation to the German people not to let the gap between the post-war generations grow too wide but

---

56   See Stephen Brockmann, *Literature and German Reunification*, Cambridge 1999, p.13ff.

57   For a discussion of the relation between collective memories and contemporary ideologies see Andrei S. Markovits and Simon Reich, *The German Predicament. Memory and Power in the New Europe*, Ithaca, NY 1997, pp.1–56, for example pp.14f: 'Collective memory, in contrast [to history], is not a record of events but a locus of tradition. If history is universalistic, collective memory is particularistic. If history is timeless, collective memory is time-bound. Above all, collective memory is always plural. [...] If history is about cognition and knowledge, collective memory is about experience and feeling. If history is a matter of the past, collective memory is a phenomenon of the present. [...] Akin to myth, only tangentially related to empirical truth, collective memory plays a key role in the symbolic discourse of politics, in the legitimation of political structures and action, and in the justification of collective behaviour.'

embark on the project of defining the present by engaging in a dialogue with the past.[58]

Critics are still looking for *the* novel of the German reunification. They conjure up Günter Grass, Thomas Hettche, Cees Nooteboom and many others. Probably they should avert their attention from the typical catch phrases of reunification and look for authors like Sebald or Alexander Kluge, for their art of creating history as an intermedial space in order to facilitate an art of commemoration outside a politics of commemoration, beyond and after 'the total breakdown of a linguistic and ideological system at once bipolar and regressive which had governed European affairs since the end of World War Two.'[59]

Bibliography

Amelunxen, Hubertus von, 'Photographie und Literatur. Prolegomena zu einer Theoriegeschichte der Photographie', in Peter V. Zima (ed.), *Literatur Intermedial. Musik – Malerei – Photographie – Film,* Darmstadt 1995, pp.209–35.

Assmann, Aleida, *Erinnerungsräume,* Munich 1999.

—— and Ute Frevert, *Geschichtsvergessenheit – Geschichtsversessenheit. Vom Umgang mit deutschen Vergangenheiten nach 1945,* Stuttgart 1999.

Assmann, Jan, 'Kollektives Gedächtnis und kulturelle Identität', in Jan Assmann and Toni Hölscher (eds.), *Kultur und Gedächtnis,* Frankfurt/M. 1988, pp.9–19.

Barthes, Roland, *Camera Lucida. Reflections on Photography,* London 1982.

Benjamin, Walter, *Lehre vom Ähnlichen,* in *Gesammelte Schriften,* II/1, ed. Rolf Tiedemann and Hermann Schweppenhäuser, Frankfurt/M. 1977, pp.204–10.

——, *Ausgraben und Erinnern,* in *Gesammelte Schriften,* IV/1, ed. Rolf Tiedemann and Hermann Schweppenhäuser, Frankfurt/M. 1984, p.400.

Boll, Friedhelm, *Sprechen als Last und Befreiung,* Bonn 2003.

Brockmann, Stephen, *Literature and German Reunification,* Cambridge 1999.

---

58 In this sense Sebald has to be seen in the wake of many post-war German writers who either saw themselves or inadvertently were regarded as a 'conscience of the nation'. See Brockmann, *Literature and German Reunification,* pp.12ff. He suggests potentially far-reaching conclusions: 'post-war German [...] literature [...] came to "watch over" Germany, "like a garrison in a conquered city." The *Kulturnation* became the warden of the *Staatsnation.*'

59 Ibid., p.45.

Caruth, Cathy (ed.), *Trauma. Explorations in Memory,* Baltimore-London 1995.

Göpfert, Rebekka, *Der jüdische Kindertransport von Deutschland nach England 1938/9,* Frankfurt/M. 1999.

Goldhagen, Daniel, *Hitler's Willing Executioners: Ordinary Germans and the Holocaust,* New York 1996.

Josephs, Jeremy, and Susi Bechhöfer, *Rosa's Child. One Woman's Search for her Past,* London 1998.

Klemperer, Victor, *Ich will Zeugnis abgeben bis zum letzten. Tagebücher 1933–1945,* Berlin 1995.

Kluge, Alexander, *Chronik der Gefühle,* Frankfurt/M. 2000.

Lacan, Jacques, *Four Fundamental Concepts of Psycho-Analysis,* Harmondsworth 1986.

Lyotard, Jean-François, *Heidegger and 'the jews',* Minneapolis 1992.

Markovits, Andrei S., and Simon Reich, *The German Predicament. Memory and Power in the New Europe,* Ithaca, NY 1997.

Niethammer, Lutz, *Posthistoire. Has History Come to an End?,* London 1992.

Paech, Joachim, 'Das Bild zwischen den Bildern', in Joachim Paech (ed.), *Film, Fernsehen, Video und die Künste. Strategien der Intermedialität,* Stuttgart 1994, pp.163–78.

——, 'Intermedialität. Mediales Differenzial und transformative Figurationen', in Jörg Helbig (ed.), *Intermedialität,* Berlin 1998, pp.14–30.

Reichel, Peter, *Politik mit der Erinnerung. Gedächtnisorte im Streit um die nationalsozialistische Vergangenheit,* Munich-Vienna 1995.

Santayana, George, *Animal faith and Spiritual life,* previously unpublished and uncollected writings by George Santayana with critical essays on his thought, ed. John Lachs, New York 1967.

Schulze, Ingo, *Simple Storys. Ein Roman aus der ostdeutschen Provinz,* Munich 1999.

Sebald, W.G., *Die Ausgewanderten. Vier lange Erzählungen,* Frankfurt/M. 1994.

——, *Die Ringe des Saturn. Eine englische Wallfahrt,* Frankfurt/M. 1995.

——, *Rings of Saturn,* trans. Michael Hulse, London 1995.

——, *Austerlitz,* Frankfurt/M. 2003.

——, *Austerlitz,* trans. Anthea Bell, Harmondsworth 2001.

Sontag, Susan, *On Photography,* Harmondsworth 1973.

Virilio, Paul, *Esthétique de la disparition,* Paris 1980.

Illustrations

Ill. 1

Ill. 2

Ill. 3

Ill. 4a

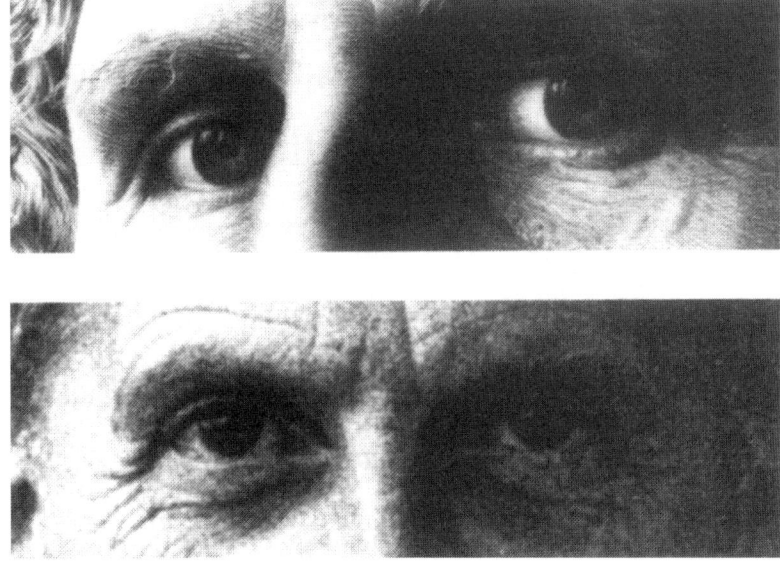

Ill. 4b

Ill. 5

Ill. 6

Andreas Böhn

Memory, Musealization and Alternative History in Michael Kleeberg's Novel *Ein Garten im Norden* and Wolfgang Becker's Film *Good Bye, Lenin!*

One basic function of narration is the building and conservation of memory. Narration links one moment in time to another, and it links the present to the past. Many of the oldest narrations we know tell stories about the mythical foundation of a society, thus explaining and legitimizing the social organization given at the time when these tales were formed. Because in most cases they are the only documents we have from these times, we don't know the circumstances of their formation, but we can suppose that they were already reactions to changes in these societies, which caused a need for restoring continuity between present and past.

This need has increased a lot under conditions of modernization and has produced different strategies of relating past and present, one of them still being narration, and another important one musealization. Historical museums have always exhibited objects which have played an important role in history and are therefore able to connect us to the past. But at the same pace the social and cultural changes accelerate, more and more items of everyday life become possible objects of musealization, even at a time when they are still used. Constant alteration causes a loss of familiarity, which is compensated by musealization.[1]

---

1   See Hermann Lübbe, *Der Fortschritt und das Museum: Über den Grund unseres Vergnügens an historischen Gegenständen* (The 1981 Bithell Memorial Lecture), London 1982; Wolfgang Zacharias (ed.), *Zeitphänomen Musealisierung. Das Verschwinden der Gegenwart und die Konstruktion der Erinnerung*, Essen 1990; Eva Sturm, *Konservierte Welt: Museum und Musealisierung*, Berlin 1991.

Musealization is closely related to the process of modernization in western societies, but it is grounded in a more general human practice. Krzysztof Pomian tries to understand the whole history of collecting as a form of cultural mediation between separated worlds or spheres, from the gathering of offerings to modern scientific collections. The collected items, which he calls 'semiophores', are taken away from everyday life, liberated of any aspect of usefulness, and given a special meaning. They represent something different from the world we know and serve to communicate between this world and another world, be it a transcendent sphere in a religious view or the past in the case of a historical museum.[2]

The strategy of musealization depends on the sensual perception of objects which are experienced as belonging to two different time levels, present and past, whereas the strategy of narration relies on the linking of events in time through story-telling, thus creating a chain between past and present. Their preferred media in modern societies are the museum on one hand and narrative literature on the other hand, but they can be combined in one medium through integration of narratives in museums or depiction of objects in literature, and even more easily in the medium of film. Period pictures tell stories which have a certain era as a background, but they also present us a musealized version of this period. The wallpapers and decorations from the 1970s in Ang Lee's *The Ice Storm* (1997) are not only scenery, but a typical expression of their time.

It is not surprising that the important historical events of the *Wende* and the German unification with its resulting social changes have provoked reactions in various cultural fields which heavily employ combinations of musealization and narration. Silke Arnold-de Simine has analysed examples from the areas of the historical museum, literature and film and concludes:

> Different memory media are increasingly convering. With the so-called *Wende-roman* and *Wendefilm* the need to present a social panorama, an exemplary examination of the twofold German history and identity, is pressing on these media. In this context the tasks associated with processes of musealization have

---

2   Krzysztof Pomian, 'Entre l'invisible et le visible: la collection', in *Collection-neurs, amateurs et curieux*, Paris 1987, pp.15–58.

also come to be imposed on film and literature. These tasks comprise an institutionalized, official version of our cultural memory, but also one with which people are able to identify.[3]

This tendency, which can be found widely, especially in the critical discourse on film and literature in Germany during the 1990s, seems to be contradicted by another way of dealing with the past which will be discussed here in its relation to musealization, the invention of an alternative history. The fictional construction of a counterfeit world, depending on at least one change of an important event in real history and unfolding its possible consequences produces the opposite of 'an institutionalized, official version of our cultural memory'. The narrative genre *What if...-Story* or *Paralleltime Novel* has been granted increasing attention in the last decades, perhaps inspired by important literary works like *The Alteration* by Kingsley Amis (1976) or *SS GB* by Len Deighton (1978).[4] But also historians have shown interest in the intellectual play with alternative history.[5] Thinking about other possibilities in the course of history can help to understand better the causes of what really happened, but it can also put into doubt the impression of a necessary development that may be produced by the writing of history and explaining the conditions of historical events. Therefore according to Jörg Helbig what he calls the 'parahistorical novel' has a strong affinity to post-modern tendencies: 'Viele Autoren nutzen die parahistorische Schreibweise als Medium, um die Verbindlichkeit historischer und empirischer Normen in Frage zu stellen und die Subjektivität der Wirklichkeitserfahrung zu betonen'. ('Many authors use the parahistoric style as a means to question the binding

---

3   Silke Arnold-de Simine, 'Themepark GDR? The Aestheticization of Memory in post-Wende Museums, Literature and Films', in Christian Emden and David Midgley (eds.) *The Fragile Tradition: The German Cultural Imagination since 1500. I: Cultural Memory and Historical Consciousness*, Oxford 2004, pp.253–280: p.277.

4   See Jörg Helbig, *Der parahistorische Roman: Ein literarhistorischer und gattungstypologischer Beitrag zur Allotopieforschung*, Frankfurt/M. 1988; Karen Hellekson, *The Alternate History: Refiguring Historical Time*, Kent, Ohio 2001; *Uchronia: The Alternate History List*, http://www.uchronia.net.

5   See Alexander Demandt, *Ungeschehene Geschichte: Ein Traktat über die Frage: Was wäre geschehen, wenn...?*, 2nd edition, Göttingen 1986.

character of historic and empiric norms and to stress the subjective character of our experience of reality.')[6]

A closer look at two examples dealing with the *Wende* and German history and combining aspects of musealization and alternative history will help to analyse the possible relations between the two strategies. Both tell stories that are located in Berlin and seem to belong to the genre *Wenderoman* respective *Wendefilm*. Michael Kleeberg's novel *Ein Garten im Norden* was published in 1998[7] and is at first sight comparable to novels like *Ein weites Feld* by Günter Grass (1995; *Too Far Afield*, 2000) or *Rot* by Uwe Timm (2001), which are both closely related to localities in Berlin and surroundings and unfold narrations that depart from the present, but extend back to the period of Fontane or the history of the generation of 1968 in the FRG, intermingling the different time layers. However, whereas Grass and Timm present an image of history which could be put into doubt from a different viewpoint, but does not at all contradict the facts of this history (or what we take for it), Kleeberg invents an alternative history to explain the fate of a fictitious site in the no-man's-land between East- and West-Berlin.

Wolfgang Becker's movie *Good Bye, Lenin!* was released in 2002 and has already become one of the most successful German films ever, not only in Germany, but also in other European countries like Britain and France and even in the USA.[8] Like Leander Haußmann's and Thomas Brussig's *Sonnenallee* (1999), another quite successful movie which has already been analysed from the point of view of musealization,[9] or Sebastian Peterson's and Brussig's *Helden wie wir* (1999; *Heroes Like Us*, 1997), it tells the story of a youth grown up in the GDR who is not primarily concerned with politics but rather with personal problems, it is dominated by comical effects and it presents a different version of the coming down of the Berlin wall. But whereas *Sonnenallee* and *Helden wie wir* present this alternative

---

6   Helbig, *Der parahistorische Roman*, p.170.
7   Michael Kleeberg, *Ein Garten im Norden. Roman*, Berlin 1998; henceforth referred to as *Garten*.
8   See http://www.79qmddr.de/index2.php.
9   See Arnold-de Simine, 'Themepark GDR?', pp.265–268.

version of history as something that really happened, although with a tongue-in-cheek-attitude, *Good Bye, Lenin!* demonstrates clearly that it is a fiction-within-the-fiction with quite personal reasons. Therefore and with regard to musealization it is comparable to *Ein Garten im Norden*. Nevertheless we will have to examine the different medial conditions of both and their consequences, too.

Ein Garten im Norden

In 1995, after long years abroad, the German writer Albert Klein returns to Germany, which he had left at least partly because of a dislike for this country and its inhabitants. His father and his cousin, who comes from the former GDR and is now doing business in real estates, show him a mysterious piece of land in the middle of Berlin, which seemingly had no identifiable owner before it was turned into a part of the no-man's-land between East and West. Albert Klein travels to Prague. In an antiquarian book-shop he acquires a strange book with empty pages, which possesses the power to turn everything written on it into reality. Albert Klein begins to write the story of someone with the name Albert Klein, living in the first half of the twentieth century, which turns into the history of the real estate in Berlin and an alternative history of Germany in this period. It is the history of a better Germany, which nevertheless ends with nazism, Hitler and the Second World War like the real history, but unfolds undeveloped possibilities. The Albert Klein of this story-within-the-story, starting without any money, gets wealthy in the finance business and uses his fortune to create an extraordinary garden in the middle of Berlin, which is used as a meeting point for the 'good' Germans, artists, scientists and politicians.

This garden forms a society-within-society with idyllic and paradisiac overtones, but open to all questions of the modern world, including politics, economics and technology. It is a utopia of enlightened civilization, based on dialogue and tolerance. Being the essence of the alternative history in the novel, it also fulfils the function of an archive and a museum. The garden itself gathers plants from all over the world, making it an image and a museum of natural beauty. The buildings in the garden not only contain a study centre, conference rooms etc., but also an audiovisual archive of human culture, which is intended to support the general purpose of building up tolerance and mutual understanding. Young students and scholars from all over the world are given the opportunity to study the documentary material, thus creating an exchange of persons, viewpoints and knowledge.

Both the creation of an alternative history and the musealization of cultural diversity are strategies against the destructive tendencies of modern civilization represented by Nazism. But they appear as closely related to those tendencies, not at all independent of them. The museum is meant to preserve, but is destroyed in the end, and the alteration of history unfolds other possibilities, which do not prevail over the rise of Hitler. Therefore both strategies seem to lead to a dead end. But the general aim of Kleeberg's novel is not to promote one strategy or one possibility of behaviour vis-à-vis the past, rather it is a very self-reflective contemplation of different strategies.

For example, the city of Berlin in the first half of the twentieth century is presented as quite ambivalent in its relation to the past. On one hand, despite its modernity and rapid change, it is orientated backwards and therefore resembles Paul Klee's famous *Angelus Novus*, which Walter Benjamin interpreted in his reflections on the concept of history:

> Wie Benjamins Angelus Novus weht es diese Stadt mit rückwärtsgewandtem Gesicht nach vorn, und ihre faktische Modernität kleidet sich in einen Digest pseudoimperialistisch-horizontaler Stadtarchitektur, deren kontinuierliches Zu-Spät-Kommen die Illustration eines sie bedingenden anachronistischen politischen Systems ist, das modernen übernationalen Kapitalismus mit den Mottenkleidern eines gottgewollten Königtums behängt. (*Garten*, 147)

> (Like Benjamin's Angelus Novus this town is blown forward with its face looking backwards. Its factual modernity dresses up in a digest of pseudo-imperialistic and horizontal urban architecture. The perpetual belatedness of which illustrates the anachronistic political system that determines it, and which dresses global capitalism up with the mothy costumes of the god-given monarchy.)

Berlin looks back, but it looks on a faked history, a historicizing camouflage of modernity, whereas on the other hand it neglects the vestiges of its real history and avoids remembrance: 'Die Stadt zerstört permanent ihr eigenes Gedächtnis, sie hat keine Zeit, sich zu erinnern, nicht einmal Zeit zu sein, sie wird.' (*Garten*, 148) ('The city permanently destroys its own memory. It has no time to remember, not even enough time to be – it becomes.')

When Albert Klein returns from a trip around the world in July 1914 and has to notice that war seems inevitable, he sees the audiovisual recordings he and his fellow traveller Lukas have brought home with different eyes:

> Und all das, was ihre beweglichen Bilder zeigten, als geschehe es hier und jetzt, würde nun also bald Vergangenheit sein und vielleicht nur mehr auf Lukas' Zelluloid weiterleben. Würde verschwinden, spurlos verschwinden und von irgend etwas neuem, dessen glattes Gesicht nichts von Erinnerung wüßte, abgelöst werden (*Garten*, 158f).

> (And everything the moving images showed as if it were happening here and now would soon belong to the past, only existing on celluloid. It would vanish without trace, displaced by something new, the smooth face of which would know nothing about memory.)

The recordings, initially just intended to transport impressions of different cultures, using the most modern techniques, are transformed into archives of a past which would otherwise be forgotten. What was intended to help building a better future turns into a means of commemorating history.

The alternative history presented in the story-within-the-story is reflected in discussions between the author Albert Klein and the antiquarian who sold him the empty book. Klein rejects the seductive perspective that in a god-like manner he could create a better history:

> 'Noch einmal', sagte ich, 'ich will nichts *verbessern*. Was immer Sie glauben, dazu bin ich zu bescheiden. Ich will nur eine andere Erinnerung. Ich begnüge mich damit, meine Erinnerung umzuschreiben.' (*Garten*, 182)

> ('Once again', I said, 'I don't want to improve anything. Whatever you think, I am too modest for that. I just want a different memory. I am content with rewriting my memories.')

He cultivates a Musilian *Möglichkeitssinn* in relation to history, like his alter ego does in relation to actual life, when he has to decide whether he will travel to Russia or India:

> Ich habe keine Lust, mich entscheiden zu müssen! Es gibt nichts Schlimmeres auf der Welt als dieses ewige Entweder-Oder. Daß wir nicht alles haben können! Rußland *und* Indien. *Mein* Leben *und* all die hundert anderen, die ich an jeder verfluchten Wegbiegung ebensogut hätte einschlagen können (*Garten*, 165).

> (I don't want to make a decision! There is nothing worse in the world than this eternal either-or. Why can't we have everything! Russia *and* India. *My* life *and* all the hundreds of other lives, which I could have chosen just as well at every damned turning.)

At the end of the novel he has changed history, and one thing he devotes his further life to is caring for the remains and documents of this history.[10]

Good Bye, Lenin!

In the summer of 1989 21-year-old Alex participates in manifestations for freedom of the press in East-Berlin. His mother, renowned as an ardent supporter of the regime, suffers a heart attack as a result of seeing her son beaten by the police. When she wakes up eight months later, the family is told that she should avoid any stress or irritation. Meanwhile the Berlin wall has come down and the old GDR is no more. Alex and his family try to revive it in their little apartment by desperately seeking GDR-goods or at least faking them by putting new western commodities in old eastern packages. They even simulate GDR-television as a way of explaining the more and more obvious changes in everyday life. Therefore they invent their own opening of

---

10   See *Garten*, 585.

the wall by the authorities of the East for the citizens of the West, who are fleeing from the devastating effects of capitalism.

In the end everything turns out to be not quite what it looked like. Alex' girl friend admits the whole swindle to his mother, who in turn admits that his father has not gone west with the intention of leaving his family behind, but that she could not follow and had to disguise her failure to go through with this plan by ostentatious support. So, the perpetuation of the GDR as a fake imitation, a museum-like revival, and its alternative ending in dignity are not the product of anyone's real opting for it, but of a misunderstanding. Musealization here is a means of creating an alternative history, which is merely a conservation of the *status quo ante*, and only transforms into a different explanation of the *Wende* under the pressure of unavoidable circumstances.

From the beginning of the movie the protagonist, who is also the narrator speaking off-screen from time to time, makes clear that he is telling a very personal story, tainted by his own memories. The visualization of these memories is presented in a mock-amateur style, as private film recordings, which are, like amateur photographs, a way of organizing personal memories by using medial objects. These amateur recordings are faked, of course, in the sense that they seem to be different from the rest of the movie because of their other material, technical and aesthetic guise, whereas in reality they are as fictional as the whole movie. But what they show is also faked, because they seem to be proving that Alex' mother was a convinced partisan of the SED. Thereby faking by playing a certain role and by using specific media is introduced as a major theme of the movie closely connected to memory.

When Alex' mother comes back from hospital into her room in the family's apartment, which has been re-decorated in GDR-style, he has to get her the goods she is used to, but which have vanished after the monetary union: *Mocca-Fix*, *Spreewald-Gurken* and *Tempo-Bohnen*. As they are difficult to get he takes new products from the West and puts them in old packages found in the garbage. Thus he is able to present his mother a typical assortment of commodities that could be displayed in a museum of GDR society and culture. In fact, items of everyday life in the GDR were pivotal objects of musealization after the *Wende*.[11]

> The German Historical Museum (*Deutsches Historisches Museum*, founded in 1987) in the West, as well as the Museum of German History (*Museum für deutsche Geschichte*, 1952–1990) in the East, launched a public appeal for contributions of objects people thought worth preserving. The motto was: 'Die DDR ins Museum!' ('Put the GDR in a museum!'). The aim was to store everyday objects that constituted a vital part of the collective socialization and would otherwise have been irretrievably lost. Even new museums such as the *Dokumentationszentrum Alltagskultur der DDR* (Centre for Popular Culture of the GDR), founded in 1993 in Eisenhüttenstadt, were established with this purpose in mind. [...] Objects were saved from the scrap-heap and transferred to the museum as if it were Noah's ark: each a representative of its whole species. Many East Germans who did not surround themselves immediately with goods from the West could encounter their own domestic environment in the museum. The effect is ambivalent: on the one hand, one's own ordinary life seems somehow ennobled; on the other, this can only be achieved by rendering it obsolete.[12]

The musealization of the GDR not only happens in museums, but also in literature, film, television and the internet, too. Jana Hensel's quite successful book *Zonenkinder* (2002; *After The Wall*, 2004), the already mentioned film *Sonnenallee* (1999) and a variety of *Ostalgie* shows on television which already have produced their specific parody[13] are just some examples. On the homepage of *Good Bye, Lenin!* we can find links to sites related to GDR-culture, some of them documenting in detail objects of everyday life in eastern Germany

---

11   See Katharina Flügel and Wolfgang Ernst (eds.), *Musealisierung der DDR? 40 Jahre als kulturhistorische Herausforderung*, Alfter 1992; Bernd Faulenbach and Franz-Josef Jelich (eds.), *Probleme der Musealisierung der doppelten deutschen Nachkriegsgeschichte*. Dokumentation einer Tagung des Forschungsinstituts für Arbeiterbildung und der Hans-Böckler-Stiftung, Essen 1993; Gerd Kuhn and Andreas Ludwig (eds.), *Alltag und soziales Gedächtnis. Die DDR-Objektkultur und ihre Musealisierung*, Hamburg 1997.

12   Silke Arnold-de Simine, 'Themepark GDR', p.259f.

13   See Stefan Niggemeier, 'Kinder, nehmt euch ein Beispiel an Walter Ulbricht. Die letzte DDR-Show ist gleichzeitig eine Parodie auf das Genre: Oliver Kalkofe nimmt sich die Ostalgie-Welle vor', *Frankfurter Allgemeine Zeitung*, 231 (6 October 2003), 40.

before 1990.[14] Consequently the reflection of musealization in *Good Bye, Lenin!* not only extends to material culture, but also to modern media. With the help of his friend Denis, a would-be movie director, Alex gathers recordings of GDR television like the daily news *Aktuelle Kamera* and the political magazine *Schwarzer Kanal* which are used to produce new transmissions. Alex' mother has to lie in her bed without the possibility of moving and therefore can see the outside world only through one window and a certain fixed perspective. This situation, comparable to Plato's cave parable in the *Politeia*, makes it easy to prevent her from noticing the ongoing changes. But when she wants to watch television another window to the world opens which has to be manipulated. First Alex and Denis simply show her old transmissions, then they begin to experiment with the montage of original scenes and new self-produced ones. In the end they create an alternative history of the German unification, fictionally realizing somehow a 'third way' between real existing socialism and western capitalism.[15] With this masterpiece of a fake Alex puts an end to his personal prolonging of the GDR, too, without disturbing his mother, as he thinks. But we as spectators know that this is not the truth. His mother has already been told about the things that had happened and about Alex' machinations, too. She does not tell him because she does not want to disappoint him. That she looks very content when watching the TV transmission does not mean that she is proud of her state, as Alex thinks, but that she is proud of her son, who has done so much for her. Personal relations prevail over relations to a nation or a state. At the end of the movie the narrator Alex makes quite clear that his memory of the GDR is basically the memory of his mother.

---

14   See http://www.79qmddr.de/links.php and http://www.ddr-alltagskultur.com/start/start.html.

15   See Hans Günter Pflaum, 'Der diskrete Charme der Ostalgie: Wolfgang Beckers "Good Bye, Lenin!" konkurriert noch um den Berlinale-Bären und kommt schon ins Kino', *Süddeutsche Zeitung*, 36 (13 February 2003), 12: 'Klug und clever demonstriert "Good Bye, Lenin!" die Willfährigkeit von Bildern und Tönen und geht dabei weit hinaus über die eigene Story: Der Fake gelingt umso leichter, als die DDR im Laufe ihrer vierzig Jahre ihrerseits die manipulierte Selbstinszenierung gepflegt hatte; da lassen sich die angeblichen Dokumente leicht umdrehen'.

On 1 October 2003 an article appeared in the German weekly *Die Zeit* which refers to *Good Bye, Lenin!*, especially to the aspect of culture shock in the movie, the trauma caused by the abrupt cultural change in the former GDR, and tries to understand the situation of East Germans as a situation of immigrants in a foreign country – a country they did not go to, but which came to them.[16] The comparison to immigration shows interesting results:

> Plötzlich erscheint auch das große Rätsel der vergangenen 13 Jahre nicht mehr ganz so rätselhaft: Warum es überhaupt so etwas gibt wie eine ostdeutsche Identität. Diese entstand erst lange nach dem Ende der DDR: Alex aus *Good Bye, Lenin!* wäre es 1990 nie eingefallen, sich als ostdeutsch zu bezeichnen. Auch die Autoren des *Sozialreports* über die Neuen Länder waren 1992 noch nicht auf die Idee gekommen, bei der Frage nach der regionalen Identifikation die Kategorie 'Ostdeutschland' einzuführen. Als sie 1999 danach fragten, fühlten sich 74 Prozent 'ziemlich' oder 'stark' als Ostdeutsche, die Zahl stieg sogar auf 80 Prozent im Jahr 2001 – ein typischer Fall von Selbstethnisierung, wie ihn die Migrationsforschung seit langem kennt. [...] Sicher wird die Identifikation mit Ostdeutschland in der zweiten Einwanderergeneration nachlassen, wenig wahrscheinlich ist, dass sie kontinuierlich verblasst und sanft entschwindet. Bei Immigranten findet sich regelmäßig ein *backlash*: die erste Generation ist oft 'separatistisch', die zweite relativ assimiliert, die dritte Generation aber 'reaffirmativ'.[17]

(Suddenly the big mystery of the last thirteen years seems less mysterious: There is such a thing as an East German identity. It developed long after the end of the GDR: Alex from *Good bye, Lenin!* would never have dreamt of referring to himself as East German. In 1992 the authors of the *Social Report* on the Neue Länder had not yet thought of introducing the category 'East Germany' when they inquired into regional identification. When they eventually did ask, in 1999, 74 per cent perceived themselves 'fairly' or 'strongly' as East Germans. The figure even rose to 80 per cent in 2001 – a typical case of self-ethnication, a phenomenon long known to migration researchers. [...] Identification with East Germany is sure to decrease in the second generation of immigrants, but it is not likely that it will simply vanish. There is a regular backlash with

---

16   Toralf Staud, 'Ossis sind Türken. 13 Jahre Einheit: In Gesamt-Westdeutschland sind die Ostdeutschen Einwanderer', *Die Zeit*, 41 (1 October 2003), 9; the article is an abridged and modified version of a contribution to: Tanja Busse and Tobias Dürr (eds.), *Das neue Deutschland: Die Zukunft als Chance*, Weimar 2003.

17   Staud, 'Ossis sind Türken'.

immigrants. The first generation is often separatist, the second generation is relatively assimilated, but the third generation tends to reaffirm its cultural identity.)

Perhaps in the case of East Germans the succession of separatist, assimilative and re-affirmative phases has already arrived at the third phase. That would mean that a young generation that does not really know the GDR through personal experience is trying to build up an identity as East Germans by using a musealized image of a bygone society and culture. *Good Bye, Lenin!* is as much a document as a reflection and critique of this tendency.

Conclusion

As Gottfried Fliedl pointed out, situations of abrupt political change, combined with destruction of former social structures and hierarchies, have always favoured musealization.[18] German unification put an end not only to the GDR, but also in a certain way to the old FRG. Discussions on the new Germany, the 'Berliner Republik', and what it could mean were boosted. In this situation it was an obvious thing to look back on German history – in particular with a musealizing gaze. Even the construction of the new Berlin was very much concerned with preserving structures and elements of the historical Berlin. For example, the urban design of the new Potsdamer Platz on the one hand eliminates the former borderline between East and West Berlin, but on the other hand tries to reconstruct the situation before the Second World War by integrating architectural remains of the Wilhelminian era. It tries to establish continuity between a distant time and the present, bypassing half a century, and creating discontinuity to the immediate past. This example may demonstrate that the relation of

---

18　Gottfried Fliedl, 'Testamentskultur: Musealisierung und Kompensation', in Zacharias (ed.), *Zeitphänomen Musealisierung*, pp.166–179: p.171; see Gottfried Fliedl (ed.), *Die Erfindung des Museums. Bürgerliche Museumsidee und Französische Revolution*, Vienna 1996.

continuity or discontinuity on one side and conservation of historical
monuments or documents on the other side is quite complex.

It has been mentioned above that musealization primarily tends
to build continuity between the present and the past, but the commemorating and reflexive gaze on the musealized objects can also create
awareness of discontinuities. Walter Benjamin described the collector
as a deeply melancholic figure, who tries different possibilities of
organizing his collection and thus experiences the relativity of every
given organization.[19] No chosen pattern seems to be necessary, each
has an alternative. The loss of familiarity and security that causes
musealization may also be the result of it. That reminds us of our two
examples. Both look back on history in a very melancholic way,
exploring alternatives to it without definitely opting for them. They
invent better endings for stories that already have ended, but also
make clear that the need for specific alternatives is a very personal
one. It is an uneasiness with the ways of German history in the
twentieth century that forms the background of these alternative
histories, which do not claim to propose outlines for a better future. As
Alex formulates them in *Good Bye, Lenin!* these alternative histories
show something one would have liked to have, but at the same time
they state that reality was different. Christa Wolf, for example,
laments about the past in *Was bleibt* (1990; *What remains*, 1993), thus
posing in the title the question what role literature or fiction in general
could play under such circumstances.[20] In contrast, *Ein Garten im
Norden* states that what remains are 'some thoughts, memories and
intentions of a few individuals'21 which nevertheless can be helpful

19   See Walter Benjamin, *Chapter H [Der Sammler]*, in Walter Benjamin, *Gesam-
     melte Schriften*, V: Das Passagen-Werk, ed. Rolf Tiedemann and Hermann
     Schweppenhäuser, Frankfurt/M. 1982, pp.269–280.
20   Christa Wolf, *Was bleibt*, Berlin 1990.
21   '"Voll, voll", sagte ich. "Irgendwo wird sich schon noch eine leere Zeile finden
     oder ein weißer Rand, auf den wir schreiben können, wie es nun weiterging und
     was schließlich bleibt." / "Was bleibt? Das fragen SIE mich!" rief der Antiquar
     und sah mich mit erstaunten, kugelrunden Augen an, und einem Lächeln, in
     dem Ironie und Zuneigung sich die Waage hielten. "Was bleibt? Nun, wie Sie
     selbst sagten: Einige Gedanken, Erinnerungen und Vorsätze in einigen einzel-
     nen Menschen…".' ('Everywhere's full', I said. 'There must be a blank some-

for the project that gives the last chapter of the novel its title: 'Zukunftsbewältigung' (*Garten*, 579) ('coming to terms with the future').

Bibliography

Arnold-de Simine, Silke, 'Themepark GDR? The Aestheticization of Memory in post-Wende Museums, Literature and Films', in Christian Emden and David Midgley (eds.) *The Fragile Tradition: The German Cultural Imagination since 1500. I: Cultural Memory and Historical Consciousness,* Oxford 2003, pp.253–280.

Benjamin, Walter, *Chapter H [Der Sammler],* in *Gesammelte Schriften,* V: Das Passagen-Werk, ed. Rolf Tiedemann and Hermann Scheppenhäuser, Frankfurt/M. 1982, pp.269–280.

Demandt, Alexander, *Ungeschehene Geschichte: Ein Traktat über die Frage: Was wäre geschehen, wenn...?*, 2nd edition, Göttingen 1986.

Faulenbach, Bernd, and Franz-Josef Jelich (eds.), *Probleme der Musealisierung der doppelten deutschen Nachkriegsgeschichte.* Dokumentation einer Tagung des Forschungsinstituts für Arbeiterbildung und der Hans-Böckler-Stiftung, Essen 1993.

Fliedl, Gottfried, 'Testamentskultur: Musealisierung und Kompensation', in Zacharias (ed.), *Zeitphänomen Musealisierung,* pp.166–179.

——, (ed.), *Die Erfindung des Museums. Bürgerliche Museumsidee und Französische Revolution,* Vienna 1996.

Flügel, Katharina, and Wolfgang Ernst (eds.), *Musealisierung der DDR? 40 Jahre als kulturhistorische Herausforderung,* Alfter 1992.

Helbig, Jörg, *Der parahistorische Roman: Ein literarhistorischer und gattungstypologischer Beitrag zur Allotopieforschung,* Frankfurt/M. 1988.

Hellekson, Karen, *The Alternate History: Refiguring Historical Time,* Kent, Ohio 2001.

Hensel, Jana, *Zonenkinder,* Reinbek bei Hamburg 2002.

Kleeberg, Michael, *Ein Garten im Norden. Roman,* Berlin 1998.

---

where or a white margin on which we could write what happened next and what remains in the end.' / 'What remains? YOU ask me!', shouted the antiquary and looked at me wide-eyed and with an amazed smile in which irony and affection mingled. 'What remains? What you said yourself: a few thoughts, memories and intentions in a few isolated individuals...', *Garten*, 557).

Kuhn, Gerd, and Andreas Ludwig (eds.), *Alltag und soziales Gedächtnis. Die DDR-Objektkultur und ihre Musealisierung*, Hamburg 1997.

Lübbe, Hermann, *Der Fortschritt und das Museum: Über den Grund unseres Vergnügens an historischen Gegenständen* (The 1981 Bithell Memorial Lecture), London 1982.

Niggemeier, Stefan, 'Kinder, nehmt euch ein Beispiel an Walter Ulbricht. Die letzte DDR-Show ist gleichzeitig eine Parodie auf das Genre: Oliver Kalkofe nimmt sich die Ostalgie-Welle vor', *Frankfurter Allgemeine Zeitung*, 231 (6 October 2003).

Pflaum, Hans Günter, 'Der diskrete Charme der Ostalgie: Wolfgang Beckers "Good Bye, Lenin!" konkurriert noch um den Berlinale-Bären und kommt schon ins Kino', *Süddeutsche Zeitung*, 36 (13 February 2003), 12.

Pomian, Krzysztof, 'Entre l'invisible et le visible: la collection', in Krzysztof Pomian, *Collectionneurs, amateurs et curieux*, Paris 1987, pp.15–58.

Sturm, Eva, *Konservierte Welt. Museum und Musealisierung*, Berlin 1991.

Staud, Toralf, 'Ossis sind Türken. 13 Jahre Einheit: In Gesamt-Westdeutschland sind die Ostdeutschen Einwanderer', *Die Zeit*, 41 (1 October 2003), 9.

Uchronia: The Alternate History List, http://www.uchronia.net.

Wolf, Christa, *Was bleibt*, Berlin 1990.

Zacharias, Wolfgang (ed.), *Zeitphänomen Musealisierung. Das Verschwinden der Gegenwart und die Konstruktion der Erinnerung*, Essen 1990.

Jonathan Bach

Vanishing Acts and Virtual Reconstructions: Technologies of Memory and the Afterlife of the GDR[1]

Introduction: Disappearance and Reappearance

What happened to the German Democratic Republic (GDR), commonly known as East Germany? It ceased to exist, of course, on 3 October 1990 when Germany was (re)unified. In keeping with the conventionally anthropomorphized status of the state we can say that the GDR died. Indeed, some of its citizens ceremoniously buried it: Daphne Berdahl, in her book on a small town in the ex-GDR, describes a scene where the residents, after lowering the GDR flag for the last time on 3 October 1990, placed it in a casket and cremated both casket and flag.[2] Perhaps this was to prevent the body from resurrection, for as we know from anthropology, death invests objects with particular powers in an uncanny way.

The legacy of East Germany is as much about (re)appearance as disappearance. As Freud famously noted, it is easier to kill than to cover up the traces, and the traces surrounding a death themselves tend to evolve into a network that becomes impossible to trace to its

---

1   The author wishes to thank Yukiko Koga and Silke Arnold-de Simine for their comments, Sheila Shettle for her assistance and insights, and Elzbieta Matynia for the opportunity to present this essay as a talk in the joint New School Graduate Faculty/New York University 2003 lecture series on 'East European Politics and Society.'

2   See the description and accompanying photograph in Daphne Berdahl, *Where the World Ended: Re-unification and Identity in the German Borderland*, Berkeley, CA 1999, pp.211–13.

origin, a network that excludes appropriation.[3] The death of East Germany is more accurately an assisted suicide, but its traces are perhaps all the more complex for this. To stay with Freud for a moment, if a people is shaped through traumatic events, what is the wound that must be sutured for the former citizens of the GDR? While the uprising of 17 June 1953 is a key moment, as is the building of the wall eight years later, arguably the most traumatic events are the end of the GDR and unification, two inextricable but not therefore identical occurrences. The end of the GDR structurally resembles, albeit in a very different register, the tension surrounding the 8 May 1945 between seeing it as defeat or liberation. The death of the GDR was notably marked by an ambiguity between the inability of the East German state to reform itself and the desire of the East Germans, after this inability became clear, to join the West. The demise of East Germany was a veritably dialectical moment – an *Aufhebung* that also marked, to invoke both Hegel and Freud, with Marx in between, the true death of the father – the infamous 'daddy state' of socialism.[4]

Thus the death of the GDR has at least two elements that alone make for a difficult case of mourning, memory and history. First, was its marking by a form of liberation through defeat (assisted suicide). Second, the speed of the transformation and the decisive discursive and institutional dominance by the West left relatively little public space for the processing (*Aufarbeitung*) of people's lived experience outside the simplistic binaries of East and West. This was accompanied by a sense of loss of control over one's own lives and future, especially as the promises of transition faded into the seeming reality of second-class citizenship.

Partially as a result of a seemingly inevitable disillusionment, pollsters find a growing sense of identification among former GDR citizens with the East. For example, the Social Report poll of 2001

---

3   Sigmund Freud, *Moses and Monotheism*, New York 1967. See also Samuel Weber, *The Joy of Killing. Violence and Guilt in the Writings of Freud* (The Ilse and Otto Mainzer Lecture, New York University, 6 March 2003).

4   In a more popular Freudian vein, Daniela Dahn interprets division and unification in explicitly sexual terms as a dissatisfying coitus interruptus. See Daniela Dahn, *Westwärts und nicht vergessen*, Reinbek bei Hamburg 1996, p.23.

found a combined total of 80 percent of the easterners asked felt 'strongly connected' (29%) or 'considerably connected' (51%) to something called 'Ostdeutschland' (East Germany), a term that in German purposely was used so as not to convey the political baggage of the East German state.[5] As Wolfgang Engler notes, the lack of representative or specifically-eastern political institutions (with the partial exception of the PDS) helped emphasize a cultural identification over political identification with the East.[6]

This cultural identification is a precarious task, since the East firmly occupies the discursive space of inferiority. In the ex-GDR the failure of the state has been followed, after a short period of euphoria, by consistent high rates of unemployment, lower wages, and social anomie. The process of unification, the rapid takeover of nearly all East German institutions by the West and the dismantling of much of the structure of the economy and the state system at all levels, was based in large part on predictable binaries where things western were good and eastern bad. One encounters in the East a certain internalization of this negative coding: as one rap song put it, *Ossis* are 'East-niggers.'[7] The question arises how people deal with this negative coding. Does one attempt to deny it by reversal, by criticizing things western, or by trying to prove the western assumptions wrong? Or is the best defense an inversion of the coding, to make a virtue out of what the dominant discourse frames as negative – in other words, we are proud of our differences? And since, practically speaking, western Germans dominate the economic, cultural, and political landscape, where do these sentiments find articulation?

---

5   Wolfgang Engler, *Die Ostdeutschen als Avantgarde,* Berlin 2002, p.20.

6   Ibid., p.21.

7   The group A.N.T.I. sings 'Eastniggers ... / are what we all are. The colour of our skin is white / yet in Germany we are the last shit', quoted in Jürgen Roth and Michael Rudolf, *Spaltprodukte: Gebündelte Ost-West-Vorurteile,* Leipzig 1997, p.97.

Alltagskultur

In this context the realm of everyday life (*Alltagskultur*) claims a heightened importance as a space that is neither entirely apolitical (since the state was omnipresent) nor explicitly political. GDR *Alltagskultur*, as the lived environment and common experience of two plus generations, is a multiply-coded space, its recapturing a form of resistance to the current social situation as well as a welcome space of ambiguity within which processing (*aufarbeiten*) can take place without drawing clear lines between good and bad – dissidents and Stasi colonels alike sang Pioneer songs when they were kids and got drunk on *Rotkäppchen Sekt*. For societies emerging from dictatorships, *Alltagskultur* is still an under-explored avenue for understanding the transition.

One instantiation of GDR *Alltagskultur* has been the questionable nostalgia known as *Ostalgie*. Previously I explored the phenomenon of *Ostalgie* as expressed through the material culture of consumption of eastern goods (*Ostprodukte*) by examining how an identity rendered voiceless bubbled up through the renewed consumption of formerly scorned eastern products, and how what seemed like a straightforward case of nostalgia was often, for *Ossis*, a longing for a style of longing, and for *Wessis* a form of distancing through camp and kitsch.[8] Ultimately both were subjected to the dynamic of marketization that turns 'authentic' subcultures into niche markets. But the GDR *Alltag* (every day) has been made to 'live on' in other ways, from societies, clubs and nostalgia parties to the contemporary adaptation of rituals such as the youth initiation known as *Jugendweihe*. But it is on the World Wide Web where the GDR, as one web site put it, is experiencing its 'virtuelle Auferstehung' ('virtual resurrection').[9]

---

8   Jonathan Bach, '"The Taste Remains": Consumption, (N)Ostalgia, and the Production of East Germany', *Public Culture*, 14/3 (Fall 2002), 545–56.

9   The term 'virtual' is used here in its double opposition to the 'real' – in a technical sense connoting a distinction between the ethereality of digital media and the materiality of traditional media (print or image), and in a social sense connoting the existence of an effect without the actual (material) basis for it.

Here is where we confront a phenomenon of what Andreas Huyssen calls new strategies of public and private memorialization, which he sees propelled by a fear of cultural forgetting and indicative of a changing relationship between memory and forgetting. Contemporary culture, Huyssen argues, pressured by a heady mix of information technologies, media worlds and consumption patterns, entails a transformation of temporality where memory and musealization are deployed in increasingly intricate fashions.[10] In this essay I focus on one instantiation of this phenomenon, the rise of the World Wide Web as a technology of memory in which we witness a virtual reconstruction of the GDR, a reconstruction that complicates the demarcation between nostalgia, memory and history and raises questions about the Web as a technology of memory. When the GDR vanished it seemed that its physical traces would only be visible in pre-fabricated apartment buildings and attics, official archives, the occasional museum exhibit, and human memory. As the GDR was imploding, however, a new technology of memory was emerging in the World Wide Web. Starting almost the year after unification, when the first web browser appeared, the fading GDR began to appear in an expanding Web that stressed personal expression and unofficial documentation. Steadily throughout the first decade of unification as the GDR disappeared into the pages of history it also reappeared in the pages of the Web. It appears there today as parody, as nostalgia, as memory, as history, as biting commentary on the present and as subtle digs at the past.

---

10   Andreas Huyssen, *Present Pasts: Urban Palimpsets and the Politics of Memory*, Stanford, CA 2003, pp.11–29.

You are Now Leaving West Berlin

In her book *Zonenkinder* (2002; *After The Wall*, 2004), Jana Hensel writes that unification made the GDR appear as belonging to a suddenly distant time which 'had the smell of fairy tales and for which we could no longer find the right words [...] [during unification] our childhood was turned into a museum that has no name and no address, and that scarcely anyone had any interest in opening.'[11] One is tempted to add that if Hensel's museum has no address, it has a URL, for since the mid-90s there has been a steady growth of sites devoted to nearly every aspect of the GDR.[12]

In 1998 one of the earliest general-interest GDR sites stated that its goal was that 'everyone should, in the Internet, be able to experience and grasp the GDR' ('die DDR soll im Internet für jeden erfahrbar und begreifbar gemacht werden').[13] Five years later what had been already many dozens of sites became many hundreds. 'GDR-Search' ('DDR-Suche'), one of at least four major search engines devoted exclusively to GDR topics, today lists 599 topics divided into numerous categories, from 'music,' to 'Stasi,' from 'transportation' to the 'national peoples army.'[14] There is a veritable GDR industry on the Web. The state and many of its organs are there, from seeming and controversial spoofs such the 'official' page of the SED government in

---

11   Jana Hensel, *Zonenkinder*, Reinbek bei Hamburg 2002, pp.24–5.
12   There are also, of course, a growing number of brick and mortar museums that
      deal with everyday life in the GDR, from the well-known Documentation
      Center for Everyday Culture of the GDR in Eisenhüttenstadt to smaller under-
      takings such as the 'DDR Museum' in Pforzheim. On the museum in Eisen-
      hüttenstadt see Charity Scribner, *Requiem for Communism*, Cambridge, MA
      2003, pp.23–44.
13   http://www.ddr-im-www.de (accessed October 1999).
14   The major search engines for the virtual GDR include 'Die DDR im WWW'
      http://www.ddr-im-www.de; DDR Suche http://www.ddr-suche.de; 'WebRing
      der DDR' http://I.webring.com, and 'DDR Web' http://www.ddrweb.de.vu/.
      The types of sites described in the following paragraphs can most always be
      found through directories or keyword searches on these sites, though as time
      passes some sites may be taken down. Sites for this essay were last accessed in
      April 2003.

exile to serious documentation of the GDR education regulations and instructions for the old procedure for applying for exit visas. The GDR military is there in full force, even in the present tense, from the National People's Army to the GDR air force and other military sites, including detailed information on military medals. The Free German Youth and the Young Pioneers are there, complete with words and melodies for the old songs and instructions for tying the red bandana. You can watch parts of GDR television such as the news show *Aktuelle Kamera*, find out about DEFA films, or listen to GDR radio, read old articles from the GDR press, look up pages of GDR jokes (both pre- and post-unification), go to glossaries and dictionaries to translate GDR-German into FRG-German. You can read up on GDR heroes such as astronaut Sigmund Jähn or villains such as Erich Honecker, or browse citizen's home pages such as 'Homepage Günter Platzdasch,' 'Camping in the GDR' ('Campen in der DDR') or 'Jens Roloff's Ostalgie Site' ('Jens Roloffs Ostalgieseite') full of photos, memories, stories, rants and guest books with numerous greetings from homepage to homepage. Of course there are pages devoted to the *Wende* and unification, the wall and the border, from the archive of the civic movement in Leipzig to chronicles of events, to the cynical half-parody 'Aktion Mauer Wiederaufbauen' ('Build up the Wall Again') and the more nuanced site named 'Begrüßungsgeld' ('Welcome Money').[15] Neither last nor least are the pages devoted to *Trabis*, *Ampelmännchen*, GDR ambulances of the Leipzig DRK hospital, ships, trucks, buses, license plates, beer coasters, matchbox covers, sports insignia, money, stamps and products of every kind, often for sale through online speciality stores. Not to mention the discussion and chat sites, GDR music, out-of-print GDR-era books, and, of course, GDR erotica ('wer zu spät kommt …').

Let us look in more detail at one site, the 'DDR-im-WWW', founded in 1998 as a private hobby and five years later operating as a large site with a staff, claiming over 5 million hits since its incep-

---

15   'Welcome Money' refers to the D-Marks given by the West German government to GDR citizens who visited the West in the period between the fall of the Berlin Wall and the currency union.

tion.[16] The first page you see contains only one image: a full-color photograph of the original sign 'You are now leaving West Berlin.' The sign indicates simultaneously a fantasy for easterners – entering the GDR from the West – and marks the beginning of a journey. A click on the sign takes you to the home page, where current news and a menu awaits.

The news for April, 2003, concerns the new PRISMA column, a new Trabi stamp, the history of the GDR *Volkskammer* (Parliament), information about the then-new film *Good Bye, Lenin!*, and an explanation of the GDR household registry book and system. The menus start with 'History', which currently comprises 1985–90, with other years promised to come. 'People' contains biographies of key GDR personalities with photograph and bibliography. 'Photographs' includes pictures submitted by guests, such as the VEB Klement-Gottwald-Werke Schwerin, or border pictures. The next section 'AK' used to have downloadable snippets of the news show Aktuelle Kamera until they encountered copyright problems. The 'Premium' category contains links to pay sites, such as a thesis on the communist party (SED) in the fall of 1989, photos of naked GDR citizens, and the downloadable GDR national anthem for your cell phone. Under 'Books' you get lists by category, reviewed with a star system, and linked to Amazon. 'Music' takes you to a 'music of the GDR' site that promises 'a musical tour through 40 years of the GDR' from composers to trends, agitpop and reviews. 'Reports' contains guest submissions, such as 'my experience as a truck driver on the Vienna to Cottbus route', 'a visit to the border museum in Schlagsdorf', and 'Winnetou, Karl May and the Stasi.' Also available under this rubric are letters to the site under the heading 'So denkt der Bürger' ('Citizen's Thoughts'). 'Interactive' currently offers seventy-one pages of discussion forum, as well as chat, bulletin board and guest book, while the 'eCards' section allows you to learn the 'ABCs of socialism' by sending postcards that recall the language and design of the GDR. 'Links' takes you to twenty-seven loosely organized categories to lose yourself in.

---

16   'Die DDR im WWW', http://www.ddr-im-www.de.

Renarration and Discovery

In moving from vintage matchbox covers to retro sport shirts to new and improved eastern brands of washing powder, the surfer of East German web sites plays the role of the flâneur. The structure of the Web calls to mind Benjamin's perception of the Arcade as a horizontal, almost ecclesiastical space with a desire to represent an overarching unity that safeguards the idea of the eternal even as it is a space within which the ephemeral is highlighted in new and contradictory ways.[17]

The classic flâneur pieces together a narrative consumption experience by associating objects and shops, creating narratives that are both path-dependent (based, perhaps, on their socio-economic background) and spontaneous (based on what they find). There is no pre-ordained sequential order to shopping in an arcade save for that which the flâneur makes for him/herself during a stroll amidst the shops.

The GDR in the Web likewise appears as a collection of citations that can be randomly assembled at the will of the surfer. This reminds one of Benjamin's predilection for history as citation, where he saw distinct perspectival advantages in tearing the historical object from its context. For Benjamin, citational history means the reader and author become blurred, not unlike the blurring of the roles of author and viewer, consumer and producer on the Web. For Benjamin, memory is not a reconstruction of the past, which he sees as one-dimensional, but always a construction, a heterogeneous history whose meaning resides in the contemporary – a 'telescoping of the past through the present.'[18] Only through a break in the imagined continuity between the past and the present can the past be made usable, can it become a locus of contradiction, debate, allegory and montage, can it assume the fragmentary form that calls forth competing interpretations to render it whole.

In this sense the GDR web *sites* are literally *cites* that paradoxically tear the historical object from its context, so to speak, while aiming to do exactly the opposite – to re-embed the GDR in its

---

17   Walter Benjamin, *The Arcades Project*, Cambridge, MA 1999, p.160.
18   Benjamin, *The Arcades Project*, pp.470–1 (Convolute N).

historical context from which it has been torn. The 'DDR-im-WWW' site articulates this re-embedding by imploring both *Ossis* and *Wessis* that 'it is not enough to know the history of the old "FRG", one must also know what has happened "over there" over 40 years.' The surfer/flâneur/reader's task is to fashion a narrative out of sites of indeterminate sequentiality.[19] A person seeking to explore childhood in the GDR, for instance, encounters a bevy of sites, personal recollections, official documents on education, serious and satirical sites on the Pioneers and FDJ (Free German Youth), and while each site has its own more or less narrative structure, the surfer/flâneur is forced to create her or his own narrative from the multitude of sites/cites. In this way the Web as Arcade allows for new relations between citational and commercial practices. But to what effect? Here we find at least three categories of potential audiences:

First, for former GDR citizens, especially the younger generation born in the last decade of the GDR, the Web as a technology of memory presents different ways to renarrate the past. It provides an ambiguous, commercialized, ironic yet occasionally touching forest of images and sentiments. Second, judging by the comments on the web sites, many visitors to the sites come from non-German countries (Denmark, France) and are looking for information on the GDR. For them the Web is a process not so much of renarration but of discovery. Looking for material for research papers or just out of curiosity, they encounter an active and complex representation of the GDR.

Third, some visitors and even web pages come from West Germans, who find a certain attractive authenticity in the easterner's web millieu. One West German site proclaims 'Warum ich Ossi Fan bin' ('Why I am an easterner fan') and goes on to say that *Ossis* are super cool, a sentiment that one finds on a number of occasions.[20] At first glance this seems to be an extension of the way in which westerners fetishize the design of GDR products because of their camp and

---

19   See Ivo Vidan, 'Time Sequence in Spatial Fiction', in Michael Hoffman and Patrick Murphy (eds.), *Essentials of the Theory of Fiction*, Durham, NC 1988, pp.434–56.

20   Warum bin ich Ossifan? http://www.hallomausi.de/Reise/DDR/S-DDR-Fan.htm.

kitsch value. This could also be read as an extension of the long-standing critique of the Western niche-society as alienating and inadequately human. One detects a degree of projection of the desire for a different West onto the somewhat glorified inter-personal relations of the East, that, in retrospect, seem somehow less alienated because of the very conditions of scarcity and repression that caused the system's failure.

This is precisely the point where easterners feel they are on strongest ground in critiquing the West. Wolfgang Engler writes that 'if the eastern German idiom has a common denominator, then it is the complaint about the shrinking of social sensitivity' after unification.[21] Western social scientists worry that the perception of coherence between the system and the individual that seems to work in the West is lacking in the East.[22] But this very incoherence is often positively coded by easterners, who take a bitter pride in pointing out how not everything is better under capitalism even if one accepts its inevitable superiority as an economic system. Good neighbourliness, time for working in the garden and for the family, trust, all these become privileged memories that loom large in the context of bankruptcy, unemployment and bad credit.

To the extent that westerners also find this nostalgic image of interpersonal relations attractive, easterners are able to at least rhetorically invert the sentiment that during the years of division West Germans became European while East Germans remained German. By presenting the core values of normal GDR citizens as closely approximating the Christian values of love-thy-neighbour, and implying that these values are the most positive legacy of the GDR, this opens the possibility to claim the GDR as the 'real' and less alienated form of the nation.

Partially because of the stereotype that easterners have deeper friendships and less shallow emotions than westerners, and partly because of the camp and kitsch attraction of the now-harmless, still residually exotic East, there is a palpable sense of a trend. The March 2003 newsletter of the DDR-im-WWW site, 'DDR-Umschau', writes

---

21   Engler, *Die Ostdeutschen als Avantgarde*, pp.29–30.
22   See Klaus Schroeder cited in ibid., p.30.

that these days 'the zone is cool.' This trend is identified as especially present in the West, where, the Newsletter notes bitterly it is exemplified by 'Joe Average ('Otto Normalverbraucher') who only knows the GDR from hearsay or from the generation that has grown up since the changes (*Wende*).'[23]

The 'DDR-Umschau' pegs the movie *Good Bye, Lenin!*, which became a runaway hit across Germany in 2002–3, as the catalyst for this trend. The film is a cultural phenomenon that has put *Ostalgie* on the map in mainstream Germany, and is an important moment in the the renarritavization of the GDR taking place simultaneously on the Internet.

Good Bye, Lenin!: A Fantasy for All

The film itself is more in the tradition of a light comedy than high art, but its incontrovertible popularity rests on its inversion of the story of unification. In the film a convinced socialist mother suffers a heart attack and falls into a coma in the period before the wall falls. She awakes after the wall has come down, and the doctor allows her son to take her home only on the condition that she experience no shocks that might cause her to relapse. The son can imagine no greater shock for his mother than learning that unification is underway, so he contrives to recreate the GDR in his mother's bedroom, hastily restoring it to the way it looked in the old days. Of course as his mother's condition improves it becomes more and more difficult to keep up the illusion that nothing has changed. She wants to watch TV, and he and a friend create fake episodes of *Aktuelle Kamera* which she watches unaware that these are both fake and from a VCR. One day she sneaks out of the house, and the son is forced to explain the presence of so many westerners and western cars. He tells his mother that things have gotten so bad in the West that westerners are fleeing to the GDR.

---

23   *Die DDR-Umschau,* 14 (2003) http://pc-special.de/nlrdr.php?nummer=552239
      &linknr=9.

Eventually, though, it becomes necessary to inform her that unification is immanent, but how? The solution appears in the form of a taxi driver who looks like (and perhaps is) the famous East German astronaut Sigmund Jähn. The taxi driver/astronaut agrees to act in a pretend newscast in which he takes over from Erich Honecker, and announces that with the full consent of the *Politburo* he is declaring the GDR such a success that, in honour of the fortieth anniversary of the Republic, he is opening the borders and unifying the country with the West. For effect this announcement is followed by the real fireworks celebrating the actual German unification, for the son has timed this for 3 October, the day of German Unity. Thus does unification occur not as a result of the failure of the GDR but because of its success.

As do all major releases these days the film has its own web site, and the site aims to create a sub-culture around the film.[24] Parts of the site are standard movie-site fare, such as interviews, actors' bios, behind the scenes pages and an online video game with GDR nostalgia prizes ('the GDR lives on! Help me in my online adventure and save the GDR in 79 square meters!'). But the site goes further than this by adopting the style of many of the GDR-sites, including its own versions of photo galleries, a column and newsletter, a dictionary of eastern vocabulary, eCards, forum, and a historical element in the presentation of 'instructional materials.' Besides the film poster, you can download parts of speeches by Walter Ulbricht and Erich Honecker and praise for young Pioneers, as if to convince a young audience that the events described in the film are indeed based on real fact. Since a major studio is not behind the film, the site lists its 'co-operation partners' including Coca Cola, Mercedes and the department store chain Karstadt.

In this way the film merges into the online world of the GDR in the Web, appearing in numerous other web sites as object of discussion or advertisement. Its tremendous success is itself a phenomenon that indicates a shift in the role that the GDR plays not only among *Ostalgie* fans but a wider German public. Its fantasy inversion of the story of the GDR plays an acceptably commercialized political role –

---

24   *Good Bye, Lenin!* website, http://www.good-bye-lenin.de/intro.php.

it gives ironic voice to both those who, like the mother, appeared to believe in the official narrative of the GDR and those who, like the protesters, sought at first reform of the GDR rather than unification.[25]

The irony runs very deep here, because this fantasy of the successful dissipation of the GDR harks back to a longing during the GDR that was premised on an unattainable object of desire, the 'fully developed Self' promised by both socialism *and* Western materialism. The longing for a socialist utopia was perversely connected to a fetishism of Western material culture, as Milena Veenis points out:

> the beautiful material [East Germans] saw [in the West], with its harmonious aesthetic compositions and its tangible, soft and sensuous characteristics, somehow seemed to be the concrete realisation and the ultimate fulfillment of all the beautiful-sounding but never-realized (socialist) promises about the Golden Future, in which we would all have a fully developed Self, while living in complete harmony with each other.[26]

The sudden possibility of unification in 1989 and 1990 held the incredible promise of instantiating these temporal and spatial fantasies. The inability of unification to act as the *Aufhebung* (sublimation) of the socialist-trained and capitalist-propelled desire for harmony resulted in a form of postunification nostalgia in the East that has as its object not the GDR itself, but the longing associated with the GDR. What had been a frozen aspiration for an indefinitely deferred future shifted to nostalgia for that aspiration. In the fantasy of *Good Bye, Lenin!* this is carried to its extreme – socialism's end is nothing other than the free-market social welfare state, and except for the older generation of economic losers (portrayed sympathetically) there is a happy ending for all.

While the film leaves little to the viewer's imagination, one thing that remains ambiguous is the politics of the eastern identity. One comment in the film's online forum agrees that there is less difference than imagined between East and West, but he sees this not as an

---

25   It turns out, however, that the mother also once planned to escape from the GDR, and her enthusiasm for socialism is in part presented as over-compensation for her inability to escape.

26   Milena Veenis, 'Consumption in East Germany: The seduction and betrayal of things', *Journal of Material Culture*, 4/1 (1999), pp.79–112: p.86.

encouraging development but as a devastating comment on West Germany's shortcomings. Rather than feeling more comfortable in his identity after seeing the film he is moved to write 'and what am I really: an Ossi? a Wessi? A Wossiossi, ossiwossi, WOSI, Ostelbiger, Oderwestlicher? I myself do not know anymore.'[27]

Cultural Survival Strategies

Perhaps the success of the film can be attributed precisely to the way in which unification is renarrativized as a process where everyone can be happy with the ending – westerners, old socialists and dissidents alike. That this fantasy is of course not true to life and open to criticism is almost beside the point. The fantasy works, in fact, to highlight the opposite empirical condition – the continuing disparities between East and West.

The link between *Good Bye, Lenin!* and the GDR in the Web as current manifestations of GDR nostalgia is the making harmless of the GDR, turning it into a parody of itself populated by well-meaning people who were capable, for the most part, of creating honest lives for themselves under adverse conditions. It is striking that among the GDR web sites most of them adopt either an ironic stance or a 'things were not that bad' message with bitterness focused on real existing capitalism.

The tongue-in-cheek nature of the sites can be seen as a distancing and disarming tool, and can be situated in an evolving understanding of the way new media technologies encourage, as Maja Mikula writes, 'the proliferation of parody as one of the modes of positive self-reference with a universal appeal akin to Bakhtinian "carnival laughter".'[28] The 'things were not so bad' message is part of

---

27   Comment posted to the *Good Bye, Lenin!* Web forum by 'MF' on 3 March 2003. http://www.good-bye-lenin.de/forum.php.

28   Maja Mikula, 'Virtual Landscapes of Memory', *Information, Communication and Society*, VI/2 (June 2003), 169–86: 169.

an understandable attempt to regain some sense of agency in a double sense: first over the GDR itself that denied agency under the all-powerful state and, second, afterwards by the relatively passive role of the ex-GDR citizens in the transition following unification. At the same time by articulating the relatively 'positive' sides of life under GDR, the relative loss of these positive associations can be attributed less as time goes by to the failures of the GDR state than to the in-ability of the western model to allow them to continue. The easterners thus become victims of the West as well as victims of their own failed regime. This sense of victimhood is part of the current identity of the East, where unemployment is disastrously higher than in the West, with devastating social consequences.

Thus one can read the subtext of the web sites and the 'East is cool' trend symbolized by *Good Bye, Lenin!* as a form of cultural survival strategy. It is an attempt to renarrate the past to supplement the official image of the gray, listless Stasi State and thereby to regain dignity and agency, even at the risk of glorification. It is also an attempt to reposition the eastern subject (in both senses of the term) in the current relation to united Germany, especially in terms of the East's deteriorating economic and social conditions. This reposition-ing can also help easterners escape the sense of failure attributed to their association with the failed East German state.

The reconstruction of the GDR on the Web, a GDR that by and large consists of ironic commentary, melancholy remembrance and a sense that although the system was bad the people were good, and in certain ways better off than today, is a supplement in the double sense of adding to the story, and replacing the narrative of unification with one where the West does not seem as positive. Taken together with other memories, the GDR in the Web helps create a nuanced view, while also serving as a critique of unification as it happened, with the message that not everything that belongs together has indeed grown together, or even should.

Technologies of Memory

It is important to note, in closing, that while the medium of the Web is often used to critique or subvert aspects of the dominant market ideology, the Web itself is a supremely commercialized sphere. Memory is literally consumed and, in part, driven by the advertising and e-commerce that is part and parcel of most web sites. The Web is itself a vast interconnected network of consumption, where the primary element at work is the visual connection to those Arcade-like 'seductively displayed, endlessly varied wares' (Benjamin) which include both actual products for purchase and the viewing of the web sites itself, especially following links for which companies pay sites that direct people to them. The GDR that appears in the Web is simultaneously a commodity *and* a form of musealized exhibit, taken out of history and displayed in a timeless form. Thus the GDR on the Web provides us both with a commodity fetish – with full exchange value through e-commerce – and with a museum fetish – that, as Andreas Huyssen puts it, 'transcends exchange value' and 'carries with it [...] a kind of memory value'.[29]

This raises the question of the emerging relation between exchange value and memory value. Is the Web a form of commercialization of collective memory, or is the notion of commercialization itself outdated by new forms of consumption and production? Will the Web as a technology of memory change the way societies remember – the way new generations access and interpret the memories of the past? It is as hard to imagine that it would not as to imagine the ways in which it will. What are the political implications that lie in the growth of an archive that is not defined by guardians with hermeneutic rights and competences, an archive with personal recollections, photo collections, unofficial and official reports, scanned historical documents, and musealized products of everyday life that are not collected, selected, maintained or presented by specialists and not geared toward

---

29   Andreas Huyssen, *Twilight Memories: Marking Time in a Culture of Amnesia*,
      New York 1995, p.33.

researchers but accessible to anyone?[30] Will the Web blur the distinction between the public and private collector, the curio-cabinet and the museum, the justificatory regimes of memory professionals (historians, curators), or might it intensify their respective claims to discrete hermeneutic rights and competences?[31]

The GDR in the Web functions in this context not only as a portal to the sentiments and resentments of a united Germany, but as part of a shifting culture of memory that accompanies the political and economic privatization of the public sphere. Perhaps we could regard the explosion of GDR sites as part of a shift toward 'distributed memory,' where, like with distributed cognition, tasks formerly concentrated in hierarchical institutions are spread among loose networks where they are undertaken simultaneously in a linked and interactive environment. While one is tempted to impute a democratic value to non-hierarchical forms of activity, it is highly uncertain what the political effect of distributed memory might be for the 'memory work' that has become a central part of contemporary German society. Whatever the ultimate effect, the memory traces of the GDR are now firmly embedded within the linked labyrinth of the World Wide Web. What Benjamin wondered about three-quarters of a century ago can be posed anew: 'We are only beginning to imagine,' he noted in his Arcades project, 'just what forms now lying concealed within machines will be determining for our epoch.'[32]

---

30   See Jacques Derrida, *Archive Fever*, Chicago 1998.

31   One also wonders how the notion of duration – so central to memory – will be affected by the transitory nature of much material on the web, where websites change constantly and appear and disappear overnight.

32   This translation is from Susan Buck-Morss, *The Dialectics of Seeing: Walter Benjamin and the Arcades Project*, Cambridge, MA 1991, p.115; See also Benjamin, *The Arcades Project*, p.155.

Bibliography

Bach, Jonathan, '"The Taste Remains": Consumption, (N)Ostalgia, and the Production of East Germany', *Public Culture*, 14/3 (Fall 2002), 545–56.

Benjamin, Walter, *The Arcades Project*, Cambridge, MA 1999.

Berdahl, Daphne, *Where the World Ended: Re-unification and Identity in the German Borderland*, Berkeley, CA 1999.

Buck-Morss, Susan, *The Dialectics of Seeing: Walter Benjamin and the Arcades Project*, Cambridge, MA 1991.

Dahn, Daniela, *Westwärts und nicht vergessen*, Reinbek bei Hamburg 1996.

Derrida, Jacques, *Archive Fever*, Chicago 1998.

Engler, Wolfgang, *Die Ostdeutschen als Avantgarde*, Berlin 2002.

Freud, Sigmund, *Moses and Monotheism*, New York 1967.

Hensel, Jana, *Zonenkinder*, Reinbek bei Hamburg 2002.

Huyssen, Andreas, *Present Pasts: Urban Palimpsets and the Politics of Memory*, Stanford, CA 2003.

——, *Twilight Memories: Marking Time in a Culture of Amnesia*, New York 1995.

Mikula, Maja, 'Virtual Landscapes of Memory', *Information, Communication and Society*, VI/2 (June 2003), 169–86.

Roth, Jürgen, and Michael Rudolf, *Spaltprodukte: Gebündelte Ost-West-Vorurteile*, Leipzig 1997.

Scribner, Charity, *Requiem for Communism*, Cambridge, MA 2003.

Vidan, Ivo, 'Time Sequence in Spatial Fiction', in Michael Hoffman and Patrick Murphy (eds.), *Essentials of the Theory of Fiction*, Durham, NC 1988, pp.434–56.

Veenis, Milena, 'Consumption in East Germany: The seduction and betrayal of things', *Journal of Material Culture*, 4/1 (1999), pp.79–112.

Weber, Samuel, *The Joy of Killing. Violence and Guilt in the Writings of Freud* (The Ilse and Otto Mainzer Lecture, New York University, 6 March 2003).

Simon Ward

Material, Image, Sign:
On the Value of Memory Traces in Public Space

In August 2003 the archaeologist Leo Schmidt from the Technical University of Brandenburg in Cottbus argued that barely noticeable remnants of the Berlin Wall (such as the light masts on Heinrich-Heine Strasse), which his team had spent two years documenting, might, as material testament to the Cold War, become a World Cultural Heritage site, joining such Berlin locations as the Museumsinsel and Sanssouci.[1] Amongst the mostly negative reactions to his suggestion, the spokesperson for the administration of city development argued that while it was important 'die Mauerreste als politisches Mahnmal zu erhalten, doch sie dafür in den Rang eines Kulturerbes zu erheben, bestehe keinerlei Notwendigkeit'.[2]

This debate about the remains of the Wall illustrates not only that archaeologists are documenting a history that is little more than a decade old. It also indicates an uncertainty about what constitutes 'politics' and 'culture' in an increasingly image-driven society and a concomitant concern with which objects deserve to be preserved and for what reason.[3] In that context, it points to the increasing number

---

1   C.v.L, 'Mauerreste Weltkulturerbe?', *Der Tagesspiegel* (7 August 2003). Many parts of the Wall (such as the towers at the Bornholmer Straße and the colourful Eastside Gallery) have long been placed under preservation orders.

2   Katja Füchsel, 'Weltkulturerbe Mauer heftig umstritten', *Der Tagesspiegel* (8 August 2003). ('while it was important that the remains of the Wall should be maintained as a political memorial, there was absolutely no need to elevate it to the status of a part of the cultural heritage.')

3   As the values of preservation policy have shifted to accept industrial architecture as a constituent part of its remit, there have been calls in recent years from some experts to limit what comes under the purview of preservation (see Nikolaus Bernau, 'Städtebauliche Wegwerfkultur', *Berliner Zeitung*, 22 Sep-

and variety of 'ungewollter Denkmale' ('unintended monuments'), to use Alois Riegl's term for those remnants of the past that play a role within public memory culture without having been specifically designed for that purpose.[4] In an era when art in general, and literature in particular, has become uncertain about its public role as a conduit for memory work, this essay looks at the processes through which physical 'memory traces' have manifested themselves as 'unintended monuments' in the public space of Berlin since 1945, paying particular attention to the period since 1989.

The shift in memory culture from the self-confidence of monuments to the contingency of traces has been considered within the context of national identity and the meaning of Holocaust monuments.[5] Running parallel to these contexts, however, is the fetishization of the material of the past in an increasingly visual culture. Writing in 1995 on the 'museum boom', Andreas Huyssen argued that, 'even if the museum as institution is now thoroughly embedded in the culture industry', it was not commodity fetishism that was at stake.[6] He argued that the 'museum fetish transcends exchange value', carrying with it something like an 'anamnestic dimension, a kind of memory value'.[7] One can identify two major forerunners to Huyssen's term. This 'memory value' does not rely on a deep knowledge of the material object (on display), and as such has strong affinities with Alois Riegl's term, 'Alterswert' ('age value'), used in his reflections

---

tember 2000) as well as attempts to focus on the difference between 'Denkmal-schutz' and 'Stadtbildpflege' (see Norbert Huse, 'Verloren, gefährdet, geschützt – Baudenkmale in Berlin', in Huse, *Verloren, gefährdet, geschützt*, Berlin 1989, pp.11–19: p.12), reflecting a more general uncertainty about the cultural-political values that underpin such institutional undertakings.

4   Alois Riegl, 'Der moderne Denkmalkultus: Sein Wesen und seine Entstehung', in *Gesammelte Aufsätze*, Vienna 1996 [1903], pp.139–84: p.144.

5   Rudy Koshar, *From Monuments to Traces. Artifacts of German Memory 1870–1990*, Berkeley, CA 2000, and James E. Young, *The Texture of Memory. Holocaust Memorials and Meaning*, New Haven, CT 1993.

6   Andreas Huyssen, 'Escape from Amnesia', in Andreas Huyssen, *Twilight Memories: Marking Time in a Culture of Amnesia*, New York 1995, pp.13–35: p.33.

7   Ibid.

on the 'modern cult of the monument'.[8] Riegl recognized that 'age value', which judged the patina of age definitive in determining the value of buildings, was gaining ground over the 'historical value', where value was determined by antiquarian knowledge of a building's history. Elsewhere Huyssen suggested that 'the newfound strength of the museum and the monument in the public sphere may be connected with the fact that they both offer something that television denies: the material quality of the object'.[9] This again echoes Riegl, who promoted a radical conservation policy by which buildings were maintained but were eventually allowed to deteriorate and amortize their full age value 'naturally'. The perception of the patina of age is dependent on the pleasure of the spectator, indicating that such age value lay more in the aesthetic impulse than the ethical. Given that the auratic power of materiality is connected with the visual pleasure of seeing the object, another important forerunner for Huyssen's conception of 'memory value' is Walter Benjamin's consideration of 'Ausstellungswert' ('exhibition value'). For Benjamin, the cultic value of the sacred object was transferred into the value imbued into the material presence of the individual (non-reproducible) art work being exhibited.[10] Both Riegl and Benjamin were attempting to describe how auratic value is established in terms of 'cultural capital'. With its roots in Riegl's and Benjamin's examination of the powerful aura of objects from the past, Huyssen's 'memory value' implies that what we may have witnessed in the last thirty years is a further stage in processes of acceleration and decomposition.

There are two major distinctions to be made, however between Huyssen and his predecessors. Firstly, both Riegl and Benjamin were writing about art and architecture, whereas Huyssen's frame of reference is much wider, indicating the expansion and increasing uncertainty of the meaning of 'culture'. Secondly, Huyssen explicitly places

---

8   Riegl, 'Der moderne Denkmalkultus', p.145.
9   Andreas Huyssen, 'Monuments and Holocaust Memory in a Media Age', in Huyssen, *Twilight Memories*, pp.249–60: p.255.
10   Walter Benjamin, *Das Kunstwerk im Zeitalter seiner technischen Reproduzierbarkeit*, in Walter Benjamin, *Gesammelte Schriften*, ed. Rolf Tiedemann and Hermann Schweppenhäuser, Frankfurt/M. 1980, I/2, pp.471–508: p.484.

'memory value' in relationship to, namely above and beyond, 'exchange value', raising the question of how this operates in public space. Huyssen writes of the power of monuments that stand in a 'reclaimed public space', implying a process that will be investigated in this paper.[11]

Henri Lefebvre argued that space is 'produced' through the interaction of three aspects – spatial practices, the development of representative spaces, and the construction of spaces of representation. He examines the meaning of the monument within 'absolute space' (which is made up of 'sacred or cursed locations [...] a space at once indistiguishably mental and social which comprehends the entire existence of the group concerned'):[12] such monuments 'offered each member of a society an image of that membership, [...] a collective mirror more faithful than any personal one'.[13] Although Lefebvre writes against any straightforward teleological development, he nevertheless describes a discernible tendency for 'absolute space' to yield to 'abstract space'. For Lefebvre, such monuments are incompatible with abstract space, which is a:

> medium of exchange (with the necessary implications of interchangeability) tending to absorb use. [...] It is in this space that the world of commodities is deployed, along with all that it entails: accumulation and growth, calculation, planning, programming. Which is to say that abstract space is that space where the tendency to homogenisation exercises its pressure and its repression with the means at its disposal: a semantic void abolishes former meanings (without for all that, standing in the way of a growing complexity of the world and its multiplicity of messages, codes and operations).[14]

An important element in this transition is the 'logic of visualization' with the visual gaining the upper hand over the other senses. It is important to remember, however, that 'abstract space is not homogeneous; it simply has homogeneity as its goal, its orientation, its

---

11   Huyssen, 'Monuments and Holocaust Memory', p.255.
12   Henri Lefebvre, *The Production of Space*, trans. Donald Nicholson Smith, Oxford, 1991, p.240.
13   Ibid., p.220.
14   Ibid., p.307.

"lens".[15] That orientation leads to the principle that 'the entirety of space must be endowed with exchange value'.

Lefebvre suggests that a monument 'does not have a "signified" (or "signifieds"); rather it has a horizon of meaning: a specific or indefinite multiplicity of meanings'.[16] This complexity increases when one considers 'unintended monuments'. As remnants, unintended monuments function differently from an 'intended monument' or museum in public space. Whereas a monument, and even more so a museum, is often allotted a privileged site, thus already implying for the user of public space some kind of 'transcendence' of banal commodified interchangeable space, the 'unintended monument', as a potential site of development, is open to, and has constantly to battle with, the commodification of space. It is a remnant whose previous function has become redundant, but where no new function or use has been established: this allows for the establishment of memory value. It is, however, not the material form of a remnant or ruin of the past itself that responds to this pressure for space to become an exchangeable value. Rather, the memory value of the trace is invoked within the discourses of the public sphere, and this essay draws on a variety of sources that play major roles in constituting and reflecting those discourses.

Without the presence of the ruined material, the monument could not operate as a surface on to which memory value could be projected. Yet it is absence, and in particular the absence of function, that enables those projections to take place. The power of the visual, and the temporal and spatial location of the spectator, are important factors in the 'construction' of a ruin. For the remnant to be a 'ruin', it has to be seen as such. Prior to, or indeed after that moment, it is regarded as meaningless, 'undistinguished' material. For Alois Riegl, a Baroque palace in a state of ruin had been an object in need of restoration, not a ruin to be admired as such, like a medieval castle.[17] Over the course of the twentieth century, processes of ruination have accelerated and what has been seen as a ruin has expanded. This paper looks at the

---

15   Ibid., p.287.
16   Ibid., p.222.
17   Riegl, 'Der moderne Denkmalkultus', p.169.

processes by which unintended monuments operate in public space: what are the discourses that surround them, how are they imbued with memory value, with what kinds of memory value are they imbued, and how are those values relate to exchange value? It focuses on four ruin sites from the post-war era, all still present in the memory land-scape of Berlin in 2005, and how the 'memory value' of these unintended monuments has been established. The Kaiser Wilhelm-Gedächtniskirche illustrates a number of paradigms of the workings of memory value in public space after 1945: the relationship between memory value and exchange value; the irrelevance of previous ideolo-gical function and architectural merit as well as the need for signs and borders to stabilize the workings of memory value and establish the exhibition value of the remnant. The *Gestapo-Gelände*, best known now as the *Topographie des Terrors* (Topography of Terror), is symp-tomatic for how a more critical form of memory value, which developed since the 1970s, has shaped the discussion of public space following German unification. As a remnant of the GDR state, the *Palast der Republik* tests the strategies by which the memory value of this particular building are played off against the demands of the new unified state as well as the plans for a reconstruction of the imperial 'Schloss' previously located on its site. The remnants on the Pots-damer Platz shed further light on the relationship between the 'urban regeneration' of post-unification Berlin, forms of 'memory value' and the dominance of the visual.

Before 1945, the Kaiser Wilhelm-Gedächtniskirche was an inten-ded monument, completed in 1895 as a memorial to the first Emperor of the new Reich. The church was built at the meeting-point of a number of busy roads during Berlin's rapid expansion into an indus-trial metropolis. By the 1920s, plans to rationalize the flow of traffic within the city had led to calls for the Gedächtniskirche to be knocked down.[18] It survived those calls, but not the bombs of the Allied raid which struck on the 23 November 1943. Although not intended to be a monument in this form, its status as a striking ruin was immediately established by photographs of post-war Berlin, and by 1949 it was

---

18   Vera Frowein-Ziroff, *Die Kaiser Wilhelm-Gedächtniskirche: Entstehung und Bedeutung*, Berlin 1982, p.335.

being referred to as the 'Wahrzeichen und Mahnmal des Nachkrieg-berlins'[19] ('landmark and memorial of postwar Berlin'). Nevertheless, calls for its removal were repeated as part of the general trend to ensure the most efficient circulation of goods and consumers. The Protestant Church, however, insisted on its place 'in the world'.[20] The vociferous newspaper campaign to maintain the ruined tower, once Egon Eiermann's plans for a modern church were revealed, invoked a particular form of 'memory value'. This was not connected with its previous imperial ideological meaning, nor with its sacred function, nor was it based on the architectural merits of the ruin. Rather, it was based on the memories of traditional spatial practices of the Berlin population which had predated the church's ruination.[21]

These practices were not, however, a major factor in the way in which the ruin has been interpreted since Eiermann's new construc-tion went up beside it. These explanations of how the ruin was supposed to function as a 'memorial' ('Mahnmal') or 'landmark' ('Wahrzeichen') were by no means unequivocal: its ethical effect was said to be achieved through its 'aesthetic power'[22] or it operated either through its 'aesthetic charm' or its 'admonishing skeleton',[23] or even as an 'impressive contrast to the pretentious gestures of its profane surroundings'.[24] Its meaning was equally unclear: it was a sign of 'good and evil remembrance'[25]; it was a 'emblem' ('Sinnbild') of loss, or it offered 'salvation in an unredeemed world' ('Heil in einer heil-losen Welt') and an indication of the 'survival of the temporal'

---

19   Karl-Joachim Reutlinger, *Und trotzdem leben wir: Als Reporter im Nachkriegs-berlin überall dabei*, Berlin 1997, p.258.

20   Stephan Hirzel, 'Kirche im Brennpunkt der Verkehrs', *Kunst und Kirche*, 28 (1965), 8–23: 8.

21   Frowein-Ziroff, *Die Kaiser Wilhelm-Gedächtniskirche*, p.336. Those (pre-war) spatial practices are wonderfully described by Siegfried Kracauer in 'Ansichts-postkarte', *Frankfurter Zeitung Morgenblatt* (26 May 1930).

22   Dietrich Worbs, *Einblicke in die Berliner Denkmal-Landschaft*, Berlin 2002, p.168.

23   Ulrich Conrads, 'Zweierlei Maß', *Bauwelt*, 48 (1957), 54–5: 55

24   'eindrucksvoller Kontrast gegen das anspruchsvolle Gebaren der profanen Umgebung'. Thomas Schmidt, *Werner March: Architekt des Olympia-Stadions 1894–1976*, Basel 1992, pp.128.

25   Ulrich Conrads, 'Zweierlei Maß', 55.

('Bestand des Zeitlichen'),[26] or rather it signified a 'temporary security' in a confusing post-war environment.[27] For Werner March, architect of the original plan for post-war reconstruction of the church, it stood in 1959 as a 'landmark' of the Berlin of 1897.[28] More recently, one critic thought that the stone remnants had been read as the 'dissolution of an ostensibly worthless material world'.[29]

If these readings illustrate the complexity of pinning down the effects and meaning of the tower ruin, then the building itself points to that difficulty. The new ensemble, combining Eiermann's buildings with the ruin, led one writer to suggest its grotesque quality made it a genuine 'landmark' of Cold War Berlin.[30] Eiermann's modernist construction, along with the commercial structures that surround it on the Breitscheidplatz, certainly accentuated the 'age value' of the tower. The whole ensemble was heightened in a material, but no less metaphorical sense by being raised above the level of the surrounding roads through a two-metre high platform made from the rubble of the old church and the synagogue in the Fasanenstraße.[31]

There are two plaques attached to the tower. The first of these points to a dual function: to the memory of Kaiser Wilhelm I, and also the 'divine judgement', 'which befell our people in the war years'. The second relates to the former entrance-hall which, with colourful frescoes celebrating the Hohenzollern dynasty, has been restored inside the tower. Marking its reopening as a 'Gedenkhalle' ('memorial hall') in 1987, the sign designates the hall 'a place of remembrance and admonishment against war and destruction, and a call to be reconciled with Jesus Christ'. This is not the only addition to the structure, however. On the opposite side of the tower, an untitled and unsigned sculpture has been grafted on to the ruin. These plaques and

---

26   Ulrich Conrads, 'Die neue Kaiser Wilhelm-Gedächtniskirche in Berlin', *Bauwelt*, 53 (1962), 95–8: 96.

27   Conrads, 'Zweierlei Maß', 855.

28   Schmidt, *Werner March*, pp.128–9.

29   'Auflösung einer scheinbar wertlosen Dingwelt'. Rolf Lautenschläger, 'Im Schatten der Superdomes', *die tageszeitung* (8 April 1994).

30   Hirzel, 'Kirche im Brennpunkt', 10.

31   Conrads, 'Die neue Kaiser Wilhelm Gedächtniskirche in Berlin', 174. This points to the role of technology in constructing the 'natural' ruin.

additions to the material of the ruin help establish its exhibition value, indicating that there is something of significance to be seen. They are, however, also important in demonstrating that the stones cannot speak for themselves, and as attempts to fix the meaning of the ruin through a specifically Christian narrative.

As a central feature of West Berlin's post-war memory land-scape, the Gedächtniskirche was affected by unification. In 1991, the *tageszeitung* ran a series considering what should be the new 'Wahr-zeichen' of the united Berlin. In 1993 a local pastor, Martin Lotz, called for the church to be redesignated with a less nationalistic dedication, to Bertha von Suttner, Paul Schneider or Dietrich Bon-hoeffer.[32] Such attempts to imbue the ruin with an identifiably different kind of memory value tally with an observation of Walter Kempowski's. He suggested that at the Gedächtniskirche 'an instru-mentalized Romanticism is grasped, but not the warning against war'.[33] Such dissatisfaction with the visually powerful 'age value' of the ruin is, as Riegl's considerations show, not a new concern. But whereas Riegl addressed the struggle between the 'historical value' and 'age value' of a site, what dominates here is the dissatisfaction with comforting narratives and a concern with how the present should judge the past. Nietzsche described such a perspective on history as deriving from the kind of historian, 'whose heart is burdened with the pressure of the present and who would love to get rid of this pressure at any price'. Such a historian 'needs to write a critical, that is a judgemental history that passes sentence on the past'.[34] This was 'critical history' and the kind of value seen in past objects in this way can be described as 'critical memory value'.

---

32 'Gedächtniskirche umbenennen', *die tageszeitung* (21 June 1993).

33 Walter Kempowski, 'Ruine – Metapher und Wirklichkeit', in Thorsten Scheer (ed.), *Stadt der Architektur – Architektur der Stadt: Berlin 1900–2000*, Berlin 2000, pp.229–35: p.233.

34 Ein Historiker 'dem eine gegenwärtige Noth die Brust beklemmt und der um jeden Preis die Last von sich abwerfen will' und der 'ein Bedürfniss zur kritischen, das heisst richtenden und verurtheilenden Historie' hat. Friedrich Nietzsche, *Vom Nutzen und Nachtheil der Historie für das Leben*, in *Kritische Gesamtausgabe*, ed. Giorgio Colli and Mazzino Montinari, Berlin 1967–, III/1, pp.239–330: p.260.

Writing from such a perspective in 1986, Dieter Bartetzko commented that the debate about what to do with the ruins of the Second World War 'got stuck in the files of repression created by a building policy which made a clean sweep under the rule of thumb: maintaining the landmarks and preserving the islands of tradition while at the same time creating radical new constructions on the fields of rubble'.[35] If the Gedächtniskirche was the maintained symbol, then the site of the Gestapo headquarters in the Prinz Albrecht Straße, which was right next to the Soviet zone after 1945, and had the Wall running along one side of it from 1961, was nearly the victim of radical new building. Regardless of the actual division of the city, West Berlin's urban planning was determined by the 'Flächennutzungsplan', established and extended since 1950, which sought to create the capital of a united Germany. The desire to produce a city suitable for automobile traffic ('die autogerechte Stadt') illustrates the tendency towards abstract space, directed to the most efficient circulation of consumers and commodities within a notional national capital. The most celebrated, and now notorious, element of that plan was the urban motorway ('Stadtautobahn'), and many of the demolitions were, ostensibly or actually, connected with this. Dieter Hoffmann-Axthelm suggested that urban planning after 1945 had no language to deal with the remains of war und 'simply demolished and allowed grass, or asphalt, to grow over everything'.[36] The language that it did have at its disposal was the grammar of abstract space. The directive that came from Bonn in 1962 regarding the 'clearing away of administrative buildings', i.e. the former Gestapo headquarters, was part of the preparations for a new urban expressway.[37]

---

35 Die Debatte 'versandete in den Verdrängungsakten eines Bauens, das unter der Faustregel: Erhalt der Wahrzeichen, Verschonung von Traditionsinseln bei gleichzeitig radikaler Neubebauung der Trümmerflächen, reinen Tisch machte.' Dieter Bartetzko, *Verbaute Geschichte*, Darmstadt 1986, pp.54–5.

36 'nur abriß und über alles Gras, oder Asphalt, wachsen ließ'. Dieter Hoffmann-Axthelm, 'Der stadtgeschichtliche Bestand', in *Dokumentation zum Gelände des ehemaligen Prinz-Albrecht-Palais und seine Umgebung*, Berlin 1983, p.36.

37 Lore Ditzen, 'Kein Ort für einen Kranz', in *Dokumentation. Offener Wettbewerb: Berlin, Südliche Friedrichstadt. Gestaltung des Geländes des ehemaligen Prinz-Albrecht-Palais*, Berlin 1985, p.43.

The 'Gelände' was not recognized as a 'ruin site' with memory value at this stage. Instead it was rendered low in exchange value by proximity to the wall. One part of it was a dumping ground for rubble from demolished buildings in nearby parts of Kreuzberg. Another, asphalted over, was a track for car-racing without a driving licence. The increasing importance of 'critical memory value' in the memory culture of West Germany, and West Berlin in particular, can be observed in the history of this site, whose function as a memory trace spans the period before and after unification. The critical form of memory work, which was instrumental in the late 1970s in 'uncovering' the site as the Gestapo headquarters, developed in relationship to the exchange value of public space. Michael Kraus recalls the moment when he introduced the question of the site's previous usage into the context of a planning meeting about the site:

Es war nicht unproblematisch, die bisherige Gesprächsebene plötzlich zu verlassen, auf den politischen und moralischen Hintergrund hinzuweisen, denn das konnte – und wurde von den Befürwörtern des Straßenbaus dann auch – als rein taktisches Manöver aufgefaßt werden, als ein unsachliches, emotionales und unfaires Ausweichen auf ein mit den bisher angewandten Kriterien nicht mehr rational faßbares Feld.[38]

(It was not unproblematic suddenly to depart from the level at which the conversation had taken place up to that point and to allude to the political and moral background, for that could be understood – and was indeed by the supporters of the road-building programme – as a purely tactical manoeuvre, as an non-objective, emotional and unfair move into an area which could not be rationally grasped with the criteria which had been used up to now.)

The invocation of such memory value at that moment radically breaks the frame of discussions about the rational ordering of space.

Descriptions of the site from the early 1980s emphasize images of absence. The site is empty, an emptiness in contrast to the traces of the site's usage over the past decades: the rubble from the building work, and the rubber tyres of the racing track. Hoffmann-Axthelm suggested that the 'essential emptiness' is the 'message itself': the site as a ruin points not towards the German past, but post-war indiffer-

---

38   Michael Kraus, 'Kein Ort für Straßen', *Arch+*, 40/41 (1978), 14–22, 18.

ence to the crimes of the Nazi state.[39] The site is discovered as an unintended monument to the repression of German history, and that lack of intention is central to its initial significance.

From the start, however, the fact that an 'unintended monument' has been intentionally discovered leads to an awareness of the ways in which the 'message itself' is made legible. The tension between aesthetic effect and ethical meaning was picked out by Hoffmann-Axthelm in considering how one might turn this 'unintended monument' into something more lasting. He pointed to the dangers of 'aesthetic legibility': 'one may not simply relate to this site in a visual manner' ('man darf sich also nicht einfach visuell zum Standort verhalten'). The last thing that should be enabled is 'a cultivated shiver down the spine' ('ein kultiviertes Frösteln über den Rücken') of the bussed-in tourists.[40] The tension between the visual, emotional impact of the location and its potential didactic role was drawn out by Ulrich Eckhardt, who made a distinction between a emotional reaction residing in 'self-satisfaction' and its (potential) status as a 'place for reflection' ('Denkort'), a 'strange, questioning location' ('seltsame[s], fragende[s] Gelände).'[41]

The potential 'critical memory value' of the site was, however, not the only value placed upon this space. Those entering the first competition, in 1983, had not only to find an adequate way of marking the site, but also had to include an area of recreation for the inhabitants of Kreuzberg. Ulrich Conrads' commentary on the 1983 winning design by Jürgen Wenzel and Nikolaus Leng is revealing:

> Was man da betritt, wird weder Hain noch Park noch Wald genannt werden können. Man wird in etwas Tot-Lebendiges hineingehen, in eine absolut

---

39   Dieter Hoffmann-Axthelm, 'Wie lesbar ist die Geschichte?', in Dieter Hoffmann-Axthelm, *Rettung der Architektur vor sich selbst*, Braunschweig 1995, pp.92–9: p.94.

40   Dieter Hoffmann-Axthelm, 'Kultiviertes Frösteln für Touristen', in *Dokumentation. Offener Wettbewerb*, pp.37–8. Similar points were made by Ulrich Conrads and Rainer Höynck.

41   Ulrich Eckhardt, 'Braucht Berlin Gedenkstätten', in *Topographie des Terrors: Ausschreibung*, Berlin 1993.

künstliche Landschaft, die doch der Natur nicht ganz entbehrt. [...] Die auf dem Boden ausgelegten Dokumente werden sagen, warum das so ist.[42]

(What one enters there can be called neither grove nor park nor wood. One will enter into something dead but alive, in an absolutely artificial landscape, which, however, is not entirely devoid of nature. [...] The documents, laid out on the ground, will say why this is the case.)

This solution combines the aesthetics of the ruin, between life and death, artifice and nature, image and materiality, with the didactic impulse of the textual. The value of the documents, reproductions of Gestapo and SS policy, is a combination of 'age value' (in their documentary authenticity), 'exhibition value' (in that they are staged) and 'critical memory value' (in that they serve a didactic purpose for the present).

The winning design was attacked by the neighbourhood groups who realized that it had not really provided them with a recreational space. It was also criticized by those who thought that the design, which sealed the ground with cast-iron plates, 'closed off' the site, rather than leaving it open. Dissatisfaction with the solutions re-asserted once more the peculiarity of this space: Hoffmann-Axthelm observed that it would have been interpreted as a cursed space by pre-modern societies,[43] while Ulrich Conrads talked of the site being 'poisoned'.[44] There is consensus for Hämer's observation that the site can have no use value,[45] while the dangers of abstract space are summoned up in Conrads' concern that compromises could lead to the influence of 'calculating administrators',[46] as well as Hoffmann-Axthelm's warning that 'administration of land development' should not be allowed to dictate the treatment of the site.[47]

A number of the 194 entries for the 1983 competition made use of architectural metaphors of excavation but the 'memory value' of

42   Ulrich Conrads, 'Schorf aus Eisen', in *Dokumentation Offener Wettbewerb*, pp.39–42: p.41.

43   Hoffmann-Axthelm, 'Der stadtgeschichtliche Bestand', p.64.

44   Conrads, 'Schorf aus Eisen', p.39.

45   Hardt-Waltherr Hämer, 'Prinz-Albrecht Palais', *Dokumentation Offener Wettbewerb*, p.32.

46   Conrads, 'Schorf aus Eisen', p.41.

47   Hoffmann-Axthelm, 'Wie lesbar ist die Geschichte?', p.92.

the site was heightened when actual archaeological finds from the Gestapo era were made during the 1986 excavations which followed on from the polemical intervention by local historical activists a year before. These remnants dealt the Wenzel-Lang plan a final blow, and greatly enhanced the auratic power of the site,[48] while also enhancing the potential legibility of the ruin: Thomas Friedrich called the uncovered cells the 'most eloquent part' of the area.[49] This question of the way in which the site communicated remained difficult. This is perhaps best illustrated by the fact that in 1981 Hoffmann-Axthelm had argued that the site was to speak 'without signs',[50] but later suggested the power of the site to speak had in fact been proved by the signs that have been erected.[51] This tension is also one between the intended and unintended monument. The 'age value' of the site had been secured by excavations displaying themselves in the centre of the city, ensuring the emotional impact of the direct, visual 'memory value' of the site; the signs ensured the exhibition value of the remnants. The question had not been solved as how to ensure the establishment of 'critical memory'.

The events of 1989 did not change the site itself, but did alter the location of the Gelände – it no longer ran along the border between East and West Berlin, and was in fact now to be found next to another remnant of the past, the Berlin Wall. This altered the potential exchange value of the site, but the consensus that the site should remain a monument was secure, even if there was no consensus on what kind of monument it should be. The second competition for designs to mark the site, held in 1993, reinforced the fact that the problem of legibility was an aesthetic one as much as an ethical one. Whereas the first competition had illustrated the limitations of an architecture of memory which sought to operate with direct expression, this competition was marked by more abstract approaches.

---

48   Lore Ditzen, 'Prüfsteine des Gewissens zu Bausteinen machen', in Leonie Baumann, *Der umschwiegene Ort*, Berlin 1986, pp.50–53: p.51.
49   Thomas Friedrich. 'Das Gestapo- und SS-Gelände im Jahre 1987', in Baumann, *Der umschwiegene Ort*, pp.81–2: p.81.
50   Hoffmann-Axthelm, 'Der stadtgeschichtliche Bestand', p.68.
51   Hoffmann-Axthelm, 'Wie lesbar ist die Geschichte?', p.98.

Perhaps the most polemical contribution came from Axel Schultes in his commentary on his design, as he imagined someone living in an apartment in the Wilhelmstraße, across the road from the 'Gelände':

> [In] der Glotze um 19 Uhr sich die bosnische Tragödie reinziehen [...], Luft schnappen auf dem Balkon der kleinen Neugier und einen Blick nach draußen werfen, auf die 'Topographie des Terrors'. Blauäugiger kann die Kommision nicht argumentieren. 'Wunde, Stadt-Wunde müßte das Prinz-Albrecht-Gelände bleiben', unbebaut deshalb vor allem an der Wilhelmstraße. 'Unvereinbar bevorzugte Wohnlage – wo ist hier die Wunde?' denken die Anlieger, nicht nur die Anlieger. [...] Stadt, die alles banalisierende Stadt also heraushalten, die Konfrontation mit dem Gelände sich nicht abnützen lassen durch die Curry-wurstbude und die Wäsche auf dem Balkon: dazu bedarf es der härtesten Abgrenzung, die herstellbar ist.[52]

> (Goggle at the tragedy in Bosnia at 7pm on the box [...], take the air on the balcony, and cast a glance over at the 'Topography of Terror'. The commission could not argue any more naively. 'A wound, an urban wound, is what the Prinz-Albrecht site must remain', and therefore above all there should be no building on the Wilhelmstrasse. 'Incompatible desirable location – where is the wound?' the residents wonder, and not only the residents. [...] The city, the city that makes everything banal, must be kept out, the confrontation with the site cannot allow itself to be degraded by the sausage stall and the washing on the balcony: for that reason, the sharpest possible demarcation is necessary.)

Schultes' vision is a reckoning with the dominance of the visual in contemporary culture, but also draws on the distinction, between the 'banal' abstract space of the city and the 'wound' that is the Prinz-Albrecht Gelände, that is part of the defining discourse of 'critical memory'. Schultes' wall shores up the 'critical memory value' of the site against 'mere' aesthetic perception. It would nevertheless have been a highly aesthetic solution. However, the jury thought his plan was a 'imposition' for those living in the Wilhelmstrasse, and it was rejected in the third round. To a certain extent, therefore, the exchange value of the accommodation nearby was a competing factor.[53]

---

52   Axel Schultes [with Charlotte Frank], 'Erläuterungsbericht', in *Topographie des Terror: Ergebnisprotokoll – Dokumentation*, Berlin 1993, pp.47–8: p.47.

53   Bericht der Jury, in *Topographie des Terrors: Ergebnisprotokoll – Dokumentation*, p.52.

The winning design in the 1993 competition, by Peter Zumthor, sought to combat the stasis of the aesthetic image by combining materiality and text in his design for the documentation centre.[54] This design stresses the materiality of the experience, and attempts to avoid the intentionality of direct expression in its form. It emphasized that the visitor would be walking on the actual ground of the site, and that this would be a building 'which speaks only of its materials'.[55] On the other hand, as with the 1983 competition winner, the legibility of critical memory would be ensured through the exhibition of the textual: it would be the documents that would speak.

At time of writing, Zumthor's design has yet to be realized, and in 2003 underwent modifications so that it might keep to budget. The financial problems that have dogged the project are a reminder that the establishment of memory value comes at a price. At the same time, the comments by Andreas Nachama, the director of the *Stiftung Topographie des Terrors* indicate how the 'trace' of the unintended monument has established itself as a paradigm of 'memory value' in the last twenty years:

> Wer [...] die drei hohlen Zähne stehen sieht, diese Treppentürme, die nirgendwo hinführen – der wird begreifen, dass dieses Gelände in der Zwischenzeit noch eine weitere Haut hinzubekommen hat. Es hat seine Tiefenhaut, das sind die barocken Steine an der Wilhelmstraße, dann kommen die Spuren des Dritten Reiches, die Trümmerberge der Nachkriegszeit, Teile der Berliner Mauer. Und dann eben diese neue Narbe. Mit diesem Anblick terrorisiert sich die Stadt selber. Im Augenblick ist das alles zusammen ein treffendes Abbild der Berliner Republik.[56]

---

54   Peter Zumthor, 'Erläuterungsbericht', in *Topographie des Terrors: Ergebnisprotokoll – Dokumentation*, p.25. Other designs were still taken with the notion of the site as an image. For example, the second prize went to Thomas Müller et al., for whom 'der Ort gleicht einem Bild voller Spuren'. Thomas Müller et al., 'Erläuterungsbericht', *Topographie des Terrors: Ergebnisprotokoll – Dokumentation*, p.33. Such readings transform the site into a 'complete' image with ALL traces, demonstrating perhaps the unavoidability of aesthetic perception and the dominance of the visual.

55   Peter Zumthor, *Three Concepts*, Berlin 1997, p.53

56   Volker Müller, 'Wie hohle Zähne: Mahnmal und "Topographie" warten auf Weiterbau – hat sich die Berliner Republik übernommen?', *Berliner Zeitung* (27 January 2003).

(Anyone who sees these three hollow teeth, these towers of stairs that lead to nowhere – they will understand that in the meantime this site has gained yet another skin. It has its deepest skin, the Baroque stones along the Wilhelm-strasse, then come the traces of the Third Reich, the rubble heaps of the postwar era, parts of the Berlin Wall. And now this new scar. The city terrorizes itself with this spectacle. At the moment, this is altogether a perfect image of the Berlin Republic.)

Nachama finds 'memory value' for the present in Zumthor's incomplete structure – he transforms this into a critique of the contemporary memory culture of the Berlin Republic.[57]

The idea of a palimpsest of material traces is one of three paradigms established by the discourses surrounding the *Topographie des Terrors* for the memory value of 'unintended monuments' in public space. It implies a complex engagement with the past, in which the critical memory value of the material trace is asserted, but its explication is complicated by the interaction of the image, materiality and the textual interpretation of the trace. The second paradigm is the assumption that demolition is a failed attempt to expunge history. Brian Ladd concludes that 'it is now clear that destroying the buildings on Prinz-Albrecht-Straße and covering their foundations neither obliterated the memory of them nor enabled Berliners to come to terms with their own history'.[58] Of course this was never explicitly the policy, and more work may need to be done on the ways in which the demands of abstract space and the trends of German memory culture dovetailed after 1945. The third paradigm is the idea that the memory value of the trace must remain an irritant against the encroachments of abstract space, to 'keep the wound open'.

These paradigms evolved within the context of a critical engagement with the Second World War and the 'abstract' urban planning which came in its wake. They have, however, been readopted in the discussion of the remnants of the GDR, as can be seen in the discussion of the *Palast der Republik*. The 'Palast' stands on the site

---

57 The term 'hohler Zahn' is an ironic reference to a popular description of the Gedächtniskirche.

58 Brian Ladd, *The Ghosts of Berlin: Confronting German History in the Urban Landscape*, Chicago 1997, p.163.

of the imperial 'Schloss', which had been damaged in the war, but was ultimately razed to the ground on the orders of Walter Ulbricht in 1950. *Neue Zeit* commented in 1991 during the debate about what to do with the Palace, that demolition had never been a good way of dealing with the past (and often, ironically, Ulbricht's treatment of the 'Schloss' has been cited as evidence of this).[59] The series of traces as a palimpsest of the historical process was invoked, for example, by Federal President Roman Herzog, who envisaged a solution that combined both the *Palast der Republik* and a rebuilt 'Schloss'.[60]

The *Palast der Republik* was built between 1973 and 1976 as a multi-function building. It was the site of the infrequent meetings of the *Volkskammer*, but precisely for that reason it can barely be considered the seat of real power in the GDR (this was not far away, where the ZK of the SED met). For many, it was and is not a symbol of the SED dictatorship, 'too civilized, too undecided and multi-layered is the message of this building'.[61] It was a place for state occasions, such as the infrequent party conferences of the SED. As a prominent marker of the shift in the GDR towards a more consumer-oriented socialism, the Palace was also designed as a place for a wide variety of cultural and leisure activities. It had been seen as a piece of international modernist architecture; 'one was – and is – proud that one had done without in order to have this one piece of world-standard architecture'.[62] The Palace was closed by the GDR government on 19 September 1990 before unification took place for health and safety reasons. The use of asbestos in its construction meant that the building needed a programme of renovation before it could be safely used. The demise of the GDR and the closure because of asbestos removed both its major functions.

---

59   Norbert Schwaldt, 'Krieg dem Palast, Friede dem Schloß?', *Neue Zeit* (4 May 1991).

60   Letter from the Bundespräsidialamt, 25 April 1996, reproduced in *Der Palast muß weg weg weg*, Berlin 1996.

61   'zu zivil, zu unschlüssig und vielschichtig ist die wahre Botschaft des Gebäudes'. Thomas Kuppinger, 'Friede den Palästen', *Zitty*, 25 (1991), 23.

62   'man war – und ist – stolz darauf, daß man sich dies einzige Stück Weltstandard vom Mund abgespart hat'. Ibid.

If, as was the case with its West Berlin counterpart, the Internationales Congress Centrum, it had simply been a ruin of a modern building technology that in only a decade had gone from being a universal practice to a byword for a creeping, invisible form of danger and decay, then this might not have provided further comment.[63] As the emblem of a modernizing socialist state, however, it could also be read as the emblematic ruin of that project, and thus two conceptions of a ruined modernity could be elided in the image of the Palace as an 'Asbest-Ruine' ('asbestos ruin'). At this stage, though, the building was not beyond renovation, nor did it appear to be a ruin, except for those who saw it as a ruin of a debased form of modernist architecture. Over the decade since it was closed, the number of personnel looking after the Palace has been continually reduced, the supply of water and electricity have been cut off. Time, that most perennial of the processes of ruination, has been working away on the Palace over this period, followed, finally, by the dramatic internal de(con)struction caused by the process of removing the asbestos.

Like the *Gestapo-Gelände*, the period of time the site spent as an unintended monument is important in the development of its meaning as such a monument. The *Palast der Republik* is different in that it has been seen as an unintended monument while the process of ruination is taking place. In discussing the reasons for the closure (and continued closure) of the *Palast der Republik*, the building becomes the projection for other concerns. Both Bruno Flierl (*die tageszeitung*, 11 May 1991) and Norbert Schwaldt argued in May 1991 that it was not closed for reasons of asbestos. Johann Friedrich Geist was even more direct, suggesting that it was 'a political act: they wanted to shut down what was popular, they wanted a spectacular victim'.[64] Others reported the Bundesministerium as arguing that it was architecturally outdated;[65] Peter Conradi (SPD), a member of parliament, suggested

---

63   The irony is, of course, that the asbestos came from Britain, and the building practice was as common in West as East Germany.

64   'ein politischer Akt; man wollte stilllegen, was populär war, man wollte ein spektakuläres Opfer'. Johann Friedrich Geist, 'Der Palast der Republik aus westlicher Sicht', in *Der Palast muß weg weg weg*, pp.23–30: p.26.

65   Eva Schweitzer, 'Palast der Republik droht jetzt doch die Abrißbirne', *Der Tagesspiegel* (4 October 1992).

in 1996 that it was being deliberately allowed to grow dilapidated, an argument also made by Professor Wolf Eisenhardt.[66]

The Palace is different from the two previous ruins in that few people argue for its preservation in a ruinous state. Nevertheless its status as a building that no longer fulfils its previous function has mobilized its memory value. One form of memory value is invoked by those who worked in and used the Palace, those whose spatial practices made this into not just a space of representation for the GDR hierarchy, but also a representative space for moments when the personal found a social location. Those demanding the maintenance of the Palace assert the value of the memories they associate with the space. The building provides the focus for those memories (and thus for an ambivalent relationship to the GDR state).[67] This form of memory value, rooted in spatial practices, offers clear parallels to the defence of the Gedächtniskirche made by the general West Berlin public in the immediate post-war era.

Other forms of memory value have been suggested. For example, for Professor Eisenhardt, the 'Palast' had cultural-historical value,[68] while Peter Strieder, then development senator in Berlin, saw the 'Palast' as having political memory value as a piece of the history of the Federal Republic (as the site where the *Volkskammer* voted to join the Republic via Article 23).[69] The variety of perspectives demonstrates that the 'Palast', as a building which has lost its function, became the projection site for different forms of memory value. The *Tagesspiegel* pointed towards the difference between spatial interaction with the building and a remnant that has been reduced to a distant image: 'The "house of the people" was, it has to be said, full of

---

66   Cited in Heinz G. Behnert, *Palast/Palazzo 1973/1998: Das Denkmalbuch zum Palast der Republik*, Berlin, 1997, pp.189 and 192.

67   For example Hans Jacobus, 'Erinnerungen', in Rudolf Ellereit and Horst Wellner (eds.), *Kampf um den Palast*, Berlin 1994, pp.81–2. Indeed many of the contributions to *Kampf um den Palast* and *Der Palast muß weg weg weg* invoke this kind of memory value.

68   Wolf-Rüdiger Eisentraut, 'Kontrapunkte', in Ellereit and Wellner (eds.), *Kampf um den Palast*, pp.73–5.

69   Report of parliamentary discussion of 17 April 1996 in *Der Palast muß weg weg weg*, p.81.

memories for those from the East; the man from the West just sees simply the dead eyes and asks what all the fuss is about'.[70]

As Otto Merk observed in 1991, tourists could have no idea what this building means: 'signs, at least temporary ones, which could say something about this building (and the others on Marx-Engels-Platz) which is scarcely to be overlooked, are presumably too expensive'.[71] The Palace itself would not seem to have had exhibition value in itself – although its paintings were displayed as a historical exhibition at the Deutsches Historisches Museum in 1996.

There are currently sixty-eight signs close to the *Palast der Republik*: these, however, posted on to the wooden fence surrounding the building, tell the history of the space now occupied by the Palace and the Schlossplatz (the history of the Palace is presented on two of these). The various forms of memory value associated with the Palace cannot be established without reference, however negative, to the exchange value of the site, for it does operate as a potential hindrance both to an increasingly abstract efficiency in the use of space, and to a drawing-board reconstruction of the heart of the Prussian city. Initially this was either in terms of whether a renovated Palace could pay for itself on the open market, or what else could be built that would be most profitable. Later there were the general consideration of cost: how much does it cost to maintain the Palace in various states of (dis)repair; how much would various forms of asbestos removal cost; how much would a renovation of the Palace cost; how much would a reconstruction of (elements of) the imperial 'Schloss' cost?

It is an irony that another form of memory value is associated with the former imperial 'Schloss' that, for many decades, had no visible material presence and has nothing to do with the recollection of spatial practices. The presence of the 'Schloss' was referred to in

---

70   'Das "Haus des Volkes" war nun einmal eine Ost-Beziehungskiste, der West-Mensch sieht heuer lediglich die toten Augen und fragt sich, was das Ganze denn nun noch soll.' n.n., 'Palast der Gefühle', *Der Tagesspiegel* (27 March 1993).

71   'Hinweistafeln, wenigstens vorläufige, die etwas über den kaum zu über-sehenden Bau (und die anderen Gebäude am Marx-Engels-Platz) aussagen, sind wohl zu teuer.' Otto Merk, 'Schandfleck der Republik', *Berliner Zeitung* (29 July 1992).

many journalistic descriptions of the building, as journalists reflected on the fact that, following its closure, the way into the Palace was through a cellar entrance which was a remnant of the 'Schloss' structure. Excavations carried out on the Schlossplatz have allowed the display of foundations whose mundanity is reminiscent of those exhibited along the Niederkirchnerstrasse at the *Topographie des Terrors*. It has often been argued that plans for a reconstructed imperial 'Schloss' would involve the erasing of historical distinctions. The façade erected around the Palace in 1993 was a blatant indication that a future reconstructed 'Schloss' will invoke memory value without even the slightest patina of age: its material presence will not even rely on the auratic power of being 'original', thus giving it a form of exhibition value which is different to that conceived by Benjamin. In the eyes of many commentators, it will be the triumph of the maintenance of the city image ('Stadtbildpflege') over both critical and antiquarian memory value.[72]

After wranglings that have gone on for a decade, it does appear that the *Palast der Republik* will be demolished in 2005. At time of writing, the asbestos removal work, although not quite the final act in the process of ruination, has meant the removal of almost all signs of the previous uses which the building had. The interior of the Palace now has the archetypal visual attraction of the ruin (this designation is practically unanimous in print media discussions of the building) with its skeletal steel structures attracting the likes of Christian von Borries to the 'hollowed-out Palace as an artificial ruin from the remains of a disappeared state' ('rückgebaute, entkernte Palast als künstlich hergestellte Ruine aus dem Nachlass eines untergegangen Staates') which provides a location 'loaded with myth and meaning' ('mythenträchtigen, extrem mit Bedeutung geladenen Ort') for his musical experimentation.[73] The ruin now offers the possibilities of a different kind of cultural value.

---

72   See, for example, Dieter Hoffmann-Axthelm, 'Zumutung Berliner Schloß – und wie man ihr begegnen könnte', in *Die Rettung der Architektur vor sich selbst*, pp.100–13.

73   Peter Laudenbach, 'Dirigent auf Montage', *tip*, 15 (2003), pp.56–7.

The discussion surrounding the Palace has undoubtedly been influenced by the different paradigms we saw in the case of both the Gedächtniskirche and the *Gestapo-Gelände*. There is the importance of previous spatial practices, the irrelevance of previous ideological significance and architectural merit for the value of the ruin. There is also, however, the employment of strategies of 'critical memory value', and the remnant as an irritant to the increasing abstraction of space. The tension between the visual form of the remnant and its legibility, which remains evident, is integral in making such remnants potential sites of debate in public space, helping in the generation of narratives and in the establishment of differing memory values.

Furthermore, however, the fate of the Palace and the future 'Schloss' points to a tendency towards the 'exhibition value' of the past in spaces dominated by 'representations of space' rather than 'representative spaces'. In the 1990s, the most prominent example of the production of abstract space dominated by visual 'representations of space' is the Postdamer Platz. The physical state of the square before 1989 was a remnant of the outcome of the Second World War: the division of Berlin into four sectors, and the building of the Berlin Wall. The ruinous condition of the Potsdamer Platz (the predication for its fetishization within memory value) was directly linked to the low exchange value of the site.

The potential of the space was transformed by the events of the *Wende*. The famous scene set in the pre-*Wende* wilderness in Wim Wenders' 1989 film *Der Himmel über Berlin* (*Wings of Desire*) demonstrated, however, that the invocatory power of the name had never fully disappeared. Indeed, the historical Potsdamer Platz was invoked by those planning the creation of a new centre in this space, most conventionally by the new owners of the space and most radically perhaps by Daniel Libeskind.[74] The construction of a new Potsdamer Platz also had to deal with the reality that the space was not empty. In contrast to the *Palast der Republik*, there were few people who could invoke the memory value of specific spatial practices associated with the site in the 1920s, and those who had used it since the Second

---

74   *Daimler Benz, Potsdamer Platz*, Berlin 1995, p.2, and Daniel Libeskind, *radix-matrix*, Munich 1997, pp.59–61.

World War, such as those living in the *Wagenburg* ('caravan community'), had a very different attitude to spatial organization. While the *Wagenburg* was moved elsewhere, there were also less mobile physical remnants: two major buildings: Hotel Esplanade and Weinhaus Huth, and a row of trees as a reminder of what had previously been the Potsdamer Strasse. It had been established that all three remnants had to be maintained in any reconstruction of the Platz. In other words, whereas those defending the *Gestapo-Gelände* and the *Palast der Republik* sought to legitimize their forms of memory value, the new Potsdamer Platz had to negotiate with an established 'memory value' of the sites. The answer was to incorporate the memory traces into the corporate citadel and by doing so reinterpret their memory value.

The remnants of the past that are to be found at the Potsdamer Platz are exhibits in the architectural display. In technologically very complex manoeuvres, Weinhaus Huth was incorporated into the surrounding buildings of the Daimler Quarter and the Kaisersaal (Imperial Hall) of the Hotel Esplanade was transplanted to be incorporated into the Sony Centre. It need hardly be said that both are sites of visual and physical consumption. The trees in the Potsdamer Strasse, which had survived the planning for Speer's Germania, and the post-war building of the Wall and the Kulturforum, were incorporated into the re-named Alte Potsdamer Strasse (Old Potsdam Street). The *S-Bahn* sign that had stood by the Wall throughout the years of the Cold War was incorporated into the Sony Tower when it was renamed Bahn Tower after the Deutsche Bahn moved its headquarters there. The other major remnant of the past was, of course, the Berlin Wall, of which, at time of writing, one slab is to be found by the entrance to the *S-Bahn*, and a further series of slabs are to the south of the square along with the remains of a former watchtower, while another slab is currently situated on the not-yet-completed Leipziger Platz. In addition, there is a reconstruction of the famous green signal box from the 1920s. Its lights change, but it has no bearing in controlling the circulation of the traffic.

Three aspects of these remnants need to be drawn out. Firstly, their artificiality. They could not have been maintained 'naturally' in their condition within all the new construction that has taken place. In that sense, not only the signal box is the simulacrum of a material remnant. Secondly, there is the use of signs. In the case of both the *S-Bahn* sign and Hotel Esplanade, these signs do not locate the meaning of these remnants in their fate during the post-war era. Rather, reference to the bullet hole in the *S-Bahn* sign relates its memory value to the Second World War, rather than, say, its emblematic quality as a remnant of divided Berlin; the Hotel Esplanade's signs point towards the hotel's role in the Wilhelmine Empire. These signs offer narratives that work against the potential for the trace as a palimpsest of historical processes. Even more striking than the use of signs is, thirdly, the employment of glass. This way of presenting traces has also become fashionable in the presentation of the memory landscape in Berlin, if one thinks of Foster's glass cupola, and more particularly the graffiti left by the Russian soldiers at the Reichstag in 1945. The meaning of the remnants on Potsdamer Platz is fixed in a quite specific fashion: a remnant is an object behind glass. They have become intended monuments whose meaning, however, is exhausted in exhibition value. The glass exhibits the aura, but also dematerializes and neutralizes it. The glass makes the objects almost invisible: instead you have a reflection of the spectator in the glass. The new Potsdamer Platz establishes the exhibition value of these remnants. These remnants are no longer irritants in the smooth efficient functioning of an interchangeable abstract space, but belong to the exhibition spectacle. This memory value is a combination of age value and exhibition value. What matters on Potsdamer Platz is the image of the past: the structures in the area make positive use of the allegorical way of seeing by using signs and putting the objects behind glass.

The meaning of material traces in public space is always in part a reflection of the values of the spectator, but not only that. The processes at work might be described through a number of paradoxes. First, the paradox that very different notions of memory value rely on the material's status as a remnant without a function to generate memory value. Second, the paradox that the fetish of materiality operates as a counterpoint to an image-dominated culture, but that the material often has to be transformed into an image in order to make its materiality legible. Third, the paradox that the material and the image cannot do without signs and written texts to ensure their meaning and indeed often their exhibition value.

Daniel Libeskind's radical 'angel trapping history' design for the Potsdamer Platz can be read as a fruitful artistic-architectural engagement with such paradoxes. That plan was not put into practice, although the more traditional memory space of the museum has been enriched by his Jewish Museum in Berlin. As the continuing wranglings over the realization of his designs for the memorial space at Ground Zero illustrate, however, the 'unintended monument' remains subject to the pressures of abstract space and exchange value.

Bibliography

Bartetzko, Dieter, *Verbaute Geschichte*, Darmstadt 1986.

Baumann, Leonie, *Der umschwiegene Ort*, Berlin 1986.

Behnert, Heinz G., *Palast/Palazzo 1973/1998: Das Denkmalbuch zum Palast der Republik*, Berlin 1997.

Benjamin, Walter, *Das Kunstwerk im Zeitalter seiner technischen Reproduzierbarkeit*, in *Gesammelte Schriften*, ed. Rolf Tiedemann and Hermann Schweppenhäuser, Frankfurt/M. 1980, I/2, pp.471–508.

Conrads, Ulrich, 'Zweierlei Maß', *Bauwelt*, 48 (1957), 54–5.

——, 'Die neue Kaiser Wilhelm-Gedächtniskirche in Berlin', *Bauwelt*, 53 (1962), 95–8.

——, 'Schorf aus Eisen', in *Dokumentation Offener Wettbewerb*, pp.39–42.

Daimler Benz, Potsdamer Platz, Berlin 1995.

Der Palast muß weg weg weg, Berlin 1996.

Ditzen, Lore, 'Kein Ort für einen Kranz', in *Dokumentation. Offener Wettbewerb*, p.43.

——, 'Prüfsteine des Gewissens zu Bausteinen machen', in Baumann, *Der umschwiegene Ort*, pp.50–53.

Dokumentation. Offener Wettbewerb: Berlin – Südliche Friedrichstadt. Gestaltung des Geländes des ehemaligen Prinz-Albrecht-Palais, Berlin 1985.

Eckhardt, Ulrich, 'Braucht Berlin Gedenkstätten', in *Topographie des Terrors. Ausschreibung*, Berlin 1993.

Ellereit, Rudolf, and Horst Wellner (eds.), *Kampf um den Palast*, Berlin 1994.

Friedrich, Thomas. 'Das Gestapo- und SS-Gelände im Jahre 1987', in Baumann, *Der umschwiegene Ort*, pp.81–82.

Frowein-Ziroff, Vera, *Die Kaiser Wilhelm-Gedächtniskirche, Entstehung und Be-deutung*, Berlin 1982.

Füchsel, Katja, 'Weltkulturerbe Mauer heftig umstritten', *Der Tagesspiegel* (8 August 2003).

Geist, Johann Friedrich, 'Der Palast der Republik aus westlicher Sicht', in *Der Palast muß weg weg weg*, pp.23–30.

Hämer, Hardt-Waltherr, 'Prinz-Albrecht Palais', *Dokumentation Offener Wettbewerb*, p.32.

Hirzel, Stephan, 'Kirche im Brennpunkt der Verkehrs', *Kunst und Kirche*, 28 (1965), 8–23.

Hoffmann-Axthelm, Dieter, 'Der stadtgeschichtliche Bestand', in *Dokumentation zum Gelände des ehemaligen Prinz-Albrecht-Palais und seine Umgebung*, Berlin 1983.

——, *Rettung der Architektur vor sich selbst*, Braunschweig 1995.

——, 'Kultiviertes Frösteln für Touristen', in *Dokumentation Offener Wettbewerb*, pp.37–8.

Huse, Norbert, 'Verloren, gefährdet, geschützt – Baudenkmale in Berlin', in *Verloren, gefährdet, geschützt*, Berlin 1989, pp.11–19.

Huyssen, Andreas, *Twilight Memories: Marking Time in a Culture of Amnesia*, New York 1995

——, 'Escape from Amnesia', in Huyssen, *Twilight Memories*, pp.13–35.

——, 'Monuments and Holocaust Memory in a Media Age', in Huyssen, *Twilight Memories*, pp.249–60.

Kempowski, Walter, 'Ruine – Metapher und Wirklichkeit', in Thorsten Scheer (ed.), *Stadt der Architektur – Architektur der Stadt: Berlin 1900–2000*, Berlin 2000, pp.229–235.

Koshar, Rudy, *From Monuments to Traces: Artifacts of German Memory, 1870–1990*, Berkeley, CA 2000.

Kracauer, Siegfried, 'Ansichtspostkarte', *Frankfurter Zeitung Morgenblatt* (26 May 1930).

Kraus, Michael, 'Kein Ort für Straßen', *Arch+*, 40/41 (1978), 14–22.

Kuppinger, Thomas, 'Friede den Palästen', *Zitty*, 25 (1991), p.23.

Lautenschläger, Rolf, 'Im Schatten der Superdomes', *die tageszeitung* (8 April 1994).

Ladd, Brian, *The Ghosts of Berlin: Confronting German History in the Urban Land-scape*, Chicago 1997.

Laudenbach, Peter, 'Dirigent auf Montage', *tip*, 15 (2003), pp.56–7.

Lefebvre, Henri, *The Production of Space*, trans. Donald Nicholson Smith, Oxford 1991.

Libeskind, Daniel, *radix-matrix*, Munich 1997.

Merk, Otto, 'Schandfleck der Republik', *Berliner Zeitung* (29 July 1992).

Müller, Volker, 'Wie hohle Zähne': Mahnmal und 'Topographie' warten auf Weiter-bau – hat sich die Berliner Republik übernommen?', *Berliner Zeitung* (27 January 2003).

Nietzsche, Friedrich, *Vom Nutzen und Nachtheil der Historie für das Leben*, in *Kritische Gesamtausgabe*, ed. Giorgio Colli and Mazzino Montinari, Berlin 1967–, III/1, pp.239–330.

Reutlinger, Karl-Joachim, *Und trotzdem leben wir: Als Reporter im Nachkriegsberlin überall dabei*, Berlin 1997.

Riegl, Alois, 'Der moderne Denkmalkultus: Sein Wesen und seine Entstehung', in *Gesammelte Aufsätze*, Vienna 1996 [1903], pp.139–84.

Schmidt, Thomas, *Werner March: Architekt des Olympia-Stadions 1894–1976*, Basel 1992.

Schultes, Axel [with Charlotte Frank], 'Erläuterungsbericht', in *Topographie des Terror: Ergebnisprotokoll – Dokumentation*, Berlin 1993, pp.47–8.

Schwaldt, Norbert, 'Krieg dem Palast, Friede dem Schloß?', *Neue Zeit* (4 May 1991).

Schweitzer, Eva, 'Palast der Republik droht jetzt doch die Abrißbirne', *Der Tages-spiegel* (4 October 1992).

Topographie des Terror: Ergebnisprotokoll – Dokumentation, Berlin 1993.

Worbs, Dietrich, *Einblicke in die Berliner Denkmal-Landschaft*, Berlin 2002.

Young, James E., *The Texture of Memory: Holocaust Memorials and Meaning*, New Haven, CT 1993.

Zumthor, Peter, *Three Concepts*, Berlin 1997.

Russel Lemmons

'Imprisoned, Murdered, Besmirched':
The Controversy Concerning
Berlin's Ernst Thälmann Monument
and German National Identity, 1990–1995[1]

Throughout their history, the Germans have repeatedly found them-selves trying to come to terms with their past. How the German people confronted this recurring problem – especially acute in the last century – has had a dramatic effect upon their national identity.[2] In 1918, for example, they were confronted by the fact that they had, in spite of unprecedented sacrifice on their part, lost the Great War. In this case, coming to terms with defeat involved little more than scapegoating those supposedly responsible for the catastrophe. The Germans made little serious effort at uncovering the long-term origins of the debacle, leaving fertile ground for the growth of a movement such as National Socialism.[3]

In 1945 the Germans faced a series of even more daunting ob-stacles in their efforts to rebuild their national identity. Not only had they survived twelve years under National Socialism, not to mention the most destructive war in European history, but they also had to come to terms with the horrific crimes committed in their name. To make matters worse, Germany would be divided for the foreseeable future, with each of the two German states seeing the events of the

1   The author would like to thank the German Academic Exchange Service, the National Endowment for the Humanities, and Jacksonville State University for providing the funds needed to complete the research for this essay.
2   Concerning the efforts to create a common German identity see Harold James, *A German Identity, 1770–1990*, New York 1989.
3   Wolfgang Schivelbusch, *The Culture of Defeat: On National Trauma, Mourn-ing, and Recovery*, trans. Jefferson Chase, New York 2003, pp.189–288.

first half of the twentieth century very differently. Each government
sought to instrumentalize the recent German past for its own ends, and
the resulting discordant accounts had dramatic implications for
German national identity, contributing to the creation of what is often
called the 'wall in the head', or very different understandings of what
it meant to be German.[4]

In general, public discourse in the Federal Republic, when it
dealt with the issue at all, tended to view the Third Reich and its
crimes as manifestations of totalitarianism. That is, Nazi Germany
was a one-party state based upon mass mobilization of the population,
an all-encompassing ideology, in addition to centrally controlled media,
a command economy, and a secret police.[5] With the advent of the
Cold War, this understanding of Hitler's Germany became increasingly popular in the West because it explicitly linked Nazism and Stalinism, thereby legitimizing the ongoing struggle against the Soviet Union
and its East German ally. As early as 1948, in the midst of the Berlin
air lift, the city's mayor, Ernst Reuter, made this association explicit
when he informed an American audience that the Germans 'Once
again' confronted 'a dictatorship that wants to oppress our people and
is trying to break our moral and political will to resist [...]. This time
we must stand up for our freedom'.[6] Reuter and others sought clearly
to link Germanness with the creation of democratic institutions. If one
accepted the contention that Stalinism and National Socialism were
'different sides of the same coin', then clearly the Federal Republic
was the only legitimate German state and the proper focus of German
national identity. Although the totalitarian model lost a great deal of
support during the course of the 1970s, it reemerged in the late 1980s.[7]

---

4   On all this see Jeffrey Herf, *Divided Memory: The Nazi Past in the Two
     Germanys*, Cambridge, MA 1997.
5   The classic exposition of the theory of totalitarianism remains Hannah Arendt's
     The Origins of Totalitarianism, 2nd edition, New York 1973.
6   Quoted in Herf, *Divided Memory*, p.265.
7   Concerning efforts to compare Stalinism and National Socialism, see Ljudmila
     Andreevna Mercalowa, 'Stalinismus und Hitlerismus – Versuch einer verglei-
     chenden Analyse', in Eckhard Jesse (ed.), *Totalitarisums im 20. Jahrhundert:
     Eine Bilanz der internationalen Forschung*, Bonn 1996, pp.200–12.

The population of the Soviet zone and the German Democratic Republic (GDR) learned to understand the recent past, as well as what it meant to be German, quite differently. The governing Socialist Unity Party (SED) adopted an antifascism model that viewed National Socialism as the natural outgrowth of industrial capitalism, still the socio-economic system of the Federal Republic. Further, the GDR was established and governed by those who had most heroically fought the fascists (Nazis) both before and after Adolf Hitler came to power. The leaders of the SED had opposed Hitler or were the heirs of those who had, and socialist East Germany was the result of this legacy (*Vermächtnis*). At the same time, the Federal Republic, because it had embraced capitalism, was linked to Germany's fascist heritage, making the GDR the only legitimate German state.[8]

Both the Federal Republic and the GDR sought legitimacy by seeking to distinguish their social and political systems from those of the Third Reich. Given this ideological dichotomy, which both governments encouraged for over forty years, it is not surprising that westerners and easterners developed very different views regarding what it meant to be German – differing national identities that remained relatively unimportant as long as Germany was divided. Because of the dramatic events of 1989–1991, however, constructing a unified national identity once again became a major concern. Much like 1918 and 1945, the Germans faced a *Stunde Null* ('Zero Hour'), a crossroads at which they had to make some major decisions regarding their future. As is always the case in the German context, how the past was perceived would have a dramatic effect upon the present and future understanding of what it meant to be German.

The city of Berlin had long been at the heart of the conflict between the rival social and political systems. In 1979, for example, SED chairman Erich Honecker publicly stated that the East German capital should 'from today forward' serve as 'a symbol for the

---

8   Antonia Gruenberg, *Antifaschismus – ein deutscher Mythos*, Reinbek bei Hamburg 1993, pp.120–45, and Feiwel Kupferberg, *The Rise and Fall of the German Democratic Republic*, New Brunswick, NJ 2002, pp.45–66.

victorious advance of socialism on German soil'.[9] Indeed, both sides of the Berlin Wall became centers for politically charged remembrance of recent German history. Not only did East Berlin have its Lenin Monument, Luxemburg Platz, and Karl Liebknecht Straße, immortalizing important figures in the history of German socialism; but the West had its Straße des 17. Juni, recalling the 1953 workers uprising, and Platz der Luftbrücke, honouring those who died during the famous 1948 airlift.[10] If, after 1989, Germany were to be culturally united, if a single national identity could be created, Berlin would necessarily be the focus of the endeavor.

Many Germans recognized this reality even before unification, and as a result the SED's version of recent events came under attack. In the months following the collapse of the Honecker regime, the historical monuments built by the SED in the East German capital became the subject of controversy. In May 1990, for example, the East German artist Joachim Scheel published an article in the West Berlin daily *Tagesspiegel*. In his essay, he attacked the 'monumental propaganda' produced by the defunct regime as 'symbols of [the] authoritarian ideology' ('Symbole alter Herrschaftsideologie') that had dominated the East German people for too long. This 'non-art' ('Unkunst') should be destroyed and the materials used to create real art. Scheel was particularly contemptuous of two of the most massive monuments in the eastern half of the city, those commemorating Soviet leader Lenin and the German communist leader Ernst Thälmann.[11] With his attack upon the Ernst Thälmann Monument, located in the Berlin's Prenzlauer Berg district, Scheel set in motion a five-year controversy that said much about the differences between easterners and westerners concerning the question of national identity.

Ernst Thälmann had been the most important German figure – eclipsed only by Lenin – in the SED's pantheon of heroes and the central figure in the party's legitimizing myth. Born in a working-

---

9   'als ein Symbol für den Siegeszug des Sozialismus auf deutschem Boden'. Quoted in *Die Zeit* (17 August 1990).

10   Brian Ladd, *The Ghosts of Berlin: Confronting German History in the Urban Landscape*, Chicago 1997, pp.175–215.

11   *Der Tagesspiegel* (15 May 1990).

class district of Hamburg in 1886, he became a dockworker and an active member of the German Socialist Party (SPD). After fighting in the trenches of the Great War, he joined the Communist Party (KPD). A relentless organizer, Thälmann played an important role in the 1923 Hamburg revolt, lauded in German communist circles as the party's Thermopylae. By 1925, he had risen to the chairmanship of the KPD's central committee and, as party leader, oversaw the Stalinization of the KPD. The Nazi 'seizure of power' in January 1933 forced him underground, and he was arrested in March. Accused of high treason, he spent the remaining eleven years of his life in prison, only to be murdered in August 1944.[12]

From the point of view of the SED leadership Thälmann had an impeccable ideological pedigree, and he became the most important figure in the regime's effort to construct an antifascist identity. Supposedly a product of proletarian roots,[13] he became chairman of the German Communist Party – a true *Arbeiterführer*. Recognizing the evil nature of the Nazi menace, he led the proletariat's struggle against 'Hitler-fascism', making the ultimate sacrifice for the cause, freely giving his life. If, as the regime's leadership contended, the GDR was the fulfillment of Thälmann's legacy, no one could question the regime's antifascist credentials or, more important, the legitimacy of a socialist alternative to the Federal Republic.

For this reason, an elaborate mythology was cultivated around the proletarian leader. Biographies appeared seeking to link the legacy of the fallen KPD chief to the GDR. East German poets lionized Thälmann, and filmmakers produced features and documentaries about his

---

12 Concerning Thälmann's life, see the highly hagiographic biography published by East Germany's Institute for Marxism-Leninism, Günter Hortzschansky, et al., *Ernst Thälmann: Eine Biographie*, Berlin/East 1985. Regarding the Hamburg communist's role in the Stalinization of the KPD, see Klaus Kinner, 'Thälmann und der Stalinismus: Das Ende des eigenständigen deutschen Parteikommunismus 1928/1929', in Peter Monteath (ed.), *Ernst Thälmann: Mensch und Mythos*, Amsterdam 2000, pp.59–80.

13 In reality, Thälmann's parents, as he admitted himself, could best be categorized as *petit bourgeois*. See Regina Scheer, '"Ich bin kein weltflüchtiger Zigeuner": Legende und Wirklichkeit einer Jugend – über die frühen Prägungen Ernst Thälmanns', in Monteath, *Ernst Thälmann*, pp.41–58.

life. Memorials were built at sites important to his political activities, and the entry-level of the SED's youth organization was the 'Thälmann Pioneers'. Anniversaries of his birth and death became important dates in the GDR's secular religion.[14]

From the very beginning of the SED regime, however, a national monument was supposed to be the cornerstone of the Thälmann legend. On 3 December 1949, just two months after the establishment of the GDR, the SED central committee called upon German artists to submit proposals for an Ernst Thälmann National Monument. The monument would be located in the former Wilhelmplatz, which, on 18 August, the fifth anniversary of the KPD leader's murder, had been renamed Thälmannplatz. A committee of ten men, including SED party chief Walter Ulbricht, minister-president Otto Grotewohl, and Thälmann biographer Willy Bredel, would choose the best proposal, which would receive a 20,000 DM prize.[15] The composition of the selection committee indicated the importance of the project, and every member was politically beyond reproach. The site chosen was important symbolically. The monument would stand in front of Hitler's former chancellery, at a location named after the one-time Kaiser, representing the ultimate victory of German socialism over imperialism and fascism. In spite of the importance of the enterprise, circumstances conspired to delay its completion. The 1961 construction of the Berlin Wall in the vicinity finally killed the enterprise completely, since the regime did not want to see its hero's name associated with a structure so embarrassing to the GDR.[16]

But Thälmann's image was too important to the ruling party's legitimacy, and the party remained determined to construct a monument in the East German capital.[17] Over the next two decades various

---

14   On the Thälmann myth see the essays in Monteath (ed.), *Ernst Thälmann*.

15   'ERNST THÄLMANN-DENKMAL: Wettbewerb', in DR1, Kulturministerium, file 1799, pp.121–2, Stiftung Archiv der Parteien und Massenorganisationen der ehemaligen DDR im Bundesarchiv (hereafter SAPMO-BA), Berlin, Federal Republic of Germany.

16   Concerning the delays in the project, see the numerous documents in DR1, files 1799 and 7695, SAPMO-BA.

17   Rudy Koshar, *From Monuments to Traces: Artifacts of German Memory, 1870–1990*, Berkeley, CA 2000, pp.277–8.

schemes emerged for the construction of a national Thälmann Monument,[18] and in 1980, the SED central committee finally produced a proposal that would bear fruit. The party leadership decided to construct a Thälmann Monument in Prenzlauer Berg, one of the largest working-class districts in Berlin. The location chosen was, at the time, a massive gas works along Greifswalder Straße. Erich Honecker and other East German leaders passed it each day on their way to their villas in Wandlitz. The memorial would be the focal point of a massive 900-unit housing complex, symbolically linking the antifascist tradition with the material benefits of 'real existing socialism'. Honecker rejected all of the suggestions presented by the East German artistic community, assuring the undying hatred of most GDR artists for the monument. The SED chief personally chose Soviet artist Lew Kerbel, most famous for his massive bronze of Marx in Karl-Marx-Stadt (Chemnitz), to design the monument. Honecker dedicated the fifty-ton, thirteen-meter high bronze bust of the KPD chief on 15 April 1986, the eve of Thälmann's one-hundredth birthday. A throwback to the massive memorials of the regime's early years, Kerbel's work depicted Thälmann giving the antifascist salute while standing in front of a Soviet flag. According to SED accounts, 100,000 East German citizens attended the ceremony. Over the next three years the site remained important to the GDR's secular religion, especially in the SED's efforts to inculcate East German youth with the proper socialist consciousness, and numerous demonstrations and festivals took place in the surrounding Ernst Thälmann Pioneer Park.[19]

When Scheel assailed the artistic merit of Kerbel's socialist realist colossus, he also challenged the legitimacy of the collapsing GDR. In addition, he maligned one of the left's most beloved historical figures. Not only was Thälmann a hero in the eyes of many

---

18   On these aborted plans see Thomas Flierl, 'Thälmann und Thälmann vor allen': Ein Nationaldenkmal für die Hauptstadt der DDR, Berlin', in Günter Feist, Eckhart Gillen, and Beatrice Vierneisel (eds.), *Kunstdokumentation, SBZ/DDR 1945–1990: Aufsätze, Berichte, Materialien*, Berlin 1996, pp.358–85: pp.375–8.

19   Flierl, 'Thälmann und Thälmann vor allen', pp.382–4; Bruno Flierl, 'Politische Wandbilder und Denkmäler im Stadtraum', in Bruno Flierl (ed.), *Gebaute DDR: Über Stadtplaner, Architekten und die Macht*, Berlin 1998, pp.103–4; Koshar, *From Monuments to Traces*, pp.278f.

Germans, but during the course of the 1950s he had become something of an anti-establishment figure. When confronted with the
travails of daily life in the GDR, East Germans would often remark
that 'If Thälmann had lived, things wouldn't be like this today'.[20] Kurt
Maetzig's two motion picture epics, *Ernst Thälmann – Sohn seiner
Klasse* and *Ernst Thälmann – Führer seiner Klasse*, remained popular
in both Germanys, continuing to attract audiences to midnight show-
ings in Hamburg well into the 1990s.[21] Many Germans who had little
sympathy for the Honecker regime believed that, because of his impeccable antifascist credentials, Thälmann's memory deserved to be
celebrated, and, in spite of its lack of artistic merit, Kerbel's bronze
adequately performed this task.

It soon became clear that Scheel's disdain for much of East
German public art, including the Thälmann Monument, was not universal. In response to demands to destroy East Berlin's monuments
and memorials, art history students from the city's universities, both
East and West, formed the 'Initiative for Political Monuments of the
GDR' ('Initiative Politische Denkmäler der DDR'). The group, while
calling for a careful study of political shrines in *both* parts of the city,
concentrated its efforts upon an analysis of GDR monuments. In
collaboration with the 'Active Museum of Fascism and Resistance'
('Aktive Museum Faschismus und Widerstand') – an organization that
had played an important role in creating West Berlin's 'Topographie
des Terror' exhibit – the 'Initiative' opened an exhibition entitled
*Erhalten, Zerstören, Verändern? Politische Denkmäler der DDR in
Ost-Berlin* ('Conserve, Destroy, Alter? – Political Monuments of the
GDR in East Berlin'). Opening in August 1990, the show concentrated
upon the four most controversial monuments in East Berlin: the nine-
teen meter tall Lenin Monument in Friedrichshain, the Marx-Engels
Memorial in the city's center, the monument to the antifascist

---

20   'Wenn Thälmann noch lebte, dann gäbe es so etwas heute nicht'. See Jörn
     Schütrumpf's introduction to Wolfram Adolphi and Jörn Schütrumpf (eds.),
     Ernst Thälmann: An Stalin, Briefe aus dem Zuchthaus, 1939 bis 1941, Berlin
     1996, p.8.
21   On Maetzig's films see Detlef Kannapin's 'Ernst Thälmann und der DDR-
     Antifaschismus im Film der fünfziger Jahre', in Monteath (ed.), *Ernst Thäl-
     mann*, pp.119–45.

resistance ('Kampfgruppen-Denkmal') in Prenzlauer Berg's Volkspark, and the Thälmann National Monument.

The exhibit presented three possible approaches to the GDR's political shrines. One alternative was simply to leave them as they were, using them as reminders of the now defunct SED state. A second option was to remove them as instruments of a now discredited totalitarian regime. A third possibility was to maintain these stone and bronze artifacts of the former government, but to provide commentary at the sites, usually in the form of billboards explaining the political history of the location. Thus the monuments could be used for political education.[22]

The exhibition encouraged open discussion concerning the fate of sites important to the GDR's interpretation of history and led to a lively discussion. Irina Rusta, an advisor on cultural matters for the Berlin city government, insisted that the monuments 'had nothing to do with art' because they were too 'burdened by ideology'. On the other hand, others made the fundamental point that 'Politicians may not define what art is'.[23] After all, the governing party's monopoly over artistic matters was one of the drawbacks of the previous regime. At a 7 August meeting, sponsored by the 'Initiative for Political Monuments', those who lived near Kerbel's bronze had the opportunity to voice their opinions. One woman wanted to see the monument removed, maintaining that 'Our Thälmann Monument is simply too massive and monumental' ('Unser Thälmann Denkmal ist einfach zu großklotzig und monumental'). The majority of those present, however, disagreed with her. One eighty-year-old resident contended: 'Thälmann was an important antifascist resistance fighter. We shouldn't simply throw him away just because the SED used him to pull its wagon.' ('Thälmann war ein bedeutender antifaschistischer Widerstandskämpfer. Nur weil die SED ihn vor ihren Karren gespannt hat, müssen wir ihn nicht gleich wegbugsieren'). Manfred Butzmann, an artist from East Berlin, offered a compromise solution. Hoping to make the site in Prenzlauer Berg more visually appealing by

---

22   Ladd, *Ghosts of Berlin*, p.194, and *Berliner Morgenpost* (18 October 1990).
23   'Politiker dürfen Kunst nicht definieren'. Quoted in *Berliner Morgenpost* (18 October 1990).

'greening' it, he wanted to plant ivy around the monument.[24] This proposal would have hidden the socialist-realist colossus from sight by encircling it in foliage. It would also have allowed commemoration of Thälmann to continue at the location. It was, however, highly unlikely that the city government would be willing to designate the financial resources needed to complete this project, especially when funds were in short supply.

While some Berliners engaged in a lively discussion concerning the fate of the Thälmann Monument, others were putting their convictions into action. On the night of 2 June, two teenagers were arrested after vandalizing the bronze bust. The police apprehended them, but no charges were filed.[25] Although those who overthrew the SED regime emphasized non-violence and respect for public property, and no statues of prominent socialist figures were toppled, spray-painting graffiti on statues throughout the GDR became common, and the Thälmann Monument, so important to the regime, was no exception. Perhaps the most interesting graffiti on the monument asked 'Don't you have it in a larger size?' ('Hattet ihr's nich 'ne Nummer größer?' [*sic*]), an astute, if facetious, comment concerning the mammoth fifty-ton bronze.[26] Later in June, hoping to distance the monument from the SED regime, Prenzlauer Berg officials removed a pair of two-meter-high stone tablets engraved with quotations from Thälmann and Honecker.[27] At a 5 September meeting the district government made the decision not to demolish Kerbel's statue. The monument, local authorities maintained, could play an important role in efforts to educate the population about Germany's past, both the antifascist traditions of the German left and the efforts of the GDR to co-opt this legacy. Simply to destroy the monument, authorities maintained, would 'hinder the current coming to terms with the past necessary for the development of a democratic community' ('für ein demokratisches Gemeinwesen notwendige aktuelle Vergangenheitsbewältigung behin-

---

24   *Berliner Morgenpost* (9 August 1990).
25   *die tageszeitung* (5 June 1990). Interview with Bernt Roder, director of the Prenzlauer Berg Museum, 15 August 2002.
26   Ladd, *Ghosts of Berlin*, p.202.
27   *Berliner Morgenpost* (9 August 1990), and *Die Zeit* (17 August 1990).

dern'). Second, and more practical, Prenzlauer Berg officials were simply unwilling to take on the expense of removing the monument, which could run to hundreds of thousands of marks. Building upon their earlier decision to remove the two stone stelae, the district approved a Green Party plan to make the site more appealing by 'greening' it, planting bushes, trees, and flowers in the vast open space at the site. On 15 September, the Greens carried out their project, only to see it destroyed, by persons unknown, within a few days. Finally, local authorities also called for an 'open competition' ('öffentlichen Wettbewerb') of proposals concerning the locale's future.[28]

Regardless of whether any of these plans for the Thälmann site and other monuments came to fruition, the discussion promoted by the 'Conserve? Destroy? Alter?' exhibit played a role in creating a democratic identity. The days between the collapse of the regime and unification were characterized by a heady idealism, during which the East German people faced the prospect of molding a new society free of the burdens of 'real existing socialism'. Untold numbers of people were politically active, and an impressive ninety-three per cent of eligible voters cast ballots in the March 1990 national elections, the only free contest in East German history.[29] While a few East Germans, especially within the intelligentsia, maintained some loyalty to the ideals of the defunct system and hoped to create a 'third way' between Soviet-style socialism and western capitalism, almost everyone supported a dramatic political liberalization.[30] The people of the GDR were developing a new national identity, one based upon a civil culture rooted in democratic institutions. Grassroots movements had toppled the previous regime, and local groups, such as the 'Initiative for Political Monuments', played a vital role in the democratizing

---

28   'Beschluß der Bezirkverordnetenversammlung vom 5. September 1990', in *Denk-Mal Positionen: Dokumentation zur Ausstellung vom 14. Juli – 13. August 1993*, Berlin 1993, p.20.

29   For the results of the election see Dirk Philipsen, *We Were the People: Voices from East Germany's Revolutionary Autumn of 1989*, Durham, NC 1993, p.401.

30   On the optimism of this period, see Philipsen, *We Were the People*; concerning the 'third way' see Konrad Jarausch, *The Rush to German Unity*, New York 1994, pp.75–94.

process.[31] The Prenzlauer Berg district government reached its decisions in an open forum, after careful consultation with its constituents, a classic example of democracy on the local level. As the debate concerning the Thälmann Monument shows, East Berliners believed that they could effect change, an important precondition for the development of liberal institutions. They expressed their opinions openly and, perhaps more important, believed that their views mattered.

The issues debated in the weeks preceding unification had dramatic implications for the East German people. The fundamental question raised in the early stages of the struggle surrounding the Thälmann Monument concerned the role of the recent past in East Germany's future. The 'children of the GDR' had to decide what part, if any, their East German identity would play in their future. Should communist heroes, such as Thälmann be remembered for their struggles against the evils of fascism, or rejected outright because of their role in legitimizing the defunct system? Although most East Germans wanted to maintain the generous social programs guaranteed by the SED, they still faced the question of whether or not they should maintain their historical identity, nurtured for over forty years. The ultimate question was whether those who came of age in the GDR should retain a separate identity based upon their historical experience, or simply adopt a broader German worldview, which in this context meant a western point of view. But before the people of the GDR had the opportunity to answer these questions, unification changed the circumstances under which they would be addressed. After the 3 October union of the GDR with the Federal Republic, many westerners would also seek to have their say. The days of heady optimism, when democracy and open public discussion were new and exciting, had come to an end. A new chapter had also begun in the discussions concerning the fate of the GDR's political monuments. Although, with reunification, East Berlin's historical monuments were defended by the Federal Republic's strict laws regarding historical preservation, the sites were not sacrosanct, and these protections could be lifted. To the chagrin of many easterners, westerners would henceforth play a

---

31   On the collapse of the GDR see Charles Maier, *Dissolution: The Crisis of Communism and the End of East Germany*, Princeton, NJ 1997.

significant role in the decision-making process. In December 1990, Berliners elected their first united city parliament in more than four decades. The resulting coalition government would play a central role in the controversy surrounding monuments in the eastern half of the city, and the debate concerning the fate of the Ernst Thälmann Monument, as well as other sites of memory, followed a dramatic new course.

These new circumstances became abundantly clear in October 1991, when Berlin's Senator for Municipal Development and Environmental Protection, Volker Hassemer, announced his determination to demolish Friedrichshain's Lenin Monument. Groups such as 'Initiative for Political Monuments' and the 'Active Museum', who favoured the preservation of the site for historical purposes, immediately attacked the decision. The nineteen-meter-tall stone statue, designed by the Soviet artist Nikolai Tomsky, had stood in Friedrichshain since 1970, they pointed out, becoming part of a familiar landscape. On the other hand, Hassemer, a member of the conservative Christian Democratic Union (CDU), insisted that Lenin was hardly a figure who should be commemorated in a liberal democracy. In a classic elucidation of the totalitarian model, Hassemer pointed out that Lenin had committed numerous crimes against the Russian people. The Soviet leader had overthrown Russia's first democratically elected body, established a secret police, built concentration camps, violently crushed the 1921 Kronstadt rebellion, and betrayed the working classes whom he claimed to represent. 'This Lenin', Hassemer contended, 'represents not only the idea of socialism, but also the reality of totalitarianism'. The monument was a 'component of the propaganda for a state that ended through a popular revolution'.[32] Throughout eastern Europe, including Lenin's Russian homeland, statues of the Soviet leader had been razed – why not in Germany as well?[33]

---

32 'Dieser Lenin steht eben nicht nur für die Idee des Sozialismus, sondern auch für die Realität der Gewaltherrschaft'. Das Monument war 'Bestandteil einer Propaganda für einen Staat, der durch eine Revolution mit Bahnsteigkarte endete'.

33 *Spandauer Volksblatt* (17 October 1991). On the origins of the Lenin statue, see Brian Ladd, 'East Berlin Political Monuments in the Late German Democratic Republic: Finding a Place for Marx and Engels', *Journal of Contemporary History*, 37/1 (2000), 91–104: 94f.

Berlin's mayor, Eberhard Diepgen, agreed, referring to the former Soviet leader as a 'despot and murderer'.[34]

Many easterners, however, were not convinced, insisting that their concerns grew out of an interest in preserving East German history and had nothing to do with Lenin. As one opponent of the demolition put it, 'For me it's not about Lenin, but rather about demonstrating our power and not letting ourselves be pushed around'.[35] Foes of the demolition circulated petitions, organized a letter-writing campaign, and staged demonstrations. Some even went so far as to shroud the granite statue with a large banner reading 'No Violence!' In spite of this resistance, the Friedrichshain district parliament passed a motion supporting the removal of Tomsky's colossus. The relatively narrow margin, forty to thirty-three, indicated the divisiveness of the issue. One legislator, Dieter Hildebrandt, a member of the Party for Democratic Socialism (PDS) – the successor organization to the SED – made his feelings abundantly clear. 'Leave us a part of our own history', he demanded, 'and don't level everything'.[36] Opponents of the removal did not give up, even after the district government's decision. Massive protests marked the beginning of the demolition, which cost half a million marks and lasted twenty-five days.[37] In the meantime, the removal of Prenzlauer Berg's 'Fighting Group' Monument engendered little protest. In this case, however, the district government alone had made the decision to remove the bronze statue.[38]

Trying to avoid future controversies like that surrounding the Lenin Monument, the Berlin city government sought to de-politicize the decision-making process concerning the former East Berlin's political monuments and allay fears that the new government sought

---

34   Quoted in Ladd, *Ghosts of Berlin*, p.197.
35   Ibid.
36   'Laßt uns ein Stück der eigenen Geschichte mitnehmen und nicht alles plattmachen'. *Berliner Morgenpost* (20. September 1991).
37   See Ladd, *Ghosts of Berlin*, pp.197–8 for the quotations. See also Helga A. Welsh, Andreas Pickel, and Dorothy Rosenberg, 'East and West German Identities: United and Divided?', in Konrad H. Jarausch (ed.), *After Unity: Reconfiguring German Identities*, Providence, RI 1997, pp. 103–36: p.131.
38   'Beschluß der Bezirksverordnetenversammlung Prenzlauer Berg vom 5. December 1991', in *Denk-Mal Positionen*, p.28.

simply to sweep aside the history of the GDR. Acting upon an idea first introduced in January 1991, on 10 March 1992, the city's Senate created the 'Kommission zum Umgang mit den politischen Denkmälern der DDR im ehemaligen Ost-Berlin' ('Commission for the Fate of the Political Monuments of the GDR in the Former East Berlin'). The special position that Berlin held in the GDR's efforts at legitimation, coupled with its role as the new German capital, made it necessary to deal with the hundreds of 'sculptures, statues, busts, memorials, stelae, monuments, [and] commemorative tablets' ('Plastiken, Statuen, Büsten, Gedenkstätten, Stelen, Gedenksteinen und -tafeln') scattered throughout the eastern half of the city. The Commission would consist of a committee of ten experts, six from the former East Berlin. Its members included artists, writers, architects, historians, and a museum director. There were only two politicians on the panel, both of whom were also experts on art, one from each half of the city. Over the following six months, they would make recommendations concerning the disposition of more than two-hundred objects. The ten members should not 'reduce' their decisions to the purely 'aesthetic-artistic aspects' of the works, but, in accordance with Berlin's 1972 'Gesetz zum Schutz von Denkmalen in Berlin' ('Law for the Protection of Monuments in Berlin'), also take their 'historical' and 'scholarly' value into consideration. The Senate ordered the Commission to go even further than the law mandated, charging it to take into account the opinions of the local population, which often came to view neighbourhood memorials and monuments as part of the urban landscape. The committee should write a report, complete with photographs, in which it suggested whether each item should be 'maintained, altered, completed, removed, commented upon, [or] moved to a museum' ('Erhalten, Verändern, Ergänzen, Verfremden, Kommentieren, Überführen in Museumssammlungen'). Ultimately, the ten experts only had the power to make recommendations, and final decisions would be made by local authorities, such as district parliaments. In addition, the Senate also rejected the CDU's politically controversial proposal to display some of the works in an exhibit of 'totalitarian art'.[39]

---

39   'Senatsvorlage Nr. 1467/92', Berlin, 19. Februar 2002, in *Denk-Mal Positionen*, pp.19–30.

Both the composition of the panel and the Senate's instructions made it clear that, overall, the Commission's inclination favoured preservation. Prenzlauer Berg's Thälmann Monument was among the most important objects to come under its purview.

Those Berliners with an interest in the ultimate fate of the Thälmann Monument did not wait upon the Commission's recommendation, however, and the site remained a subject of public interest. On May Day 1992, for example, the neo-Nazi Free German Workers' Party (FAP) staged a demonstration at the site on Greifswalder Straße. The demonstration succeeded in inciting the monument's supporters, and counter-demonstrators chanting 'Nazis raus!' greeted the skinheads. Violent clashes resulted, and rocks and bottles were thrown. In the end, only one young man, a counter demonstrator, was arrested and ultimately given a nine-month suspended sentence.[40] On 7 May, the Prenzlauer Berg district assembly passed a resolution maintaining that 'the [Thälmann] Monument should not remain in its current form' ('Das Denkmal sollte in der jetzigen Form nicht erhalten werden'). Calling upon Berlin's Senator for Culture to put the process in motion, the assembly repeated an earlier call for an open competition in which artists could submit their proposals for changes to the site. Finally, the resolution concluded, 'The district office will install a panel at the site containing information about the decision-making process'. Local officials hoped for a 'continuous updating' ('fortlaufende Aktualisierung') to the entire endeavour.[41]

With no end to the controversy in sight and the Monument Commission's report long overdue, in January 1993 the Prenzlauer Berg assembly took up the subject of the Thälmann Monument again. Acting upon a resolution introduced by the Social Democrats, it decided to make the area more suitable by planting foliage, the goal being to make Thälmann Park more useful to the neighbourhood. The assembly had no idea where it would get the money needed for the

---

40   *die tageszeitung* (22 April 1993).
41   'Das Bezirkamt installiert umgehend auf dem Denkmalsgelände eine Informationstafel über den Prozeß der Entscheidungsfindung'. 'Bezirksverordnetensammlung Berlin-Prenzlauer Berg, Beschlußnummer 451/92', 7 Mai 1992, in *Denk-Mal Positionen*, p.32.

improvements, however, and significant changes simply could not be carried out.[42] Further, any alterations might be affected by the recommendation of the Monuments Commission. Although public discussion on the issue remained relatively sedate while people waited on the Commission, the fate of the site remained a concern for the district government.

The debate regarding the fate of the Thälmann Monument gained new momentum, however, when the Monument Commission finally issued its report on 15 February 1993. Concerning the Greifswalder Straße site, the committee's recommendations were brief and to the point. The Commission maintained that Kerbel's work was 'monumental Leninist propaganda'. The SED had co-opted the memory of the KPD leader, and the monument, which reflected its subject 'uncritical[ly]' as a 'symbolic figure', had nothing to do with the historical Thälmann, and was therefore not an appropriate memorial to his legacy. 'By a large majority the commission recommends: The Monument is to be removed' ('Die Kommission empfiehlt mit großer Mehrheit: Das Denkmal ist abzureißen.'). Its ultimate fate should be 'Demolition and modification of the location' ('Abbau und Neugestaltung des Standortes'), which might involve the creation of a 'park with sculptures and the inclusion of artists' whose works could not be 'exhibited in the park during the time of the GDR' ('ein Park mit Skulpturen [...] solcher Künstler, die bei der Gestaltung des Platzes zu DDR-Zeiten nicht berücksichtigt wurden') making the proposed artistic competition redundant. Finally, attempting to placate some of the monument's supporters, the report concluded that 'the abandonment of this object must not mean a similar abandonment of remembrance of Thälmann'.[43]

There was an immediate response to the Commission's proposals regarding the Thälmann Monument. The Christian Democrats and the

---

42   'Bezirksverordnetenversammlung Prenzlauer Berg von Berlin, Drucksache Nr. 197/93', 27. Januar 1993, in *Denk-Mal Positionen*, p.38.

43   'Der Verzicht auf dieses Objekt muß nicht zugleich Verzicht auf das Andenken Thälmanns bedeuten.' *Bericht der Kommission zum Umgang mit den politischen Denkmälern der Nachkriegszeit im ehemaligen Ost-Berlin*, Berlin 1993, pp.33–4 and 85.

Liberal Democrats (FDP) applauded the recommendation. Hoping to use the socialist-realist behemoth for anti-communist political education, they had long supported its removal and hoped to see it transported to a monument park similar to those outside Budapest and other eastern European cities. The Social Democrats, while supporting the Monument Commission's recommendation, did not back the CDU's efforts to instrumentalize the fifty-ton bronze politically. Rather, the SPD emphasized the importance of converting Thälmann Park into a green space that would be more useful to the neighbourhood.[44] The 'Initiative for Political Monuments', contending that 'the monuments are not only witnesses to the history of the city, but also document worldwide historical developments', continued to oppose the removal of any monument or memorial from the former East Berlin.[45] Allied with the Greens and the PDS, the 'Initiative' sought to maintain the Thälmann monument, albeit in an altered form. Any changes, they suggested, should have two goals. First, the modifications should make the massive bronze less of an eyesore. Insisting that the CDU proposal would remove the object from its historical context, the three groups further maintained that any alterations should make the monument more useful to the study of the GDR's history. Taking up the suggestion made by the Prenzlauer Berg district government, all three groups wanted to have a competition, open to all artists and architects, to choose the best design for the future of the monument. Finally, the Communist Party of Germany (KPD) and the German Communist Party (DKP), small groups consisting of unreconstructed Stalinists, demanded that the monument remain unaltered.[46]

The situation became even more complicated four days after the Monument Commission issued its report. On 19 February, Joseph Kurz, who possessed a collection of eight monumental statues from Czechoslovakia and the GDR, offered to remove the monument on

---

44   *Denk-Mal Positionen*, p.6.
45   'Die Denkmalsgruppen sind nicht nur Zeugnisse der Stadtgeschichte, sondern sie dokumentieren weltweite historische Entwicklungen'. 'Denkschrift der "Initiative politische Denkmäler" Arbeitsgruppe des Aktiven Museums Faschismus in Berlin', Februar 1933, in *Denk-Mal Positionen*, p.13.
46   *Denk-Mal Positionen*, p.7.

Greifswalder Straße for free, providing he could take it to his museum in the Bavarian city of Gundelfingen. Kurz's exhibit boasted a triple monument commemorating martyred SPD leader Rudolf Breitscheid as well as Lenin and Thälmann, which he had earlier removed from the city of Dresden. The private monument park already had images of Stalin and East German politician Klement Gottwald, and Kurz eagerly awaited the delivery of ten statues from Lithuania and Poland. The addition of Kerbel's work would enhance his budding enterprise dramatically. Kurz insisted that his proposal was the best solution for nearly everyone, both those who wanted to remove the monument and the groups who wanted it preserved. The scheme had the added advantage of being efficient. Since he would pay for the removal of the monument himself, the city of Berlin would save at least half-a-million marks, and the removal of the fifty-ton bronze would only take a couple of days. Welders would simply cut it into sections with a blowtorch and haul the pieces off to Bavaria, where the statue would be reassembled. When asked about his motivations, Kurz insisted that he had 'no ideological axe to grind' ('keine ideologischen Scheuklappen'), and that he 'simply [did] not want to see the monuments destroyed' – in short, he sought to give the Thälmann Monument 'asylum'.[47]

The CDU agreed that Kurz had devised the ideal solution to the controversy. The socialist-realist colossus would be removed – at no cost to the city of Berlin – but not destroyed. Much to the chagrin of the CDU, however, Kurz's suggestion did not bring an end to the controversy, and numerous objections arose. Some simply objected to the idea of giving away fifty tons of bronze and demanded that Kurz pay for the monument.[48] In addition, the plan did not, as Kurz and the Christian Democrats had hoped, placate the groups, such as the Greens, the 'Initiative for Political Monuments', and the PDS, who wished to see the monument preserved. They maintained that relocating the piece to Bavaria would take it completely out of its historical

47   'Ich will einfach nicht, daß die Denkmäler zerstört werden.' *die tageszeitung* (22 February 1993).

48   *die tageszeitung* (5 June 1990). Interview with Bernt Roder, director of the Prenzlauer Berg Museum, 15 August 2002.

context, rendering it useless to any effort to understand the experience
of those who lived in the GDR. The PDS, while conceding that the
East German regime had misappropriated the martyred KPD leader's
memory, and that the 'monumental statue does an injustice to Thälmann's reputation' ('Monumental-Plastik beschädigt Thälmanns
Ansehen'), insisted that the monument must be left where it was.
Although some wanted to see him erased from German history, the
PDS demanded 'justice for Ernst Thälmann'. In spite of what conservatives thought, Thälmann was undeniably an important historical
figure. He had ardently opposed the Nazis, and, as a result, they had
murdered him. Therefore, the PDS held, the monument 'must stay in
its place until a better, more artistic and politically correct form of
assessment is possible' ('muß so lange an seinem Ort bleiben, bis eine
bessere, künstlerisch wie politisch gerechtere Form der Würdigung
möglich ist'). In the meantime, the party hoped that the site could be
made more visually palatable.[49]

The objections of the tiny DKP and KPD went even further.
According to one of their fliers, 'Ernst Thälmann is a symbol of the
resistance against fascism' who had died in the fight against Nazism.
'Anticommunists', engaged in 'demagoguery', dominated the 'discussion concerning the form of the monument' commemorating the KPD
leader. These non-communists sought ultimately to obliterate his memory, but 'The Thälmann Monument must remain exactly as it is
today, where fascism is being revived' ('Das Thälmann-Denkmal muß
erhalten bleiben – gerade heute, wo der Faschismus wieder auflebt').
The flier concluded with an invitation to a demonstration. To be held
at the monument on 16 April, Thälmann's 107th birthday, its goal was
to 'protest [...] against the destruction of our history'.[50] The PDS
would also participate in the demonstration.[51]

---

49   'Presseerklärung der PDS Prenzlauer Berg zum 107. Geburtstag von Ernst
      Thälmann', 16. April 1993, in *Denk-Mal Positionen*, p.12.
50   '[P]rotestiert [...] gegen die Vernichtung unserer Geschichte'. 'Flugblatt der
      Parteien KPD und DKP zum 107. Geburtstag von E. Thälmann', 16. April 1993,
      in *Denk-Mal Positionen*, p.14.
51   *Berliner Morgenpost* (16 April 1993).

One of the members of the 'Monument Commission', Barbara Teuber, publicly responded to the pro-preservation organizations. The goals of the Commission and the protestors were not all that different, she contended. Her distaste for the mammoth bronze was not politically grounded. She simply found the 'unaesthetic, propagandistic monument' ('unästhetische, plakative Denkmal') unappealing and had no objection to commemorating Thälmann's sacrifice and recommended that a new, more tasteful memorial be constructed on the same site. Teuber's suggestion was doomed from the outset, however. District officials did not even have the half-million marks needed to remove the monument, much less to build another one, however modestly designed.[52]

Hoping that the city government would ultimately foot the bill, in mid-May the Prenzlauer Berg district parliament voted to follow the Monument Commission's recommendation. The relatively narrow margin of the vote – twenty-two to sixteen – in favor of demolishing Kerbel's behemoth reflected the contentiousness of the issue. Prenzlauer Berg officials still had no idea who would pay for the demolition, and the monument's supporters took comfort in this fact. In response to the assembly's vote, Eberhard Elfert of the 'Active Museum of Fascism and Resistance' reiterated his group's position. It would be far better, not to mention less expensive, to keep the monument, 'examine [it] critically', and modify it artistically.[53]

Refusing to give up on its plan, the 'Active Museum' was among the groups, along with the 'Initiative for Political Monuments' and two artists' organizations, sponsoring a 4–5 June symposium at the 'Kulturhaus' ('Culture House') in Thälmann Park.[54] The symposium would permit artists to share their proposals concerning the aesthetic and political modification of the site. Hopefully, Elfert pointed out, this would lead to an official competition sponsored by the district or city government and the ultimate preservation of this 'historical document of the GDR' ('Geschichtsdokument der DDR').[55]

---

52 Ibid.
53 *Berliner Morgenpost* (14 May 1993).
54 'Einladung zum Ernst-Thälmann-Symposium in der Wabe vom 4. bis 5. Juni 1993', in *Denk-Mal Positionen*, p.40.
55 *die tageszeitung* (7 June 1993).

The gathering witnessed the introduction of some interesting ideas. One proposal would have built a 'viewing stand' to permit people 'to look deep into Thälmann's eyes' ('Thälmann tief ins Auge zu schauen'). Ruth Baumeister wanted to put the fifty-ton colossus on a rotating platform, but Fritz Heisterkamp favoured the demolition of the monument, seeking to replace it with an 'airship' ('Luftschiff') bearing the martyred communist leader's name. The most popular – not to mention practical – proposal, however, was that of Manfred Butzmann, who in 1990 had suggested planting ivy at the site. By 1993, however, his idea had evolved dramatically.[56] Building upon his vision of 'greening' the site, Butzmann now proposed encircling it with trees. Further, the Berlin artist wanted to surround the memorial with water, placing it upon what amounted to a small island, making it 'a place to reflect and ponder, surrounded by trees and a quiet pool'.[57] This proposal would not only have hidden the socialist-realist colossus from sight by cloaking it in foliage, but it would also have created the impression of an imprisoned Thälmann, thereby emphasizing that the monument would now commemorate his incarceration and murder at the hands of the Nazis, rather than his place in GDR political propaganda. While Butzmann's proposal did have much appeal, it was highly unlikely that either the city or district government would be willing to assign the financial resources needed to bring this or any of the other suggestions to completion, and all of the proposals were stillborn, in spite of the publicity they received at an exhibit housed in the Prenzlauer Berg Museum.[58]

Ultimately, the site in Thälmann Park remained largely unchanged. Krenz's death ended the possibility of the monument being moved to Bavaria, and neither the district nor the city could pay to remove it. Other concerns, such as the economic dislocation caused by German unification, would place the fate of the Thälmann Monument and other East German sites in the background. In April 1995, the district

---

56   *Der Tagesspiegel* (9 June 1993).
57   'Ein Platz zum Nach- und Bedenken, von Bäumen umstanden und einem stillen, dafür viereckigen Teich umspült'. Quoted in *Der Tagesspiegel* (19 February 1993).
58   *Der Tagesspiegel* (15 July 1993), and *Neues Deutschland* (15 July 1993).

mayor of Prenzlauer Berg, Manfred Dennert, announced that the fifty-ton bust would remain where it was for the foreseeable future.[59] The only alteration made was to stencil three words on its base: 'Eingekerkert, Ermordet, Beschmiert' ('Imprisoned, Murdered, Besmirched'). Thälmann was 'imprisoned' and 'murdered' by the Nazis but 'besmirched' by the SED dictatorship. Officials hoped that this brief comment would place the massive statue in its proper historical context.[60]

Before unification, the debate concerning Berlin's Ernst Thälmann Monument could be viewed as an early exercise in democracy at the grassroots level. Discussion about the monuments of Berlin was carried out in the context of an emerging liberal ethos. As Wolfgang K., an eastern trade union official put it: 'It was sort of a liberating moment. The pressure was gone all of a sudden. When you have been scared to speak up for such a long time, it just feels incredible to be able to say what you think'.[61] The people of the GDR were determining their own fortunes for the first time in decades and molding a new national identity, one characterized by a democratic political consciousness.

Following the October 1990 unification, however, the tenor of the discussion changed dramatically. Henceforward, westerners would play a central role in determining the fate of the former East Germany. This, coupled with the economic dislocation engendered by the unification process, fostered a great deal of resentment, not to mention cynicism.[62] To add insult to injury, westerners who had never lived under the SED dictatorship saw fit to explain life in the GDR to those who had personally experienced 'real existing socialism'. Many easterners, therefore, resented it when the central city government decided the fate of East Berlin's Lenin Memorial, making them determined to defend the city's Ernst Thälmann Monument, one of the most important symbols of the GDR. Many easterners found themselves disillusioned in the face of 'real existing democracy'. Once again Wolfgang K. characterized this change in attitude:

---

59 *Der Tagesspiegel* (29 April 1995).
60 Ladd, *Ghosts of Berlin*, p.203.
61 Quoted in Philipsen, *We Were the People*, p.289.
62 Maier, *Dissolution*, pp.285–329.

I think we need to look out for ourselves. In fact, we should have done that all along. You see, in the opinion of West Germans pretty much everything we've done, everything we've had here, was somehow wrong, or at least deficient. In their eyes we are basically all failures, whether it was our fault or not. I don't think that's correct, and I certainly don't think it's fair. I am not going to let them steal my whole past, and I don't want to be a second-class citizen for the rest of my life.[63]

The brief honeymoon characterizing the weeks leading up to reunion came to an end, and the resulting re-emergence of a distinct East Germany identity should come as no surprise. After all, for over forty years, the governments of both Germanys had cultivated identities emphasizing the distinctions between the two systems. Couple this with all the problems manifested by reunification, and it is not surprising that East Germans have once again emphasized their distinctiveness, their unique outlook, based upon common experiences shared for over four decades. These intra-German differences have manifested themselves in a widespread nostalgia for the GDR, emphasizing the things easterners perceive as having been positive accomplishments of the regime; hence the re-emergence of an appetite for notoriously inferior East German consumer goods.[64] Overcoming this 'wall in the head' will probably take much longer than rebuilding the German economy, and disagreements between *Wessis* and *Ossis* will remain a challenge for the new Germany in the foreseeable future. The dispute concerning Prenzlauer Berg's Thälmann Monument can best be understood in this context. The honouring of Thälmann, who had given his life in the struggle against National Socialism, was, in the eyes of many from the East, one of those 'good' things about the GDR and should continue. While few would defend Kerbel's metal monstrosity on artistic grounds, many former East Germans, including most who lived in the shadow of the monument, wanted to maintain it not only as a relic of a flawed, but not entirely evil, regime, but also as a commemorative site honoring a true German hero. Even today, well over two hundred locales – among them streets, schools, memorials,

---

63   Quoted in Philipsen, *We Were the People*, p.381.
64   Paul Betts, 'The Twilight of the Idols: East German Memory and Material Culture', *The Journal of Modern History*, 72 (2000), 731–65.

and town squares – in the former GDR continue to bear Thälmann's name.

The fifty-ton bronze representation of the martyred KPD chief still stands along Berlin's Greifswalder Straße. It has been altered only slightly since Erich Honecker unveiled it to much fanfare in 1986, and fifteen years of unification have done little to assimilate the statue into the political life of the united Germany. Few people visit the site today, which has neither been preserved as a historic relic of the GDR, nor effectively altered to make it useful in political education. Indeed, as the chief of the Prenzlauer Berg Museum, Bert Roder, put it, the monument, in its current state, 'has no theme'.[65] Perhaps this makes it an appropriate metaphor for an understanding of recent German history. Ultimately, it is up to the Germans themselves to provide a proper 'theme' for twentieth-century German history and thereby help to create a common identity, a process for which all will need a great deal of patience.

Bibliography

Adolphi, Wolfram, and Jörn Schütrumpf (eds.), *Ernst Thälmann: An Stalin, Briefe aus dem Zuchthaus, 1939 bis 1941*, Berlin 1996.

Arendt, Hannah, *The Origins of Totalitarianism*, 2nd edition, New York 1973.

Betts, Paul, 'The Twilight of the Idols: East German Memory and Material Culture', *The Journal of Modern History*, 72 (2000), 731–65.

Bericht der Kommission zum Umgang mit den politischen Denkmälern der Nachkriegzeit im ehemaligen Ost-Berlin, Berlin 1993.

Denk-Mal Positionen: Dokumentation zur Ausstellung vom 14. Juli – 13. August 1993, Berlin 1993.

Flierl, Thomas, 'Thälmann und Thälmann vor allen: Ein Nationaldenkmal für die Hauptstadt der DDR, Berlin', in Günter Feist, Eckhart Gillen, and Beatrice Vierneisel (eds.), *Kunstdokumentation, SBZ/DDR 1945–1990: Aufsätze, Berichte, Materialien*, Berlin 1996, pp. 358–85.

---

65   *die tageszeitung* (5 June 1990). Interview with Bernt Roder, director of the Prenzlauer Berg Museum, 15 August 2002. Original in English.

Gruenberg, Antonia, *Antifaschismus – ein deutscher Mythos*, Reinbek bei Hamburg 1993.

Herf, Jeffrey, *Divided Memory: The Nazi Past in the Two Germanys*, Cambridge, MA 1997.

Hortzschansky, Günter et al., *Ernst Thälmann: Eine Biographie*, Berlin/East 1985.

Kannapin, Detlef, 'Ernst Thälmann und der DDR-Antifaschismus im Film der fünfziger Jahre', in Monteath (ed.), *Ernst Thälmann*, pp.119–145.

Kinner, Klaus, 'Thälmann und der Stalinismus: Das Ende des eigenständigen deutschen Parteikommunismus 1928/1929', in Monteath (ed.), *Ernst Thälmann*, pp.59–80.

Koshar, Rudy, *From Monuments to Traces: Artifacts of German Memory, 1870–1990*, Berkeley, CA 2000.

James, Harold, *A German Identity, 1770–1990*, New York 1989.

Jarausch, Konrad, *The Rush to German Unity*, New York 1994.

Kupferberg, Feiwel, *The Rise and Fall of the German Democratic Republic*, New Brunswick, NJ 2002.

Ladd, Brian, *The Ghosts of Berlin: Confronting German History in the Urban Landscape*, Chicago 1997.

——, 'East Berlin Political Monuments in the Late German Democratic Republic: Finding a Place for Marx and Engels', *Journal of Contemporary History*, 37/1 (2000), 91–104.

Maier, Charles, Dissolution: *The Crisis of Communism and the End of East Germany*, Princeton, NJ 1997.

Mercalowa, Ljudmila Andreevna, 'Stalinismus und Hitlerismus – Versuch einer vergleichenden Analyse', in Eckhard Jesse (ed.), *Totalitarisums im 20. Jahrhundert: Eine Bilanz der internationalen Forschung*, Bonn 1996, pp.200–12.

Monteath, Peter (ed.), *Ernst Thälmann: Mensch und Mythos*, Amsterdam 2000.

Philipsen, Dirk, *We Were the People: Voices from East Germany's Revolutionary Autumn of 1989*, Durham, NC 1993.

Scheer, Regina, '"Ich bin kein weltflüchtiger Zigeuner": Legende und Wirklichkeit einer Jugend – über die frühen Prägungen Ernst Thälmanns', in Monteath (ed.), *Ernst Thälmann*, pp.41–58.

Schivelbusch, Wolfgang, *The Culture of Defeat: On National Trauma, Mourning, and Recovery*, trans. Jefferson Chase, New York 2003.

Welsh, Helga A., Andreas Pickel, and Dorothy Rosenberg, 'East and West German Identities: United and Divided?', in Konrad H. Jarausch (ed.), *After Unity: Reconfiguring German Identities*, Providence, RI 1997, pp.103–36.

Contributors

Silke Arnold-de Simine is Assistant Professor of German at the University of Mannheim, where she teaches literatur and film. She is the author of *Leichen im Keller: Zu Fragen des Gender in Angstinszenierungen der Schauer- und Kriminalliteratur, 1790–1830* (2000), and is researching the organization of memory in the media of literature, film and the museum.

Jonathan Bach is Core Faculty at the New School Graduate Program in International Affairs in New York City. He is the author of *Between Sovereignty and Integration: German Foreign Policy and National Identity After 1989* (St. Martin's Press) and has published in *Public Culture, Theory, Culture and Society, Studies in Comparative and International Development* and *Geopolitics*.

Andreas Böhn is Professor of Modern Literature and Media at the University of Karlsruhe. He has published on German literature since the eighteenth century, film, intermediality, mimesis, musealization and genre parody. He is the author of *Das Formzitat. Bestimmung einer Textstrategie im Spannungsfeld zwischen Intertextualitätsforschung und Gattungstheorie* (2001) and, most recently, editor of the volume *Formzitat und Intermedialität* (2003).

Friederike Eigler received her Ph.D. from Washington University in St. Louis, Missouri and is Associate Professor of German at Georgetown University, where she teaches German and Austrian literature and culture from the late nineteenth century to the present, as well as literary and cultural theory. She has published widely on post-war and contemporary German literature and is the author of a monograph on Elias Canetti, coeditor of *Cultural Transformation in the New Germany: American and German Perspectives* (1993) and *The Feminist Encyclopedia of German Literature* (1997). Her research and publications in recent years have focused on issues of cultural memory and inter-generational memory in contemporary literature and culture. Her book-length study on *Generation und Geschichte in Generations-romanen seit der Wende* has recently been published.

Birgit Haas completed her doctorate on *Das Theater des George Tabori* at the University of Heidelberg in 1998. From 1999 to 2004 she had been teaching as a DAAD-Lektorin at the University of Bristol (UK). She currently teaches and researches at the German Department of Heidelberg University. Her main research interests are drama and theatre of the twentieth and twenty-first century, dramatic performance, and comparative studies. She has published widely on modern drama, most recently her book-length studies on *Wende-theater – Theater der Wende* (2004) and on *Political Drama in Germany 1980–2000* (2003).

Marc Oliver Huber studied in Munich, Vienna, Berlin, and Oxford, and is currently writing his PhD on cultural memory in the writings of Thomas Mann.

Russel Lemmons is Professor of History at Jacksonville State University in Jacksonville, Alabama. A 1988–1989 Fulbright scholar at Berlin's Free University, he received his doctorate from Miami University (Ohio) in 1991. The author of *Goebbels and Der Angriff* (1994), his current research project focuses upon the development of the Ernst Thälmann myth from its creation in the final years of the Weimar Republic through the collapse of the GDR.

Bernhard Malkmus, studied English and modern languages at the Universities of Würzburg, Cambridge and Konstanz, held teaching and research fellowships at the Charles University (Prague) and Harvard University, and is currently working on a PhD thesis on political implications of twentieth-century picaresque fiction at Cambridge University.

Anne Friederike Müller is currently an AHRB fellow at King's College London. She studied history and social anthropology at

Tübingen, Paris, and Cambridge, where she obtained a PhD in 2001. She has worked and published on everyday life in seventeenth-century France, political metaphors in Imperial Germany, human rights issues in contemporary Germany and France, as well as social theory.

Ruth J. Owen studied and taught at the University of Oxford. In 2002–3 she held a research fellowship at the Humboldt-Universität in Berlin. She is currently research associate and lecturer at the University of Leeds, where in 2004 she co-organized the conference *Interactions: Contemporary German Literature's Dialogue with the Arts*. Recent publications include *The Poet's Role: Lyric Responses to German Unification* (2001) and essays on various aspects of contemporary, post-war and early-twentieth-century poetry, particularly focussing on science, cities and the body.

Rolf Parr is Professor for Modern German Literature at the University of Bielefeld. He has published widely on German literature and culture since the eighteenth century, on mythical historical figures, literary societies, media discourses, semiotics, discourse theory and the imagery of the collective. He published *Historische Mythologie der Deutschen 1776–1918* (1991) and is the co-editor of *(Nicht) normale Fahrten. Faszinationen eines modernen Narrationstyps* (2003).

Simon Ward is Lecturer in German at the University of Aberdeen. He is the author of a monograph on Wolfgang Koeppen, and has published articles on many aspects of the literature and cultural history of Germany in the twentieth century. He is currently writing a book on ruins and modernity in post-war Berlin.

Index

CULTURAL HISTORY AND LITERARY IMAGINATION

EDITED BY CHRISTIAN EMDEN & DAVID MIDGLEY

This series promotes inquiry into the relationship between literary texts and their cultural and intellectual contexts, in theoretical, interpretative and historical perspectives. It has developed out of a research initiative of the German Department at Cambridge University, but its focus of interest is on the European tradition broadly perceived. Its purpose is to encourage comparative and interdisciplinary research into the connections between cultural history and the literary imagination generally.

The editors are especially concerned to encourage the investigation of the role of the literary imagination in cultural history and the interpretation of cultural history through the literary text. Examples of the kind of issues in which they are particularly interested include the following:

- The material conditions of culture and their representation in literature, e.g. responses to the impact of the sciences, technology, and industrialisation, the confrontation of 'high' culture with popular culture, and the impact of new media;

- The construction of cultural meaning through literary texts, e.g. responses to cultural crisis, or paradigm shifts in cultural self-perception, including the establishment of cultural 'foundation myths';

- History and cultural memory as mediated through the metaphors and models deployed in literary writing and other media;

- The intermedial and intercultural practice of authors or literary movements in specific periods;

- The methodology of cultural inquiry and the theoretical discussion of such issues as intermediality, text as a medium of cultural memory, and intercultural relations.

Both theoretical reflection on and empirical investigation of these issues are welcome. The series is intended to include monographs, editions, and collections of papers based on recent research in this area. The main language of publication is English.

Vol. 1   Christian Emden & David Midgley (eds): Cultural Memory and Historical Consciousness in the German-Speaking World Since 1500. Papers from the
         Conference 'The Fragile Tradition', Cambridge 2002. Vol. 1.
         316 pp., 2004. ISBN 3-03910-160-9 / US-ISBN 0-8204-6970-X

Vol. 2   Christian Emden & David Midgley (eds): German Literature, History and
         the Nation. Papers from the Conference 'The Fragile Tradition', Cambridge
         2002. Vol. 2.
         393 pp., 2004. ISBN 3-03910-169-2 / US-ISBN 0-8204-6979-3

Vol. 3   Christian Emden & David Midgley (eds): Science, Technology and the German
         Cultural Imagination. Papers from the Conference 'The Fragile Tradition',
         Cambridge 2002. Vol. 3.
         319 pp., 2005. ISBN 3-03910-170-6 / US-ISBN 0-8204-6980-7

Vol. 4   Forthcoming.

Vol. 5   Silke Arnold-de Simine (ed.): Memory Traces. 1989 and the Question of
         German Cultural Identity.
         343 pp., 2005. ISBN 3-03910-297-4 / US-ISBN 0-8204-7223-9

Edric Caldicott / Anne Fuchs (eds.)

Cultural Memory

Essays on European Literature and History

Oxford, Bern, Berlin, Bruxelles, Frankfurt am Main, New York, Wien, 2003. 422 pp.
ISBN 3-03910-053-X / US-ISBN 0-8204-6294-2 pb.
sFr. 103.– / €* 70.80 / €** 66.20 / £ 43.– / US-$ 78.95

* includes VAT – only valid for Germany and Austria   ** does not include VAT

Memory and culture are terms which are now fashionable, if not over-used, but they need careful handling. This book explores their use in a variety of contexts: in European creative writing, in the spheres of national celebration, mourning, and administration of the arts, and in concepts of translation and history. The editors' introduction maps the surrounding theoretical terrain, and each of the following twenty-two essays explores related issues within the specific brief of a local context, whether in France, Germany, Ireland, Italy or Spain, organized under five thematic lines of enquiry: Memory as Counter-History, Narrativity and Remembering, Locating Memory, Remembering and Renewal, Remembering as Trauma. Coming into prominence after the Holocaust and the fall of European dictatorships, studies in Cultural Memory have been fuelled by the works of Walter Benjamin, Aby Warburg, the rediscovery of Maurice Halbwachs, and more recently by Pierre Nora's notion of 'sites of memory'. Furthermore, they have benefited from the reflections of a range of contemporary theorists in this area, including Paul Ricœur, Michel de Certeau and Jan Assman. The studies in this volume, however, go beyond the present to show how, in earlier times, the devices of memory and commemoration were exploited both for and against the state. Within the sphere of the present, the expression of memory in narrative is shown to be an essential source of inspiration for the creative writer, discovering renewal in a sense of loss.

With contributions by: Edric Caldicott – Anne Fuchs – Jeanne Riou – Carol Baxter – Síofra Pierse – Angela Reinicke – Sabine Egger – David Rock – Eamonn Jordan – Deirdre Byrnes – Patrick Crowley – Douglas Smith – Guy Beiner – Christian J. Emden – Phyllis Gaffney – Gillian Pye – Deirdre O'Grady – Susan Bassnett – Patrick O'Donovan – Alison Ribeiro De Menezes – Tom Quinn – Carmel Finnan – Catherine O'Leary – Silvia Ross.

PETER LANG

Bern · Berlin · Bruxelles · Frankfurt am Main · New York · Oxford · Wien

Christian Emden / David Midgley (eds.)
Cultural Memory and Historical Consciousness in the German-Speaking World Since 1500
Papers from the Conference 'The Fragile Tradition',
Cambridge 2002. Volume 1

Oxford, Bern, Berlin, Bruxelles, Frankfurt am Main, New York, Wien, 2004. 316 pp.
Cultural History and Literary Imagination. Vol. 1
Edited by Christian Emden and David Midgley
ISBN 3-03910-160-9 / US-ISBN 0-8204-6970-X pb.
sFr. 80.– / €* 55.– / €** 51.40 / £ 36.– / US-\$ 61.95

* includes VAT – only valid for Germany and Austria ** does not include VAT

This is the first of three volumes based on papers given at the conference 'The Fragile Tradition: The German Cultural Imagination Since 1500' in Cambridge, 2002. Together they provide a conspectus of current research on the cultural, historical and literary imagination of the German-speaking world across the whole of the modern period. This volume highlights the ways in which cultural memory and historical consciousness have been shaped by experiences of discontinuity, focusing particularly on the reception of the Reformation, the literary and ideological heritage of the Enlightenment, and the representation of war, the Holocaust, and the reunification of Germany in contemporary literature and museum culture.

Contents: David Midgley/Christian J. Emden: Introduction – Aleida Assmann: Four Formats of Memory: From Individual to Collective Constructions of the Past – Christian J. Emden: History, Memory, and the Invention of Antiquity: Notes on the 'Classical Tradition' – Ortrud Gutjahr: Literary Modernism and the Tradition of Breaking Tradition – Marc Oliver Huber: Memoria in Zeiten des Zeitenbruchs: Nietzsches *Zweite Unzeitgemäße Betrachtung* als Indikator einer Gedächtniskrise – Susanne Rau: Reformation, Time, and History: The Construction of (Dis)Continuities in the Historiography of the Reformation in the Early Modern Period – Wilhelm Ribhegge: German or European Identity? Luther and Erasmus in Nineteenth- and Twentieth-Century German Cultural History and Historiography – Stefan Busch: Ideals and Life in German Literature of the Late Enlightenment Period: The Grotesque as *reductio ad absurdum* of Providentialism – Laura Benzi: Die Entstehung der Lyrik in der zweiten Hälfte des 18. Jahrhunderts und die spätaufklärerische Affektenlehre – Ritchie Robertson: Joseph II in Cultural Memory – Kristin Veel: Topographies of Memory: Walter Benjamin and Daniel Libeskind – Silke Arnold-de Simine: Theme Park GDR? The Aestheticization of Memory in post-*Wende* Museums, Literature and Film – Karen Leeder: 'rhythmische historia': Contemporary Poems of the First World War by Thomas Kling and Raoul Schrott.

PETER LANG
Bern · Berlin · Bruxelles · Frankfurt am Main · New York · Oxford · Wien